16

INTRODUCTION TO OPINION AND ATTITUDE MEASUREMENT

INTRODUCTION TO OPINION AND ATTITUDE MEASUREMENT

H. H. REMMERS

PROFESSOR OF PSYCHOLOGY AND EDUCATION
DIRECTOR, DIVISION OF EDUCATIONAL REFERENCE
PURDUE UNIVERSITY

GREENWOOD PRESS, PUBLISHERS
WESTPORT, CONNECTICUT

The Library of Congress has catalogued this publication as follows:

Library of Congress Cataloging in Publication Data

Remmers, Hermann Henry, 1892–
    Introduction to opinion and attitude measurement.

    Original ed. issued in Harper's psychological
series.
    1. Attitude (Psychology)--Testing. I. Title.
[BF323.C5R44 1972]   301.15'42   74-138127
ISBN 0-8371-4166-4

Originally published in 1954 by Harper & Brothers,
New York

Reprinted with the permission of Harper & Row,
Publishers.

Reprinted in 1972 by Greenwood Press,
a division of Congressional Information Service, Inc.
88 Post Road West, Westport, Connecticut 06881

Library of Congress catalog card number 74-138127
ISBN 0-8371-4166-4

Printed in the United States of America

10 9 8 7 6 5 4 3 2

CONTENTS

· · • ● • · ·

PREFACE

· · • ● • · ·

Nearly 20 years ago G. W. Allport said, "The concept of attitude is probably the most distinctive and indispensable concept in contemporary American social psychology." What was true then is even more true today. Scientific work both "pure" and "applied" related to the concept—under the name of attitude and a variety of synonyms—has produced a large and rapidly growing literature. William James would very likely find this literature more nourishing than the literature on emotion that he found no more rewarding than would have been counting the stones on a New England farm. Attitudes toward the individual's world and toward himself have become central not only in social psychology but in other, applied areas as counseling, psychotherapy, advertising, and public relations.

College and university courses on the psychology of attitudes have been introduced in many institutions as a function of the growing interest in this area of social psychology. Despite this, there has not been, to my knowledge, a suitable textbook available. This volume represents the major content of a course I have been teaching for a number of years.

Not all the techniques that have been used in attempts to study attitudes have been included. Content analysis might well be judged by some of my interested colleagues to have merited a chapter. Inferring attitudes from overt, nonverbal behavior—effort expended for a cause, relative amounts of money spent for good and services, etc.—is another such possibility. These, however, were judged methodologically less amenable to measurement and hence not included. Their value and relevance are not, of course, thereby called into question.

Acknowledgments

The author's thanks are extended to the following for permission to quote from their publications: Dun's Review; Gordon Company; Harper & Brothers; Harvard University Press; International Journal of Opinion and Attitude Research; Journal of Abnormal & Social Psychology; Journal of Applied Psychology; Journal of Consulting Psychology; Journal of Educational Psychology; Journal of Social Psychology; Macmillan Company; Personnel; Personnel Journal; Princeton University Press; Psychological Bulletin; Rinehart & Company; Sociology and Social Research.

Without the assistance of many of my students this book could not have been written. They are too numerous to mention them all by name. Specific mention, however, is due the following of my former students and three of my present colleagues. Those whose assistance is identified with particular chapters are the following: R. B. Aledort, Chapter X; P. C. Baker, Chapter III; Lois Remmers Dean, Chapter XI; A. J. Drucker, Chapter II; D. N. Elliott, Chapter IX; R. B. Kirk, Chapter XII; J. A. Norton, Chapter IV; and B. Shimberg, Chapter VIII. Miss Leigh Van Ausdall gave valuable help in preparing the Subject Index. For careful and meticulous help in typing and proofreading I am indebted to Mrs. Barbara Clapp, my secretary.

It goes without saying that if any sins of omission or commission appear in this book, they are chargeable only to me.

H. H. REMMERS

November, 1953

PART ONE

· · · ● ● · · ·

Techniques in Opinion
and Attitude Measurement

CHAPTER I

· · · ● ● ● · ·

Attitudes—A Preliminary Overview[1]

The ways of looking at things and persons, forms of readiness, approaching and withdrawing behavior, feelings of rightness and wrongness, and liking or disliking for objects or values differ from emotions though they are related to them. They have been fused in the working concept of *attitude* which may be defined as an affectively toned idea or group of ideas predisposing the organism to action with reference to specific attitude objects. Thomas and Znaniecki (*34*), two sociologists, first studied social attitudes and approximated the concept as currently used by social psychologists. Since then psychologists have been increasingly concerned with attitudinal study, for attitudes are theoretically a component of all behavior, overt or covert.

As thus defined the number of identifiable attitudes is the same as the number of things to which the organism can respond, and the concept is coterminous with, or closely related to, a considerable number of other psychological concepts, such as interests, appreciations, motives, mores, morality, morale, ideals, complexes (in the psychoanalytic sense), values, prejudices, fears, sentiments, loyalties, ideologies, character, and the like. From the point of view of society the system of

[1] This chapter is, with slight modifications, the same as my Section 2, "Social Attitudes," pp. 10-15, in D. H. Fryer and E. R. Henry (eds.), *Handbook of Applied Psychology*, New York: Rinehart & Company, Inc., 1950, and is included here with permission of the publishers.

3

morals and customs in operation is the social attitudes which constitute the matrix of attitude patterns of the individuals in society. From the point of view of the individual, attitudes constitute the individual's own evaluation of his conduct and desires in relation to the system of social values as he understands them. The functional psychoses thus have their origin in the attitude patterns of the individual.

The purpose of this chapter is to give the student a preliminary orientation to the psychological role of attitudes in human behavior. We shall discuss briefly the following: (1) development of attitudes in the individual, (2) measurement and the standardization of measurement, (3) attitudes of contemporary societies and social groupings, and (4) the value of attitude measurement to society. These general topics along with others growing out of them will be expanded and elaborated in later chapters.

DEVELOPMENT OF ATTITUDES IN THE INDIVIDUAL

Genetic Development

Environmental modification of the human organism begins with conception. Apart from embryonic development, the changes wrought by environmental contact are manifested from birth on during the early years or even months of life. Here the individual acquires his first attitudes and exhibits his first learned behavior. In brief, he develops personality. Original drives are overlaid by social experiences organized into attitudinal systems.

The newly born child quickly acquires certain feeding habits and comes to regard favorably those who contribute to the gratification of his needs and unfavorably those who frustrate his activities. The baby's attitudes toward his parents will carry over to others. As the child grows in his capacity to respond to those outside his family group, his social attitudes, e.g., coöperativeness, selfishness, dominance, conformity, and the like, will become definite.

As the child acquires "human nature" which will equip him for life in a society of human beings, the area of his relevant experience expands and the attitudinal patterns become incorporated in his personality. Attitudes will be modified, through learning, in accordance with his own goals and drives. This means that he will acquire attitudes like those of his parents, his friends, and the other primary groups (permanent face-to-face groups) of which he is a member. As the individual grows older, secondary groups (non-face-to-face or temporary face-to-face groups) with which he is associated will elicit certain attitudes. In general, the closer the relationships between an individual and others, the greater will be the potency of such relationships in the formation of attitudes.

The growth and development of attitudes involves the integration of numerous specific responses of a similar type. Such attitudes determine the entire adjustment of the individual. If a child is frustrated by his classroom teacher and believes that the teacher is discriminating against him, he will tend to react negatively to the teacher's future criticisms. Accordingly, the term "attitude" is merely a convenient way of referring to the preparedness that exists within the organism for some future activity. It is to be emphasized that such preparedness is neither automatic nor routine, but possesses cognitive and conative aspects differentiating it from habits and reflexes as commonly regarded. Furthermore, attitudes toward inanimate forces, institutions, and values, while culturally determined, vary in intensity between individuals and within the same individual at different times.

The baby grows into childhood, youth, and adulthood with attitudes as an important aspect of his learned behavior. Attitudes are evolved from association with his family group, with children in his play and school group, and in general through social-psychological interaction. As an adult, occupation and the responsibilities of citizenship and parenthood are important in attitude development. It is inconceivable that cultural stability, language, and dependability in human affairs could exist without attitudes. Yet the fact that attitudes do change accounts for social innovations, social conflicts, and social changes.

Stability of Attitudes

To what extent can attitudes be modified, to what extent do they remain constant over a period of time, and what factors are related to change or constancy of attitudes? Some of these questions are answered in studies which show that attitudes can be changed and that these changes persist for some time. Buck (6) suggested that marked changes persist for attitudes toward unemployment and socialism were definitely related to changed mores in the population at large and resulted from widespread economic conditions. Peterson and Thurstone (26) demonstrated that the changed attitudes from seeing a single movie persisted for as much as a year and a half. Knower (20) measured modification of attitudes toward prohibition by oral argument and printed material, discovering changes in the directions anticipated. Remmers and his students (29) have made similar findings. After studying materials on social insurance, capital punishment, conservation measures, and labor unions, high school pupils showed significant shifts in attitudes in the direction planned, and these changes persisted for at least a school year. Attitudes toward the Negro differed significantly after students were given material pointing out unfairness toward and discrimination against the Negro. Elementary school children under a pupil self-government plan were significantly more favorable toward law enforcement than otherwise similar children. Significant shifts toward liberalism occurred in college students during the period 1931-1937 and toward Germans, Jews, Japanese, and Nazis from 1935 to 1947.

Such studies are important in indicating the effect of various types of stimulation in shaping and maintaining attitudes, and point to the tremendous importance of school and community indoctrination in creating beliefs consistent with our aims and values.

MEASUREMENT AND STANDARDIZED MEASURES

Scientific treatment of attitudes requires quantification. In most measurement of attitudes we are really measuring opinions. Opinions, therefore, are expressed attitudes. These may deviate from underlying self-attitudes with or without the awareness of the subject. In the literature they are frequently distinguished as "public" and "private" attitudes.

Method

Certain assumptions must be made in order to measure attitudes: that attitudes are measurable, that they vary along a linear continuum, and that measurable attitudes are common to the group, that they are held by many people. Limitations of attitude measurements not implicit in these assumptions include the fact that they may be temporary and changeable and subject to rationalization and deception.

While attitudes may be inferred from overt behavior (effort expended for a cause, relative amounts of money spent for goods and services, and the like), most systematic psychological work has concerned itself with opinions expressed or endorsed as indices of attitudes. We shall, therefore, consider the various types of scales that have been developed.

Types of Scales

Attitude scales may be classified according to methods of constructing attitude measuring devices such as the interview, a priori "scales," psychophysical scales, sigma scales, master scales, rating scales, behavior scales, and analogous measurements of various sorts. These devices differ markedly in their theoretical and practical adequacy.

A Priori Scales. The crudest method of measuring attitudes is that of the case method, closely followed by ballot counting, as exemplified in various public opinion polls. Such polling devices are in effect two-point "scales." For example, in measuring attitude toward capital punishment the relevant item might be, "Capital punishment is necessary." The proportions of "yes" and "no" votes would then be taken as an index of the existing social attitude for a given population.

A slight refinement is introduced by adding qualifying statements to the main proposition, such as "always, sometimes, rarely, never"; or "strongly agree, agree, undecided, disagree, strongly disagree." Such devices have been criticized on the ground that they are not "scales" in the rational sense of equal units on the scale. A classic example is that of Bogardus' (5) a priori scale to measure social distance, in which he attempted to measure differences in group mores related to individual willingness to admit members of particular groups to this or that social relationship.

Psychophysical Scales. In 1927 Thurstone (35) applied psychophysical scaling methods to the problem of measuring attitudes. While the rationale of his method is too lengthy to be included here, in essence it consists of arranging a series of opinions relevant to a given attitude object, ranging all the way from most favorable to most unfavorable, in equally spaced, experimentally determined units along a continuum. The average scale value endorsed by a subject thus becomes a measure of his attitude with reference to the attitude object. We shall explain the method in some detail in Chapter IV. For the assumptions underlying the method and for the criteria for selecting attitude items the reader must consult the relevant technical literature.

Thurstone himself has pointed out as possible limitations that attitudes may not be on a single continuum but may be discrete, and that the scale values derived from a population of judges is not necessarily applicable to other populations. Hinckley (15) reported correlations ranging from 0.94 to 0.98 between scale values, of items independently scaled by Negroes and whites with reference to attitude toward the Negro. Pintner and Forlano (27) similarly reported a correlation of 0.98 between two scalings of groups of students known to differ widely when the items of Thurstone's patriotism scale were the consideration.

Sigma Scales. Likert's (21) modification of the Thurstone methods makes the doubtful assumption that attitudes are distributed normally. On this assumption, he measured attitudes using standard deviation units. Between scale values obtained by this method and that of arbitrarily assigning numerical values from 1 to 5 to the various alternative responses, he obtained a correlation of 0.99. He also reported higher coefficients of reliability by this method than by the Thurstone scoring technique. Equating the number of items used, he obtained higher coefficients of correlation for ten different attitude scales and every group measured.

Likert's method has been criticized on the ground that it makes the doubtful assumption of normality of distribution and also because scales constructed without the use of judges have correlated only 0.65 to 0.71 with scales using the Thurstone technique of construction. Such findings, it is argued, do not warrant discarding the judging group, especially if measurement of individuals rather than groups is desired. Remmers and Sageser (31) and Remmers and Ewart (30) have shown that adding an arbitrary scale of from 3 to 7 points to each opinion item in a scale increased the reliability in accordance with that predicted by the Spearman-Brown prophecy formula (see Chapter VII). Guttman (13) has proposed a rational scheme based on matrix algebra for eliminating items not on the principal continuum for any type of psychological trait. It is relatively simple in application and much less laborious than factor analysis methods. See Chapter IV.

Master Scales. Another modification of the Thurstone method is that of the Remmers (29) generalized or master scale method. The essential difference from the Thurstone method is that the opinions which constitute the scale are incomplete sentences without subject, this being supplied at the time of measurement, so that attitudes toward any one of a large group or class of attitude objects can validly be measured on a single scale. Examples of such scales are Scales to Measure Attitudes Toward Any: Advertisement, Disciplinary Procedure, Homemaking Activity, Play, Practice, Proposed Social Action, Racial or National Group, School Subject, Social Institution, Teacher, and Vocation.

The scaling method used is based, like Thurstone's method, upon the principle that equally often observed differences are equal, with the median scale value of the opinions endorsed becoming the subject's score. Such a series of master scales eliminates much of the laborious process of collecting statements about each attitude to be measured and the extensive labor involved in the scaling. Practically, it is useful in that it is immediately available to measure an issue of current interest. For example, when it was announced that President Roosevelt would address the nation via radio on his proposed enlargement of the Supreme Court, the Scale to Measure Attitude Toward Any Proposed Social Action was used to survey a group of high school pupils before and after they listened to the speech to determine the change in attitude which occurred as the result of the speech. A number of studies have shown that these scales are internally consistent and give substantially the same results as Thurstone's scales for the same attitude object (Grice, *12*, Kelley, *19*).

Behavior Scales. Rosander (*33*) developed a scale to distinguish verbalized opinions from behavior. He attempted to measure attitudes toward the Negro by the subject's acceptance or rejection of items such as the following.

1. In the community where you live a Negro marries a white girl. You do nothing about it (6.2).
2. You are bathing at a beach. Some Negroes approach and enter the water near you. You start to fight with them (1.2).
3. A Negro family moves into a residential district where you live. You invite them to your house (11.5).

The parenthetical scale values following the statements were obtained by the usual psychophysical scaling methods based upon the equally often observed difference principle.

Eckert and Wilson (9) constructed a scale on a somewhat similar assumption, that verbal descriptions of specific situaations designed to afford some measure of the allegiance of scales as those of Thurstone, Likert, Remmers, and others. Their scale, entitled "What Would You Do? A Survey of Student Opinion," was not constructed according to the refined methods previously described. It presented specific situations designed to afford some measure of the allegiance of pupils to the "basic tenets of American democracy." The face validity of such scales appears to be good. Their validity as related to behavior must, as is the case for other types of scales, be determined by further research.

Analogous Measurements. Attempts to measure attitudes by the use of scales not directly drawn up for this purpose have not been wanting. These include personality scales, interest blanks, advertising experiments (consumer surveys), polls of public opinion, observation of overt behavior (as group membership, ways of spending money), acceptance-rejection scales (Fitz-Simmons), and the like.

The possibilities of ambiguity and misinterpretation, either conscious or unconscious, have long been stumbling blocks in the use of verbal scales, because of the possible lack of correspondence between expressed attitudes and other, nonverbal behavior. It should be pointed out in this connection that for a large variety of attitude objects verbal response is the only possibility for most individuals. For example, one's response to the notion of a world court or a supranational government could hardly take other than verbal form. So it is with many other issues.

Hartshorne and May's (14) studies of character represent one attempt to measure the difference between expressed attitudes and behavior. A similar attempt is the study of attitudes by projective techniques, in which attitudes are inferred through interpretations of various types of stimuli or behavior situations. The term "projective technique" implies a field of unstructured material on which the individual can project his personal way of seeing life, his meanings, significances, patterns, or feelings. Such methods differ from standardized tests in that they do not seek so much to interpret individuals in terms of cultural norms as to describe the specific dynamic organization within a particular individual. A further difference from standardized tests is the avoidance of explicit formulation of the issue involved; in this way, the aim is to eliminate conscious falsification or inability (emotionally or intellectually) to respond. A criticism, of course, is the difficulty in applying statistical measures of reliability and validity.

Among the better known types of projective technique is that of play therapy, in which the child is allowed to express his conflicts, guilt feelings, aggression, or other motivations or attitudes through spontaneous creations of clay, finger paints, dough, or mud. In this way, the child is said to project his feelings into the formless materials, meaningless in themselves. In the same way, he may use dolls or small toys to represent emotionalized persons or situations and thus work through emotional stresses, which could be verbalized only with prolonged and strenuous effort. For example, sibling rivalry and feelings of rejection or inferiority can often be brought to light in the maladjusted child who could not verbalize them directly, even if he were willing to coöperate.

In the same manner, pictures, music, ink blots have been presented for individual interpretation. The Rorschach test, a series of ten cards, was devised to allow free association, projection of unconscious patterns of affectivity, perception, and thinking upon unstructured stimuli. Morgan and Murray's Thematic Apperception Test (23), while still allowing individual interpretation, is less plastic, in that it is composed of definite pictures which the individual interprets according to his own experiences and attitudes. In a test designed for use with children, one of the pictures shows a boy fishing near a "No Fishing Allowed" sign. Responses of necessity involve the child's attitudes toward law enforcement, independence, fear of being caught, and others.

Numerous studies, such as Wright's (37) toy situation to measure constructiveness in play, the Horowitz (17, 18) measurements of social and race attitudes by preference for pictures, Fite's (10) dramatic play with dolls to indicate the child's attitudes toward aggression, suggest the possibilities of these techniques. Two relatively recent books (2, 4) provide detailed and systematic description and criticism of projective techniques.

Another technique is that of psychodrama, wherein the individual expresses his feelings and attitudes by acting them out. Moreno (22) cites examples of a ten-year-old boy who hit his mother before bedtime and at parties, of a wife suffering from violent fits of rage; both behavior patterns were eliminated after dramatic situations allowed complete expression of them.

Such methods, still largely in the experimental stage and quite different from the usual test or scale, provide a new and interesting approach to attitude study and, so far as evaluated, seem to offer definite contributions to the field. It is to be noted that all behavior is in some sense "projective" as it would be interpreted by a clinical psychologist.

ATTITUDES OF CONTEMPORARY SOCIETIES AND SOCIAL GROUPING

The attitude patterns of all societies can best be understood against the background of the anthropological concept of culture. Man as a biological organism is, with the exception of a few obvious and largely irrelevant differences in color and size, everywhere the same. Everywhere he faces the same persistent life problems: to gain subsistence, shelter, and security, and to perpetuate the species, to form some sort of group life in which the individual can function in the common affairs of life, to regulate human conduct through the transformation of simple impulsive behavior into behavior patterns consonant with the strivings of the group. This process of socialization or acculturation is perhaps the most distinctively "human" characteristic of the species. Psychologically the values, the mores, the loyalties, the ideals, or, in short, the attitude patterns thus formed, may be thought of as the dynamics of social behavior.

The great diversity of existing cultures, so great as to appear completely different and unrelated to each other, nevertheless have this common denominator of coming to terms with the conditions of life. From the point of view of the group, socialization is successful when the individual produces no undue tensions and frictions within the group. From the point of view of the individual, success is a matter of achieving individual goals in relation to the multiplicity of institutionalized attitude patterns. Illustrations of the failure of socialization in our culture from either point of view are such things as crime and delinquency, divorce, inability to hold a job, and last, but not least, the functional psychoses.

Within each culture, however defined, are many subcultures—social groups (often pressure groups) with which, in various relations, the individual identifies himself. Much of social tension is explicable in terms of clashes and conflicts of such subcultures occasioned by special attitudes toward religion, race, labor, capital, government, vocations, industry, and business. These may or may not parallel defined social values and needs of the majority. Psychologically the clash in culture known as World War II has its explanation in the conflict of ideologies, systems of values, basically related to the persistent tasks of life previously mentioned.

It is also the characteristic of each culture to magnify its virtues and to overlook its deficiencies and blind spots. The Germans were by no means the first to think of themselves as a *Herrenvolk*, or master people. Such an attitude as an unstated major premise is present in all cultures. In terms of written records the notion of a "chosen people" is several thousand years old. The names of various American Indian tribes were, according to cultural anthropologists, given them by other tribes. Each tribe, for itself, called itself *the people*.

Within our own nation the subcultures are as many and varied as are the social groupings that we can identify. Labor and capital, white and colored, urban and rural, town and gown, the social set and "the people across the tracks" are a few commonplace illustrations of the many dichotomies and attitudinal oppositions that exist. Social activities inevitably become institutionalized and develop integrated and involved social hierarchies within the activity. Roethlisberger (*32*) shows that this is true in industrial plants. Anyone at all familiar with college and university life can easily see such patterns—the extent to which individuals and the groups to which they belong "rate."

VALUE OF ATTITUDE MEASUREMENT TO SOCIETY

The realization is rapidly growing that attitudes, the way individuals and groups feel about the various aspects of their world, are probably more determinative of behavior than mere cognitive understanding of this world. When this is granted, the importance and value of attitude measurement becomes at once obvious. On the basis of experimental evidence psychologists agree on the majority of psychological issues of importance in the determination of happy, need-gratifying individual existence. Areas about which there is substantial agreement include mental hygiene, intelligence, race differences, nutrition, specific aptitudes, and educational methods. Turning from the individual to society, from which he is inseparable, it is essential that the body of knowledge on which there is professional agreement and for which there is objective substantiation be utilized for the realization of the individual's capacities and happiness and for his integration in terms of the general welfare.

Among the prerequisites for the fulfillment of the promise of psychology and the other social sciences are the cultivation of attitudes favorable to (1) social change and social invention, (2) public responsibility and open discussion of public issues, and (3) the fruitfulness of free inquiry. Nothing less in the areas of social attitudes will permit the extension of knowledge for free men in a democratic society. A few specific means of fostering these attitudes suggest the necessity of a continuous and vast program of adult education, equal opportunity of expression, growth of the free press, the expansion of public service by such organizations as public opinion polling agencies, municipal reference bureaus, student opinion surveys, the Educational Policies Commission of the National Education Association, the Town Meeting of the Air, and the modification of the programs of our schools to secure the desired affective outcomes.

Psychologists and other social scientists have a definite responsibility of transmitting their findings to the people and assisting a popular understanding of the importance and implications of these findings. This obligation is no less real, for example, than that of the medical profession. In recent years there is growing evidence that psychologists are becoming acutely aware of this responsibility and are bringing their knowledge and methods to bear on crucial social problems.

SUMMARY

The role of attitudes in human behavior has been developed by pointing up the importance of this concept in psychology applied to human problems. The acquisition of "human nature" by the individual as a process of learning in a cultural setting, methods of measuring attitudes, their functioning in social groupings, and the value of scientific study of attitudes have been described. The concept of attitudes is thus a central one in the development of a science of society.

Questions

1. A recent novel, *Out of Control,* relates that a little girl with the connivance of her mother got a tricycle that she wanted by

hiding the valuable dog of the local bank president in the cellar for three days and then returning him under the pretense of having found him caught in a foxtrap in the woods. She got the tricycle as a reward. Since then she does not like dogs.

Is this description psychologically plausible? Explain.

2. A recent writer in one of the technical psychological journals, reporting an experiment on the growth of "race" attitudes in a school system in a mixed population, stated: "Attitudes are the personality." Do you agree? Explain.

3. A study by the Purdue Opinion Panel shows that high school students whose college-trained parents received a general education had more desirable citizenship attitudes than did the students whose parents received a technical professional college education. An earlier study by Robert Pace showed that the same kind of attitude differences exist among college graduates with these two kinds of education. What inferences can you draw from these facts?

4. Show in terms of a specific functional psychosis that its origin is the attitude pattern of the individual.

5. Is it useful, as is often done, to distinguish between expressed opinion and behavior? Explain.

6. Is there any fundamental difference between the problems of measurement in the physical sciences and those of the measurement of opinion and attitude? Compare the measurement of temperature with measuring attitude.

7. What is meant by the statement, "All behavior is in some sense 'projective' as it would be interpreted by the clinical psychologist"?

8. Explain how the functional psychoses illustrate the failure of socialization in our culture.

9. Can you give further examples of individual or group ego-inflation exemplified by the concept of a *Herrenvolk?*

10. Over a period of several years the Purdue Opinion Panel has repeatedly polled its national sample of high school students on the question, "Are or are not racial prejudices inborn?" About one-fourth of the respondents have repeatedly said that such prejudices are inborn. How do you account for this biological superstition? What kinds of facts refute it?

Bibliography

1. Allport, G. W., "Attitudes," In Murchison, Carl (ed.), *Handbook of Social Psychology,* Worcester, Mass.: Clark University Press, 1935.
2. Anderson, H. H., and Anderson, Gladys L., *An Introduction to Projective Techniques,* New York: Prentice-Hall, Inc., 1951.
3. Bain, R., "Theory and Measurement of Attitudes and Opinions," *Psychol. Bull.,* 1930, *27:*357-379.
4. Bell, J. E., Projective Techniques, New York: Longmans, Green & Co., Inc., 1937.
5. Bogardus, E. S., "Measuring Social Distance," *J. appl. Sociol.,* 1925, *9:*299-308.
6. Buck, W., "A Measurement of Changes in Attitudes and Interests of University Students over a Ten Year Period," *J. abnorm. soc. Psychol.,* 1936, *31:*12-19.
7. Day, Daniel, "Methods in Attitude Research," *Amer. sociol. Rev.,* 1940, *5:*395-410.
8. Dunham, H. W., "Topical Summaries of Current Literature," *Amer. J. Sociol.,* 1940, *46:*344-375.
9. Eckert, Ruth E., and Wilson, H. E., "What Would You Do? A Survey of Student Opinion," Cambridge, Mass.: Committee on Publications, Harvard Graduate School of Education, 1939.
10. Fite, M. D., "Aggressive Behavior in Young Children and Children's Attitudes Toward Aggression," *Genet. Psychol. Monog.,* 1940, *22:*151-319.
11. Frank, L. K., "Projective Methods in the Study of the Individual," *J. Psychol.,* 1939, *8:*389-413.
12. Grice, H. H., "The Construction and Validation of a Generalized Scale to Measure Attitude Toward Defined Groups," *Purdue Studies in Higher Education,* 1934, no. 26:37-46.
13. Guttman, Louis, "A Basis for Scaling Qualitative Data," *Amer. sociol. Rev.,* 1944, *9:*139-150.
14. Hartshorne, H., and May, M., *Studies in the Nature of Character,* New York: The Macmillan Company, 1928-1930, vols. I-III.
15. Hinckley, E. D., "Influence of Individual Opinion on Construction of an Attitude Scale," *J. soc. Psychol.,* 1932, *3:*283-296.
16. Hinckley, E. D., and Hinckley, M. B., "Attitude Scales for

Measuring the Influence of the Work Relief Program," *J. Psychol.,* 1939, *8:*115-124.

17. Horowitz, E. L., "The Development of Attitude Toward the Negro," *Arch. Psychol.,* New York, 1936, no. 194.

18. Horowitz, R., and Murphy, L. B., "Projective Methods in the Psychological Study of Children," *J. exp. Educ.,* 1938, *7:*133-140.

19. Kelley, I. B., "The Construction and Evaluation of a Scale to Measure Attitude Toward Any Institution," *Purdue University Studies in Higher Education,* 1934, no. 26:18-36.

20. Knower, F. H., "Experimental Studies of Changes in Attitudes: I. A Study of the Effect of Oral Argument on Changes of Attitude," *J. soc. Psychol.,* 1935, *6:*315-347.

21. Likert, R., "A Technique for the Measurement of Attitudes," *Arch. Psychol.,* New York, 1932, no. 140:1-55.

22. Moreno, J. L., *Who Shall Survive? A New Approach to the Problem of Human Inter-Relations,* Washington, D. C., Nervous and Mental Disease Publishing Co., 1934.

23. Morgan, C. D., and Murray, H. H., "A Method for Investigating Fantasies: The Thematic Apperception Test," *Arch. Neurol. Psychiat.,* Chicago, 1935, *34:*289-306.

24. Murphy, Gardner, Murphy, Lois B., and Newcomb, E. M., *Experimental Social Psychology,* New York: Harper & Brothers, rev. ed., 1937, chap. 13.

25. Nelson, E., "Attitudes," *J. genet. Psychol.,* 1949, *21:*367-427.

26. Peterson, R. C., and Thurstone, L. L., *Motion Pictures and the Social Attitudes of Children,* New York: The Macmillan Company, 1933.

27. Pintner, R., and Forlano, G., "The Influence of Attitude upon Scaling of Attitude Items," *J. soc. Psychol.,* 1937, *8:*39-45.

28. Remmers, H. H., "A Generalized Attitude Scaling Technique," *Psychol. Bull.,* 1933, *30:*710-711.

29. Remmers, H. H., "Studies in Attitudes—Series I, II, and III," *Purdue University Studies in Higher Education,* 1934, no. 26; 1936, no. 31; 1938, no. 34.

30. Remmers, H. H., and Ewart, E., "Reliability of Multiple-Choice Measuring Instruments as a Function of Spearman-Brown Prophecy Formula, III," *J. educ. Psychol.,* 1941, *32:*61-66.

31. Remmers, H. H., and Sageser, H. W., "Reliability of Multiple-Choice Measuring Instruments as a Function of Spearman-Brown Prophecy Formula, V," *J. educ. Psychol.,* 1941, *32:* 445-451.

32. Roethlisberger, F. J., *Management and Morale,* Cambridge, Mass.: Harvard University Press, 1941, 26 and 194.

33. Rosander, A. C., "An Attitude Scale Based upon Behavior Situations," *J. soc. Psychol.,* 1937, *8:*3-16.

34. Thomas, W. I., and Znaniecki, F., *The Polish Peasant in Europe and America,* Boston: R. C. Badger, 1918.

35. Thurstone, L. L., "Attitudes Can Be Measured," *Amer. J. Sociol.,* 1928, *33:*529-554.

36. Thurstone, L. L., and Chave, E. J., *The Measurement of Attitude Toward the Church,* Chicago: University of Chicago Press, 1929.

37. Wright, M. E., "Constructiveness of Play as Affected by Group Organization and Frustration," *Character & Pers.,* 1942, *2:* 40-49.

CHAPTER II

· · ● ● ● · ·

Sampling in Opinion and Attitude Studies

INTRODUCTION

Investigations in the social studies are frequently directed toward making some generalizations of observations or measurements regarding a population. It is often desired to estimate a particular statistic of the population, such as the total proportion of voters who endorse a certain presidential candidate or the average age of college freshmen in a specified area. It is relatively rare that an entire population is observed, where data on every unit of the total population are collected and classified, although the United States Census may be said to make such an attempt every 10 years.

The usual procedure in social science investigations is to take a sample representing data only for a small but representative part of a total population. The plating inspector examining a bin of silvered buckle tongues may proceed in this fashion. Since it may be impracticable or too expensive to examine every tongue, he samples the total load by taking a few at the top, sides, or bottom of the bin or he may thoroughly examine every tenth or twenty-fifth bin that comes through his hands. By so taking a sample he may then conclude within specified "limits of confidence" that the entire batch is good, poor, or otherwise, according to his judgments of the sample. If it is both feasible *and* desirable to take a census, that is, to examine every piece in the job lot, this is done. But even if it were always possible to take a complete census, there are sometimes good reasons for not doing so. For example, in a test to determine the breaking point of electric light bulbs, a "census" would serve no useful purpose. Or the taking may affect the population. In a test on a human population, where the subject is to give the name of his Representative in Congress, the population might become changed in respect to the test item in that it would thenceforth become "Representative-conscious."

In dealing with human groups from which to make generalizations, there is actually little danger of thus corrupting an entire population. The designer of a vocational interest questionnaire may desire to discover the true proportion of personnel managers in this country expressing a preference for speech-making. It would be a mountainous and financially impossible task to question all the personnel managers in the country to obtain the desired information, so a sample is necessarily taken as representative of that total group, just how representative being a matter of the extent to which various parts of the country's industrial centers and by-nooks are included in the population proportions.

TERMINOLOGY

In sampling a *sampling unit* is the basic identity whose characteristic is to be studied. It can be individuals, the family, farm, school, industry, crop, or even judicial decision (29:297). A *sample* is a mass of such sampling units taken in some specified manner from a larger group of which it is a part. If it is a representative sample it is, within the allowable sampling error, a replica of the larger group with respect to the characteristic or characteristics under study (23). Taking a sample, if properly done permits estimating with a calculable degree of reliability the means, percentages, and other statistical quantities of the given population at a given cost, using only a small fraction of the population (39). It is a research technique for the social sciences using controls over observations and measurements. It is a technique devised to obtain the correct group for study in lieu of the data of a population or universe (29:286), for sampling implies that a census is either not feasible or desirable or both.

The *statistical population or universe* is a term that defines all the measurements or observations of the attribute of the phenomenon being studied. For practical purposes such a population may be considered hypothetical in that even though it may be theoretically possible to measure or enumerate all its units, it may not be feasible to do so.

Defining the Population

As already stated, it is required that the sample be representative of the whole group or population of which it is a part. But before that condition can be satisfied, there is definite need that the population or universe to be studied be defined precisely. The investigator may, within limits, define as he pleases the universe which he wishes to study (23). If, for example, he wishes to study the attitudes on given labor issues of a given group of college students in and of themselves and intends no generalizations for any larger group, he has defined his population as the attitudes of a given group on given issues. In another situation the same attitudes may be a sample of attitudes where in the strictest sense they are believed to comprise a replica of a larger population of attitudes under investigation.

Frequently, however, the conveniently grouped sophomores of Psychology I classes are studied in the hope that in a given measured characteristic they are representative samples of some larger, complete population. Occasionally they actually are. Miller (27), for example, found that college students as a group are not distinguishable in national morale from the adults who live in the same area. But the charge has been made that too many attitude studies have been made on atypical groups, such as those comprised of college students, which are not sufficiently heterogeneous to generalize for a larger group (25).

Two considerations basic to this charge may be noted. The one is the feasibility of obtaining a sample "large enough to permit numerous subclassifications of the total sample, and to permit checks on the meaning of identical questions and responses in different subsamples" (4). The other is that the broader the population selected for study, the more complex it becomes for a scientific study of attitudes and opinions. The number of questions that may be asked is limited. The nature of the questions asked is restricted because of vocabulary difficulties, lack of information, inability to handle complex ideas, and the like at the lower levels of a large social or political group. It is possible that a unidimensional scale (see Chapter IV) would not retain its unidimensionality when applied to a highly heterogeneous group, since identical terms might not have identical meaning for different parts of the sample, nor identical responses have uniform significance. Finally, few generalizations are likely to hold uniformly for all segments of a broad population (4).

BIAS IN SAMPLING

Bias Versus Chance Fluctuations

How can data be collected so that a sample is truly representative of the population that it is from? Here is a major problem in sampling. The inexperienced housewife who samples cake ingredients for sweetness before she has thoroughly mixed them in a bowl may not get a representative sample of the quality. What she tastes may be too sweet or not sweet enough and she may conclude erroneously that she has too much or too little sugar in her mixture. The discrepancy between the tasted sweetness and the actual amount of sugar in proportion to the bulk of the mixture is the bias in her sample.

When a seventh-grade class above average in achievement is taken as a sample of all seventh-grade classes (where the investigation is to deal with scholastic achievement), such a sample is unrepresentative or biased, or when in a mail questionnaire survey only the returns are used as a sample of the total population, and the unreturned questionnaires are forgotten, a biased sample may be the result.

Bias, or lack of representativeness, is one of the two major types of error commonly recognized in sampling. The other main type of error is the sampling variability or fluctuation that can be expected to occur as a result of chance, where the sample is randomly selected. The sampling variability of the quality of sweetness of a thoroughly mixed bowl of cake ingredients will be negligible, but may be considerable in the case of selecting a representative group of seventh graders in general scholastic achievement, even though random methods of selection are used. This topic will be discussed later in more detail.

Errors of measurement or observation, such as arithmetic and clerical errors, are sometimes recognized as a third category. In some instances they are thought to balance out and hence are ignored. Supposedly, in a census the only errors are those of observation and measurement (29:285), for there is normally no possibility of selection bias or sampling fluctuations. All cases are employed and simple enumeration is all that is required of the data.

In stratified or controlled sampling the chief source of error is the failure to obtain a random sample of observations or measurements for each control stratum that should be controlled for the universe sampled. Bias results because not all related variables have been taken into account in the stratification. As we shall see later, size of sample is not nearly so potent a source of error. Randomization is the primary control factor in all sampling to reduce bias to a minimum. To the extent that randomization is not possible, which is generally true for the widespread and heterogeneous populations usually dealt with in the social sciences, stratification is used to compensate for the errors or bias (*29*:311).

Sampling fluctuations will generally occur whenever a random sample is taken. If we know that the true proportion of a given characteristic is a certain percentage, we still do not expect that any random sample will equal that proportion but only that it will come within a certain range of tolerance within a certain level of confidence. It is impossible to predict what the sample proportion of a single sample will be, but it is possible to control to a certain extent the width of the range of tolerance of sample fluctuations by increasing the size of the sample. Sampling fluctuations become zero, of course, when the sample is 100 percent of the population or is the population itself. As Deming (*8*) has shown, errors in sampling may be combinations of the above three mentioned, with errors of measurement and observation perhaps playing a minor role. Four possible combinations pointed out by Deming include heavy bias with a wide sampling tolerance, heavy bias with narrow sampling tolerance, a negligible bias with wide sampling tolerance, and a negligible bias with a narrow sampling tolerance. These combinations, illustrated in Figure 1, may be likened to four rifle marksmen shooting at targets. If we assume that only two variables can affect the proximity of hits to the bull's-eye—mechanical adjustment of the sights and the actual shooting accuracy of the marksman (or his ability to hold his rifle steady)—the vertical line in the figure is then the target, the bias the lack of adjustment of the sights, and the sampling tolerance the accuracy of the marksman. Obviously, to improve marksmanship the rifleman must first eliminate the constant bias of his rifle, i.e., adjust his sights. Until he does his chances of hitting the target are particularly poor because he has two sources of error to contend with. In obtaining a representative sample it is also desirable to eliminate sources of bias first, so that only fluctuations of the sampling itself need be dealt with.

Then attention can be paid to reducing sampling fluctuations by increasing the size of the stratified or random sample.

Some Sources of Bias

Important sources of bias have been listed by Deming (8):

The method of selecting respondents. Information obtained from one segment of the population may not be valid for another

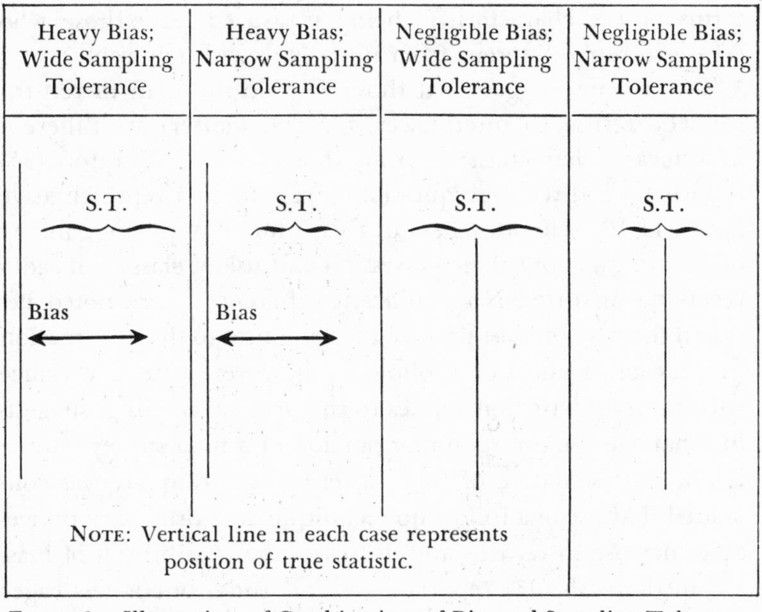

Heavy Bias; Wide Sampling Tolerance	Heavy Bias; Narrow Sampling Tolerance	Negligible Bias; Wide Sampling Tolerance	Negligible Bias; Narrow Sampling Tolerance
S.T.	S.T.	S.T.	S.T.
Bias	Bias		

NOTE: Vertical line in each case represents position of true statistic.

FIGURE 1. Illustrations of Combinations of Bias and Sampling Tolerance.

segment. This is the type of bias or constant error that random sampling precludes and that stratification seeks to reduce.

Bias of nonresponse. It is suspected that nonrespondents would not reply to questionnaires in quite the same manner as do respondents.

Bias of the questionnaire wording, including leading questions, emotionally "loaded" words, and the like.

Bias arising from errors in response, including intentional or unintentional mistakes in response and errors caused by the type of inquiry, those caused by the interviewer, and those injected by the auspices of the study, as when the respondent is motivated to protect self-interests.

Bias of Incomplete Returns.   Undoubtedly because of its convenience, the mail questionnaire is very frequently used. Since the percentage of returns in a given survey is seldom, if ever, complete, there is reasonable suspicion of bias in the responses of those that do send in returns. Do they represent a significantly unrepresentative portion of the population in terms of the characteristic being measured? Are those who refuse to reply different from those who willingly reply?

Two studies suggest that those who do not mail in returns (or who refuse an interviewer, for that matter) are different in relevant characteristics from those who do. Stanton (*35*) reports on a three-page questionnaire sent to a representative list of 11,169 schoolteachers in this country inquiring, among other things, about their possession and use of classroom radio receiving facilities. No significant differences were noted between the first and last parts of the responses to the information in question. Results of a follow-up, however, were at variance with findings based on replies to the original mailing, suggesting that the usual responding portion of a mail survey sample is not representative of the nonreturning group. It was concluded that use of a follow-up technique does produce a noticeable increase in returns and decreases the possibilities of bias.

Shuttleworth (*33*) reports a similar study, but is less eager to advocate generalizations therefrom. A questionnaire was sent to alumni to determine the percent unemployed. The first 184 returns from 327 indicated only 0.5 percent were unemployed, but later 125 returns from the same group showed 5.6 percent unemployed. Shuttleworth concludes that even if results of early returns are the same as those of later returns, this is no proof that the obtained proportion is representative, but that the only real check is against complete returns. He advocates that each questionnaire situation receive intensive study, including a complete return from at least a portion of the total population. Then future questionnaires can be planned to eliminate or minimize bias.

In another study (30) differences between college persons responding and not responding to a mailed questionnaire in a given situation were studied. Here background information on both respondents and nonrespondents was available, making comparisons possible. Information was classified into five major categories of intelligence, length of stay in college, community background, family background, and sociability. Of these, higher intelligence and scholarship records, loyalty or ties to the questionnaire sponsor, and a rural background all seemed to be positively associated with the tendency to respond.

In measuring attitudes toward the retail store, Hancock (11) compared the following four methods for obtaining responses to an attitude scale:

1. Sending the measuring instrument with an explanatory letter to a predetermined number of individuals.
2. Sending the instrument and 25 cents to a second group of individuals with instructions in the accompanying letter to return the quarter and the unused instrument in the return envelope if the recipient did not wish to coöperate.
3. Sending the instrument to a third group of individuals together with an appropriate letter instructing them to fill out the instrument and return it, and that upon receipt of the filled-out instrument 25 cents would be sent to the addressee.
4. Holding a personal interview with a fourth group of individuals using the instrument to record the responses on, as in the three mailing methods.

Method 1 yielded 9.56 percent returns. Method 2 yielded 47.2 percent returns. Method 3 yielded 17.6 percent returns. Method 4 yielded 85.5 percent returns. Despite these large discrepancies in returns for the different methods, a negligible sampling bias occurred, the four methods being found to measure the attitudes in question with equal accuracy.

Methods of controlling bias in mail questionnaires are given by Clausen and Ford (3). The problem as they see it is twofold:

(1) to maximize response by every means possible in order to cut down the size of the nonresponding group whose characteristics and attitudes are unknown, and (2) to make allowance or correction for any bias that may exist in incomplete returns. In mail follow-ups personalized salutations and true signatures were tried without significant increases over nonpersonalized salutations and mimeographed signatures, but use of special delivery letters did result in significant increases. A multiphasic survey, covering several potentially interesting topics, yielded higher rates of response than did a single subject survey of the same population and also greatly lessened an interest bias in response. These authors feel that if returns from successive mailings are tabulated separately, the trends in returns will often aid in estimating the characteristics of those still missing.

Reporting in connection with consumer research surveys, Hilgard and Payne (15) find that "people easily found at home on the first call differ significantly from those found at home only after repeated calls. The latter occur in large enough proportions to make it important for repeated calls to be made in order to represent them in sample surveys," or else too large a proportion of responses from households with the characteristics of the stay-at-homes will be obtained.

Not so potent a bias is represented by intended respondents who refuse to coöperate in a survey, since their number is quite small. Refusals analyzed were found most frequently among the poor, women in large cities, and among older people (14:123).

Interviewer Bias. Apparently there is justification in the charge that it matters who asks the questions in surveys. In all likelihood results of interviews of the same subjects by a socialist and by a prohibitionist in a survey to assign causes of unemployment would reveal some startling discrepancies. Detailed mention is made here of two studies relative to bias introduced by interviewers.

Katz (19) compared the findings of white-collar interviewers of the American Institute of Public Opinion with the findings of working-class interviewers, both groups working under the same instructions. His conclusions are summarized here:

1. White-collar interviewers find a greater incidence of conservative attitudes among lower-income groups than do interviewers from working classes.
2. The more liberal and radical findings of working-class interviewers are more pronounced on labor issues.
3. Differences in answers reported by white-collar workers as against working-class interviewers increase when union members, or their relatives, are interviewed.
4. Working-class interviewers find more support for isolationist sentiments among lower-income groups than do white-collar interviewers (before World War II).
5. Experience in interviewing lowers the incidence of conservatism found by the white-collar interviewer.
6. Results suggest that one source of constant bias of the public opinion polls in underpredicting the Democratic vote lies in the exclusive reliance upon white-collar interviewers who fail to discover the true opinions of the labor voter. (See quota sampling.)[1]
7. The above findings do not mean necessarily that the interviewer should have membership-character in the group he is interviewing. For some types of information the subject will respond more completely and accurately to an outsider with the proper prestige.

In a Blankenship study three experienced interviewers interviewed similar samples with ten questions each in a study conducted in Irvington, New Jersey, to measure interviewer effect, "all other factors being a constant." Each interviewer himself answered the questions as well. The results secured by

[1] In explaining the failure of his poll to predict properly the election of Mr. Truman in 1948, George Gallup has stated: "Some of our critics have said that our sample was at fault, that we did not interview enough persons of low income. While this statement was undoubtedly true in earlier elections, I am reasonably sure that this was not the case in 1948." He explains further that two errors in judgment accounted for most of the error in his 1948 prediction—his decision to eliminate the "undecided" voters in the sample and the failure to take a last minute poll and thereby take account of the last minute shifts in favor of Mr. Truman (26:181).

each interviewer were *essentially similar*. The attitudes of the interviewers in general were correlated with the results they secured in the questions and differences obtained between interviewers were real differences. The conclusion was then drawn that even trained interviewers show bias. This bias can be checked in practice by noting whether any results of individual interviewers are very much out of line and then balancing them (*1*).

Cantril's findings and conclusions somewhat bear out the above (*2*:118).

1. The opinions interviewers report have been found on certain questions to correlate with the opinions of the interviewers themselves.
2. Apparently there is an inverse correlation between the degree of relationship between interviewers' and respondents' opinions and the size of the town in which the interviewing is done.
3. Interviewers who are highly experienced show as much bias as less experienced interviewers.
4. Discrepancies between interviewers and respondents on the ground of race or class definitely hamper rapport and create distortion of true opinion.
5. Biases of interviewers tend to balance out and the overall percentage of opinion is not likely to be far off. Investigators should choose an equal number of interviewers who are biased in different directions. Error due to lack of rapport, however, does not necessarily cancel out.

Statistically the reliability or consistency of interviewer ratings may be measured by two methods. The correlation coefficient between observations of the same individuals by the same interviewer with his observations of the same subjects at a later date may be computed, or the correlation of the observations of one interviewer with those of other interviewers of the same subjects may be employed. (The first method is, of course, analogous to test-retest reliability and the second to reliability of equivalent forms of the same test.) With the first method a correlation coefficient of 0.79 between ratings on income was reported, 0.97 on age. With the second method correlation coefficients of 0.63 on income and 0.91 on age were reported (28:106).

One way of measuring validity of sampling as the ability of observers to classify what they are supposed to classify is to correlate judgments of interviewers as to a given characteristic for the same subjects with the judgments of experts. Other methods have also been used. A correlation coefficient between interviewers' ratings on economic status and reported income was 0.73. That between respondents' subjective classification of their income groups with the interviewers' classification was 0.60, and that between respondents' classification of themselves and the income they say they receive was 0.58 (28:106).

Avoiding Bias in Data Collection

Random Samples Versus Stratified-Random Samples. After deciding upon the population for investigation and after defining it in terms of the elements comprising it, the investigator turns his attention to drawing his sample or samples. If he draws them so that each sampling unit in the total population has an equal chance of being selected, his sample is random. This type of sampling is adequate if the population is defined in a clear-cut manner and is such that a random selection of sampling units can easily be made and investigated. When objects such as industrial products are to be inspected, random sampling is quite naturally used. For random sampling of individual persons a complete listing of sampling units is a great convenience. Techniques such as selecting every tenth or twentieth case or assigning case numbers and then using a table of random numbers are customary.[2] When the object of the survey is people this type of sample is not likely to be suc-

[2] A table of random numbers may be found in E. F. Lindquist *Statistical Analysis in Educational Research,* Boston: Houghton Mifflin Company, 1940, pp. 262-264.

cessful in that various factors affecting the characteristic in question (or are related to it—traits, social and economic status, etc.) will not have been controlled adequately.

In order to obtain a representative sample of populations of people, frequently some sort of stratified-random sample is employed. The essential principle of stratification is that the total population is broken up into major groups or divisions or strata before the sample is drawn. A random sample is then taken from each stratum in the proper proportion. Peatman (29:299) defines stratified-random sampling as a sample consisting of "two or more random samples drawn from two or more subdivisions or strata of the universe, each stratum having been established with respect to one or more secondary control factors, the size or weight of the sample from each stratum corresponding to the proportionate size or weight of the control factors in the universe being studied." The total sample result is therefore derived from a series of random samples.

The secondary control factors in stratified-random sampling are traits or behavior that are known or assumed to be correlated to some degree with the attribute to be investigated. They are the criteria on the basis of which a universe is subdivided into two or more strata, or combination of strata, each of which is then sampled. Two assumptions are basic to the above procedure: (1) that there is a significant correlation between the control factors and the trait or behavior to be studied; (2) that the necessary information about the universe is available so that stratification can be based on facts and not merely on guesswork.

In general, a representative sample is one that is a reasonable replica of the universe sampled. But this representativeness refers to the trait being studied and not to some other factor or characteristic. There is some question, then, whether the stratified-random sample may be a typical cross section of the universe in secondary control factors such as residence, socioeconomic status, age, sex, etc. Therefore, Peatman suggests, it might be better to refer to a stratified-random sample as a typical cross section of the sampling units of the universe, and then to describe the control factors used in the stratification, than to refer to such samples as representative samples (29:312).

Technique of Stratification. By means of preliminary "test tube" surveys, the possible relevance of one or more secondary control factors can be determined. First, one may determine by tetrachoric correlation or other means an idea of the relationship of these factors with the characteristic to be measured, say the factors of educational status and sex with attitude toward a proposed labor law. Correlated control factors reduce the sampling error (that attributable to chance fluctuations) since a single random sample cannot be expected to give a truly representative result for the attitudes of the universe studied (29:300).

Sampling units of some subuniverses are relatively easy to identify (geography, location, or socioeconomic status by resident areas); others are more difficult, especially when units are people and stratification factors are individual differences of people. Those factors commonly used in public opinion polls and in market research are sex, age, socioeconomic status, education, residence, geographical or sectional region in the United States, and occupation. Also skin color, nationality background, religious affiliation, and politics are often used.

For a given size of sample the results with a stratified-random sample will be more precisely representative of the universe than those obtained with an unstratified-random sample, two controls—randomization and stratification—accounting for the increase in accuracy of results. With no correlation between the attribute or behavior and stratifying factors the overall random sample will yield a result that is equally as satisfactory. It must be noted, however, that the amount of sampling error can be validly estimated (calculated) only for a truly random sample.

"Accidental" Samples. Data yielded by mere collections of cases are not without value in the opinion of Cornfield (6). They may give the investigator greater insight into his subject,

may strengthen his intuitive grasp, may possess a high order of intrinsic interest. They lack, however, the ability to provide statements of a known order of accuracy about a parent population, as was seen in the unfortunate *Literary Digest* poll of 1936 presidential preference. Peatman suggests that samples drawn in unplanned or haphazard fashion, that is, convenient collections of cases, are accidental and not necessarily random. He terms them *ignorant* samples, as representing no known universe and as having no character and hence no place in scientific research (*29*:316). The daily sidewalk interviews of four to six people that are run by newspapers under titles such as "The Inquiring Reporter," usually including photographs of the interviewees, are based upon such accidental samples. They hardly present "scientific" findings.

Sampling from Files and Lists. In the problem of obtaining a representative sample, randomization always plays some part, whether it is the stratified factor or element or whether it is the entire sample that is randomized. The method of selecting the sample must be entirely unrelated to the data it is intended to get from the sample—another way of saying that bias should be avoided in the selection of cases. Random sampling should be done according to some mechanical principle which is unconnected with the subject and purpose of the study. To this end frequently every nth case is selected from an alphabetized list or sometimes a table of random numbers is employed, each case being assigned a number and the numbers drawn in accordance with the random pattern of the table.

Such sampling from files is easiest, of course, if the files are truly representative of the whole. But care must be exercised that if some units are missing they will be given their chances of being selected unless one knows they are just like the ones included in respect to the relevant characteristics. Even a listing like a city directory may not be representative. Stock (*37*:133) indicates that in one Southern city only one-third of the Negro population was represented because two-thirds of them lived in alleys and the book did not include alleys. The time lag in using city directories is an even more apparent source of error. And Cornfield (6) points out that a sample of families obtained by drawing names from a pay roll listing earners may be worse than a mere convenient collection of cases since the chances of a family's being included may be too dependent upon the number of earners it has.

RELIABILITY AND VALIDITY IN SAMPLING

A statistical program must possess five general characteristics: comprehensiveness, so that correct interpretations may be made; uniformity of definitions, procedures, units, and measures to avoid misleading interpretations; speed, which is to say that the data must be timely; reliability or representativeness of the figures used; and validity or the use of figures that represent answers to the questions that one thinks they answer (8).

Size

A primary question arising in connection with planning the sample that is going to be drawn from a given population is how may cases will comprise it. Size of the sample to be drawn is a function of the character of the sample, which involves knowing the methods used to obtain it and the extent to which it predicts the behavior expected of the universe. Once character of the sample is determined to be satisfactory, size can be considered, bearing the following principles in mind: (1) In voters' preferences the size of the sample required depends upon the closeness of the poll result. Larger samples are required for smaller differences to be significant. (2) When the universe is finite (all elements comprising it at least theoretically capable of being measured) a random sample of a given size will yield a more precise result for a small than for a large universe. (3) The more heterogeneous the character of the universe to be sampled, the larger will be the sample required and conversely, the more homogeneous the character of the universe, the smaller will be the sample required (29:314).

To sample the blood count of an individual, for example, the doctor needs only a drop of blood and he will have a representative sample. If, however, an investigator wishes to obtain an idea of the total number of pain receptors in a human body, he will probably be forced to sample skin areas from many different parts of the body. Similarly, in the social sciences, sampling the racial attitudes of liberal arts college students of a given socioeconomic status (a relatively homogeneous population) would require a comparatively smaller sample than sampling the same attitudes of persons from all social and economic and educational walks of life.

By and large, the larger the sample, the greater the accuracy, provided the sample is at least a fairly representative one. Bias is not removed or even diminished by merely increasing the size of any sample except where the size of the sample is near 100 percent of the population. The now-classic example of a combination of nonrepresentativeness and size of a sample is the *Literary Digest* straw poll of 1936, which failed rather ignominiously to predict the President-Elect. It compiled the preferences of more than 100,000 individuals, using, however, as a source of data, persons listed in telephone directories and persons from lists of car owners. In the national public opinion surveys, the sample sizes range from 1500 to 50,000 with maximum errors ranging from 4 to 2½ percent, although a high level of stability can be reached with as few as 400 interviews in any subsection with only an 8 percent maximum error (9).

Relatively small samples of from 200 to 500 have been used rather successfully to get a quick, inexpensive, and superficial sounding of the drift of public opinion in elections. In well-organized surveys such small samples have been called telegraphic polls. The investigator usually has worked out a small sample of 200 to 500 cases and has interviewers carefully distributed throughout the country (in a national survey) who have already been instructed about the number and distribution of cases they are to interview. Replies are then sent in by telegram. Validated against three elections, they are reported to have had an average error of less than 5 percent, which compares quite favorably with the regular national samples of polling organizations. Telegraphic samples, however, are not an adequate substitute for regular national samples. They are highly unlikely to represent opinion faithfully unless opinion is fairly uniform throughout an area and within different interest groups and unless such differences are already fairly well known. Finally, they allow no possibility of a reliable breakdown or other detailed analysis (2:169-171).

Adequacy

A sample is adequate if it is both representative and precise. Its adequacy is specific to the investigation and is dependent upon the sampling methods used. While size is an important element in determining the adequacy of a sample, the criterion is whether a sample is large enough for generalization about certain characteristics, rather than what is the ratio of the size of the sample to the total population (37:129). A random sample of clerical workers in a large business organization may give results on a clerical efficiency test that will constitute a sample sufficiently representative and precise for that universe to be an adequate basis on which to develop test norms for all clerical workers in that one organization, but the same sample will be inadequate for the development of test norms for clerical workers generally, or in another business organization.

Garrett (10) has suggested as one of the simplest tests of adequacy of a sample the drawing from the population of a second sample of approximately the same size as the first and concluding that if the mean and standard deviations of the second sample are of nearly the same size as the mean and standard deviations of the first, the sample is probably representative of its population. The taking of successive samples is considered of value *only* when the sampling is random or is otherwise unbiased, their chief value being that of a confidence-strengthener. McNemar (*24*) has replied to the effect that if it is known that the sample is random or otherwise unbiased, then there is no need for a second sample. If it is not known, of course, a similar second sample could easily duplicate any influence of selection bias present in the first sample.

Accuracy

Accuracy of a sample result refers to its evaluation in terms of the extent to which any measure derived from it agrees with that value of the measure for the universe sampled *when it is known*. In the absence of universe values, one recourse is to a consideration of the method of drawing the sample (*23*). It was actually possible at the time the *Literary Digest* straw ballot was being conducted to predict a Roosevelt victory in 1936 from the data compiled by the *Literary Digest*. In taking the percentage of that sample which had voted for Hoover in 1932, it was noticed that the percentage was not the same as that of the total 1932 vote. Hence, by proper weighting of these ballots, a fairly accurate Roosevelt majority was predictable (*6*).

Another method sometimes used or recommended for use is the quality check or a reinterview of the population or of a sample of the population. This may be an effort to repeat an interview under the same essential conditions or to repeat it under vastly improved conditions of better qualified and better trained interviewers, with more time, and greater intensity of questioning (*26*:79).

Gallup frequently tests his cross sections by adding to his battery of questions an information question, the answer to which he knows from census figures (*9*).

Precision is dependent upon a number of interacting variables. One is the variability of the characteristic being measured within the group being studied. Generally, the more homogeneous the group, the smaller is the sample required. Another is the size of the sampling unit which is inversely related to precision or representativeness. A sample of many small units, each randomly chosen, is almost without exception to be preferred to an equal sample of a few large units, even though they appear to be well chosen. Precision is further related to the effectiveness of the stratification or the degree to which the sampling method adopted ensures the proper representation of each class of the total group under study. Finally, size of the group, and adequacy, have bearing upon the representativeness of a sample (2:130-131).

Attitudes and Behavior

In the foregoing sections concerning size, adequacy, and accuracy (or precision) of a sample, the question of how well a population is being represented by a sample was discussed. This is actually the question of reliability.

It was said before the 1948 presidential election that recent political election results had "made" the national public opinion surveys. The elections provided some measure of proof through election poll behavior that the opinions of people actually were what the polls said they were. Otherwise, it was maintained, the polls would be mere curiosities. This is the problem of validity in sampling. Do the answers of subjects give a true picture of their behavior?

A little thought leads to the conclusion that the basic criterion for validating opinion must be corresponding behavior. When one measures validity on a verbal level, the connection with actions must be established (22). Polling agencies realize more fully now that the poll must occur as shortly before the election as possible; otherwise there may be a discrepancy introduced through changes of opinion before election, as clearly happened in the 1948 presidential election. The replies of consumer market research subjects are validated by comparing them with accounts of purchasing behavior. There is much evidence establishing the high validity between consumer research replies and use of various products. Correlates, moreover, have been successfully established between public attitudes and actions regarding attendance at World's Fair exhibits, listening to a company's radio program, knowledge of a company's advertising, and presence or absence at traveling exhibits (22).

Hyman's study on behavior of people replying to questions of a survey indicates people do not necessarily give a true picture of their behavior as to redemption of war bonds, display of grocery posters, and absenteeism in industry where traditional random polling resulted in much more distortion than did the intensive interviewing of known absentee offenders (18). It is believed by many social scientists that some groups deliberately falsified their voting intentions to 1948 presidential polling interviewers.

SAMPLING ERROR THEORY

Sampling error theory describes a statistical method for evaluating errors due to sampling or chance fluctuations. A sample is drawn from a population as an estimate of a particular statistic (a "parameter") of that population. A hypothetical value of the population's statistic is set up. The statistic of the sample is then compared to the hypothesized parameter and the arithmetical difference between the two is the *sampling error* which is evaluated by using a measure of the normally expected (or chance) dispersion of the statistic of samples of the same size that are drawn at random from the population. This measure of dispersion is the standard deviation of the sampling distribution and is also known as the *standard error* of the particular statistic whose sampling error we are testing. The sampling distribution is the distribution of a given statistic—of means, for example, of 100 random samples—and differs from the distribution of the data of a sample which is a distribution of *frequencies* of a single sample. The mean of a sampling distribution is assumed to be the parameter or true population statistic.

The sampling distribution is expected to be normal, particularly of means and proportions or percentages, although as a matter of fact the sampling distribution of most statistics is not yet known. The hypothetical statistic or parameter is set up. Let us say it is the percentage, 60 percent, of the total population that the investigator hypothesizes is the true percentage of persons in favor of daylight saving in a given community. A sample selected at random from this population, or at random within specified stratification controls, reveals a percentage of 65 in favor of daylight saving. The question may then be asked, "Assuming that the percentage of the sample comes from a population of percentages with the parameter or true percentage at the mean of the sampling distribution of percentages, how many times in a hundred in the course of many similar random samplings, i.e., as a matter of chance, would we get a departure, that is, a difference between the parameter and the sample statistic, as large or larger than that of 5 percent which was found?" The reply is in terms of the ratio between this obtained difference and the standard error of a percentage, the latter being a function of the number in the sample. Since the sampling distribution is assumed to be normal, the ratio just obtained, frequently called a *critical ratio,* is referred to normal probability tables where the ratio is transferred into a probability statement that an observed statistic or percentage, in this case, would deviate from the parameter as much as did the sample percentage. This probability is the "level of confidence" or "level of significance" expressing the *degree* of confidence with which the hypothesis (in this case that the true percentage is 60) would be rejected.

If a high level of confidence is obtained, corresponding to a small probability, the stated hypothesis is rejected and the statement may be made with the appropriate level of confidence that the sample could not have come as a result of chance fluctuations from a population having that particular hypothesized parameter. The hypothesis is then disproved, but it cannot be proved. If it cannot be disproved by this method, then the statement may only be made that the hypothesis is tenable or reasonable. Note, however, that while a hypothesis that the parameter percentage is 60 may be tenable, other hypothetical parameter values may also be tenable. The hypothesis cannot be stated in terms of the probability that a true difference exists. The only workable hypothesis is that no real difference exists between a given parameter and a sample statistic. The general concept here is that of the null hypothesis.

In practice it is often preferred to get an idea of where the parameter does lie before the various hypotheses concerning parameters are tested. Based upon predetermined levels of confidence and standard error measures, the statement is made that the sample statistic may lie within certain limits of the parameter, these limits being the specified confidence limits. Generally speaking, the larger the sample the more accurate will be the results or, to state it differently, the narrower will be the confidence limits. Formulas for the computation of measures of standard error, normal probability tables, and more detailed discussion concerning techniques of sampling error theory will be found in any elementary statistics book. Chapter III in this book provides the elements of statistical theory relevant to our present interests.

Mention should be made of differences between statistics from pairs of random samples. Such differences may themselves be regarded as statistics and can therefore be tested for significance. Wilks (39) mentions that an increasing number of public opinion surveys involve such tests for differences in percentages obtained over a lapse of time, reflecting changes in attitudes, the test being whether such changes could occur as a result of chance fluctuations or whether something has occurred during the lapse of time to make for a "real" or significant change in attitude. Ryan (32) points out that in psychological investigations of all kinds an obtained difference between statistics may have three degrees of pertinence. A difference might be (1) large but statistically insignificant, (2) large and significant, or (3) small and significant. Generally, a large and significant difference is of greatest value, although a small and significant difference, say of percentages when the parameter percentage is close to 50, may be extremely important as was the case in the presidential election polls in 1948. In that election Gallup's error, though it was shown to contain systematic bias, was actually smaller than it was in the 1936 election which largely established his reputation in preëlection polling. The important difference was that in view of the 1936 Roosevelt landslide the error was largely overlooked, while the close 1948 election (in addition to last minute shifts in opinion) led to his failure in prediction.

SOME SAMPLING PRACTICES

Basic Sampling Practices

Since most populations involving human beings are not very homogeneous, it is usually advisable to select some sort of controlled sample to ensure that the sample will be a replica of the population or that at least there will be a close degree of representativeness. Public opinion polling and market research agencies make regular use of devices known as stratified-quota, area and block, master and panel samples. Other psychological investigations which involve and depend a great deal upon choice of a representative sample of the population make use of devices that are similar, at least in principle, to the above in certain respects. Norms set up for nationally known and used college "scholastic aptitude" tests may be based upon the systematic stratification of such controls as national regions, size of schools, or perhaps school curricula. Populations in investigations such as the setting up of test standards are probably more homogeneous than are those whose attitudes on nation-wide issues are to be measured, where several elements of the national population are to be included and represented. In practice, the system of stratification used probably will **not** have to be as elaborate as the following techniques which are directed in the main toward economy of operation as well as representativeness.

Stratified-Quota Method. This method of controlled sampling consists essentially in predetermining the elements of the universe to be studied so that the people selected for the sample will be in the same proportion as they are in the total population sampled. First there is a choice of selected characteristics of the population to be sampled, which are used as "controls." These characteristics are known or assumed to be correlated with the responses to be obtained. Then there is a determination of the proportion of the population possessing the characteristics selected as controls. Finally quotas are fixed for the enumerators who select the respondents so that the population interviewed contains the proportion of each class as determined above (*13*). Stock (*37*:139-141) gives an example of the selection of a national sample of adults for a desired public opinion poll: The country is divided into geographic sections. Each section is divided into various layers according to the degree of urbanization. Interviewers are employed who live in or near points decided upon in the sample. They are instructed to select a specified number of people in different economic status groups, a specified number of Negroes, and a specified number of farmers. Hence the sample is shown to be controlled on five variables: section of the country, size of town, economic status, color, and farm or nonfarm. Further, interviewers are instructed to control for sex and age, that is, to get half men and half women, half over forty and half under forty, this not being necessarily in proportion to the population.

This is an inexpensive method but is to be used with caution because of the wide latitude to interviewer choice which, as has been shown, may be biased. In addition to being relatively inexpensive, there is reportedly greater speed in executing the sample design and the field work (*16*).

Hansen and Hauser (*13*) criticize the quota method on the grounds that such samples cannot provide sample estimates for which the risk of error can be measured because they do not provide for the selection of persons in a way that permits knowing the probabilities of selection. Estimates made of the sampling error of the quota sample usually are erroneous. The quota method is regarded as of value only if rough estimates are wanted and if small samples will be employed. Area or probability methods, instead, are recommended by these authors if results of a specified reliability need to be obtained and if there is a fairly heavy loss involved with incorrect results. Hochstein and Smith (*16*) recommend the quota method as more efficient if surveys dealing with issues and reasons for opinions are desired. The quota sample cannot possibly be representative of all characteristics of the population, as other opponents point out. "It is physically impossible to ask the interviewers to select a person over the age of fifty, who is a Presbyterian, with two years of college, and who belongs to five organizations, who lives in a certain part of the state, who had measles at the age of six and reads so many magazines. It would take them years to locate more than three or four persons with all those characteristics, and unless in the theoretical design you have a system so that after selecting on three characteristics you at the same time are getting a complete coverage of all other characteristics, you are running into extreme difficulty, theoretically" (*26*:257).

Area Sampling. Another common method used for selecting a representative cross section in public opinion surveys is known as area or probability sampling. This method is a special form of a simple random sampling in which the universe area is divided, subdivided, and subdivided again down to a number of sampling units, all by randomizing devices, and these sampling units only are covered completely or sampled. A sample of such areas is drawn and all sampling units within those areas are then combined. This sample of areas then is used to establish stratified-random samples for a city, county, large rural area, state geographical section, or entire nation (*13*).

The area method is taken from agricultural surveys where the stress is upon geographical subdividing of the universe to be sampled.

Theoretically, in extreme forms of the area method randomness applies throughout and the interviewer has no choice even within a household. Area sampling is said to be less subject to bias in that interviewers are not responsible for selecting the final respondents. Practically, however, the problem of finding at home and then interviewing all persons in a given subdivided area is usually an impossible one and interviewers usually must exercise some judgment in selecting substitutes to interview. Hochstein and Smith (*16*) point out that under certain conditions a "domal sample" (dwelling unit sample where not blocks or areas but houses and dwelling units within the blocks are predetermined in a systematic way with quotas for one or more characteristics being assigned) will produce about as good a cross section as will an area sample. The area method is of advantage in periods of rapid shifts in population or changes in the economic structure; and there need be no concern about numbers in each of the assigned categories (*9*). It is likewise of advantage if the purpose of the sample is to measure exact quantities. A disadvantage lies in the fact that there must be a constant search for new areas. Reliability can be measured and controlled as the various elements in the population are known. Costs of this method are higher because of rates for interviewing and the necessity of making callbacks.

The Master Sample.   This method attempts to achieve the advantages of small-unit area sampling by means of a cross section of area samples for the universe to be studied, rather than by the subdivision of the complete universe into areal units. As in total area sampling, it has the advantage of eliminating freedom of choice on the part of the field workers, for the sampling for an investigation can be completely designed in advance in the central office by means of appropriately stratified and randomized techniques (29:309).

The Panel. This type of controlled sample is perhaps best used where changes in attitude are to be investigated. It appears to be common in consumer research where there is necessity for an instrument to give a continuous and comparable picture of consumption in the home, and there are numerous instances of it in educational work. The panel consists of a relatively small group of persons, chosen for certain controlled factors, whose attitudes are sampled periodically. The simplest form of the panel is a single reinterview of people who have been interviewed before (20). It has been used to find out what changes in opinion occurred in the 2 weeks immediately prior to elections. Groups used to study changes after lessons, radio talks, or films are in essence panels. Other advantages of the panel have been enumerated by Lazarsfeld and Fiske (21):

1. It is useful for detailed comments to questions where an original effort has been successful with a given group.
2. If one is interested in relating the opinions of people to their personal characteristics, a repeated interview, as in the panel, is better.
3. Statistical reliability of the panel is greater than in other forms of controlled samples per number of cases; hence the number of cases may be smaller for a given reliability desired.
4. In studying the attitudes of people toward an event which is itself extended in time, such as a radio broadcast, a panel organizes a ready group.
5. In certain cases a panel is a substitute for use of a control group, since often the controls can be introduced by the investigator, as when certain farmer members of a panel are given radios and their radio attitudes are compared with those of nonradio holders.
6. A final advantage is a saving in cost of sampling.

The same authors mention the following problems or disadvantages in using panels: patience of the participators; the growing articulateness of participators; the representativeness of their opinions as time passes; the "critical set" of panel members when they are asked ahead of time to judge an event; and the "freezing" of opinions. The term "panelitis" has been applied to the distortions that may or do result.

The extent to which members of a panel will coöperate is probably the chief concern of investigators. Frequently a member drops out or fails to do something after he has promised to do it. As panels have been known to operate, it is very rare that more than two-thirds coöperate at any given time. Consequently the practice has been to get twice as many as are needed to start with. The same principle has been observed in the selection of members with regard to stratification factors, it having been discovered that advanced cultural level and interest in a particular issue make for better coöperation in a Town Hall project (20). To offset the customary mortality of this group, more of those with lower interest and lower cultural level were selected. In a consumer research investigation, Stonborough (38) reports the successful use of monetary incentives to overcome the obstacles of lack of coöperation, and predicts the extension of the fixed panel into other fields with the use of material incentives.

Effect of panel participation in influencing the opinions of panel members is also discussed by Lazarsfeld (20). He suggests that possibly one should make distinctions between issues where a member is already concerned and where he has no opinion. But still one cannot tell whether the member is more susceptible to influence or whether he will tend to stick to an opinion once it is attained. Many people will not admit changes of opinion for fear of losing "prestige" or face. A panel, however, permits the investigator to spot a large percent of panel members who do admit a change and through interviews to investigate the causes of their shifts. In the panel of reader-reporters used by the *Woman's Home Companion*, bias resulting from increased articulateness in the members due to participation in the panel is reduced by rotating the member-ship so that each year one-third is completely replaced (*31*).

Typical Sampling Programs

The 1940 Population Census. The 1940 United States Census was a combination of complete enumeration and systematic sampling. Statistical information regarding unemployment, occupational shifts, and population growth was obtained in response to a set of supplementary questions to be asked concerning a sample of one in twenty. Supplementary questions included parentage and mother tongue, veteran status, social security, occupation, and fertility data (age at first marriage and number of children). The method of sampling was as follows: Schedules were printed with notes in the margin that designated two of forty lines on each side as sample lines, thus including 5 percent of the total. Exactly 5 percent of all lines in each geographical area was selected and in this respect the sample was stratified for geographical differences in population characteristics. Several possible sources of bias were noted— "line" bias, a process bias arising from a systematic procedure specifying the order of enumeration within blocks and within households, and an enumerator's bias arising from failure to follow directions and tendencies to cover territories in certain patterns. Varying the schedules helped eliminate line bias (*36*).

A word on sampling is injected by Stephan, Hansen, and Deming, reporting on the above survey. A complete enumeration is considered in itself but a sample. Even a "perfect" 100 percent sample is but one of the many perfect yet distinct 100 percent samples that might have resulted from the same social and economic cause systems existing at the time of the census.

The NORC (National Opinion Research Center at Chicago University) (17). The NORC uses a quota control method of sampling, in which three types of control factors normally play a role: *impersonal* (beyond individual control), such as geographical data; *personal, unchangeable* factors, such as sex, age, race; and *personal, changeable* factors, such as education, occupation, religion, political factors, and standard of living. NORC's social cross section of the civilian adult population is controlled by geographical distribution of the population (regional and rural-urban) and by sex, color, and standard-of-living level. Age is partially controlled by assignment of age quotas under and over forty years of age. Variables are controlled by proportions reported by the 1940 census. With the exception of age, where instructions are mainly to get a good spread over and under forty, there is objective control of these stratification factors; they are not subject to individual and personal determination by interviewers.

The Purdue Opinion Panel.   The Panel usually conducts three opinion polls a year among high school pupils all over the country. A nationally representative sample of about 3000 is selected from a total of 10,000 to 15,000 returns using stratification figures based upon the latest available census data. The stratification variables consist usually of sex, grade in school, religious preference, geographical region (rural-urban status), and economic-cultural status. Economic-cultural status is ascertained as the score a subject makes on the seven-item House and Home Scale, an adaptation of the Kerr-Remmers American Home Scale, included in each questionnaire. Urban-rural status merely refers to the size of the community of residence, rural being communities of less than 2500 population. Depending upon the nature of the opinion questions asked, other stratification items such as "race" or educational level of the parents are included in the questionnaire. Since the Panel is conducted as a mail questionnaire, with the high school pupils recording their answers on mark-sensing International Business Machine ballot cards, interviewer bias is avoided (there being no interviewers). Validity of these data used for stratification purposes rests of course upon the responses made by the subjects themselves, although the accuracy of such data has occasionally been checked for consistency to reveal less than one percent inaccuracy in certain types of personal data.

A Survey of Higher Education Enrollment (5). The method of stratified-random sampling was used to survey the fall enrollments in certain institutions of higher learning for the year 1946. Strata variances in enrollments for previous years were used as a basis for stratification in this sampling. It was found that the stratified plan used was almost 80 percent more efficient than the unrestricted random sampling would have been. Of chief value to the investigators was the fact that by using such available information about a universe (enrollment in teachers colleges) with techniques that produce desired reliability, the number of returns required in the sample was reduced.

Sampling in Experimental Psychology. A satisfactory control and an experimental group can be set up by drawing two random samples from the same universe. They are then matched in one basic factor only—randomization. Any difference between two such groups at the beginning of an experiment should be no greater than would be expected on the basis of chance alone. Hence, any difference at the conclusion of the experiment that is greater than could be expected on the basis of chance would be attributable to the experimental variable, provided, of course, other conditions for both groups were kept similar during the experiment (29:321). Thus one could select at random two groups of high school tenth graders from a given population of tenth graders and, having ascertained by a Thurstone-type attitude scale that they hold similar attitudes toward unionization, subject them to a series of lessons, and again measure their attitudes at the conclusion of the talks. If the experimenter is reasonably certain the subjects have not been subjected to other influences during the course of the experiment, he may conclude that any significant differences are the result of the lessons.

This holds if one can assume that the initial measurements did not appreciably alter both the experimental and control groups by sensitizing them both to the experimental variable—by inducing, as it were, a kind of panelitis. Solomon (*34*) has shown experimentally that this does happen and provides an experimental design to control this factor by adding a second or even a third control group.

Sometimes samples are matched to establish equated groups providing one more control where it is known or assumed that there are factors present that are correlated with the experimental variable (*29*:318). If in a given experiment it is believed that intelligence or scholastic level is a factor in attitude toward unions, the groups may be matched with respect to some index of these characteristics, and again any significant change that occurs may be attributable to the experimental influence.

Practical Considerations in Planning a Sample

"The purpose of any survey, sample or complete, is to provide factual evidence that presumably will be useful in formulating a course of action in the solution of some problem" (*12*). The aim desired in designing a sample is to devise procedures that will (1) operate within the available budget and limitations of time and man power; (2) operate also within other imposed administrative limitations or restrictions; yet (3) produce the maximum amount of information that is possible within the limitations of (1) and (2); (4) give results that are reasonably sure to fall within a certain allowable sampling error, which for any survey will be predetermined by the administrative uses that are to be made of the data (*12*).

Deming (*8*) lists the one, two, three of planning a sample:

1. Decide what sort of survey or experiment would be feasible and whether funds are available.
2. Lay plans for reducing errors and biases.
3. Decide sampling error tolerance.
4. Design the sample to meet tolerance at the lowest cost.
5. Put sampling plans into practice.
6. Interpret data.

Professionally a job of sampling has certain characteristics mentioned also by Deming (8). Selection of respondents is automatic with relentless follow-up. The sampling process and computation procedure are laid out in advance. An error formula for calculating precision exists.

Methodological and statistical procedures of many surveys have been under recent attack (25) because of a lack of emphasis which would, in the words of Crespi (7), "seem to excommunicate a whole new area of modern statistical development which is concerned with the fashioning of relatively imprecise statistics which are, however, of remarkable efficiency in terms of information obtainable per unit cost in time and money." Academic quarrels aside, to consider the administrative and budgetary hurdles any survey must cross or circumvent, weight undoubtedly must be given the criterion suggested by Hansen and Deming (12): Does it "provide factual evidence that presumably will be useful in formulating a course of action in the solution of some problem?" If so, there seems to be little justification in insisting upon a perfection that may not be achieved in this day.

SUMMARY

Most psychological investigations of attitudes of human subjects are based upon the responses of samples of people taken from some larger population which must be precisely defined. There are errors in sampling to the extent that the drawn sample is not truly representative of the population from which it is drawn and to the extent that sample statistics will fluctuate in value from true statistics within chance limits. The first type of error is referred to as bias, which may easily arise in the case of incomplete returns or where the influence of interviewers may weigh unduly or where methods of data collection are not adequate. Reliability of sampling is related to the factors of size, adequacy, and accuracy. Validity of sampling is seen as the degree of relationship between expressed attitudes and behavior. Common types of controlled samples are the quota, area, and master samples, and the panel. Practical considerations are often stressed over theoretical ones in planning a sample.

Questions

1. Is it feasible and useful to think of samples of such universes as: Railroad freight cars? Ions? Telephone sets? Twelve-year-old, rural, white boys? Opinion questions about a world government? The reading vocabulary of John Doe? Students of opinion and attitude measurement?
2. What is wrong (if anything) with "The Inquiring Reporter" technique used by many newspapers?
3. Find in the psychological literature or invent an example of the violation of the requirements of representativeness in a sample used for study and generalization about a population.
4. Can you think of concrete examples that will illustrate each of the four conditions of sampling shown in Figure 1?
5. In the light of what is known of the psychology of perception, how far is it possible to avoid bias resulting from question wording?
6. What factors might increase or decrease the reliability of interviewers' ratings?
7. How might the inverse relationship reported by Cantril (see quotation p. 32, paragraph numbered 2) be accounted for?
8. If you wished to ascertain the attitude of the United States adult population toward the United Nations by means of a stratified sampling procedure, what factors would you stratify on and why?
9. If there is no relationship between stratifying factors and the characteristic(s) under study in a sample, what difference will there be between this sample and a strictly random one?
10. Which will yield the more precise result of a poll on voting intention in a state: a one percent sample of the population of Nevada or a one percent sample of the population of California?
11. In the Purdue Opinion Panel a total self-selected sample of

between 10,000 and 18,000 senior high school students is obtained. This sample is largely of unknown composition. How may representativeness be more nearly obtained? On a question concerned with high school students' attitude toward labor legislation, how would you proceed?

Bibliography

1. Blankenship, A., "The Effect of the Interviewer upon the Response in a Public Opinion Poll," *J. consult. Psychol.*, 1940, *4*:134-136.

2. Cantril, H. (ed.), *Gauging Public Opinion*, Princeton, N. J.: Princeton University Press, 1944.

3. Clausen, J. A., and Ford, R. N., "Controlling Bias in Mail Questionnaires," *J. Amer. Statis. Ass.*, 1947, *42*:497-512.

4. Conrad, H. S., "Some Principles of Attitude Measurement: A Reply to 'Opinion-Attitude Methodology,'" *Psychol. Bull.* 1946, *43*:570-589.

5. Cornell, F. G., "Sample Plan for a Survey of Higher Education Enrollment," *J. Exp. Educ.*, 1947, *15*:312-318.

6. Cornfield, J., "On Certain Biases in Samples of Human Populations," *J. Amer. statis. Ass.*, 1942, *37*:63-68.

7. Crespi, L. P., " 'Opinion-Attitude Methodology' and the Polls —a Rejoiner," *Psychol. Bull.*, 1946, *43*:562-569.

8. Deming, W. E., "On Training in Sampling," *J. Amer. statis. Ass.*, 1945, *40*:307-316.

9. Gallup, G., *A Guide to Public Opinion Polls,* Princeton, N. J.: Princeton University Press, 1944.

10. Garrett, H. E., "The Representativeness of a Sample," *Amer. J. Psychol.*, 1942, *55*:580-581.

11. Hancock, J. W., "Four Methods of Measuring Unit Costs of Obtaining Attitudes Toward the Retail Store," Ph.D. Thesis, Purdue University, 1939.

12. Hansen, M. H., and Deming, W. E., "On Some Census Aids to Sampling," *J. Amer. statis. Ass.*, 1943, *38*:353-357.

13. Hansen, M. H., and Hauser, P. M., "Area Sampling—Some Principles of Sample Design," *Publ. Opin. Quart.*, 1945, *9*:183-193.

14. Harding, J., "Refusals as a Source of Bias." In Cantril, H. (ed.), *Gauging Public Opinion,* Princeton, N. J.: Princeton University Press, 1944, 119-123.

15. Hilgard, E. R., and Payne, S. L., " 'Those Not at Home': Riddle for Pollsters," *Publ. Opin. Quart.,* 1944, *8:*254-261.

16. Hochstein, J. R., and Smith, D. M. K., "Area Sampling or Quota Control—Three Sampling Experiments," *Publ. Opin. Quart.,* 1948, *12:*73-80.

17. *How NORC Builds Its Cross Section,* Denver: National Opinion Research Center, University of Denver, *Statistical Department Memorandum,* 1946.

18. Hyman, H., "Do They Tell the Truth?" *Publ. Opin. Quart.,* 1944, *8:*557-559.

19. Katz, D., "Do Interviewers Bias Poll Results?" *Publ. Opin. Quart.,* 1942, *6:*248-268.

20. Lazarsfeld, P. F., "Panel Studies," *Publ. Opin. Quart.,* 1940, *4:*122-128.

21. Lazarsfeld, P. F., and Fiske, M., "The 'Panel' as a New Tool for Measuring Opinion," *Publ. Opin. Quart.,* 1938, 2:596-612.

22. Link, H. C., and Freiberg, A. D., "The Problem of Validity Versus Reliability in Public Opinion Polls," *Publ. Opin. Quart.,* 1942, *6:*87-98.

23. McNemar, Q., "Sampling in Psychological Research," *Psychol. Bull.,* 1940, *37:*331-365.

24. McNemar, Q., "In Reply to Garrett," *Amer. J. Psychol.,* 1942, *55:*581-582.

25. McNemar, Q., "Opinion-Attitude Methodology," *Psychol. Bull.,* 1946, *43:*289-374.

26. Meier, N. C., and Saunders, H. W. (eds.), *The Polls and Public Opinion,* New York: Henry Holt and Company, Inc., 1949.

27. Miller, D. C., "National Morale of American College Students in 1941," *Amer. sociol. Rev.,* 1942, 7:194-213.

28. Mosteller, F., "Reliability of Interviewers' Ratings." In Cantril, H. (ed.), *Gauging Public Opinion,* Princeton, N. J.: Princeton University Press, 1944, pp. 98-106.

29. Peatman, J. G., *Descriptive and Sampling Statistics,* New York: Harper & Brothers, 1947.

30. Reuss, C. F., "Differences Between Persons Responding and

Not Responding to a Mailed Questionnaire," *Amer. sociol. Rev.* 1943, *8*:433-438.

31. Robinson, R. A., "Use of the Panel in Opinion and Attitude Research," *Int. J. opin. attit. Res.,* 1947, *1*:83-86.

32. Ryan, T. A., *Work and Effort,* New York: The Ronald Press Company, 1947.

33. Shuttleworth, F. K., "Sampling Errors Involved in Incomplete Returns to Mail Questionnaires," *J. appl. Psychol.,* 1941, *25*:588-591.

34. Solomon, R. L., "An Extension of Control Group Design," *Psychol. Bull.,* 1949, *46*:137-150.

35. Stanton, F., "Notes on the Validity of Mail Questionnaire Returns," *J. appl. Psychol.,* 1939, *23*:95-104.

36. Stephan, F. F., Deming, W. E., and Hansen, M. H., "The Sampling Procedure of the 1940 Population Census," *J. Amer. statis. Ass.,* 1940, *35*:615-630.

37. Stock, J. S., "Some General Principles of Sampling." In Cantril, H. (ed.), *Gauging Public Opinion,* Princeton, N. J.: Princeton University Press, 1944, pp. 127-142.

38. Stonborough, T. H. W., "The Continuous Consumer Panel: A New Sampling Device in Consumer Research," *Appl. Anthrop.,* 1942, *1*:37-41.

39. Wilks, S. S., "Representative Sampling and Poll Reliability," *Publ. Opin. Quart.,* 1940, *4*:261-270.

CHAPTER III

· · · ● ● ● · ·

Statistics of Opinion and Attitude Measurement

INTRODUCTION

Purpose

The elevation of the study of human behavior to the level of a true and exact science has been accomplished almost entirely by the application of statistical methods to investigations of human behavior. It is the purpose of this chapter to describe briefly the more basic statistical concepts and their application to opinion and attitude measurement. We shall discuss methods of presenting data and methods of describing these data. The most common statistics used to describe data are the *measures of central tendency: the mean, the median, and the mode.* If we wish to present more information about the data we may describe the degree to which the values tend to cluster about the mean value with a *measure of variability.* If we have the opinions expressed on two issues by a group of people we may wish to describe the relationship between the attitudes toward these two issues and we shall present a *measure of relationship.* Some of the more powerful tools will be discussed briefly in order to indicate to the student the elegance and economy of more advanced statistical analysis.

TERMINOLOGY, NOTATION, DEFINITIONS

Variable	Any attribute, quantity, or quality in which the members of a sample differ from each other.
Sample	See Chapter II.
x_i	A score, measurement, or observation of the ith individual on variable x.
Array	A series of scores, measurements, or observations.
Continuous	A variable is said to be continuous when x_i may assume any value among an infinite number of values between two specified limits. Variables of measurement or growth are usually considered to be continuous.
Continuum	A variable such that, between any two values, no matter how close together they may be, it is always possible to have a third value.
Discrete	A variable is said to be discrete when there is a natural grouping of that variable; when it is discontinuous; when x_i may assume only certain specified (usually equidistant) values along a scale of values.
Σ	Sigma, upper case, means "the sum of"; thus, Σx_i means the sum of all scores, measurements, or observations in an array.
f	Frequency.
N, n	The number of scores, measurements, or observations.
$\dfrac{\Sigma x_i}{N} = \bar{x}$	The arithmetic mean equals the sum of all scores divided by the number of scores.
$\tilde{x}$	The arithmetic mean of the population; the "true" mean.
$x_i - \bar{x}$	The deviation of x_i from the mean; the difference between x_i and the mean score.
$\Sigma(x_i - \bar{x})$	The sum of such differences.

σ_x $\sqrt{\dfrac{\Sigma(x_i - \bar{x})^2}{N}}$, the standard deviation of the x's.

$\dfrac{(x_i - \bar{x})}{\sigma_x}$ The amount of deviation from the mean of x_i in standard deviation units.

Sampling Distribution of a Statistic: A frequency distribution of an array of similarly obtained statistics, most frequently refers only to a hypothetical distribution.

PRESENTING DATA

Frequency Distribution

When an array of scores has been assembled in which any particular score has been duplicated, it is often not advisable to present each score separately if economy and efficiency of presentation are desired. Rather, it is convenient to list each possible score and indicate the number of observations (frequency) that yield that score. When an array has been thus ordered it is called a *frequency distribution.*

When the range of possible scores is large (usually more than 15) scores are grouped into classes, each containing the same number of distinct possible scores, 2, 3, 5, 10, or any convenient number. An array so ordered is called a *grouped frequency distribution.* When the variable being measured is continuous in nature it becomes necessary to order observations of this variable by means of a grouped frequency distribution. Grouping, in this case, is accomplished by dividing that portion of the continuum occupied by the array into a series of equal steps or classes. Usually between twelve and fifteen such classes are adequate. Each class has a mid-point or mid-value and two class limits, an upper and a lower. When presenting a distribution it is customary to describe the classes by their mid-points. A value thus indicated is called a *class index.*

Histograms and Frequency Polygons

If we wish to present a frequency distribution in graphic form we construct a *histogram.* The score values are arranged along a base line; the frequency of each score or the frequency in each class interval is represented by the relative height of a rectangle constructed on the base line. Thus, the frequency distribution *A* in Figure 2 would appear as histogram *A* in Figure 3.

Score	*f*
70	5
60	7
50	28
40	44
30	13
20	3
	100

A
Scores Made by 100
Men on Attitude Scale

Rating Given	*f*
Superior	487
Above average	264
Average	152
Below average	94
Poor	3
	1000

B
How 1000 Men
Rated This Product

FIGURE 2.   Frequency Distributions.

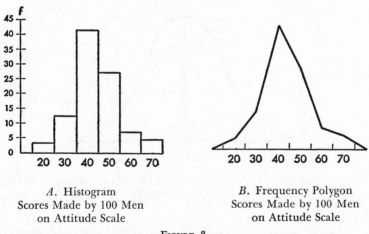

A. Histogram
Scores Made by 100 Men
on Attitude Scale

B. Frequency Polygon
Scores Made by 100 Men
on Attitude Scale

FIGURE 3.

If instead of constructing rectangles on the base line we join the mid-points of the class intervals by a broken line we have a frequency polygon as in *B*, Figure 3. It is a matter of personal choice which type of graphical presentation will be used. The histogram seems to emphasize the differences and irregularities between the classes whereas the frequency polygon seems to minimize these variations.

The Normal Curve

The normal curve is a mathematical ideal; as an ideal it is never found but only approached. Early mathematicians studying the frequency distributions of errors of observations made by groups of astronomers found that their histograms approached a characteristic bell-shaped curve. They called this curve the *normal curve of error.*

Other mathematicians studying the frequency distributions of certain natural phenomena found many of their histograms approaching this same bell-shaped curve. For a time it was thought that this curve represented the *natural law of distribution.* The curve was labeled the *normal frequency curve.*

Still other mathematicians studying the laws of probability found that the behavior of things which are controlled only by

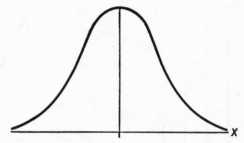

FIGURE 4.   The Normal Curve.

chance (the toss of a coin, the roll of a die) could be described quite accurately with this curve, hence, the title the *normal curve of probability.*

In each case the mathematicians, through the application of higher mathematics to the known characteristics of the curve, found that the ideal curve which their data approached could be expressed by the formula:

$$y = \frac{1}{\sqrt{2\pi}} e^{-\frac{x^2}{2\sigma^2}}.$$

Since the ideal curve is the same in each case, we now speak of it as simply the *normal curve.*

The importance of the normal curve in the study of opinion and attitude measurement cannot be overemphasized. Its importance stems from the fact that errors in observation and measurement are described by this curve and the probability of making a certain error can be determined. Furthermore, when we find our statistics to be normally distributed, or when we can prove them to be normally distributed, then they become subject to the elegance and rigor of analysis by the mathematical laws governing the normal curve.

Characteristics of the Normal Curve.   The normal curve is usually described as a bell-shaped, unimodal, bilaterally symmetrical curve which is asymptotic to the base line. This means that the curve has one maximum value or high point, that it is the same on both sides, and it approaches the base line but never quite reaches it no matter how far extended in either direction.

A second way to describe the normal curve would be to show the relationships between the heights of the ordinates of the curve erected at various points along the base line. If the maximum ordinate is taken as the unit, all other ordinates can be expressed as definite fractions of it.

The third and most important way to describe the normal curve for our purposes is in terms of the area under the curve. If we take the area under the entire curve as the unit (i.e., equal to one) then the area under the curve between any two ordinates can be expressed as a fraction of the total area. Some of these area relationships are indicated in Figure 5. The units along the X-axis are standard deviation (or sigma) units, the significance of which will be brought out in the section on variability.

For a finer gradation of these relationships we present in Table 1 an abbreviation of the table computed by Karl Pearson. This table shows the percentage of the total area under the normal curve between the mean ordinate (the ordinate at the zero point) and ordinates erected along the base line at intervals of one-tenth of a standard deviation unit. Since the curve is the same on both sides only one-half the curve is described in Table 1. Thus, the percentage of the total area between the mean ordinate and an ordinate 1σ above the mean is the same as the percentage of the total area between the mean ordinate and an ordinate 1σ below the mean ordinate. If one wishes to find the percentage of the total area between an ordinate 2σ above the mean and an ordinate 1σ above the mean it is neces-

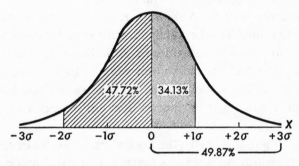

Figure 5.   Area Relationships Under the Normal Curve.

sary only to subtract the area between the mean ordinate and the ordinate 1σ above from the area between the mean and the ordinate 2σ above. Thus,

% total area between mean and ordinate $+ 2\sigma = 47.72$

% total area between mean and ordinate $+ 1\sigma = 34.13$

% total area between $+ 1\sigma$ and $+ 2\sigma = 13.59$,

or 13.59% of the total area under the normal curve falls between the ordinate erected at 1σ above the mean and the ordinate erected at 2σ above the mean.

Question: What percentage of the total area falls between $+1\sigma$ and -1σ?   *Answer:* 68.26%

What percentage of the total area lies above 2.5σ?

Answer: 00.62%

TABLE 1. Percent of Total Area Under Normal Curve Between Mean Ordinate and Ordinate Sigma Units from the Mean

% of Area		% of Area		% of Area		% of Area	
0.0	00.00	1.0	34.13	2.0	47.72	3.0	49.875
0.1	03.98	1.1	36.43	2.1	48.21	3.5	49.97674
0.2	07.93	1.2	38.49	2.2	48.61	4.0	49.99683
0.3	11.79	1.3	40.32	2.3	48.93	4.5	49.99966
0.4	15.54	1.4	41.92	2.4	49.18	5.0	49.99997
0.5	19.15	1.5	43.32	2.5	49.38		
0.6	22.57	1.6	44.52	2.6	49.53		
0.7	25.80	1.7	45.54	2.7	49.65	$\sigma = \dfrac{x - \bar{x}}{\sigma_x}$	
0.8	28.81	1.8	46.41	2.8	49.74		
0.9	31.59	1.9	47.13	2.9	49.81		

SOURCE: Karl Pearson (ed.), *Tables for Statisticians and Biometricians*, London: Cambridge University Press.

PERCENTAGES AND PROPORTIONS

One of the most common statistics used in opinion and attitude measurement is p, the proportion or percentage of a sample which possesses such-and-such an attitude, or the proportion of a sample who answer a poll question "yes." It is found by simply dividing the number who answer the question "yes" by the total number who were asked to answer the question; or by dividing the number of cases found to possess the attribute in question by the total number of cases examined. The companion symbol q is defined as the proportion of the cases examined who do not have the attribute in question. Since $p =$ those who do, and $q =$ those who do not, $(p + q) = 1$, $q = (1 - p)$, and $p = (1 - q)$.

If we think of the question asked or the attribute examined for as a test, we can score this single item as "1" for the correct answer and "0" for the incorrect answer or lack of the attribute. Then each individual examined receives a score of "1" or "0" depending upon whether or not he answers the question correctly or has the attribute in question. In this case, $p = \dfrac{\Sigma x_i}{N}$. In this sense p is the mean score of a sample on this single item.

Measures of Central Tendency

When we use the word "average" in everyday language we usually refer to some attribute or measure that is in some sense typical of a group, assuming that some of the group have more and some have less of the attribute. In other words, we refer vaguely to some central measurement. The term "average" in statistical language is more specifically designated as *measure of central tendency*.

The Arithmetic Mean. The most important measure of central tendency is the *arithmetic mean*. Mathematically the arithmetic mean is defined as:

$$\bar{x} = \frac{\Sigma x_i}{N}.$$

This means to "sum all of the scores on variable x and divide by the number of such scores." The arithmetic mean has the following important characteristics: (1) The sum of the deviations from the mean is zero. (2) The sum of the squares of the deviations from the mean is a minimum, i.e., less than the squared deviations from any other point or value. (3) It is the best score to guess or estimate if such an estimate is needed in predicting the score that an individual will achieve. (4) The mean is the most stable or least variable statistic under sampling; it is least likely to show extreme variation from the "true" mean of the population. (5) It is not "terminal"; that is, it is subject to further mathematical manipulation such as combining the means from several samples.

The Median. The median is defined as that value in an array so located that one-half of the values in the array are greater than and one-half of the values are less than it. It is the "middle" value.

The Mode. The mode is defined as the most "popular" score or measurement. It is the score with the greatest frequency in a frequency distribution; it is the score value under the highest point on the frequency curve. More generally, it is any point in a frequency distribution where there are more measures than on either side of that point.

VARIABILITY

If all the scores in an array of scores are not identical, there must be some variation in them; they tend either to scatter out or to cluster about the central point. We wish to have some measure of the relative tendency of scores to cluster closely about the mean score or to scatter out from the mean score.

The Range

One such measurement is the range. The range is a simple statement of the highest and the lowest scores in an array of scores. It tells us, in a crude manner, the scores above which and below which we do not expect any cases to fall.

Standard Deviation

The most valuable measurement of variability is the standard deviation. Mathematically, we define the standard deviation as:

$$\sigma_x = \sqrt{\frac{\Sigma(x_i - \bar{x})^2}{N}}.$$

This formula says: (1) Find the amount of deviation from the mean score of each individual score, $(x_i - \bar{x})$. (2) Square all of these deviations, $(x_i - \bar{x})^2$. (3) Add together all of these squared deviations, $\Sigma(x_i - \bar{x})^2$. (4) Find the mean of these squared deviations, $\frac{\Sigma(x_i - \bar{x})^2}{N}$. (5) Take the square root of the mean squared deviation.[1]

---

[1] For actual computation, the procedure can be somewhat simplified by using these alternate formulas. The first is best for machine computation.

$$(1) \qquad \sigma_x = \sqrt{\frac{N\Sigma x_i^2 - (\Sigma x_i)^2}{N}}$$

$$(2) \qquad \sigma_x = \sqrt{\frac{\Sigma x_i^2}{N} - \left(\frac{\Sigma x_i}{N}\right)^2}$$

Standard Deviation and the Normal Curve

Above it was pointed out that the area relationships under the normal curve are defined in terms of the percentage of the total area between the mean ordinate and ordinates erected at various standard deviation units from the mean. Thus, we might find in a frequency distribution of data which is "normally" distributed the following statistics.

$$\text{Arithmetic Mean} = 50$$
$$\text{Standard Deviation} = 10$$
$$N = 100$$

We should then expect to find about 34 percent of the cases to have scores between the mean (50) and a score one standard deviation above the mean (50 + 10 = 60); or 34 cases have scores between 50 and 60. We would also expect to find only 16 percent of our cases to have scores above 60 since we would have 50 percent with scores below 50 and 34 percent with scores between 50 and 60 (100% − 50% − 34% = 16%).

Question: What percentage of the cases would have scores less than 30?   *Answer:* 2.28%

This relationship between the normal curve and frequency distributions leads to two useful operations. (1) We can test our data to see if they are "normally" distributed or we can determine what adjustments in our instrument are necessary to yield scores that are "normally" distributed. If our data are known to be "normally" distributed we can predict the number of cases in a sample that will get scores of such-and-such a value and above, etc.

Variability of Statistics

Just as individual scores are found to vary from one person to another, so other statistics are found to vary from sample to sample. If we were to take the mean scores on an attitude scale from several different samples it is extremely unlikely that these mean scores would all be identical; they would undoubtedly exhibit variation. Furthermore, we could calculate the amount of variation among these mean scores in the same way that we calculated the standard deviation of an array of individual scores. When we speak of the *standard deviation of an array of similarly obtained statistics* we label it the *standard error* of that statistic; thus, there exist standard errors of means, standard errors of standard deviations, standard errors of differences, standard errors of percentages, etc.

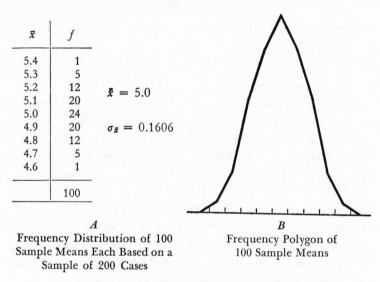

$\bar{x}$	f
5.4	1
5.3	5
5.2	12
5.1	20
5.0	24
4.9	20
4.8	12
4.7	5
4.6	1
	100

$\bar{\bar{x}} = 5.0$

$\sigma_{\bar{x}} = 0.1606$

A
Frequency Distribution of 100
Sample Means Each Based on a
Sample of 200 Cases

B
Frequency Polygon of
100 Sample Means

FIGURE 6.

Note that above we spoke of the standard deviation of an array of similarly obtained statistics. One of the elegant features of the mathematical nature of statistics is that we can calculate the standard error of a statistic without going to the trouble of getting a frequency distribution of similarly obtained statistics; that is, it is unnecessary to determine the sampling distribution of the statistic empirically. Actually, in most cases, it is impossible to get an array of such statistics. For purposes of illustration, however, let us assume that we have a frequency distribution of 100 means, each mean score having been obtained on a sample of 200 cases.

The following important facts can be proved mathematically: (1) The mean of this distribution of means approaches the "true" mean of the population from which the samples were drawn, as we increase the number of samples or the size of the samples $(\overline{\overline{x}} \rightarrow \tilde{x})$. (2) The standard deviation of this distribution of means (S.E.$_m$) equals the standard deviation of the population divided by the square root of N, the size of each sample $\left(\sigma_m = \dfrac{\sigma_{pop}}{\sqrt{N}} \right)$. (3) The standard deviation of this distribution is equal to the standard deviation of one sample divided by the square root of $N - 1$ $\left(\sigma_m = \dfrac{\sigma_{sample}}{\sqrt{N-1}} \right)$. (4) This distribution is normally distributed.

Testing an Obtained Mean or Testing an Exact Hypothesis. Suppose now that we had another sample of 200 cases with a mean of 4.84. This mean would fall in the interval 4.75 to 4.85 in our frequency distribution above. We see that there are 36 means farther away from the "true" mean than our last sample mean. Since there are 100 means in the frequency distribution and we find that there are 36 of these means that are farther away from the true mean than our obtained mean we can say that "the chances are 36 in 100 that an obtained mean equal to our sample mean would lie this far away from the true mean." Suppose now that our obtained mean were equal to 4.40. In this case there are no means in the frequency distribution which lie this far away from the true mean or the population mean. We would, therefore, conclude that (1) our sample is not truly random or (2) our sample was not drawn from the same population. In other words, there is something about our sample that makes it different from the other samples, and different from the population from which the other samples were drawn.

Similar illustrations could be made for all statistics; however, it is not necessary to find a frequency distribution of similarly obtained statistics in order to calculate the characteristics of that frequency distribution. We can calculate these characteristics from *one* sample. Thus we can list the standard errors (the standard deviations of the sampling distributions) of the following statistics.

FORMULAS FOR THE STANDARD ERROR OF VARIOUS STATISTICS

(1) S.E. of a Mean $$\sigma_m = \frac{\sigma_{sample}}{\sqrt{N-1}}$$

(2) S.E. of a Proportion $$\sigma_p = \sqrt{\frac{pq}{N}}$$

(3) S.E. of a Median $$\sigma_{mdn} = 5/4 \; (\sigma_m)$$
$$= \frac{5 \; (\sigma_{sample})}{4 \sqrt{N-1}}$$

(4) S.E. of a Standard Deviation $$\sigma_\sigma = 0.707 \; \sigma_m$$
$$= \frac{\sigma_{sample}}{\sqrt{2 \; (N-1)}}$$

(5) S.E. of a Difference $$\sigma_{diff} = \sqrt{\sigma_{x_1}^2 + \sigma_{x_2}^2}$$

Formula 2 tells us, for example, that if we had an array of similarly obtained proportions the standard deviation of that array would be $\sqrt{\frac{pq}{N}}$.

Formula 5 says: "The standard deviation of an array of similarly obtained differences would equal $\sqrt{\sigma_1^2 + \sigma_2^2}$."

NOTE: This holds for uncorrelated measures only. For correlated measures the formula is $\sqrt{\sigma_1^2 + \sigma_2^2 - 2r\sigma_1\sigma_2}$. This obviously reduces to Formula 5 when $r = 0$.

TESTING OF HYPOTHESES

In opinion and attitude measurement we shall frequently be concerned with such questions as: "Is there any significant difference between the attitudes of college freshmen and college seniors toward their professors?" "What are the chances (probability) that the 'true' mean score of all white-collar workers on our test, Attitude Toward Labor, is equal to 73?" "What are the chances that the President will be reëlected?"

From these questions one can formulate verifiable hypotheses. Statistics enable us to verify or refute these hypotheses and answer the questions, e.g., "the chances are 95 in 100 that the hypothesis is true."

Suppose that the city council has proposed a certain tax measure and they wish to know in advance the chance of a bill to receive a majority vote in a city referendum. To determine the probability, pollsters are sent to question citizens at random on their attitude toward the proposed measure. A sample of 400 citizens is polled and 230 (or 58 percent) are found to favor the bill. To pass in the referendum, the bill would have to receive more than 50 percent of the votes. The question is then, "With what confidence can we predict that the measure will pass?"

We reason thus: If the "true" proportion of voters favoring the bill is 50 percent then an array of percentages based on a sample of 400 cases would have a mean of 50 percent and a standard deviation of 2.5 percent.

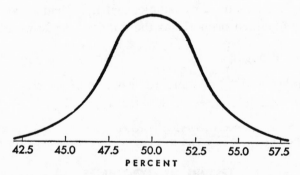

PERCENT

FIGURE 7. Distribution of Percentages Around 50 Percent, Each Sample Containing 400 Cases.

If this were true then we have found a percentage which is three standard errors above our hypothetical mean percentage of 50 percent. From Table 1 we see that out of all such percentages only 1 in 1000 lie so far above the mean. Thus, if we were to choose at random from among all such percentages the chances are only 1 in 1000 that we would obtain one this far above a hypothetical mean of 50 percent. A gambler could, therefore, afford to bet odds of about 999 to 1 that the measure will pass.

In mathematical notation this problem would be worked like this:

$$p - \tilde{p} = 58 - 50 = 8\%$$

$$\sigma_p = \sqrt{\frac{50\ (100\ -\ 50)}{400}} = 2.5$$

$$\text{C.R.} = t = \frac{p - \tilde{p}}{\sigma_p} = \frac{8}{2.5} = 3.20$$

$$\text{Prob.}_{(t\,=\,3.2)} = 0.0013.$$

And we would conclude that it is very likely that the bill will pass; the odds are 9,987 to 10,000 for it.

Critical Ratio

Above we introduced the critical ratio (t) which we now define as *any statistic divided by the standard error of that statistic*. The critical ratio tells us how many standard error (standard deviation) units our obtained statistic lies away from the mean value of the sampling distribution of that statistic. From Table 1 we can determine the probability associated with critical ratios of various sizes, where we read the proportion of cases that lie above or below certain points, that is, above or below a certain number of standard deviation units away from the mean. This *percentage of cases* can be interpreted as *chances in 100*, or the probability of an obtained statistic arising on the basis of chance alone. When we find that probability we are capable of answering the question posed in the hypothesis. We can conclude that the hypothesis is supported or refuted, as the case may be. If a hypothesis is supported by the findings, many writers state that they are "confident at the $p\%$ level" or the "hypothesis is supported or rejected at the $p\%$ level of confidence."

The Significance of Differences

One of the more common tests of significance encountered in opinion and attitude measurement is the test of the significance of the difference between means. Such a problem would arise if the question to be answered were, "What is the difference between men and women on a test of attitude toward drinking?" We would have the scores made by N_1 women on the test with a mean score of $\bar{x}_1$ and a standard deviation of σ_1. N_2 men have a mean score of $\bar{x}_2$ and a standard deviation of σ_2. The question to be answered is, "If there is no difference, on the average, between men and women on this test, what are the chances that whatever difference was obtained would have arisen by chance alone?" In this case our interest centers around a hypothetical distribution of *differences between means* with the average of these differences equal to zero. Our obtained difference is $\bar{x}_1 - \bar{x}_2$. How many standard error units above or below the mean (zero) does this difference lie?

$$t = \frac{x_1 - x_2}{\text{S.E.}_{diff}}$$

What is the standard error of this difference? S.E. $= \sqrt{\sigma_{m_1}^2 + \sigma_{m_2}^2}$.

Hence, $t = \dfrac{x_1 - x_2}{\sqrt{\dfrac{\sigma_1^2}{N_1 - 1} + \dfrac{\sigma_2^2}{N_2 - 1}}}$.

Note here that we have substituted for the S.E. of the Mean the formula used for computing the S.E.$_m$. What is the probability of such a difference occurring if the "true" or population difference is equal to zero? Find t in Table 2. Find the percentage of cases that lie this far away from the mean.

Here we come to the questions, "Suppose t is negative?" or "Suppose we call the men's mean score $\bar{x}_1$?" In a case of this kind when the direction of the statistic from the mean is unknown or is unimportant we use both tails of the normal curve. Our difference could be at the upper or lower tail of the curve; $p\%$ could lie above our obtained difference, or $p\%$ could lie below. But, $2p\%$ will be as far away in either direction as our obtained difference. Hence, we conclude that we

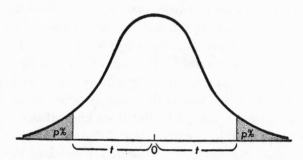

FIGURE 8. Note here that the two shaded areas at the tails of the curve taken together represent the total proportion of cases that lie as far away from the hypothetical mean as our obtained value.

are confident at the $2p\%$ level that a real difference does exist between the attitudes of men and women toward drinking as measured by our test.

When the hypothesis being tested is that the "true" difference is equal to zero, it is said that the *null hypothesis* is tested and accepted or rejected, as the case may be.

Illustration. For purposes of illustration assume the following values for the above example and find the level of confidence at which we can reject the null hypothesis.

$$N_1 = 146 \qquad\qquad N_2 = 146$$
$$\bar{x}_1 = 9.1 \qquad\qquad \bar{x}_2 = 11.6$$
$$\sigma_1 = 8.0 \qquad\qquad \sigma_2 = 9.0$$
$$Answer:\ t = 2.5$$
$$p = 0.01$$

Conclusion: The null hypothesis can be rejected at the 1% level of confidence. This means that, if the true difference is zero we have found a difference that would be found only 1 time in 100 on the basis of chance alone.

STANDARD SCORES

If we say that individual A made a score of 30 on one of our attitude scales (X) and a score of 2.5 on another of our attitude scales (Y) we cannot conclude that he has a more favorable attitude toward the things in scale X than he has toward those in scale Y. If we know that the mean score on scale X is 20 and the mean score on scale Y is 2, we can say that he is above average on both, but we still cannot say how much above the average for it is obvious that the raw score units on the two scales are not comparable. But if we know that the standard deviation of scale X equals 10 and the standard deviation of Y equals 1, we know that A scored 1 standard deviation unit above the mean on scale X and only $\frac{1}{2}$ standard deviation unit above the mean on scale Y. Hence, we can now conclude that individual A has a more favorable attitude toward those things in scale X than in scale Y. What we have done here is to compute his standard scores on the two attitude scales.

$$t_x = \frac{x - \bar{x}}{\sigma_x} = \frac{30 - 20}{10} = 1$$

$$t_y = \frac{y - \bar{y}}{\sigma_y} = \frac{2.5 - 2.0}{1} = 0.5$$

Note that t_x and t_y are comparable since they are both in terms of standard deviation units.

It can be pointed out that the t as a standard score and the t as a critical ratio are essentially the same, for a critical ratio is but a statistic divided by its standard error. The standard error of a single measure is the standard deviation of the array from which it was taken.

MEASURES OF RELATIONSHIPS

Let us now suppose that we had many individuals who, like individual A above, had taken both scales X and Y; and we noticed that several individuals, like A, had scores that were above the mean scores on both scales, and several other individuals had scores that were below the mean scores on both scales. It might occur to us that a high score on one scale would tend to indicate a high score on the other scale, and a low score on one scale would indicate a low score on the other. *A relationship between the two scales would become apparent.* The problem is to arrive at some measure of relationship as the coefficient of correlation:

$$r = \frac{\Sigma t_x t_y}{N},$$

which says r, the coefficient of correlation, equals the mean of the cross product of the standard scores made on the two instruments by N individuals. The coefficient of correlation will be found to have a value some place between $+1$ and -1. When the sign of r is plus it indicates a positive relationship between X and Y; a person scoring high on X will score high on Y. When the sign of r is minus it indicates an inverse relationship between X and Y; a person scoring high on X will score low on Y. When $r = 0$ it indicates that there is no relationship between X and Y; a person scoring high on one variable might score either high, low, or in the middle on the other variable. The absolute numerical value of r is indicative of the strength of the relationship between the two variables; the closer r approaches 1 the stronger the relationship. When $r = 1$ there is a perfect relationship; a given standard score on one variable will be matched by the same standard score on the other variable. If $r = -1$ a standard score on one variable will be matched with the same standard score on the other variable but on the other side of the mean.

When we come to compute r we shall use a formula which enables us to use raw scores rather than standard scores. It can be derived in the following manner:

$$r = \frac{\Sigma t_x t_y}{N} = \frac{\Sigma\left(\frac{x-\bar{x}}{\sigma_x}\right)\left(\frac{y-\bar{y}}{\sigma_y}\right)}{N} = \frac{\Sigma(x-\bar{x})(y-\bar{y})}{N\sigma_x\sigma_y}$$

$$= \frac{\frac{\Sigma xy}{N} - \left(\frac{\Sigma x}{N}\right)\left(\frac{\Sigma y}{N}\right)}{\sqrt{\frac{\Sigma x^2}{N} - \left(\frac{\Sigma x}{N}\right)^2}\sqrt{\frac{\Sigma y^2}{N} - \left(\frac{\Sigma y}{N}\right)^2}} = \frac{N\Sigma xy - (\Sigma x)(\Sigma y)}{\sqrt{N\Sigma x^2 - (\Sigma x)^2}\sqrt{N\Sigma y^2 - (\Sigma y)^2}}$$

Prediction

If we had two tests that correlated perfectly ($r = 1$) it would be useless to give both tests to a group of individuals, for we could predict exactly from the first test the scores that each would make on the second test. If a person made a score of one sigma above the mean on the first test he would make a score one sigma above the mean on the second test. We almost never find two tests that correlate perfectly, but we do occasionally find two tests that show a strong relationship ($r = 0.90$). We could, in a case like this, predict the scores that would be made on the second test from our knowledge of the scores made on the first test. We would arrive at our predicted score with the following formula which says the predicted standard score on test Y equals the obtained standard score on test X multiplied by the coefficient of correlation.[2]

$$t_y = r_{xy}t_x$$

[2] In terms of raw scores the prediction formula takes the following form.

$$t_x = \frac{(x-\bar{x})}{\sigma_x}$$

$$t_y = \frac{(y-\bar{y})}{\sigma_y}$$

$$\frac{(x-\bar{x})}{\sigma_y} = r\frac{(x-\bar{x})}{\sigma_x}$$

$$y = r\left(\frac{\sigma_y}{\sigma_x}\right)(x-\bar{x}) + \bar{y}$$

The prediction made with this formula would work quite well, but, of course, with the relationship being less than perfect ($r = 0.90$) we would be in error from time to time; our predicted score would not exactly equal the score that would be obtained on the second test. As with any measure we could compute the amount of error in each case and calculate the mean and standard deviation of these errors. But again this is not necessary. We can show that the mean of these errors is equal to zero and we can show that the standard deviation of these errors can be computed from the following formulas.

FORMULAS FOR THE STANDARD ERROR OF ESTIMATE

(1) Predicting Y from X: $\sigma_{yx} = \sigma_y \sqrt{1 - r^2}$

(2) Predicting X from Y: $\sigma_{xy} = \sigma_x \sqrt{1 - r^2}$

For purposes of illustration let us assume that test X is a test of mathematical aptitude and that test Y is the final examination in a course in mathematics. We have found that X and Y correlate $+0.90$. This relationship can be illustrated graphically with a *scattergram*. In Figure 9 we have plotted the scores on the two variables. To plot a point we take the two values for one individual. We go to the right along the X-axis until we come to the score of that individual, we then go up until we reach his score on Y. We there make a tally mark. It can be seen that all people who make the same score on X tend to make about the same score on Y, or in our illustration, those who score high on the mathematics aptitude test tend to make the better grades in the final examination.

If we have given the mathematics aptitude test at the beginning of the course we can predict what grade each student will receive at the end of the course. Of course, we will not always be correct, but we can tell in advance what amount of error we can expect in our predictions by use of Formula 1. Take, for example, all the individuals who made a score of 70 on test X. From the scattergram we see that they range between 45 and 85 on variable Y. But we will have predicted a score of 68 for each of them. If we wish to be accurate and admit that our estimate is likely to be in error we can state that a person receiving a score of 70 on the aptitude test will receive a grade of 68 ± 9.1 on the final examination. Such a statement shows that our best guess of the predicted score is 68 but that

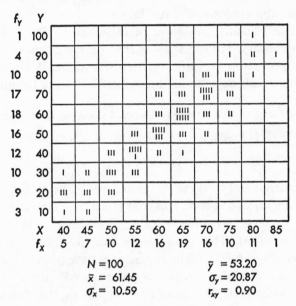

FIGURE 9.   Scattergram X Versus Y.

we are certain to make some errors in our predictions and that the standard deviation of these errors (the standard error of estimate) will be 9.1. In other words, 68 percent of all cases who receive a score of 70 on X will fall between 77.1 and 58.9 on Y.

Other Measures of Relationship

When we wish to measure the degree of relationship between two variables that are two-valued, or between two single-answer questions, or between two attributes that have no quantitative values, we resort to a more simple measure of relationship involving proportions.

$$\varphi = \frac{ad - bc}{\sqrt{p_1 q_1 p_2 q_2}}.$$

We can define the values in the above formula by means of a two-category scattergram.

$a =$ proportion of cases in category 1 on X and category 1 on Y.

$b =$ proportion of cases in category 0 on X and category 1 on Y.

$c =$ proportion of cases in category 1 on X and category 0 on Y.

$d =$ proportion of cases in category 0 on X and category 0 on Y.

$p_1 = a + b \qquad q_1 = c + d$

$p_2 = a + c \qquad q_2 = b + d$

	1	0	X
1	a	b	p_1
0	c	d	q_1
Y	p_2	q_2	1.0

Tetrachoric Correlation.   Another measure of relationship, beyond the scope of this book, is the tetrachoric correlation coefficient. It is useful when two multivalued variables have been dichotomized for the sake of simplicity, or when it is not possible accurately to measure the multivalued variables to a finer degree than two values. The problem then becomes one of finding a normal bivariate surface which, if dichotomized in the same manner as our data, would fit our data and show a certain coefficient of correlation.

Biserial Correlation.   The biserial r is used as a measure of relationship between two variables, one of which is two-valued or dichotomous and the other multivalued. It is useful in measuring the relationship between a simple attribute or a single-answer question and a total test score. One form of the biserial r makes the assumption that one of the variables is normally distributed and has been forced into a dichotomy. The product-moment form of the biserial r makes the assumption that one variable is dichotomous in nature.

MORE POWERFUL TOOLS

The field of statistics is becoming marvelously full of techniques and methods with which every research worker must be acquainted. We shall mention a few and indicate the nature of each.

Multiple Correlation

In many instances it will be found that one single variable will correlate only poorly with another variable which we wish to predict and the errors of prediction will be great. But, when we combine other variables with the first variable we find that each of the added variables contributes a little more until we find that we can predict the desired variable with very slight error in our prediction. The variable to be predicted is usually some *criterion* measure, some variable such that if we could predict a person's achievement on it, certain advantages would accrue to us. When such a variable can be predicted from a group of variables we say that there is a high degree of multiple correlation between the criterion and the predictor variables.

Analysis of Variance

The technique labeled "analysis of variance" is, in effect, a test of the significance of several differences at once. It thus represents considerable economy. Suppose, for example, that we have scores on an opinion scale from several samples such as day laborers, factory workers, white-collar workers, sales persons, supervisors, and executives. To test the significance of the difference between the mean score of each group and the mean score of every other group would require fifteen operations. With analysis of variance these fifteen operations are reduced to one operation which is scarcely more involved than each of the fifteen.

Factor Analysis

Factor analysis is a scientific method that is probably more used to *formulate* hypotheses than to *support* hypotheses. As an approach to the study of mental life it holds great promise.

It grew out of the fact that most measures of mental ability tend to be positively correlated, and the correlation between measures of certain faculties or skills are of a rather stable nature. The mathematics of the procedure are couched in hyperspace geometry and matrix algebra so we can only hint at the general nature of factor analysis.

One theory views the *mind* as composed of general areas or pools of abilities such as verbal skills, number skills, memory skills, visualization skills, etc. Each of these general areas is subdivided into small, more specific areas or pools of abilities. When a group of persons are tested, certain of these areas are *tapped*. If the test is a paper-and-pencil test of arithmetic, the people must of course be able to read and understand the problems. Obviously, we are fishing in the pools of verbal skills and visual skills although our main intent is to fish in the pool of numerical skills. How much of the variation in test scores is due to variation in verbal skills and visual skills is a question that factor analysis attempts to answer. Factor analysis aims at an accurate description of the various pools and subpools of mental activity and a determination of the interrelations of these activities when performance of a specific kind is called forth.

SUMMARY

For a complete explanation of the statistical methods we have discussed see any standard textbook on statistics.

An easily comprehended algebraic development of factor analysis is given in Peters and Van Voorhis (5). A complete description of the method can be found in Thurstone (6) and Holzinger and Harmon (1).

The other books listed in the bibliography are well-rounded elementary texts in statistics applied to psychology.

Questions

1. In Figure 2, what are the integral limits of the interval whose class index is 50? What are the real limits?

2. Classify the following as either continuous or discrete variables: chairs, ions, election votes, children per family, attitude toward birth control, weights of athletes in pounds, ratings on a five-point arbitrary scale.

3. In the example of predicting the final examination grade of all those who made a score of 70 on the aptitude test, how do we know that about 68 percent will fall between 58.9 and 77.1?

4. In the example, what percent will fall between 49.8 and 86.2?

Bibliography

1. Holzinger, Karl J., and Harmon, Harry H., *Factor Analysis,* Chicago: University of Chicago Press, 1941.

2. Kelley, Truman Lee, *Fundamentals of Statistics,* Cambridge, Mass.: Harvard University Press, 1947.

3. Lindquist, E. F., *A First Course in Statistics,* Boston: Houghton Mifflin Company, 1942.

4. Peatman, J. G., *Descriptive and Sampling Statistics,* New York: Harper & Brothers, 1947.

5. Peters, C. C., and Van Voorhis, W. R., *Statistical Procedures and Their Mathematical Bases,* New York: McGraw-Hill Book Company, Inc., 1940.

6. Thurstone, L. L., *Multiple Factor Analysis,* Chicago: University of Chicago Press, 1947.

CHAPTER IV

· · · ● ● ● · · ·

Scaling Techniques

INTRODUCTION

Our discussion of techniques for constructing an attitude scale falls more or less naturally into two major subdivisions. There are first the two "classical" scaling techniques which have been extensively used in opinion and attitude research since the early 1930's—the method of equal-appearing intervals, associated with the name of L. L. Thurstone (*42, 43, 44, 45*), and the method of summated ratings, due to Rensis Likert and co-workers (*30, 34*). There are a host of trick schemes and minor and major variations on these basic techniques. Second, there are the recent developments in the theory of attitude scales which have taken place during the war years and since, centering around the concept of "unidimensionality."

THE METHOD OF EQUAL-APPEARING INTERVALS

The method of equal-appearing intervals, as developed by Thurstone and associates, was an application of a well-known psychophysical technique to the problem of attitude scaling, and represented an attempt to develop a "rational" scale, based on psychologically defined units. The procedure may be outlined as follows.

First a large number of simple statements or propositions which express *some* kind of opinion about the attitude object under study are collected. (Thurstone and students used 100 or more.) These statements should express an opinion rather than a matter of fact; they should all refer rather directly to the one attitude object in question; they should be as unambiguous as possible (double-barreled statements, for instance, are unsatisfactory for this purpose); and they should cover the entire continuum of attitude toward the object in question, from extreme unfavorableness on the one hand to extreme favorableness on the other.

This collection of opinion statements is then given to each of a large group of judges. Various investigators have used anywhere from 50 to 300 or more judges, but it is usually desirable to have at least 100 or more. These judges need not be in any sense "experts" in attitude measurement, but they should be persons who will give some care to the task assigned them. Neither does it matter what the make-up of the group of judges is as regards their own attitudes toward the attitude object involved. Each judge is instructed to sort the opinion statements into eleven piles—an eleven-point scale—it being made clear that his own opinions should play no part in the process. The pile at one end is defined as the place for statements expressing an extremely unfavorable attitude toward the attitude object; at the other end go those attitudes strongly favorable toward the object; and the middle—sixth—pile is for statements expressing a neutral attitude. The positions intermediate between these three positions are not defined by the investigator for the judges, but instead each judge is instructed to sort the items into the eleven piles in such a way that the opinions which the piles represent seem to be spaced along the attitude continuum from one extreme to the other at intervals which are, *in his opinion,* equal. This is the reason for the name, "method of equal-appearing intervals."

Seashore and Hevner (*38*) showed experimentally that if the opinion statements are mimeographed and the judges are instructed to encircle a number from 1 to 9 before each statement (they used a nine-point scale instead of the eleven-point scale of Thurstone) the scaling results agree substantially with those obtained by the more time-consuming, card-sorting procedure of Thurstone.

Distributions are then tabulated for each statement showing the frequency with which it was placed in each of the eleven (or nine) categories by the group of judges. Two statistics are required from each of these distributions: the median and the distance between the 25th and 75th percentile points, or Q. These are computed by interpolation or other smoothing method to perhaps one decimal place. A convenient method is to express each distribution in the form of a distribution of cumulative proportions, and plot these cumulative proportions on graph paper for the eleven scale points laid out on the horizontal axis. A smooth ogive (cumulative frequency) curve may then be drawn through the points thus plotted and the median and 25th and 75th percentile points read off the horizontal scale at the points where this smoothed curve crosses the 50, 25, and 75 percent lines, respectively. For distributions of extreme statements, which crowd up near the ends of the horizontal scale, only part of the complete ogive may be adequately represented by the actual data, and it is necessary to extrapolate beyond the ends of the scale to obtain the best estimate for a median (i.e., extend the partial ogive until it crosses the 50 percent line). In such cases, also, probably the most satisfactory estimate of Q is to get the difference between the extrapolated median and the 25th or 75th percentile point, as the case may be, and double it, rather than attempting to extrapolate further out to the other quartile point needed.

The two statistics thus obtained for each opinion statement now serve as the criteria for building our attitude scale. The median judgment for an item is taken as the scale value or position along the attitude continuum for that item. The statistic Q serves as a measure of ambiguity or other fault in the opinion statement. That is, if Q is small, it indicates that the judges were relatively in agreement about the proper position of that statement along the attitude continuum. If Q is large, it indicates relative disagreement among the judges, and therefore that for some reason—ambiguity, irrelevance, or something else—the statement is not suitable for use in our attitude scale.

The attitude scale is now built up by choosing a number of items (usually twenty or more) which have low Q-values, and whose scale values cover the entire scale as evenly as possible. Thurstone and his students followed the practice of constructing two parallel forms of an attitude scale from the original large collection of opinion statements, each about twenty to twenty-two items long and each constructed as indicated above. The statements chosen may be presented on the final instrument in scrambled order as far as scale value is concerned. This is the method actually used by Thurstone. It makes scoring a laborious process, however, since the statements endorsed by each subject must be averaged. A study by Sigerfoos (*39*) showed that arranging the items in ascending or descending order of scale value and using the median scale value of the items endorsed as the individual's score gave results as valid as arranging the items in random order and using the arithmetic mean of the scale values of the items endorsed. This vastly reduces the cost in time and labor and is, therefore, the method recommended in constructing such scales.

The attitude scale is now ready for use. A subject whose attitude is to be measured is instructed to read each statement and check each one which he would endorse as expressing his own sentiment, opinion, or attitude. The subject's attitude score is then taken to be the mean or median of the scale values of the statements which he checked. If the scale had complete internal consistency, and the items were perfectly reliable, a subject would endorse only statements in a very short range on the scale where his true attitude fell. This will not generally occur in practice—the statements will not have the same "scale values" for every individual tested. By the use of a reasonably large number of items, however, and an average

A SCALE FOR MEASURING ATTITUDE TOWARD ANY INSTITUTION

Ida B. Kelley   Edited by H. H. Remmers

Form B

Please fill in the blanks below. (You may leave the
space for your name blank if you wish.)

Name_____

Male   Female   (encircle one)   Date_____

Age_____   Class if in school_____

Directions:

Following is a list of statements about institutions.
Place a plus sign (+) before each statement with which
you agree with reference to the institution or institutions
listed at the left of the statements. The person in
charge will tell you the institution or institutions to
write in at the head of the columns to the left of the
statements. Your score will in no way affect your grade
in any course.

Institution

1. The world could not exist without this
   institution.
2. Is an ideal institution.
3. Has done more for society than any
   other institution.
4. Benefits everybody.
5. Has more good points than any other
   institution.
6. Appeals to man's highest nature.
7. Develops good character.
8. Furthers the most lasting satisfactions
   in life.
9. Has a long useful life before it.
10. Is a powerful agency for promoting
    individual and social efficiency.
11. Is of real value to the civilized
    individual.
12. Gives real help in meeting economic
    problems.
13. Encourages moral improvement.
14. Is fundamentally sound.
15. Is retained in the civilized world
    because of its value to mankind.
16. Offers opportunity for individual
    initiative.

(OVER)

91

Institution

17. Is increasing in its value to society.
18. Is necessary as a means of controlling society.
19. Is improving in its service to mankind.
20. Is in the process of changing and will come out a fit instrument.
21. Is not sufficiently appreciated by the general public.
22. Its good and bad points balance each other.
23. Has not yet proved itself indispensable to society.
24. Is too conservative.
25. Is retained in the civilized world because of sentiment.
26. Is decreasing in its value to society.
27. Is too changeable in its policies.
28. Regulates the individual's life too minutely.
29. Grew up in frontier days and does not fit our industrial civilization.
30. Is too radical in its views and actions.
31. Is unfair to the individual.
32. Is a tool of the mercenary.
33. Is disgraced by its past.
34. Is a tool of the unscrupulous.
35. Is developing into a racket.
36. Is fundamentally unsound.
37. Is out of control of society and is running wild.
38. Appeals to man's lowest nature.
39. Is an enemy of truth.
40. Has always cheated society.
41. Thrives on the avarice, jealousy, hatred, and greed in man.
42. Must be discarded immediately.
43. Has more bad points than any other institution.
44. Is the most despicable of institutions.
45. Is the most hateful of institutions.

of the scale values of the statements endorsed by any individual as that individual's score, it has been found that this technique yields a reasonably satisfactory attitude measurement.

Remmers (*36*) evolved a modification of the Thurstone technique of considerable practical value that makes it possible, with a single scale, to measure a very large number of attitudes. The essential difference of the method from that developed by Thurstone lies in the assumption that an attitude toward any one of a large *group* or *class* of objects can validly be measured on a single scale. "Object" is here used in the logical sense as opposed to "subject." An object in this sense is any affective stimulus to which an individual may react. It may range, therefore, from a very concrete phenomenon to the most abstract ideas possible. Considerable experimentation based on this hypothesis demonstrated its general validity with a large variety of attitude objects (*36, 37, 39*).

Thus a relatively small number of scales enable the measurement of an incalculable number of attitudes. Examples are Scales to Measure Attitudes Toward Any: Social Institution, Racial or National Group, Practice, Vocation, School Subject, Teacher, Proposed Social Action, Home-Making Activity, etc.

A few illustrative items will make clear the general nature of the Remmers generalized or master scale. The Kelley-Remmers Scale for Measuring Attitude Toward Any Social Institution is illustrated on pages 91 and 92.

One other notable reduction of labor is in the scoring. While in the Thurstone scales the items are arranged in random order of scale values of the items and are scored by computing the arithmetic mean of the items endorsed, the master scale items are arranged in descending order of scale value of the items and are scored by obtaining the mid-point of the scale values of the items endorsed. This modification was validated in an extensive series of experiments by Sigerfoos (*39*).

A central question, of course, for the validity of the method of equal-appearing intervals is whether or not the scale values obtained from the sorting of the judges are actually independent of the attitudes of the judges toward the attitude objects in question. Several investigations have dealt with this (10, 26, 35), and the results rather consistently indicate that judges actually are able to make a sort of "absolute" judgment about the proper position of a statement on the attitude continuum independent of their own attitudes in the matter. This conclusion, however, must still be taken as relative to a given time and culture pattern. What is extreme in one culture pattern may not be so extreme in another, and, similarly, over a relatively long period of time cultural shifts may take place within the same social structure so that scale values would not remain invariant (9).

THE METHOD OF SUMMATED RATINGS

This method, generally associated with the work of Rensis Likert, is an application to attitude scaling of item-analysis procedures borrowed from test-construction techniques. The fundamental steps in the process are as follows.

First, as in the method of equal-appearing intervals, a large number of statements or propositions relating to the attitude object in question are collected. These may, however, either refer directly to the attitude object, or they may, in the opinion of the investigator, be related to the attitude to be measured. These items should be carefully edited by the investigator to eliminate ambiguous, irrelevant, and otherwise faulty items.

The items are then drawn up in the form of a questionnaire or attitude test, each item being given multiple response categories of "strongly agree, agree, undecided, disagree, strongly disagree." The statements should be so constructed that for about half of them an "agree" response represents a favorable attitude toward the attitude object in question, and for the other half a "disagree" response represents a favorable attitude.

This experimental instrument is then administered to a reasonably large group of subjects (again it is well to have 100 or more) who are asked to indicate *their own* attitudes by checking the response to each item which most nearly expresses their feeling on that item. The questionnaires are then scored for each subject by assigning arbitrary weights of 1, 2, 3, 4, and 5 (or 0, 1, 2, 3, and 4) to the five response categories of each item in such a way that the highest weight is always assigned to the response that tends toward one end of the attitude continuum (say the favorable end), while the lowest weight is always assigned to the response categories which tend toward the opposite end. A subject's score is the sum of the weights assigned to the responses which he made.

The items are then analyzed for their discriminatory power with respect to measurement of the attitude in question, by any one of several item-analysis procedures available. Perhaps the simplest index (though a rough one) is to take the top and bottom 10 percent (or 27 percent, or any other percent) of subjects on the distribution of total scores, and calculate the mean of the responses to each item for each of these groups separately. Those items are the most discriminating which show the greatest discrepancy in mean response between high and low extreme groups. If more sensitive quantified indices of item discriminating power are wanted, the phi coefficient may be used (*16, 28*), or—to avoid dichotomizing the items— multiserial correlation (*27*) or other item-test correlation procedures may be employed.

The final attitude scale is then constructed by choosing the twenty to twenty-five items from the total list which show the greatest discrimination. These items are used with the same five "agree-disagree" response categories, and scoring is done in the same way.

It should be noted that while the Thurstone scaling procedures give absolute meaning to scale units, and therefore to an individual score achieved on an attitude instrument constructed by these procedures, no such situation exists with the Likert techniques. In the latter case, an individual score can only be interpreted by reference to sets of norms for defined populations, since the units of the scale are not "rational" in the sense of having been defined (psychologically) as equal and equally spaced along the attitude continuum.

A little careful consideration will also reveal that the two types of attitude scales discussed in the preceding paragraphs differ fundamentally in the nature of the process of measurement which is involved. In the Thurstone-type scales, a subject is expected to endorse statements which lie close to his true position on the attitude continuum, and the further away from this position *in either direction* along the attitude continuum a statement is, the less likely he is to endorse it. That is, we may think of a more or less bell-shaped probability distribution representing the likelihood of endorsement of statements with scale values along the range by an individual with a given "true" attitude score. The maximum ordinate of this probability distribution would be expected to come at the point on the scale which represents the individual's "true" attitude score. Loevinger (*32*) refers to this type of measurement as a "differential" test or scale.

In the Likert-type scale, on the other hand, a subject makes some response to every item. A high score (let us suppose this means a highly favorable attitude) is obtained by the subject who makes more strongly favorable responses to more of the items than the subject with less favorable reactions. This represents, then, a sort of *cumulative* type of measurement—the subject's attitude position being determined by the "amount" of favorable response which accumulates in his answers to the items.

An understanding of the cumulative nature of this type of measurement will be helpful in grasping the concept of unidimensionality to be discussed in the next section.

UNIDIMENSIONALITY: THEORY AND PROCEDURES
OF SCALE ANALYSIS

The Meaning of a Score

When an individual is assigned a "score" or an attitude "test" or "scale" (or on an achievement test, or an intelligence test, or any other similar psychological "measuring instrument"), what is that score intended to represent? Usually we wish to take such a score as an index of the position of that individual on the underlying variable which the test or scale was intended to measure—"how much" he is prejudiced against some racial group, or "how much" he knows about algebra. Further, if A has a "higher" score than B, we wish to be able to say that A is "more" prejudiced than B, or knows "more" algebra than B, and if C and D have the same score, we wish to be able to say that C and D are "equally" prejudiced, or know the "same amount" of algebra. In fact, ordinarily we restrict ourselves to requiring that a score be an indication of *rank-order* position of individuals with respect to the underlying variable. In social or psychological measurement it is too much to ask that units have the same meaning throughout the scale. Even though E's score may be as much higher than A's as A's is higher than B's, still we can only *rank* them $E, A, B,$ from high to low; we *cannot* say that E is *as much more* prejudiced than A as A is more prejudiced than B. Our arbitrary scoring units are not that good.

Suppose, now, that we had been foolish enough to include items designed to measure prejudice against some racial group and items to test knowledge of algebra in the same test, and that by some means we derived a single total "score" for each individual to whom we gave this test. These "scores" would now be ambiguous and would not have the desirable properties outlined above. A's score might be higher than B's either because he is more prejudiced than B, and knows the same amount, or less algebra, or because he knows more algebra than B, but is equally, or less prejudiced. And though C and D have equal scores, one may be more prejudiced than the other, and know less algebra, or vice versa. To give a more realistic example, from the field of intelligence testing, the American Council on Education Psychological Examination yields a total score and two subscores, one called Q for a measure of ability in quantitative thinking or manipulation, and one called L for a measure of linguistic facility. The total score is taken as a measure of the individual's "intelligence," or scholastic aptitude. But suppose that the abilities measured by the Q and L scores, whatever they may be, are *both* quite important in determining scholastic success. An individual might have a quite acceptable total score on the test by virtue of having a very high Q-ability and a very low L-ability, in which case *total score* alone might prove to be badly mistaken. The separate Q and L scores would also have to be taken into account, which is, of course, why they are also given when a score on the test is reported. But we have been assuming here that the Q and L scores themselves are each unambiguous measures of some single ability, and this is not necessarily the case unless by some means they have been shown to be so.

The above examples are intended to illustrate the desirability of having a test or scale from which we derive a single score be a measure of one factor and one factor only—i.e., be *unidimensional*. Some of the techniques currently used in attitude and achievement measurement do not necessarily guarantee this property. Standard item-analysis techniques, for instance, attempt to achieve "internal consistency," as it is called, by (1) approximating zero-order linear correlation coefficients between each item and a total score based upon arbitrary weights assigned to the items (or their subcategories); (2) excising from the test all those items which do not correlate sufficiently well with the total scores, "sufficiently well" being defined variously but usually involving a simple sampling test of significantly positive correlation; and (3) then assigning differential weights to the remaining items based on their correlation with the total score. It has been pointed out (*17a* and *b*) that if this correlation procedure is to have any consistent rationale, it must be looked upon as an approximation, and frequently a bad one at that, to multiple linear regression between the total score and performance on all the items of the test simultaneously, and that the sampling notions that are then introduced into the process are inadequate for the complex situation that really obtains.

In the Thurstone method of equal-appearing intervals for

the construction of attitude scales that we have already discussed, the criterion for item selection is based upon the variability among the positions on the scale to which the various judges have assigned the item. As a general measure of ambiguity, this criterion may serve to spot some items measuring a different and disturbing variable in the minds of some judges, as well as catching just poorly constructed items, but it cannot be counted on to separate two or more factors which definitely do belong to an attitude area that has been too broadly defined (*33*).

The Rationale for a Scale Variable

What, then, is a proper criterion for unidimensionality of a scale or test? Guttman, who is principally responsible for the theory and techniques of "scale analysis" that we are discussing in this section, has proposed the following (*17b, 19*): If a single, quantitative score is to represent, *without ambiguity,* the behavior of an individual on a group of items, then we must require that it be possible, knowing the individual's score, to know his behavior *on each and every item* in the group. Guttman has called this the principle of *reproducibility.* If this criterion is perfectly satisfied, then a given score on a scale or test stands for one pattern of responses to the items of that scale or test, *and one only,* and it would not be possible, as in our illustrations above, for two or more individuals to get the same score by combining differing amounts of two or more factors that may exist within the test.

For those who like to chew over a rigorously constructed definition, we may, following Guttman (*19*), restate this idea.

1. First, we define the concept (from mathematical logic) of *one-to-one* correspondence; a variable y is said to have a one-to-one correspondence with a variable x if, to each value of the variable x, there corresponds one and only one value of the variable y, and conversely.
2. Now suppose that y is an attribute (or *qualitative* variable), such as a given item in a test, or on an attitude questionnaire,

and suppose that this qualitative variable takes on certain "values," such as getting the item right, or getting it wrong, on the test, or has various response alternatives, as on the attitude questionnaire; if the quantitative variable x (whose units of measurement may be arbitrarily fine) can, however, be divided into a certain number of intervals in such a way that these *intervals* will have a one-to-one correspondence with the "values" taken on by the attribute, or qualitative variable y, then y is said to be a *simple function* of x.

3. Now we come to the definition: "For a given population of objects (in attitude and opinion measurement, these 'objects' will be people) the multivariate frequency distribution of a universe of attributes (items, or questions) will be called a *scale* if it is possible to derive from the distribution a quantitative variable (scores) with which to characterize the objects (people) such that *each* attribute is a *simple function* of that quantitative variable. Such a quantitative variable is called a *scale variable*" (*19*).

We recognize the concept of *simple function* as that required by the statement of the reproducibility criterion in the first paragraph of this section. If *each* item is a simple function of the scale variable (scores), and if we know the value of the scale variable for an individual, we can, by determining what *interval* of the scale variable appropriate to each item his score falls within, say what "value" of each qualitative variable, or item, he assumed. That is, we can *reproduce* his answer, the response that he made on every item.

There are two aspects of this definition of particular importance, and these are the terms "*population* of objects" and "*universe* of attributes." Thus, Guttman's formal definition of a scale involves both an infinite universe of items all pertaining to the same area of attitude, or of knowledge, or whatever the universe of attributes, and also a population of people whose behavior with respect to this universe of attributes we are interested in. In practice, of course, we have only a finite sample of items from the universe, and a finite sample of people from the population.

To illustrate how Guttman's criterion does ensure unidimensionality, let us borrow a simple illustration from Festinger (*13*). Suppose that we wanted to measure the heights of people, but that a standard unit of measurement, such as a foot rule or a yardstick, was not known and was not available to us. Lacking any predetermined unit of measurement, suppose that we chose, as a measuring instrument, ten sticks, each of a different length.

The operation of measurement would be to stand each stick up alongside each individual and to record whether he is taller or shorter than the stick. We record a plus if he is taller and a minus if he is shorter. Our data for each individual then consist of ten marks, each of which may be either plus or minus.

We might now determine how many individuals received a plus on each of the measuring sticks. We could then arrange our sticks in order from the one where the greatest number of people received a plus down to that stick on which the smallest number of people received a plus.

We would now find that any individual who received a minus on stick "1" would have received minuses on all the other sticks; an individual who received a plus on stick "1" and a minus on stick "2" would have received minuses on all of the subsequent sticks, and so on. The individual who received a plus on stick "10" would have received pluses on all of the other sticks. Each individual would thus have fallen into one of eleven "patterns of response." These patterns could be arranged in order from "tallest" to "shortest" and we would thus have a scale for measuring height. It may be noted that since this instrument was unidimensional, it would have been impossible for an individual to have received a minus on stick "1," a plus on stick "2," and a minus on stick "3." In fact, there are 1013 possible "patterns of response" which would *not* have occurred (*13*).

A picture called a *scalogram* could be made of the eleven "patterns of response" made by the people on our ten-stick

Table 2. A Perfect "Scale"

Stick number	1		2		3		4		5		6		7		8		9		10		Scale Score
"Response" category	+	−	+	−	+	−	+	−	+	−	+	−	+	−	+	−	+	−	+	−	
Arbitrary weights	1	0	1	0	1	0	1	0	1	0	1	0	1	0	1	0	1	0	1	0	
Q	x		x		x		x		x		x		x		x		x		x		10
A	x		x		x		x		x		x		x		x		x			x	9
Z	x		x		x		x		x		x		x		x			x		x	8
X	x		x		x		x		x		x		x		x			x		x	8
S	x		x		x		x		x		x		x			x		x		x	7
W	x		x		x		x		x		x		x			x		x		x	7
E	x		x		x		x		x		x			x		x		x		x	6
D	x		x		x		x		x		x			x		x		x		x	6
C	x		x		x		x		x		x			x		x		x		x	6
V	x		x		x		x		x			x		x		x		x		x	5
F	x		x		x		x		x			x		x		x		x		x	5
R	x		x		x		x		x			x		x		x		x		x	5
T	x		x		x		x			x		x		x		x		x		x	4
G	x		x		x		x			x		x		x		x		x		x	4
B	x		x		x		x			x		x		x		x		x		x	4
N	x		x		x		x			x		x		x		x		x		x	4
H	x		x		x			x		x		x		x		x		x		x	3
Y	x		x		x			x		x		x		x		x		x		x	3
U	x		x		x			x		x		x		x		x		x		x	3
J	x		x			x		x		x		x		x		x		x		x	2
M	x		x			x		x		x		x		x		x		x		x	2
K	x		x			x		x		x		x		x		x		x		x	2
I	x			x		x		x		x		x		x		x		x		x	1
L		x		x		x		x		x		x		x		x		x		x	0
P		x		x		x		x		x		x		x		x		x		x	0
f	23	2	22	3	19	6	16	9	12	13	9	16	6	19	4	21	2	23	1	24	

(Left margin, spanning rows V through L: INDIVIDUAL)

102

measuring instrument, and it might be something like Table 2 (each row representing "responses" for one person, and each pair of columns, the distribution of marks for one stick, first the pluses, then the minuses—ignore, for the present, the "arbitrary weights").

The "quantitative scale variable" which we seek to determine from the "multivariate frequency distribution" of responses is indicated at the right. It may be obtained merely by assigning rank-order numbers to each successive different pattern of response, running from that pattern characterizing the shortest individuals to that characterizing the tallest. These could be any numbers, as long as the rank order is preserved. They need not start with zero. Or they need not be numbers at all. Any designation would do, such as an alphabetical one, as long as we know the rank order. However, we are used to thinking of scores in terms of numbers, and the numbers will prove useful for other purposes later.

We see that this perfect "scale" satisfies Guttman's definition and the criterion of reproducibility that we laid down previously. Knowing the structure of this scale, we now know, for instance, that anyone with scale score 6 received pluses (i.e., is higher than) sticks "1" through "6," and received minuses on (i.e., is shorter than) sticks "7" through "10." We know that this is the *only* way that one can achieve a scale score 6 on our instrument. And we know, without any ambiguity whatsoever, that anyone with scale score 6 is higher than anyone with scale score 5, and shorter than anyone with scale score 7. Since height is undeniably a unidimensional variable, this artificial example illustrates how Guttman's proposed criterion will be fulfilled if the underlying variable is actually unidimensional. Instead of measuring sticks, in practice we shall have ten items on an attitude scale, say, which we have administered to a group of people. If a consistently reproducible pattern such as this emerged (it would not, of course, ever be perfect in practice), then we would have evidence that the underlying variable we are measuring is unidimensional, and we can attach unambiguous meaning to an individual's score on this attitude scale.

This example has also served to give a foretaste of one of the methods of testing for "scalability" in practice.

The Universe of Content and the Hypothesis of Scalability

Now let us go behind this relatively simple idea of unidimensionality to see what are some of the fundamentals of the theory of scales, as developed by Guttman, and some of their implications for attitude research. When we think of constructing an instrument to measure an attitude, we do not suppose that the particular items which we use on our instrument exhaust the possibilities of verbal expression of the attitude (for it is verbal behavior that we must actually observe with a paper-and-pencil method). There are, in fact, an infinite number of different items that might be used, all of which would seem to measure some aspect of the attitude that we are trying to get at. That is, the possible verbal expressions of the attitude form an infinite universe. That is why the formal definition of a *scale* speaks of a "universe of attributes."

When we set out to do a piece of attitude research, then, the first thing that we must do is to define carefully the universe of attributes, or universe of *content,* in which we are interested. This having been done, we construct some items which seem to represent adequately the various aspects of the universe of content in which we are interested. We shall think of these items as a *sample* from a hypothetically infinite universe of items of *similar content.* It is important to notice that this "sampling" process is highly subjective, and by no means a random one, so that usual sampling theory is of no use to us in interpreting the behavior of our sample of items.

We must define next a population of individuals (also perhaps hypothetically infinite) whose behavior with respect to the universe of attributes we are interested in observing. Having defined this population, we must obtain a sample of individuals from it to whom we can administer our attitude instrument. This sampling can and should be obtained by some carefully planned sampling process, whether random, stratified-random, or other controlled sampling (see Chapter II). Thus the formal theory behind scale analysis involves a double sampling process—the sampling of a universe of items, and of a population of individuals.

Now we are ready to state, and test, the following hypothesis: that the universe of attributes, which we have sampled, forms a *scale,* as defined above, for the population of individuals we have sampled—i.e., is unidimensional with respect to that population of individuals. Notice that this hypothesis of scalability is stated for the *universe* of attributes, and the *population* of people. It is the universe which is the *scale,* according to the formal definition, but any sample of items from a perfectly scalable universe will necessarily form a unidimensional hierarchy among themselves, and it is for this reason that we are able to use our *sample* of items from the universe to test the hypothesis of scalability. And the hypothesis must also be stated with respect to a particular population of individuals. A universe of attributes which forms a scale for one population of individuals need not necessarily do so for an entirely different population of individuals, as, for instance, a completely different cultural group with respect to a racial attitude.

The behavior of our sample of individuals upon our sample of items now affords the means for testing this hypothesis. Guttman has indicated (*19, 22*) that samples of a dozen items from the universe and about 100 individuals from the population are sufficient to test the hypothesis of scalability. If the structure of response patterns for our sample meets the criteria for scalability, which we shall presently state, then it may be inferred that the universe of attributes which we have sampled *does* form a scale with respect to the population of individuals we have sampled. As is true of any inference from sample to population, this is not infallible.

Techniques for Performing the Scale Analysis

There are at least four available techniques for performing the actual job of a scale analysis, all of which yield essentially equivalent results via different approaches. The technique which Guttman originally devised (17b) is no longer considered feasible for ordinary work. It was a laborious procedure based on the least-squares principle of minimizing errors of prediction, and its primary purpose was, in fact, not so much to discover a scale pattern, if such existed, as to provide a series of values for all the categories in order to yield, as a total score, the best possible quantitative scale variable. Guttman has since stated (23) that the problem of category weights is of minor importance in scale theory, and that the primary focus of interest should be the *structure* of the universe of attributes, as exemplified, for instance, in our measuring-stick illustration. If a universe were perfectly scalable, the same rank order of individuals, by total score, would be obtained no matter what weights were assigned to the categories of the items, so long as the size of the assigned weights maintained the proper rank order *within* the categories of each item.

In the work of the Research Branch, Information and Education Division, Army Service Forces, the standard technique was a *scalogram board*, constructed with movable rows and columns on which the responses of the individuals on each item could be indicated, and then these movable rows and columns manipulated in a manner to achieve, if possible, a pattern similar to that exemplified above.

The two techniques most immediately available to research workers are the frequency tabulation technique, devised by Goodenough (15), and a trial scoring and graphic tabulation technique, dubbed by Guttman the "Cornell technique" (22). The latter will be described in some detail, since it seems to be the technique most likely to be feasible in the greatest variety of situations.

The Cornell Technique

Having obtained the behavior of a sample of individuals from the population in which we are interested upon a sample of items from the universe of content in which we are interested, we are now ready to test the hypothesis of scalability, as stated above. This involves, by the technique which we shall describe, manipulating the responses in an attempt to produce, within suitable limits of approximation, a consistent structure for the patterns of response present in our data, similar to that shown for the perfect example of our ten-stick measuring instrument.

The basic principle of the Cornell technique is to obtain a rough approximation to the scale rank order of individuals, if such exists, on the basis of total scores obtained by assigning arbitrary integral weights to the categories of each item and totaling the weights of the categories checked by an individual to obtain his total score, as in the method of summated ratings. The structure of response patterns (scalogram) presented by the rank order thus obtained is then inspected to see whether or not it meets the empirical criteria for scalability, which we shall outline below. The entire procedure is set forth here, step by step (22).

1. Weights are assigned to each category of each item, using the integers beginning with zero. This is done in such a way that the weights assigned to the categories of an item are in accordance with the rank-order relationship that those categories are judged to have with respect to the basic variable which the entire instrument was intended to measure. Thus, in an attitude scale which is intended to measure tolerance for, or favorableness toward, some attitude object, the categories of any one item are arranged in rank order from most tolerant to least tolerant, or most favorable to least favorable, and the arbitrary weights assigned accordingly, the least tolerant or least favorable response being weighted zero, and successively higher integers being assigned to the others, on up until the highest

weight needed for the item in question is assigned to the most tolerant, or most favorable response.

Thus, in a five-response item, the weights would range from zero to four. Or, if our scale were conceived as measuring prejudice toward some attitude object, in the positive direction, then we would merely assign the weights in the opposite direction, giving zero to the least prejudiced response, and the highest weight to the most prejudiced response for any one item. It makes no difference, as long as the same direction is maintained for all the items, and this, of course, determines which direction the total scores will go, if the instrument is unidimensional. In our measuring-stick example, we might assign *zero* to the minus "response" for each "item," because that represents being shorter with respect to that "item," and *one* to the plus "response," because that represents being taller, and we wish our scale to measure increasing height in the positive direction. This weighting procedure is carried out for every item in our sample (on our instrument—test, questionnaire, scale, what-have-you).

It will be noted that the rank order of the categories of an item appropriate to the scale variable that we hope to get out of the instrument is a matter entirely for subjective judgment at this stage. In most cases, there will be little doubt as to the proper rank order if the item has been well constructed, but in cases of doubt the structure of response patterns in the first trial scalogram will indicate if a misjudgment has been made.

2. A total score is obtained for each individual by adding up the weights assigned to the categories into which he falls, the response alternatives which he chose. For instance, in Table 2 individual *Q* would have total score 10, individual *U* total score 3, etc.

3. The questionnaires, or answer sheets, or whatever we have on which the responses for each individual are recorded, are then shuffled into rank order according to total score, from high-to-low or low-to-high—it doesn't matter.

4. A table is prepared for the first trial scalogram, with one column for each category of each item, and one row for each individual, like the table for our measuring-stick illustration, Table 2. In our example, each item has only two possible re-

sponse alternatives, plus or minus, but this of course is not necessarily the case for any instrument. There would be as many columns for each item as there were response alternatives for that item.

5. The responses made by each individual to every item are indicated on this table by putting an "x" in the row for each person in the column for each response alternative which he chose. The responses for individuals are entered in this table in descending (or ascending) order of total score, as shown in our example. The arrangement of people with the same total score is arbitrary. This table completely summarizes the data we have obtained from our sample of people on our sample of items.

6. At the bottom of each column of this table, enter the total frequency of response in that category (as done in Table 2) which will equal the total number of people in our sample.

7. Now we come to an important part in the test for scalability (although not the only one—see Criteria for Scalability, below). If the universe of content which we have sampled on the basis of trial-total-scores-from-arbitrary-weights is the true scale rank order, or closely approximates it, then our scalogram should have much the same kind of regular pattern as appears in the perfect scale in Table 2. That is, for any item, the people who made the response given the greatest weight for that item should all be ranked (by total score) above the people who made the response given the next greatest weight for that item, who, in turn, should all be above the people who made the response given the next greatest weight for that item, etc., for all the categories in the item (usually not more than five). And this should be true for *every* item in the group. This, as we have seen, is what is meant by each item being a *simple function* of the rank-order scale scores. The "staircase" effect in Table 2 comes about, of course, only because we have listed the "items" (sticks) in order of increasing height. Ordinarily it would turn out that the items fall in this regular increasing order, unless we consciously arrange them that way ahead of time, and this can only be done for items that are all dichotomous anyway. If there are items with three or more categories, the "steps" will jump around the table.

A perfect pattern, as illustrated by Table 2, is not, of course, to be expected in practice, and the first part of our test for scalability is to see how well the pattern of our scalogram approximates a perfect pattern. This is done by establishing *cutting points* between the categories of each item. A cutting point is a point in the order of responses on our scalogram table such that most of the responses in a higher category are above the cutting point, and most of the responses in the next adjacent lower category are below the cutting point. For instance, the cutting point for item 1 in Table 2 is between individual *I* and individual *L*, the cutting point for item 5 is between individuals *R* and *T*, etc. A cutting point is established between each pair of adjacent categories in an item so that each item will have one less cutting point than it has response alternatives.

In an actual scalogram there will not ordinarily be the unique and clear-cut determination of where to place the cutting points that there is in our perfect example of Table 2. No matter where the cutting point is placed, there will be some individuals with responses in the higher category who are *below* the cutting point in the rank order, and some individuals with responses in the lower category who are *above* the cutting point. These responses are *errors of reproducibility* for any given placement of a cutting point.

In determining where to place each cutting point in an actual scalogram, we consider each possible placement of the cutting point, and count the errors of reproducibility there would be below it to the left, and above it to the right, for each possibility. Then we place it in the position for which this total number of errors of reproducibility around the cutting point is the smallest possible. If there are several possible positions with the same minimum number of errors, the placement may be arbitrary, or it may be partially determined by some of the considerations to be mentioned in the next section.

Now we can see why these out-of-place responses are referred to as errors of reproducibility. After all the cutting points have been established in our scalogram, we can extend them, either mentally, or with dotted lines as in Table 2, across the entire table, so that they break up the rank-ordering of people into several groups. The number of groups will be one more than the total number of cutting points in the entire table, or the total number of response categories (columns) in the entire table minus the number of items plus one. If the scale were a perfect one, as in Table 2, then all the people included between any two successive dotted lines would have *exactly the same pattern of responses to all items.* In an actual example this will not be the case, but our cutting points have been so placed that all the people between any two successive dotted lines have response patterns that are as nearly alike as possible, and are, in fact, exactly alike *except for* the misplaced responses which we have called errors.

We may ignore the trial total scores, which were merely a means of approximating the scale rank order among individuals and have no intrinsic claim to representing the "true" order exactly since they are affected by the "misplaced" responses. Instead, we shall consider those people falling between any two successive dotted lines as being all of one kind, as far as behavior with respect to our sample of items is concerned, and we give these groups new rank-order designations, either with numbers, or alphabetically. Ordinarily, except in the case of a perfect scale, these new groupings of people with like response patterns will not coincide exactly with the previous groupings of people all of whom had the same trial total score, but it is the *new* groupings which we now take to be an approximation to the true scale rank order among our individuals, if such exists.

Now we are in a position to deal with the concept of *reproducibility.* We have noted that all the people in any one of our new groupings have response patterns that are as nearly alike as possible. If we were told that an individual fell into such-and-such a scale rank-order group, we could then attempt to *reproduce* his responses to the individual items by setting down the pattern of responses which characterizes that scale order group. If we did this for all the individuals in our sample, the only places where we would be wrong would be on all those responses which we found to be unavoidably "misplaced" when we established our cutting points. These responses are, in truth, errors of reproducibility—we err on each such response when we predict that an individual made the response characteristic of the scale order group into which he falls when, in fact, he did not, but made some other response not characteristic of the scale order group into which he falls.

This concept now forms the basis for computing a statistic which becomes *part* of our test of the hypothesis of scalability. We count up all errors of reproducibility in the entire scalogram table, subtract from the total number of responses in the table, and then express this number as a proportion or percent of the total number of responses recorded in the entire table. When expressed as a proportion, we refer to this statistic as the *coefficient of reproducibility,* or if expressed as a percentage, we say that we have such-and-such percent reproducibility. For instance, in Table 2 there are $25 \times 10 = 250$ responses recorded, and there are no errors of reproducibility, so we have a coefficient of reproducibility of $250/250 = 1.00$ or 100 percent reproducibility, which expresses the fact that this sample of responses to this sample of items was perfectly scalable.

Criteria for Scalability.   We are now in a position to apply a preliminary test of our hypothesis of scalability (preliminary because, except in the case of all dichotomous items, the data may be manipulated further if the first test fails—see below). The essential criteria which must be met before we can accept the hypothesis of scalability are four in number.

1. *Homogeneity of content:* The items of our "measuring instrument" must, on the face of them, pertain to the same area of attitude, achievement, or some other designated psychological dimension. It is possible for an item to scale with a group of items from a defined area and yet not have the content defining that

area; its content may be a correlate of the area, rather than part of the definition of the area. The question of homogeneity of content is a matter for subjective and intuitive judgment, at least at the present stage of development of scale theory. The problem has, of course, to be met in the process of constructing the instrument, before the other aspects of the test for scalability are ever applied. A preferred procedure is to make use of the combined judgment of several people considered "expert" in the area in question. We shall speak later of a subsequent development which provides for the use of judgments, among other things—the "scale discrimination" method of attitude scaling (8).

2. *Reproducibility:* In order for a universe of content to be considered scalable with respect to a given population of individuals, it has been judged necessary that a sample of items from the universe exhibit 90 percent reproducibility or better when administered to a sample of individuals from the population.

3. *Range of marginal frequencies:* Before a reproducibility coefficient can be considered high enough, even though it be 0.90 or greater, we must consider the distribution of total frequency of response among the various response categories of each of several items. This is because no individual item can have a percent reproducibility less than the percent of the responses to that item that fall in the most popular response category—the "modal" category. Consider, for instance, an item for which the modal frequency is 90 percent of all the responses to the item. Then, even if the cutting points are pushed all the way to the top and/or bottom of the scalogram table, the very maximum number of errors—misplaced responses—that this item could have would be only 10 percent of the total, and even though the item provides no cutting points between one scale rank-order group and the next, we still could predict responses to that item correctly for 90 percent of the people in our sample. If all the items on our instrument were items of this type, with modal response categories containing 90 percent or more of the responses to the item, then obviously the coefficient of reproducibility which we would obtain from a scalogram would be 0.90 or higher, even though in the most extreme case there might be no determinable cutting points at all in the entire table. Such a situation does not yield any division of our sample of individuals into rank-order groups; they are all 90 percent or better alike in their

response patterns to these items, and therefore no evidence is presented, one way or the other, about the scalability of the universe of content sampled by these particular items.

For this reason it is necessary in applying the test for scalability, if the reproducibility requirement is met, to examine next the range of marginal frequencies in the response categories of the items. If the modal response frequency for each item, in proportion or percent form, is as high, or nearly as high, as the coefficient of reproducibility obtained for the entire scalogram, then there still is no evidence of scalability. If, however, there are some items with low modal response frequencies (near 50 percent for dichotomous items, 33 percent for trichotomous items, etc.), then a reproducibility coefficient of 0.90 or better may be taken as good evidence of scalability. There is no satisfactory method of testing objectively whether or not this criterion is sufficiently satisfied. Guttman has suggested as a requirement that every response category in the scalogram contain more *nonerror* responses than error, or "misplaced," responses.

Even though this test is applied, it is still desirable to inspect the actual range of marginals. The most desirable situation is to have items whose modal frequencies range all the way from their theoretical minimum on up, since the low ones render the coefficient of reproducibility more meaningful, but the high ones provide cutting points near the ends of the range in our rank order of individuals, which is also desirable.

4. *Random scatter of errors:* A final consideration in testing the hypothesis of scalability is to examine the pattern and position of those responses which remain unavoidably "misplaced" as errors of reproducibility. There should be no conspicuous "bunching" of the error responses in any particular response category within a narrow range of the overall rank order of individuals. Such a bunching would imply that there are a substantial number of people whose response patterns to all items are essentially similar (since they fall together in the rank order of individuals) and whose responses to the particular item where the bunching takes place are also alike, but are *different from the response to that item supposed to characterize individuals with that rank-order position.* That is, we would have a number of people (those whose responses to the item in question constitute the "bunch" of error responses)

whose response patterns are alike among themselves, and whose response patterns to all other items are like those of the other individuals in their rank-order group, but who make in common a response to that particular item different from the other individuals in their rank-order group.

Such a situation clearly violates the basic concept of a scale variable, that for an individual to have any particular scale position implies one particular pattern of response to all the items, and one only. If any substantial frequency of such a typical response pattern does occur in the scalogram, it signifies the presence of a significant "nonscale type," as it is called, and thus implies that we are not justified in accepting the hypothesis of scalability for the universe of content, as defined by the items used, with respect to the population sampled.

It is for these reasons that the fourth and final consideration in applying the test of the hypothesis of scalability is to make sure that the 10 percent or fewer responses remaining as error responses in our scalogram are scattered more or less randomly throughout their respective response categories, and do not tend to bunch up in any substantial numbers at any point in the rank order of individuals.

If all the items on an instrument are dichotomous, then the above steps, and the subsequent examination to see whether the criteria for scalability are or are not met, represent the "end of the line" for this particular sample of items on this sample of individuals. The hypothesis of scalability of the universe of content sampled is either accepted, rejected, or remains dubious due to borderline situations with respect to one or more of the several criteria, and that is that. If, however, there are items present with more than two response categories, and the criteria for scalability are not met in the first trial, it is possible that there is another explanation for this failure than actual unscalability of the universe of content sampled. Guttman says (*23*):

It has seldom been found that an item with four or five categories will be sufficiently reproducible if the categories are regarded as distinct. One reason for this is the verbal habits of people. Some people say "strongly agree" where others say "agree," whereas they have essentially the same position on the basic continuum but differ on an extraneous factor of verbal habits. By combining categories, minor extraneous variables of this kind can be minimized.

Reproducibility may thus be low in our first trial scalogram simply because the people whose responses fall in two adjacent response categories of an item differ, not basically on the underlying variable, but only in their verbal habits with respect to the response alternatives offered. Let us test this supposition.

The appropriate procedure is to combine into a single response category adjacent response categories for which the above seems to be true, as evidenced by the scalogram structure of responses. We examine the first trial scalogram for adjacent categories within an item in which the responses seem to "intertwine" or scatter up or down the rank order of individuals more or less together—that is, the response checks in one category do not taper off and the response checks in the next adjacent category begin within any relatively narrow range on the rank order. We decide to combine such categories.

We now have a new set of response categories for each of the items on our instrument, representing combinations from the original. The next step is to assign new arbitrary weights to these new response categories for each item, and obtain new trial total scores for each of our individuals on the basis of these new scoring weights. In assigning these new arbitrary weights, we proceed as we did on the first trial, using weights from zero up in the appropriate predetermined direction.

If there are items with differing numbers of the new combined categories, better results will be obtained if the *range* of arbitrary weights used within each item is kept as nearly alike from item to item as possible. For instance, if some items now have three categories, while others have only two, weights of 0, 1, and 2 are used with the trichotomous items, and weights of 0 and 2 with the dichotomous items. This consideration also holds in the first trial scoring, if the items as they originally appeared on the instrument had differing numbers of response categories. The rescoring of individuals may be done without reference to the original answer sheets, merely by making up a key strip with divisions corresponding exactly to the columns on the first trial scalogram, putting the new weights on the strip, and then placing the key under each individual's row, in turn, on the first trial scalogram, and computing his new trial total score.

The procedure is now exactly as that described before. A new scalogram table is made up with the number of columns for each item being the number of response categories for that item *after combination*. The individuals are entered on the scalogram table in the order of their new trial total scores, and their responses are entered in the table as now classified with reference to the new, combined response categories, rather than the original ones. Cutting points are then established, and reproducibility computed as before. The criteria of the test for scalability are then applied to the new scalogram, the hypothesis now being that the universe of content sampled is scalable for the population of individuals sampled, after extraneous variation in verbal behavior with respect to the original response categories of the several items has been removed.

A word of caution is in order on the matter of combining response categories for the purpose of a second trial scalogram. Care should be taken that the combination of categories does not merely have the effect of increasing the modal response frequency of each item in such a way that the increased reproducibility is due merely to high modal response frequencies in the several items.

The process of combination of response categories and drawing up of new trial scalograms may be repeated as often as necessary or desirable, until all items have been reduced to dichotomies, when the process necessarily ends. If, at any stage, the criteria for scalability are satisfied, we are able to accept the hypothesis which we set out to test. If not, we must in general reject the hypothesis for the universe of content defined for the sample of items used, or permit it to remain in doubt.

There are several courses of action which may then be indicated, and these will be discussed in a subsequent section on nonscalable situations.

Quasi Scales

One nonscalable situation warrants separate treatment, however. This is the situation where *all* the criteria for scalability are satisfied *except* the matter of reproducibility. In such a situation, we say that we have a *quasi scale*. It is important to emphasize this definition: A universe of content may be considered to be a quasi scale with respect to a defined population if, for a sample of items homogeneous in content (the content being that defined for the universe), the best possible scalogram for the responses of a sample of individuals from the population exhibits reproducibility less than 90 percent, but has, nevertheless, a range of marginal frequencies with a reproducibility somewhat higher than that to be expected on the basis of the modal response frequencies alone, and, most important of all, *for which the errors are randomly scattered.* This situation implies that although the universe cannot be considered a scale in the sense that a single response pattern is associated with a given rank-order position, there is one dominant variable determining the response behavior of the individuals, and the random scatter of the responses which depart from a scale pattern reflect the influence of many other small factors—there is no outstanding secondary variable present. Quasi-scalable areas have certain desirable properties in common with scalable ones, as we shall see in the next section.

Properties of Scales and Quasi Scales. The most outstanding characteristic of a universe of content which forms a scale for a population of people is the unidimensionality feature already discussed: There exists a rank-order relationship among the people, for the area, which is unambiguous in the sense that a given rank-order position implies one particular pattern of behavior with respect to the area, and one only (within the acceptable limits of errors of reproducibility—10 percent or less), and it is meaningful to speak of persons as "higher" or "lower" in the area. These properties are stated for the universe of content and the population of persons. It follows, however—and this is the feature which is important for attitude research—that the responses of a *sample* of persons from the population on a sample of items from the universe will serve to establish the rank order of those persons with respect to the entire universe, within the limits of the ability of the particular items in the sample to discriminate.

As can be seen from an examination of the relationship between cutting points and the number of rank-order groups obtained on a scalogram, the more items that are used on an instrument (or rather, strictly, the more response categories that are satisfactorily reproducible, whether they be in the same or different items), the finer will be the rank-order discriminations among the persons. This fact also has important implications for attitude research. While it is necessary to use a dozen or more items from the universe of content to *test* the hypothesis of scalability, once the hypothesis has been accepted for an area it is necessary to use on the final instrument only as many items as are required for the desired fineness of rank-order discriminations among the persons, and this may often be less than that necessary to test the hypothesis.

A quasi scale, on the other hand, does not have the clear-cut unidimensionality characteristic of a scale because it lacks the essential feature of near-perfect reproducibility—the "simple function" concept discussed earlier. Yet by virtue of the requirement of random scatter of errors in the definition of a quasi scale, it is still true that, to the extent one person is higher than another in the rank order established by the dominant factor in the quasi scale, his probability of being in a higher category of any item is correspondingly greater. Therefore, provided the sample of items on an instrument is large enough, the rank order obtained for a sample of persons may be taken to be essentially their rank order with respect to the dominant variable present in the quasi scale. No information is obtained, however, about the characteristics of the persons with respect to the many minor variables in the universe of content which account for its failure to meet the requirements of a scale.

An extremely important statistical property of a scalable universe of attributes is the following: If for a population of persons the relationship between a universe of attributes and some external variable is desired, the multiple correlation between the external variable and all the elements of the universe of attributes is the appropriate measure of the relationship, but if the universe is scalable, this multiple correlation is equal to the zero-order correlation between the external variable and the rank-order scale variable for the universe. This property continues to hold, essentially, whether we are dealing with a sample of items from the universe or a sample of persons. If the universe is scalable, then the simple correlation between the external variable and the rank-order scale variable obtained for our sample of items equals the multiple correlation between the external variable and all items of the sample; and it is an estimate of the relationship holding for the population of persons on the universe of attributes, the degree of precision of the estimate depending on the size and nature of our samples at hand.

Moreover, this statistical property holds also for quasi scales. Because the errors of reproducibility vary in a random manner, it is still true that the simple correlation between an external variable and the rank order established by the dominant variable in the quasi scale equals the multiple correlation between the external variable and the items of the quasi scale, even though the reproducibility is low. It is for this reason that quasi scales have been singled out for special mention from the several possible nonscalable situations; even though the rank-order variable for a quasi scale has less *internal* meaning than a scale variable has, it is nevertheless fully as efficient for relating the area to an *external* variable. In order to make practical use of this property of the quasi scale, it is important to be quite exacting about the requirement that the nonscale response behavior present be distributed in a random fashion.

Nonscalable Situations

It should not be inferred from the previous discussion that there is something wrong with a universe of content that is found not to be scalable. It is perfectly possible for a well-defined area which is quite homogeneous in the sense of content not to be a scale for a given population of people. This happens when the area of content in question is not "well structured," as the psychologists say—not integrated into a functional unity—for the population under discussion (3). To say that such an area is not scalable is only another way of saying what is intuitively obvious: that it does not make much sense to speak of one person as "higher" than or "lower" than another person on such an area. We can only deal with the characteristics of individuals separately; we cannot compare them with one another, because there is no basis on which to make the comparison.

Where an area is adjudged to be a quasi scale, as discussed above, we may say that there is one dominant variable plus many small variables making up the area, or we may say that the area is only partially structured for the population in question. The two points of view are essentially equivalent.

But there are also certain other alternative conclusions which seem possible when the hypothesis of scalability must be rejected on the basis of a trial scalogram on a group of items, and we shall discuss these here. It is a strong temptation, for example, simply to toss out certain items that seem to be spoiling the scale pattern, and to try again with the reduced instrument. If the new subset of items then did prove to be scalable, or if we obtained a scalable subset of items after repeating this process a few times, we might be tempted to conclude, uncritically, that we still had a sample of items from the original universe of content, that we had shown this universe to be scalable, and that the items thrown out were either just badly constructed items or else did not belong in the universe. Such a process, however, is not justifiable from the theory of Scale Analysis since, in a sense, it puts the cart before the horse. Guttman says (*21*):

> Finding scalable subsets of items *may* sometimes imply that the original universe of content can be divided into subuniverses, at least one—or perhaps all—of which are scalable separately. To test the hypothesis that a scalable subset is part of a scalable subuniverse, *it is necessary to show that the content of this subuniverse is ascertainable by inspection,* and is distinguishable by inspection from that of the rest of the universe. The practical procedure to test this hypothesis is as follows: Construct new items of two types of content, one type which should belong to the apparently scalable subuniverse, and one type which should belong in the original universe but should not belong to the scalable subuniverse. If the new items designed for the apparently scalable subuniverse do scale, and scale together with the old subset, and if the new items designed not to be in this subuniverse do not scale with the sub-scale, then the hypothesis is sustained that a subuniverse has been defined and has been found scalable. Each hypothecated subuniverse should be tested in this way.

And again:

> Scale analysis as such gives no judgment on content; it presumes that the area of content is already defined, and merely tests whether or not the area is representable by a single variable. It might serve as an *auxiliary* argument with respect to content in a special case where there is controversy over but one or two items of a large sample of items in which the remaining items are scalable. . . . It should be emphasized that this kind of inference is but *auxiliary*—there must be a cogent initial argument based on content.

And regarding the possibility of badly constructed items:

> There are at least two possibilities as to why some items do not scale while others in the same area do: (*a*) the universe is not scalable as a whole, but contains a scalable subuniverse; (*b*) the items have been imperfectly constructed. This latter reason is so easy and glib that it is best to avoid it as much as possible. If the vast

majority of a sample of items do scale, then it may be plausible to blame faulty construction for the nonscalability of one or two items. This hypothesis can be tested by rebuilding the apparently faulty items and retesting them.

The moral is that the evidence from a given trial scalogram of a sample of items on a sample of persons is not, by itself, adequate for item selection, or a "factor analysis" among the items of the sample. "There must be a cogent initial argument based on content," and any second guesses about the structure of the universe of content should be tested with new items constructed in the light of the new hypothesis.

Some investigators, e.g., Gage (*14*), in basing item-selection procedures on the evidence of a scalogram, have guarded against the dangers of artificial selection of an item sample which happens to scale for the responses of a particular sample of persons by readministering the selected items to a new sample of persons and verifying that the scalability continues to hold. This is probably an acceptable compromise procedure for avoiding the error of conclusions based on restricted selection and may be considered to demonstrate that the selected subsample of items comes from an area of content which is scalable for the population sampled, but it must be realized that this content area may be only a subsidiary part of the universe of interest originally defined.

Another kind of nonscalable situation occurs when what should be the scale pattern is quite clear and well defined, but one or more nonscale types of response patterns appear in sufficient numbers so that the hypothesis of scalability must be rejected. This situation calls for subdividing the population of persons sampled, rather than subdividing the area of content involved, in order to reach meaningful results. If the persons who are the nonscale types in the first scalogram can be identified to represent a definable subpopulation of the original population sampled, then the one or more subpopulation so identified may be resampled and retested, and scalability perhaps established for them separately. If subpopulations cannot be so identified and defined, then we may have to accept the area of content as nonscalable for the population, but the instrument may serve a useful purpose by making it possible to pick out, individually, these nonscale types, or deviants, in the population for clinical study.

Intensity Function

One of the greatest methodological problems for opinion polling and attitude surveys has revolved around the attempts to divide a population into pro and con groups on an issue, or "favorable" and "unfavorable" groups with respect to an attitude, etc., and to estimate the proportions of the population that fall into these classes. It has been found that no matter how careful the item construction, how extensive the pretesting and other attempts at standardization, different investigators (or even the same investigation) using differently constructed questions on the same area will arrive at differing conclusions regarding the proportions of the population in the "pro" and "con," "positive" and "negative" classes. This is the problem of question bias. And since it is apparently not possible to tell, even with the greatest amount of care, when a question is "biased" and when it is not, the desired proportions remain essentially indeterminate by the usual methods.

Probably the most important contribution of the theory of scale analysis to opinion-attitude methodology is a solution to this problem of question bias. According to Guttman, the mathematical development underlying the scale analysis procedures indicates that each scale variable, as defined above, has associated with it a series of higher "components" or functions of the scale variable. The first such component is a U- or J-shaped function of the scale variable, and each higher component has one more "bend" in it than the preceding one. Guttman and his associates have done considerable experimenting with this first component and have called it the "intensity function" of the scale variable (*20, 25, 40*).

It is this intensity function which provides the key to the

determination of the psychological zero point on an attitude continuum. The reasoning is as follows: The intensity function of an attitude continuum, measured by techniques which we shall outline shortly, has actually been found to form a U- or J-shaped curve when plotted against the attitude continuum. The low point on this curve is the point of least intensity, or greatest indifference, with respect to the attitude area, and can logically be considered as the point at which the attitude variable changes "sign," so to speak, from positive to negative, "pro" to "con." Two individuals with the same intensity score but on opposite sides of the "indifference" point on the attitude variable must hold attitudes which tend toward opposite poles of the attitude continuum.

The intensity function has been measured in several ways, but the most satisfactory procedure seems to be to include an intensity item after each content, or attitude item, in the scale or questionnaire. These intensity items may all be of the same form, or they may take different forms, depending on what is most appropriate to the nature of the content item referred to. Some forms that have been used are: "How strongly do you feel about this?" with answer categories of "very strongly, fairly strongly, not so strongly, not at all strongly"; or "How sure are you of your answer?"; or "How hard was it for you to make this choice?"; each question of course has appropriate response categories. It is best to keep all reference to content out of the intensity item, the content item being clear since it immediately precedes the intensity item in each case. Another procedure for measuring intensity, which combined content and intensity in the same response, was found to be unsatisfactory because the intensity responses were not experimentally independent of the content responses.

Analysis of the data obtained from the administration of such a questionnaire now involves two scale analyses, by the procedures indicated above: The content items are subjected to scale analysis to test for the existence of a content scale variable, and the intensity items are subjected to scale analysis, separately, to test for the existence of an intensity scale variable. Experience has shown that if the content items are scalable, the intensity items will also be scalable, unless faulty techniques of intensity measurement have been used. If both sets of items are scalable, then we have two scores for each individual, a content scale score and an intensity scale score. The next step is to set up a two-way frequency distribution, tabulating intensity scale score against content scale score for all individuals in our sample. The column for each content scale score will then contain an "array" distribution of intensity scores of people having that content score. The median intensity score in each array should also be located.

In order to graph the curve of the intensity function for our sample, it is better to convert the content and intensity scores to a "percentile metric." This is done as follows: Consider each content scale score as a class interval to be given class limits which are the highest and lowest percentile ranks on content for the entire sample in that interval, and then assign a class index or mid-point to each such class interval in the usual way. Do the same for the total distribution of intensity scores.

We may now ignore the content and intensity scale *scores,* and consider that we have a two-way frequency tabulation based on class intervals which are in units of percentile rank, one axis representing content percentile rank, and one axis representing intensity percentile rank. Now determine the percentile rank for the median of *each* of the array distributions at content intervals, interpolating into intensity class intervals in the usual way. The curve of the intensity function for the sample may now be graphed by plotting on the horizontal axis the value of the mid-point of each content percentile-rank interval and, vertically, the intensity percentile value of its array median.

The intrinsic intensity function of the scale variable for the universe of content would be a smooth curve, U- or J-shaped, opening upward and touching the horizontal (content) axis at its lowest point. This point is the psychological zero point for the attitude content continuum. However, since we have a limited number of items in our scale, and our techniques for measuring intensity are subject to much error, this is not true of the intensity curve for our sample—it will not touch the content axis, and it is made up of a series of straight line segments, proceeding by jumps.

Therefore we cannot, from our data, determine the exact psychological zero point for the attitude axis, but only the range in which it falls. The zero point must lie between the content percentile values for the next-to-the-lowest points on either side of the lowest point of our sample intensity curve, and we can say that *at least* such and such a percent of the population sampled are positive, or "pro," on this attitude, and *at least* such and such a percent are negative, or "anti." The more items from the content universe that are included in our instrument, especially those that break somewhere near the true percentage division, the more closely will the range for the zero point be narrowed down, so that we may, if necessary, add more items in order to determine the "zero range" more closely.

Guttman and others have done some experimentation with these techniques for determining the zero range of an attitude variable and have found it to be essentially invariant under different (even intentionally biased) wordings of content items, different arrangement of content items, different forms of intensity items, and other sources of variation. That is, the zero point (or rather, zero range) as determined by these methods seems not to be affected by the various types of biases that have previously caused difficulty in attitude measurement. They have also found that the shape of the intensity function curve yields certain additional information about the attitude area for the population sampled. For instance, if the intensity function is very flat-bottomed, it indicates a relatively large amount of indifference toward the particular attitude area, or if it is sharp-pointed and V-shaped, this indicates that the population is sharply divided on the attitude area with relatively few individuals professing indifference.

They have applied the same techniques to an instrument in which the content items were matters of fact, i.e., an instrument of the same nature as an achievement test, with intensity items of the "How sure are you of your answer?" form. The intensity curve in such cases turned out to have no bend in it, but was, rather, a curve steadily rising from low to high content score. This is consistent with our concept of the nature of "knowledge"—that is, ordinarily we do not consider the possibility of "negative" knowledge. Knowledge of facts represents a sort of special or degenerate case of an attitude continuum in which the negative half of the axis is not present.

General Comments

The theory and procedures of scale analysis detailed above have been the subject of much discussion, experimentation, and criticism since their introduction (2, 5, 7, 13, 29, 32). One source of dissatisfaction with scale analysis procedures in their present form is, of course, their lack of "methodological precision"—the absence of objective, quantified criteria for establishing cutting points, testing for random scatter of error, testing for degree of "spuriousness" in obtained reproducibility coefficients due to high modal frequencies, etc. Another focus of criticism is the entirely subjective nature of the selection of the original sample of items from the "content universe" for testing the hypothesis of scalability. The objection is that, since this sampling process is incapable of being analyzed in a manner similar to that for the sampling of a population of individuals or other defined entities, it is improper to infer from the scalability of a particular set of items that the universe of content which the investigator had in mind is also scalable; it may only be some relatively narrow subuniverse that has been shown to be scalable.

Nevertheless, the concept of unidimensionality is for the most part accepted as an important one for psychological measurement generally, and the properties of a scalable set of items exhibiting unidimensionality are recognized to be valuable— unambiguous and essentially invariant rank-ordering of individuals and maximum efficiency of prediction to an outside criterion through use of zero-order correlation with the scale variable. It is to be hoped that further research will be directed at overcoming the shortcomings discussed above. Certain advances and improvements have already been suggested. One of these, the scale discrimination technique of Edwards and Kilpatrick (8), attacks the problem of selection of the initial set of items to be tested for scalability. This is discussed in the next section.

THE SCALE DISCRIMINATION TECHNIQUE

In some preliminary investigations on the behavior of attitude items under the various scaling procedures which we have discussed, Edwards and Kilpatrick (4, 7) observed two empirical relationships operating: first, that the cutting points and response frequencies of an item are related to its scale value under the Thurstone scaling procedure, extreme items tending to have high modal response frequencies one way or the other, and neutral items tending to have more nearly even distribution of response frequencies; second, that the reproducibility of an item from the trial total score tends to be related to the discriminatory power of items as calculated in the item-analysis procedures of the Likert technique—the more an item discriminates between extreme groups, the higher its reproducibility tends to be. They further observed that items with neutral Thurstone scale values tended to have poorer reproducibility, there being more or less equal probability of endorsement by individuals from opposite ends of the attitude continuum, and that the Thurstone criterion for item selection—Q—did not seem to have much relationship to the discriminatory power of an item.

From these findings they reasoned that a combination of the Thurstone scaling procedures and item-selection techniques as in the Likert method ought to provide an objective method for selecting a group of items for the final attitude scale which would have a good chance of meeting Guttman's criteria of scalability. This is truly a synthesis of the methods previously discussed, and has been dubbed the "scale discrimination technique" by its authors. In the few applications of the technique which have so far been published, it has lived up to expectations quite well. The following paragraphs outline the steps of the procedure in some detail.

As in the Thurstone and Likert procedures, a large number of opinion statements in the attitude area to be scaled are first collected, using various sources such as books and articles, invited essays and statement of opinion, etc. This original collection should be edited to meet certain informal standards, among which Edwards and Kilpatrick suggest the following: Items should not be retained which could be endorsed by individuals with opposed attitudes; which are statements of fact, or could be so interpreted; which are irrelevant; which are so extreme as to be likely to be either accepted or rejected unanimously by subjects; which seem subject to ambiguous interpretation; or which contain vocabulary too difficult for prospective subjects. The collection of retained items, after such editing, should number perhaps 100 to 150.

This reduced collection of items is now subjected to a Thurstone scaling procedure by a group of perhaps 100 judges, exactly as described under the method of equal-appearing intervals. The judges are instructed to avoid expressing their own attitudes, and to place the items at the points along the continuum so that the intervals between points appear to them to be equal. A nine- or an eleven-point scale may be used. Edwards and Kilpatrick used a nine-point scale. The original card-sorting procedure of Thurstone may be used, but simplified judging procedures like those of Ballin and Farnsworth (1) or Seashore and Hevner (38) would reduce the labor considerably. After eliminating the records of those judges who appear not to have followed directions in one way or another, the judgments from the rest of the judges are tabulated, and the scale value and Q computed or read graphically for each item, as previously explained.

The items are now plotted in a two-way distribution with scale values along the base line and Q values along the vertical axis. The median Q-value for all items is determined, and a horizontal line drawn across the scatter plot at this value. All items above this line are rejected, and only the items falling below this line are retained for further steps. This amounts to applying the Thurstone criterion of ambiguity, or disagreement among the judges for some other reason, and we select for further steps only the 50 percent of the items which show the least ambiguity or disagreement, as measured by Q.

The remaining 50 percent of the items are now drawn up in a Likert-type questionnaire with multiple-choice response categories on an agree-disagree continuum. Edwards and Kilpatrick used a six-point "forcing" scale of "strongly agree, agree, mildly agree, mildly disagree, disagree, strongly disagree," but presumably a five-choice scale or some other number would be equally suitable. This questionnaire is then administered to a large group of subjects who are to indicate *their own* attitudes by checking the response to each item appropriate for them. It is well for this group of subjects to number from 200 to 300 or more, if possible, and more satisfactory results are obtained if a wide range of attitudes on the attitude object involved is represented.

The items are now subjected to item analysis on the basis of the responses of this group of subjects. Weights are assigned to the response categories of each item, the proper direction for the weights within each item being determined in accordance with its scale value as previously determined, and a total score derived for each subject. The discriminating power of each item is then obtained by any of several procedures—although in this case it is necessary to have an actual quantitative index of the discriminating power of each item. Edwards and Kilpatrick used the phi coefficient (*16, 28*), though presumably biserial or multiserial correlation (27) or other item-test correlation procedures could equally well be used. An advantage of the phi coefficient is that it involves less computational labor than most other procedures.

A new two-way distribution of the items is now plotted, with scale values (from the original Thurstone-type scaling) along the base line, and the index of discriminating power—say phi coefficients—along the vertical axis. This is the point at which the final selection of items for the scale (or scales, if two equivalent forms are to be constructed) takes place. The principle is to select the most discriminating items from each of several intervals into which the horizontal (scale) axis may be arbitrarily divided, but how fine these intervals shall be, or how many items are to be selected from each, will depend on each particular case.

Edwards and Kilpatrick divided their nine-point scale axis into half-unit intervals, yielding eighteen intervals in all. Only seven of these intervals contained any items, however, by the time they reached this stage of the process, and they accordingly selected the four items with highest phi coefficients from each of these intervals in order to construct two equivalent fourteen-item scales. Each investigator using these procedures will have to make his own decisions at this point, based on how well spread throughout the scale his remaining items are, and how many items he wants to select. Edwards and Kilpatrick also imply that it would be well for the investigator to set some minimum standard of discriminating power, and in no case to select items with discriminating power less than the minimum. In their example no item selected had a phi coefficient of less than 0.58. Such a criterion, they point out, would probably tend to exclude all "neutral" items except those with exceptional promise as far as reproducibility is concerned.

The procedures outlined above[1] constitute a suggested

[1] After this chapter was written a highly important series of four books was published that the serious student of the psychology of attitudes cannot ignore: S. A. Stouffer and others, *The American Soldier*, I, *Adjustment During Army*

method for the *selection* of items for the attitude scale, which, as we have seen, is one of the weak points of scale analysis theory in its present stage of development. As the final step in the process, the instrument thus constructed should be tested for scalability, by the procedures outlined in the section on scale analysis. As mentioned earlier, the little experience so far obtained with this method indicates that the items thus selected are quite likely to exhibit satisfactory unidimensionality.

Questions

1. Is an attitude scale constructed on the equal-appearing-intervals principle for all practical purposes a unidimensional scale?
2. What is the equal-appearing-intervals principle?
3. What is meant by psychological unidimensionality?
4. The span of attention or span of immediate perception for adults has been experimentally shown to be limited to about six or seven items. What implications may this fact have for the construction of attitude scales by the Thurstone technique, where attitude items are required to be sorted into eleven piles? Can you suggest an experimental design to test such implications?
5. What is a "rational" scale?
6. Discuss: "In the construction of attitude scales, the method of equal-appearing intervals and the method of summated ratings differ fundamentally in the nature of the process of measurement involved."
7. Because increasing the number of alternate responses to a scale item increases the intricacies of the scalogram and accordingly lessens the chances of a group of items of being scalable, it would appear desirable to minimize the number of alternate responses, possibly limiting them to two. What other factors must be given consideration, and what might be the disadvantages of such a procedure?

Life; II, *Combat and Its Aftermath;* III, *Experiments on Mass Communication;* and IV, *Measurement and Prediction,* Princeton, N. J.: Princeton University Press, 1950. As its title implies, vol. IV is particularly relevant to this book. In vol. IV the Guttman scaling technique is developed and illustrated very extensively, as is also the *latent structure* theory of Paul F. Lazarsfeld. The entire four volumes are a landmark in scientific development in the social sciences.

8. Attack or defend: "The theoretical background of attitude measurement implies that an instrument that fails to meet the criteria of scalability has no value as a measuring instrument."

9. Is it logical to assume that all errors will have the same weight with regard to reproducibility?

Bibliography

1. Ballin, M. R., and Farnsworth, P. R., "A Graphic Rating Method for Determining the Scale Values of Statements in Measuring Social Attitudes," *J. soc. Psychol.*, 1941, *13*:323-327.

2. Clark, K. E., and Kriedt, P. H., "An Application of Guttman's New Scaling Technique to an Attitude Questionnaire," *Educ. psychol. Meas.*, 1948, *8*:215-224.

3. Coombs, Clyde H., "Some Hypotheses for the Analysis of Qualitative Variables," *Psychol. Rev.*, 1948, *55*:167-174.

4. Edwards, A. L., "A Critique of 'Neutral' Items in Attitude Scales Constructed by the Method of Equal-Appearing Intervals," *Psychol. Rev.*, 1946, *53*:159-169.

5. Edwards, A. L., "On Guttman's Scale Analysis," *Educ. psychol. Meas.*, 1948, *8*:313-318.

6. Edwards, A. L., and Kenney, Kathryn Claire, "A Comparison of the Thurstone and Likert Techniques of Attitude Scale Construction," *J. appl. Psychol.*, 1946, *30*:72-83.

7. Edwards, A. L., and Kilpatrick, Franklin P., "Scale Analysis and the Measurement of Social Attitudes," *Psychometrika*, 1948, *13*:99-114.

8. Edwards, A. L., and Kilpatrick, Franklin P., "A Technique for the Construction of Attitude Scales," *J. appl. Psychol.*, 1948, *32*:374-383.

9. Farnsworth, P. R., "Shifts in the Values of Opinion Items," *J. Psychol.*, 1943, *16*:125-128.

10. Ferguson, L. W., "The Influence of Individual Attitudes on Construction of an Attitude Scale," *J. soc. Psychol.*, 1935, *6*:115-117.

11. Ferguson, L. W., "The Requirements of an Adequate Attitude Scale," *Psychol. Bull.*, 1939, *36*:665-673.

12. Ferguson, L. W., "A Study of the Likert Technique of Attitude Scale Construction," *J. soc. Psychol.*, 1941, *13*:51-57.

13. Festinger, L., "The Treatment of Qualitative Data by Scale Analysis," *Psychol. Bull.*, 1947, *44:*149-161.

14. Gage, N. L., "Scaling and Factorial Design in Opinion Poll Analysis," *Purdue University Studies in Higher Education, Further Studies in Attitudes, Series* X, 1948, No. *61.*

15. Goodenough, Ward H., "A Technique for Scale Analysis," *Educ. & psychol. Meas.*, 1944, *4:*179-190.

16. Guilford, J. P., "The Phi Coefficient and Chi Square as Indices of Item Validity," *Psychometrika,* 1941, *6:*11-19.

17. Guttman, Louis: (*a*) "An Outline of the Statistical Theory of Prediction," 253-311; (*b*) "The Quantification of a Class of Attributes: A Theory and Method of Scale Construction," 319-348; (*c*) "Empirical Studies of Weighting Techniques," 349-364. *In* Horst, Paul, and others, *The Prediction of Personal Adjustment,* New York: Social Science Research Council, *Bulletin* No. 48, 1941.

18. Guttman, Louis, *The Desire of Enlisted Men for Post-War Full-Time Schooling: An Example of a Scale,* Washisgton, D. C.: Research Branch, Information and Education Division, Army Service Forces, mimeo., 1943.

19. Guttman, Louis, "A Basis for Scaling Qualitative Data," *Amer. sociol. Rev.,* 1944, *9:*139-150.

20. Guttman, Louis, *Experiments on the Measurement of the Intensity Function and Zero Point in Attitude Analysis,* Washington, D. C.: Research Branch, Information and Education Division, Army Service Forces, *Report* D-1, mimeo., 1945.

21. Guttman, Louis, *Questions and Answers About Scale Analysis,* Washington, D. C.: Research Branch, Information and Education Division, Army Service Forces, *Report* D-2, mimeo., 1945.

22. Guttman, Louis, "The Cornell Technique for Scale and Intensity Analysis," *Educ. & psychol. Meas.,* 1947, 7:247-279.

23. Guttman, Louis, "On Festinger's Evaluation of Scale Analysis," *Psychol. Bull.,* 1947, *44:*451-465.

24. Guttman, Louis, "Suggestions for Further Research in Scale and Intensity Analysis of Attitudes and Opinions," *Int. J. opin. attit. Res.,* 1947, *1:*30-35.

25. Guttman, Louis, and Suchman, E. A., "Intensity and a Zero Point for Attitude Analysis," *Amer. sociol. Rev.,* 1947, *12:* 57-67.

26. Hinckley, E. D., "The Influence of Individual Opinion on Construction of an Attitude Scale," *J. soc. Psychol.,* 1932, *3:* 283-296.

27. Jaspen, Nathan, "Serial Correlation," *Psychometrika,* 1946, *11:* 23-30.

28. Jurgensen, C. E., "Table for Determining Phi Coefficients," *Psychometrika,* 1947, *12:*17-29.

29. Kriedt, Philip H., and Clark, Kenneth E., " 'Item Analysis' vs. 'Scale Analysis,' " *J. appl. Psychol.,* 1949, *33:*114-121.

30. Likert, R., "A Technique for the Measurement of Attitudes," *Arch. Psychol.* New York, 1932 (no. 140): 1-55.

31. Likert, R., Roslow, S., and Murphy, G., "A Simple and Reliable Method of Scoring the Thurstone Attitude Scales," *J. soc. Psychol.,* 1934, *5:*228-238.

32. Loevinger, Jane, "The Technic of Homogeneous Tests Compared with Some Aspects of 'Scale Analysis' and Factor Analysis," *Psychol. Bull.,* 1948, *45:*507-528.

33. McNemar, Q., "Opinion-Attitude Methodology," *Psychol. Bull.,* 1946, *43:*289-374.

34. Murphy, G., and Likert, R., *Public Opinion and the Individual,* New York: Harper & Brothers, 1937.

35. Pintner, R., and Forlano, G., "The Influence of Attitude upon Scaling of Attitude Items," *J. soc. Psychol.,* 1937, *8:*39-45.

36. Remmers, H. H., "Generalized Attitude Scales—Studies in Social-Psychological Measurements," *Purdue University Studies in Higher Education: Studies in Attitudes—A Contribution to Social-Psychological Research Methods,* 1934, no. 26:7-17.

37. Remmers, H. H., and Silance, E. B., "Generalized Attitude Scales," *J. soc. Psychol.,* 1934, *5:*298-312.

38. Seashore, R. H., and Hevner, K., "A Time-Saving Device for the Construction of Attitude Scales," *J. soc. Psychol.,* 1933, *4:* 366-372.

39. Sigerfoos, Charles C., "The Validation and Application of a Scale of Attitude Toward Any Vocation," *Purdue University Studies in Higher Education: Further Studies in Attitudes Series,* II, 1936, no. 31:177-191.

40. Suchman, E. A., and Guttman, Louis, "A Solution to the Problem of Question Bias," *Publ. Opin. Quart.,* 1947, *11:*445-455.

41. Thurstone, L. L., "The Method of Paired Comparisons for Social Values," *J. abnorm. soc. Psychol.,* 1927, *21*:384-400.
42. Thurstone, L. L., "Attitudes Can Be Measured," *Amer. J. Sociol.,* 1928, *33*:529-554.
43. Thurstone, L. L., "Theory of Attitude Measurement," *Psychol. Rev.,* 1929, *36*:222-241.
44. Thurstone, L. L., "The Measurement of Social Attitudes," *J. abnorm. soc. Psychol.,* 1931, *26*:249-269.
45. Thurstone, L. L., and Chave, E. J., *The Measurement of Attitude Toward the Church,* Chicago: University of Chicago Press, 1929.

CHAPTER V

. . . ● ● ● . . .

The Single Question

INTRODUCTION

In this chapter we shall examine and evaluate the single-question technique of polling. Involved in this are the usual problems of validity and reliability.

The problem of validity may be stated as being that of predicting other, often nonverbal, behavior from the responses obtained to opinion or attitude questions. We should not overlook the fact, however, that much of human behavior is verbal and symbolic, and that in many situations, therefore, the criterion for validity would be verbal or symbolic behavior of some sort. Most of us will never be able to express our attitudes toward, let us say, the United Nations in any way other than by stating these attitudes, or voting for persons who in our judgment will implement our attitude—a verbal, symbolic response. So it is with many situations. Political behavior and much of all social behavior in general is this kind of verbal, symbolic behavior. An individual who feels strongly about an issue may write a letter to the editor of his newspaper, which is, again, a verbal response to a situation.

In much of market and consumer research it is possible, obviously, to check verbal responses to questions about the purchase or nonpurchase of given items of merchandise against the actual sales in neighborhood stores or in a given geographical area. One of the most dramatic tests of validity of recent times was that of the prediction from attitude studies in the armed forces before the end of World War II that 8 percent of the veterans would avail themselves of the GI Bill of Rights. Actually, 8.1 percent presented themselves for admission to institutions for further education.

Another general consideration is that behavior is conditioned in many and often subtle ways. In the early psychological and sociological literature concerning attitudes, there was much discussion of "public" versus "private," or "real" opinions and attitudes. In a given context an expressed attitude is just as "real" as any expressed attitude in a different context. The individual's perception of the situation, his previous experiences with similar situations, will determine what attitude he expresses. The "publicness" of an attitude, or its "privateness," is a relative matter. There are, in fact, all degrees of "publicness" and "privateness" possible for the same expressed attitude and the same individual, depending upon the social context—the "public" in whose presence the attitude is expressed as perceived by the respondent.

VALIDITY

With these preliminary considerations in mind, let us now turn to the problem of *validity*. If we are interested only in knowing what the present attitudes of a given group are, we can equate validity with reliability. For example, if a group of students are asked anonymously to give their opinions of their teachers, it can be argued that since we are interested only in knowing these opinions, with no implications for further behavior on the part of the students, the validity of the observation will be as high as the reliability—the two terms in this situation become synonymous.

There are, however, frequently other criteria which can be used as the basis of prediction. The best known illustrations, of course, are the preëlection polls, carried out by such organizations as those of Gallup, Roper, Crosley, the National Opinion Research Center, and many newspapers, the latter especially for state or local elections. Another criterion is the agreement of the answers to questions with known previous social commitments. Clearly, membership in the Temperance League or the Prohibition Party would validate certain kinds of answers to questions about the sale and use of alcoholic beverages; membership in the Seventh Day Adventist sect would validate questions about the desirability of Sunday observance.

A third type of criterion not infrequently used is the judgments of experts as to the best answers on what are, for all practical purposes, opinion statements. Questions designed to get at citizenship attitudes were used in a survey of approximately 10,000 college graduates by *Time* Magazine (*14*). The questions were validated by submitting them to political scientists, psychologists, sociologists, and educators; and those questions which produced the most substantial agreement as to the best answer of three alternatives, "agree, disagree, or doubtful," were used in the survey.

A fourth type of criterion is nonverbal, usually future, behavior. The prediction of the proportion of veterans who would take advantage of the GI Bill of Rights has already been mentioned as one such instance. Market and consumer research are other instances of this type of criterion. The General Motors Corporation, for example, has for a good many years been studying consumer preferences in automobile design and presumably bases its engineering at least in part upon the results of such study. Many newspapers and journals carry on readership studies to determine what kind of content is best liked by what kinds of reading audiences. The movie industry makes consumer surveys to determine in advance the box office appeal of movies, and the Hooper rating of radio is an index, presumably, of the number of radios over the nation tuned in on a given program. Similar ratings for television programs further illustrate the point.

Constant Errors

Under the general heading of validity comes the problem of constant errors. The *sampling bias* of which the 1936 *Literary Digest* preëlection poll is the classic example illustrates this hazard in polling to a very high degree. The failure to predict the outcome of the 1948 presidential election in the United States, on the other hand, appears to have been not so much a case of bias in sampling, but a case of such a close election that prediction beyond the sampling error was not possible.[1]

Interviewer bias is another hazard in polling. It has been shown, for example, that the interviewer's own attitude may color his record and report of the interviews. The story is told of two interviewers of unemployed persons during the economic depression of the 1930's to determine among other things to what the individuals interviewed attributed their lack of employment. One of the interviewers, an ardent prohibitionist, found a majority of his interviewees attributing their unemployment to alcohol. The other interviewer, a Socialist, found a majority of his interviewees attributing their unemployment to the malfunctioning of the capitalistic economic system.

The *group membership* of the interviewer and of the respondent have been shown in a number of studies to affect the results of opinion attitude surveys. Hyman reports (7:365-366) that in two National Opinion Research Center surveys, samples of Christian respondents in New York City were asked whether Jews in America had too much influence in the business world. Both Christian and Jewish interviewers were used. Of those interviewed by Christian interviewers, 50 percent said the Jews had too much influence, but only 22 percent of

---

[1] The factors in the failure of the predictions in the 1948 presidential election were complex, as they must necessarily be in such a situation. For a careful, critical review by a distinguished committee of social scientists, see F. Mosteller and others, *The Pre-Election Polls of 1948*, New York: Social Science Research Council, 1949.

those interviewed by Jewish interviewers said so. In another survey which he reports, respondents were asked whether they agreed with the statement, "Prison is too good for sex criminals; they should be publicly whipped or worse." Among women respondents who were interviewed by men interviewers, 61 percent agreed with this statement, but when women were interviewed by women, only 49 percent agreed (7:356).

In another survey where both white and Negro interviewers were used, the question was asked whether the Army is unfair to Negroes. The Negro interviewers obtained 35 percent "yes" answers to this question, but of those interviewed by whites only 11 percent agreed that the Army was unfair to Negroes. In general, it has been well established that responses vary with the disparity between the interviewers' and respondents' sex, class, color, religion, and other group membership factors. The systematic behavior of these effects is such that they should be attributed, not to the unreliability of the measurement, but to the kind of person interviewed and the way in which he altered his behavior in accordance with the kind of person who did the interviewing (8:248-268; 3: ch. 8).

Question Wording

One of the greatest problems of public opinion research is that of presenting a question to groups of people who may differ widely in cultural background, education, past experience, etc., and presenting that issue in such a way that it is equally clear and meaningful to everyone concerned, so that an answer may be obtained and interpreted validly. The problem of semantics (in the present context, the meaning of questions) therefore is one of the basic problems in opinion polling and attitude measurement.

The problems of semantics and their investigation have received increasing attention by such writers as Korzybski, Ogden, and Richards, and more popularly by Hayakawa and Stuart Chase. The "tyranny of words" has plagued and will continue to plague those concerned with measuring opinions and attitudes through verbal symbols. At best it will be possible to minimize the errors from this source; they cannot be completely eliminated.

Since meanings are built up for the individual through experience, and since no two individuals have the same experiences, it follows necessarily that in strictest logic no verbal symbol, no word, can have exactly the same meaning for any two or more individuals. "Meanings are in persons' minds, not in words," says Thorndike. "At least 99 percent of meanings depend upon the past experience and present attitude or 'set' of the hearer (or reader)" (*17*:613-632).

Research concerning this problem of the wording of attitude questions has been directed toward a quest for objectivity, and this quest is, in the light of the above statements on meanings, ultimately futile, for all words and other symbols that have meanings have some amount, greater or less, of affective tone for the hearer (or reader). Thus the social scientist who makes a fetish of "objectivity," seeking neutral, objective phrasings of an issue, is to a considerable extent pursuing a will-o'-the-wisp. Communication in terms of completely colorless and "objective" words can never be a reality. At most, affective loadings can be experimentally determined and allowed for.

Much of the investigation in the field of question wording has been directed toward eliminating emotionally toned words, stereotypes, and prestige words. Selden Menefee (*11*:614-621) investigated the effect of stereotyped words upon judgments by comparing the approval or disapproval of 742 subjects to proposals under the conditions of (1) grouping under labels, such as communism, radicalism, fascism, pacifism, and the like, and (2) no grouping under any label. He found the proposals grouped under the headings mentioned were favored less than when the same proposals were offered without the label.

Blankenship (*1*:12-18) found "danger words"—those "which arouse the emotions and prejudices of the respondent," and lists a number of these words, such as fascism, capitalism, communism, etc. "A complete list of danger words and their possible effect is a great need of the poll technician," he states. "The important thing is for the investigator to decide exactly what he wants to measure, and if he wants to measure an attitude involving an emotionally colored word, there is certainly no objection to his doing that, as long as it is made clear in the analysis just what was done."

Rugg (15:91-92) experimented with comparable cross sections of the population to show how differences in phrasing of the issues can affect the response. In one of his examples, one of the subsamples was given the question, "Do you think that the United States should allow speeches against a democracy?" A second comparable subsample was given the question, "Do you think that the United States should forbid speeches against a democracy?" In this case, 62 percent replied "no" to the first question, while 46 percent replied "yes" to the second question. The difference, says Rugg, appears to be the use of the term "forbid" in which case the "implied threat to civil liberties was more apparent."

One of the better studies of the meaning of questions is that of Cantril (3). He selected for studies "certain areas where misinterpretation or obscurity of meaning seemed likely, where answers to questions did not seem consistent with observable facts or other opinions." Using information gathered in intensive interviews with forty subjects, Cantril obtained valuable information in these areas. He used questions taken from national surveys by the American Institute of Public Opinion, National Opinion Research Center, and *Fortune* poll. His method was that of asking the questions chosen and then eliciting more specifically the meanings of the questions to the respondent. He found the following difficulties.

1. Questions too vague to permit precise answers.
2. Questions obscure in meaning.
3. Questions getting at some stereotype or overtone implicit in the question, rather than the meanings intended.
4. Questions misunderstood because they involve technical or unfamiliar words.

5. Questions presenting issues not sufficiently circumscribed.
6. Questions whose implications are not seen.
7. Alternatives provided for answers not exhaustive.
8. Alternatives too many or too long.
9. Questions concerned with only a portion of the population and therefore meaningless to many people.
10. Questions getting only surface rationalization.
11. Questions getting only stereotyped answers.

Cantril's results point up these problems, demonstrating a widespread lack of agreement among respondents as to the meaning of questions and alternatives given as answers. The disagreement led to the same response from individuals who actually differed widely in their view, or in some cases, different responses from respondents who essentially agreed upon the issue.

In another study, Blankenship concerned himself with question forms (2:27-30), reporting an experiment in which a question regarding the legalization of horse racing and pari-mutuel betting was stated in five different ways: objective, positive objective, negative objective, positive objective with check list, and subjective. The poll was made in New Jersey, shortly before an election on that issue was to be held. Blankenship therefore had in the election results an outside criterion. He concluded from his study that the "objective" form was the best in this situation. He therefore recommends "considerable wording experimentation" with questions, but fails to give the reader any hint as to how the investigators shall determine whether the objective form will be the best for his particular problem, or how the final wording is to be selected in the absence of election returns or other validating data.

Proposed legal changes included in the question can often evoke different responses on the issue or phrase without pointing out that a law must be changed (3). Opposition is apparently created on the part of many respondents when they find that some legal change must be made.

Under the general heading of the *mechanics of questioning*,

McNemar (10:318) summarizes the factors that may affect the responses to questions even if these are clear and provide a frame of reference: "positive versus negative statement of the questions; attempted balancing of positive statements by end-ing with 'or not'; loading by introducing emotionally charged words or phrases; the presence of contingent or conditional ideas; the influence of juxtaposed questions; suggestive ele-ments; alternate wording; prestige elements; personalization of the question; stereotypes; technical words; biased wording; etc." Obviously, a number of words in this catalogue overlap each other but they do point out the complexity of the seman-tic problem.

McNemar (10:317) gives an amusing example of how words in a question may carry different connotations for individuals of different cultural backgrounds or of lower educational levels. He reports that a surprising number of the members of a minority group, interviewed orally, seemed opposed to governmental control of profits. Further probing brought out the belief that "God alone should exercise control of prophets!"

A recent work by Terris (16:314, 319) casts more light upon this area of vocabulary limitations. The study attempted to gauge the language of the polls to determine the likelihood of its being understood by all levels of the American population. He used the Flesch and Dale-Chall formulas for predicting readability, and applied them to American Institute of Public Opinion, National Opinion Research Center, and *Fortune* polls. The questions, totaling 144, were selected at random from the polls reported in the *Public Opinion Quarterly* from Spring, 1946, to Winter, 1947-1948. Terris found that over 90 percent of the questions on the three polls were too difficult for 12 percent of the population, and that about 70 percent of the questions are beyond the grade-comprehension level of nearly 50 percent of the American population. Such studies clearly indicate the need for close attention to vocabulary diffi-culty and for pretesting of opinion and attitude questions.

McNemar (10) and Cantril (3) have both pointed out the

importance of providing a frame of reference and standards of judgment to the respondent. Cantril finds that people having standards of judgment resulting in stable frames of reference will be inclined to answer a given issue in the same way, regardless of the particular wording used. No absolute frame of reference for all individuals is, of course, possible; but the investigator can make clear through the context of one question in a list of many questions the meaning of the question. Using the interview to provide standards of judgment would not be measuring public opinion, but shaping it. It appears that for determining areas of ignorance, the polls do a good job. For determining what people actually think concerning the various aspects of a given issue, the single-question polls are not as valid as they could be. Considerable doubt exists that the single question, whether of the simple yes-no type or with multiple-choice alternatives, will ever be as valid as other methods.

Krech and Crutchfield (9) state the issue thus: "Perhaps the safest solution to the problem of biased wording of questions is to accord relative rather than absolute significance to the percentages of answers based on these questions." Trends can be indicated, groups can be compared, but percentages should not be quoted (as journalistically they are) with such absolute interpretation. Since bias cannot be completely eliminated, and no question can be found which is neutral, unambiguous, and uniform in meaning for all groups, the use of the single question alone carries with it too great a hazard for the careful, conscientious investigator.

RELIABILITY

Thus far the discussion has been concerned with one of the two general classes of errors—that of constant, or biasing, errors. All such errors can be subsumed under the general heading of validity. The problem of *reliability* has to do with the second general class of errors, i.e., those of the random or variable sort. For an attitude scale, reliability is easily calculated if two forms are available, by correlating form against form, or possibly by the so-called split-half method. While not a few experimental studies have appeared in the literature in which both forms of a Thurstone type of attitude scale were administered, and the reliability of both forms estimated by the Spearman-Brown formula, there is considerable doubt that that formula is valid for such a purpose (5:291-295).

Another possibility with attitude scales is the test-retest in which the same attitude scale is readministered after an interval of time.

But for the single question, these methods, except the test-retest, are obviously not feasible. In the test-retest method the time interval must be long enough to preclude the possibility that respondents give the same answers because they remember their previous one. This, however, runs the hazard of the possibility that real changes have taken place in the attitude during the interval. Stating questions in alternate form is a possibility, but to state questions in alternate forms that are *comparable* is difficult. The reliability of responses to a single question involves categorizing an individual into one of a few categories. Stated differently, the question is would the individual give the same response and therefore be given the same classification if he could be asked the same question under conditions such that he had forgotten his original response, and precluding real changes in the attitude in the interval? The variable response errors to the single question will tend to be canceled in computing the percentage of a group that has expressed itself as holding a given opinion. McNemar points out (10:313) that the effect of such errors can be reduced still further by asking the group several questions on the issue, computing the separate percentages, and then taking their average. This procedure is essentially that of the summated questionnaire, which is discussed in Chapter VI.

Not very much has appeared in the literature by way of investigations of the reliability of the single question. Cantril (3) reports the reliability of this question: "Do you think

Roosevelt is doing a good job, only a fair job, or a bad job running the country?" For a group of 286 persons he reports an interview and reinterview agreement of 79 percent, which for the given situation, approximates a correlation coefficient of 0.90. The same group gave 87 percent consistent answers to a question concerning whom they voted for in the last presidential election, and 86 percent on whether they owned a car or not. If one can obtain such reliabilities for single questions, generally, such measurements would compare rather favorably with the better psychological measuring instruments of all sorts. Unfortunately, this cannot be assumed.

In a study of the correlations obtained by means of a consistency of responses to positively and negatively worded statements, Hayes (6:359-398, 503-552) reports concerning two issues, armaments and war debts, that the degree of consistency as computed by the tetrachoric correlation coefficient varied from 0.60 to 0.70. For government ownership, taxes on risks, tariff, unemployment relief, and veterans' relief the coefficients ranged from 0.40 to the 0.60's. For five other current issues the agreement ranged from the 0.30's down to 0.10. These coefficients, however, may be to a considerable extent as much a measure of the failure to construct comparable questions as they are adequate estimates of the reliability. In other words, biasing factors may have caused serious underestimates.

We should note that while few reliability coefficients for single questions have been published, much research is available in the literature reporting correlates of responses to single opinion and attitude questions (usually, to be sure, in terms of differences of percentages rather than coefficients of correlation) from which at least a kind of "lower bound" of reliabilities may be inferred. Obviously, as a matter of statistical logic, zero reliability for a question would also produce zero correlation with any other variable. The literature is, however, replete with reports of many significant correlations of answers to single questions with variables such as sex, age, socioeconomic status, membership in various groups such as religious,

fraternal, political, and many others; and from any such correlations, the minimum reliability necessary to produce the
observed correlation can be inferred.

ORGANIZING AND EXECUTING A POLL

The planning, organizing, and execution of a poll probably
seems to the casual observer a simple process. Naïvely, all that
appears to be involved is asking people some questions. Actually, however, it is a complex process, as the following "Dimensions of a Poll" by Stuart C. Dodd will show (4).[2]

Dimensions of a Poll

A job analysis, or operational definition, of a poll is often called
for. Practitioners want to train employees for their jobs, social
agencies need to coach all volunteers in a community survey, and
teachers want a complete analysis of polling for their students in
courses on public opinion. The analysis given here will serve as a
rough guide to be modified as needed for the various types of
polling. The model here is for a "quickie" poll taking two weeks
from inception to report, or 1000 man-hours of work. It is a volunteer type, involving no budget, by using University students. It
included 300 interviews, areally sampled, in a section of a city.
(It happened to poll interracial attitudes in a white district newly
confronted by an influx of Negro tenants.) The plan, outlined
below to serve as a check list for a poll director, was made up as
presented here before the poll started and was carried through on
schedule (though the number of man-hours are only approximate).
It is thus a case analysis of an actual poll as well as a generalizable
guide to the steps and materials needed in polling.

The degree of itemization is arbitrary. It is itemized here into
fifty steps under the six standard processes of designing, sampling,
question drafting, interviewing, tabulating, and reporting. Each
step is an action for which someone is responsible. Its man-hours,
degree of skill, and consequent budget can thereby be planned.

The "tensions" or "motivation" column lists the incentives for

[2] Stuart C. Dodd is Director of the Washington Public Opinion Laboratory in
Seattle, and a member of the Department of Sociology, University of Washington. Reproduced by permission of the author.

a volunteer survey. If the personnel are paid, this column would list items of budgeted or expected expense and, alongside, the actual expense account.

For each step, its deadline and location can be fixed, the persons assisting or interacting with the responsible agent for that step can be set, the materials needed and documents to be used or produced can be specified. These are the dimensions of a poll. They define a demoscope. They can be written, as below, in algebraic formulas integrating polling practice with systematic theory in sociology. They can also be written in folk terms as answers to the questions: Who? does what? with what? with whom? when? where? why? and how? in polling. [See "Dimensions of Demoscopes" on the following pages.]

Technical note: The job analysis (following) develops systematic sociological theory[3] in building on:

1. The four basic dimensions of time (T); space (L); people (P) and all residual characteristics (I) in any recorded situation or set of data (S); a poll is thus a particular case of the dimensional formula (without scripts) for any human situation: $S = T$; L; P; I;

2. Compounding various social processes and forces as the accelerating (T^{-2}) of administrative changes in people;

3. Compounding two characteristics—desiderata (V) and intensity of desire (D)—to define tension (E) measuring people's motivation or internal stimulation;

4. Compounding social control as the triple correlation (here expected to exceed 0.9) of three indices (I^3), namely:

   a. The intentions of the controllers (the committee of local civic leaders) to poll their community

   b. The instruments used by the controllers; i.e., the demoscope here dimensionally analyzed

   c. The influence on the controllees (the interviewees) in getting them to assert their opinions.

5. Compounding social organization as the specialized interacting, in a system of social controls, by three parties (P^3), namely:

---

[3] For this dimensional analysis developed in full see: Stuart C. Dodd, *Systematic Social Science,* Seattle: University of Washington Bookstore, 1947.

DIMENSIONS OF DEMOSCOPES

An Operational Definition for Predicting and Controlling the Polling

Names of Dimensions in General[a]	Indices of Actions	Time Deadline Dates	Time Man-Hours	Space	People: Agents	People: Clientele	People: Publics	Tensions	Material	Situations
Symbols	T^I	T_T	T^T	L_1^2	P_A	P_C	P_P	$E = D/V$	I_E	S
Administrative process (in any organizing)	Programming or job steps	Scheduling		Mapping	Staffing	Sampling	Publicizing	Motivating	Equipping	Recording
Question (in folk terms) to be answered	What is done?	When is it done?		Where is it done?	Who is it done by?	Whom is it done to?	Whom is it done for?	Why is it done?	What is it done with?	How is it done?
Summary of this illustrative demoscope	Interracial opinions were polled	Between Nov. 1-10, 1948, in 1000 man-hours of work		In Greenwood (115-125 Sts. & Greenwood-Aurora) Seattle	By university professors and 40 students	Among 400 residents	For the Greenwood and other publics interested	Toward civic unity & scientific research	With equipment listed below	Using techniques as recorded below

[a]See Technical Note.

DIMENSIONS OF DEMOSCOPES *(continued)*

Steps	Deadline Dates	Man-Hours 1000	Place	Persons Responsible	Persons Interacting	Persons Concerned	Reward Basis	Equipment Needed	Documents Produced
I. Designing		35							
1. Defining the poll situation	Oct. 28	8		Director		Local committee	"Selling" the poll to the committee by a talk	Autos, typewriters, mimeograph	Minutes of the committee
2. Defining the objectives	Committee meets Oct. 28	8	In local school	"		"			List of members
3. Formulating hypotheses	Oct. 29	4	"	"		"			
4. Planning all steps below	Committee meets Oct. 29	6	"	"		"	Appeal in classes		
5. Communicating all plans	Oct. 30	4	In Univ. classes	"	Assistants	No publicity	A graduate wanting experience		
6. Revising plans	Oct. 31	5	In office	"	"				

DIMENSIONS OF DEMOSCOPES (*continued*)

Steps	Deadline Dates	Man-Hours 1000	Place	Persons Responsible	Persons Interacting	Persons Concerned	Reward Basis	Equipment Needed	Documents Produced
II. Sampling		18							
7. Designing the sample	Nov. 2	1	In office	Director	"Parent population" fixed			Maps	Memo; map copies traced
8. Getting maps	Oct. 27	3	"	Assistant					
9. Getting lists	Nov. 2	4	"	"					Prelisting memo
10. Drawing the units	Nov. 3	1	"	"	Respondents selected				Memo on folders
11. Assigning to interviewers	Nov. 3	1	"	"					Control sheet
12. Controlling the execution	Nov. 6	2	In the field	"					Work sheets
13. Checking the execution	Nov. 6, 7	4	"	"				Calculating machines	"
14. Computing sampling errors	Nov. 7	2	In office	"					

Steps	Deadline Dates	Man-Hours 1000	Place	Persons Responsible	Persons Interacting	Persons Concerned	Reward Basis	Equipment Needed	Documents Produced
III. Question drafting		95							
15. Collecting used questions	Oct. 27, 31	8	Library	Assistant A			Students wanting experience	Paper	
16. Inventing new questions	Oct. 27, 31	8	At school	Staff					
17. Judging the questions	Nov. 1, 7 P.M.	20	"	"		Local committee		Mimeo.	Typed questionnaires
18. Mimeographing version A	Nov. 2, 8 A.M.	2	Office	Secretary B			Paid for scientific research	Clip-boards	Mimeo. questionnaire A
19. Briefing pretesters	Nov. 2, 1 P.M.	6	In class	Director					
20. Pretesting: 25 interviews	Nov. 2, 2-6 P.M.	20	In town	6 pretesters	25 respondents (not in final sample)		Civic appeal to respondent		Experience noted down
21. Revising questionnaire	Nov. 3-5	6	In office	Director & Staff					
22. Repeat last four steps as often as needed	Repeat Num. 17-21	25	Repeat Num. 17-21	Repeat Num. 17-21	Repeat Num. 20				Mimeo. version B, etc.; instruction; mimeo.

DIMENSIONS OF DEMOSCOPES *(continued)*

Steps	Deadline Dates	Man-Hours 1000	Place	Persons Responsible	Persons Interacting	Persons Concerned	Reward Basis	Equipment Needed	Documents Produced
IV. Interviewing		540							
23. Contacting possible interviewers	Oct. 27, 28	18	In classes	Director			Appeals to civic interest & academic credit		List of volunteers
24. Selecting the interviewers				"					Instruction manual
25. Training them	Nov. 2, 5	50	Class-rooms	"					Control sheet; folders of schedules
26. Assigning their jobs	Nov. 6	6		Assistant					
27. Canvassing	Nov. 6, 7	400	In field	40 interviewers	400 respondents in Greenwood	Civic interest			Time record
28. Reporting to office	At 8, 12, & 6 P.M.	40	In office	"					
29. Supervising	Nov. 6, 7	24	In field	Assistants				Autos	
30. Rewarding the interviewers		2		"					Notes

DIMENSIONS OF DEMOSCOPES (*continued*)

Steps	Deadline Dates	Man-Hours 1000	Place	Persons Responsible	Persons Interacting	Persons Concerned	Reward Basis	Equipment Needed	Documents Produced
V. Tabulating		202							
31. Editing schedules	Nov. 6, 7	3	In office	Assistants					
32. Coding	Nov. 7	15	In office				Paid	IBM cards, punch, verifier	Coding key
33. Punching IBM cards	Later in Nov.	5	"	Clerk			"		Punched cards
34. Laying out tabulations	Nov. 5	5	"	Assistant			"	IBM tabulator	Dummy tables
35. Sorting cards	Later	5	"	Clerk			"		
36. Subsorting cross-tabs	Later	6	"	"			"		
37. Filling out tables	Nov. 7 P.M.	160	"	"				Typewriter	Filled-out tables
38. Typing	Nov. 7 P.M.	4	"	Typist					Typed tables
39. Computing	Nov. 7	4	"	Assistant				Calculator	Work tables
40. Checking	Nov. 7	4	"	"					

DIMENSIONS OF DEMOSCOPES (*continued*)

Steps	Deadline Dates	Man-Hours 1000	Place	Persons Responsible	Persons Interacting	Persons Concerned	Reward Basis	Equipment Needed	Documents Produced
VI. Reporting									
41. Planning the write-up	Nov. 8	50	In office	Director			Research interest		Drafts
42. Drafting it	"	10	"	Assistant					"
43. Graphing	"	4	"	"					"
44. Typing	"	4	"	Typist			Paid	Typewriter	Final draft
45. Editing	"	5	"	Assistant					
46. Submitting report to critics									
47. Printing	Nov. 9	15	At press	Director					Mimeo. report
48. Distributing	Nov. 10	4	In office	Assistant		300 recipients in community		Press	Journal article?
49. Publicizing	Nov. 10	5	"	Assistant Director					
50. Filing all records	Nov. 10	3	"	Clerk				Files	Album of all records above

  a. The agents (P_A), the pollers
  b. The clients (P_C), the interviewees
  c. The public (P_P), the citizenry interested.
6. All compounding up to the dimensional formula for any poll (or demoscope more fully) namely: $S \equiv T^{-2}$; L^2; P^3; I^3 yielding the classificatory quantic numbers of 8; 2; 3; 3.

This job analysis of a poll can serve as a guide to the prospective practitioner of opinion and attitude measurement. It is included here not because its use is restricted to the single question, however. Obviously, it is quite general, and can be applied with the use of the best and most refined measuring instruments possible. For an exhaustive treatment of such and similar problems, see Parten (*13*).

SUMMARY

In this chapter we have examined some of the major problems related to polling, particularly to the single-question type of polling, under the two general subjects of validity and reliability. Factors that have been shown to be significant are the frame of reference of the respondent, the interaction of interviewer and respondent, semantic difficulties including vocabulary difficulty, emotional loading of questions, and the psychological problems inherent in the differences in psychological, social, and cultural background of those concerned in the process of polling and attitude measurement. A job analysis of a poll has also been presented.

Questions

1. In considering current social, economic, scientific, and cultural trends in the American population, would you say that the difficulty of polling and attitude measurement is increasing or decreasing?
2. A two-alternative single question (yes-no) may be thought of as a "scale" with two "units" of measurement. Is such a "scale" unidimensional? Would adding more alternatives such as "strongly agree, mildly agree," etc., change your conclusion? Explain.

3. Do "danger words" change from time to time or from place to place? Give examples.
4. What is meant by the "frame of reference" of respondents? Give examples of how different frames of reference lead to different responses.
5. Is the man-on-the-street pollster concerning a controversial issue justified in presenting background or explanatory information? What hazards or advantages are involved?
6. How would you outline the logic of equating validity with reliability in some attitude surveys?
7. Can you give several different operational definitions for each of a number of specified attitudes such as, let us say, toward labor unions, United Nations, eating olives, double-feature movies, etc.?
8. In the job analysis of a poll, a great deal of detailed work is described. Can you suggest three areas of possible neglect in setting up a poll?
9. In the reports of research, find a few instances of statistically and socially significant correlates of attitudes as measured by single questions, and estimate the minimum reliability required to produce the observed relationship.

Bibliography

1. Blankenship, A., "The Choice of Words in Poll Questions," *Sociol. soc. Res.*, 1940, *25*:12-18.
2. Blankenship, A., "Does the Question Form Influence Public Opinion Poll Results?" *J. appl. Psychol.*, 1940, *24*:27-30.
3. Cantril, H. (ed.), *Gauging Public Opinion*, Princeton, N. J.: Princeton University Press, 1944.
4. Dodd, Stuart C., "Dimensions of a Poll," *Int. J. opin. attit. Res.*, 1949, *3*(no. 3):414-420.
5. Hancock, John, "Reliability of Generalized Attitude Scales as Related to Length of Scale," *Purdue University Studies in Higher Education; Further Studies in Attitudes*, Series II, 1936, no. 31: 291-295.
6. Hayes, S. P., Jr., "The Inter-relations of Political Attitudes: II. Consistency in Voters' Attitudes; III. General Factors in Political Attitudes; IV. Political Attitudes and Party Regularity," *J. soc. Psychol.*, 1939, *10*:359-378, 379-398, 503-552.

7. Hyman, Herbert, "Problems in the Collection of Opinion-Research Data," *Amer. J. Sociol.*, 1950, *55*(no. 4):362-370.
8. Katz, D., "Do Interviewers Bias Poll Results?" *Publ. Opin. Quart.*, 1944, *6*:248-268.
9. Krech, David, and Crutchfield, R. S., *Theory and Problems of Social Psychology*, New York: McGraw-Hill Book Company, Inc., 1948.
10. McNemar, Q., "Opinion-Attitude Methodology," *Psychol. Bull.*, 1946, *43*:289-374.
11. Menefee, S., "Effect of Stereotyped Words on Political Judgment," *Amer. sociol. Rev.*, 1936, *1*:614-621.
12. Mosteller, F., and others, *The Pre-Election Polls of 1948*, New York: Social Science Research Council, 1949.
13. Parten, Mildred B., *Surveys, Polls and Samples*, New York: Harper & Brothers, 1950.
14. *Preliminary Report on the U.S. College Graduate Survey*, New York: *Time*, 1948.
15. Rugg, Donald, "Experiments in Wording Questions," *Publ. Opin. Quart.*, 1941, *5*:91-92.
16. Terris, Fay, "Are Poll Questions Too Difficult?" *Publ. Opin. Quart.*, 1949, *13*:314-319.
17. Thorndike, E. L., "Psychology of Semantics," *Amer. J. Psychol.*, 1946, *59*:613-632.

CHAPTER VI

• • • ● • • •

The Summated Questionnaire

INTRODUCTION

The preceding chapter considered the hazards and short-comings of the single question. In this chapter we shall draw the necessary logical consequences of the previous chapter's discussion, and proceed to consider the problems of combining single (related) questions into meaningful wholes, and the related problems of validity, reliability, and dimensionality.

Further Definition of Attitude

To lay the ground work for the purposes of this chapter, let us first consider certain concepts more or less closely allied to attitudes, some of them essentially synonyms or near-synonyms, since they are frequently used, not only in popular discussion, but in technical literature as well. Such concepts are *interests, motives, instincts, appreciations, tastes, mores, morality, morale, ideals, social distance,* and *character.* Other similar concepts could be listed but these will serve the present purpose, which is to show that each of these concepts from a dynamic, functional point of view is constituted of attitudes.

Interests as observed are presumably the reflection of attractions and aversions in our behavior, of our feelings of pleasantness and unpleasantness, likes and dislikes. In terms of action they are characterized by seeking-acceptance at one end of the scale and by avoidance-rejection at the other (*19*:15).

A distinction may be made between attitudes and interests in that the latter merely indicate the degree to which the individual prefers to hold an object before his consciousness, whether he acts approvingly or disapprovingly toward the object, while attitudes indicate his reaction in terms of its direction, pleasantness or unpleasantness, agreement or disagreement. But since we do not prefer to hold an object before our consciousness unless we agree with it or find it pleasurable, the distinction is a very fine one, and attitudes and interests are for practical purposes identical. If this be granted, why do we use the term attitude instead of interest?

The answer is that theoretical and experimental social psychology has produced a vast literature around this concept and has used the word "attitude" to denote it. In vocational psychology and guidance, however, the term "interest" has been mainly used. Thus Bingham (7:62) defined interest as a "tendency to become absorbed in an experience and to continue it." The similarity of this definition of attitudes is apparent. The use of a separate term for such a tendency serves only to complicate our thinking and to hinder the application of experimental and theoretical work in attitudes to the field of interest. For this reason we shall here use the term attitude as inclusive of such mental functions as vocational psychologists and guidance workers have called "interest."

Motives are related to attitudes in that the latter, with their directionality and feeling-tone, may constitute an important aspect of motives. Thus a highly favorable attitude toward a particular individual may motivate another individual toward emulation of the first individual. Hero worship is an extreme but illustrative form of attitude operating as motive. Here again the two concepts are so closely related that any distinction between them is difficult to make. However, attitude refers more specifically to the goal of a motive, toward the attitude object; while a motive refers to the force, derived in part from the attitude, which is used in overcoming obstacles to the individual's achievement of a satisfactory relationship with the attitude object.

Values may be thought of as the interiorized mores (see below)—the subjective appreciation of what is good, worthwhile, excellent behavior. This holds for the culture or subculture with which the individual identifies himself. Thus the upright citizen has one set of values, the member of a racketeering mob another. The saint differs from the gangster chiefly in his system of values. Both behave in accordance with their value systems.

Appreciations are considered in the plural rather than the singular in order to retain the perspective of the operational point of view, whereby concepts are defined in terms of the operations performed in observing or knowing them. The term "appreciation" is loosely used in at least two widely different senses. "I appreciate your point of view" obviously uses the term with the connotation of understanding or comprehending—a cognitive, intellective meaning. Appreciation of literature, music, graphic, and plastic arts—in short, aesthetic appreciation—on the other hand, connotes emotionalized affective processes. It is in this latter sense that the term concerns us. Its kernel here is the acceptance-rejection notion and this is readily subsumed under the concept of attitude.

Taste as a term is used practically synonymously with *appreciation*, although it, like the term appreciation, carries a cognitive connotation. It implies also the acceptance-rejection, likes and dislikes, meaning, and therefore operationally falls under the heading of attitude.

Mores, morality, and *morale* are three terms conveniently treated together. In their linguistic and their social-psychological meaning they are closely associated. Mores are defined by Sumner (*34*:59) as "the ways of doing things which are current in a society to satisfy human need and desires, together with faiths, notions, codes, and standards of well-living which inhere in those ways, having a genetic connection with them." The mores "are special rituals in which we all participate unconsciously" (34:62); they define "right" and "wrong" for a particular social group. Though usually having a rational origin, many of the mores become obsolescent to changing social conditions, but tend nevertheless to continue as categorical imperatives, and tend as such not to be questioned. They are subjectively highly emotionalized and violations of them are "wrong," "sinful," "obscene," "in bad taste," and in general not tolerated by the group. Their emotional loading brings them readily within the purview of the concept of attitude, at least from the operational, measurement point of view.

The term *morality* in its popular meaning has come in this country to be restricted largely to sex morality but it is properly to be used as referring to all social sanctions implemented by the mores. The moral act, then, is one which is in harmony with the mores, either in doing what they demand or in refraining from doing what is contrary to them. The moral person is one who observes the mores. The connection of morality from the point of view of social psychology with the notion of attitude was indicated at the beginning of this discussion.

Morale refers to the *esprit de corps*, the emotional integration of a group. Its essence psychologically is the integrative pattern of attitudes which exist with reference to attitude objects judged to be of vital concern to the group, these being frequently of a threatening nature; or these attitude objects imply goals, the achievement of which is endangered by the absence of morale. Thus we have the morale of an army, or of the civilian population in war, the morale of the classroom, of an industrial organization, of a teaching staff, and so on.

Ideals are the conscious aspects of the mores (8:472-473). Conscious striving toward "ways of doing things" most acceptably is the essence of ideals. They are the individual's conscious adjustment to the demands of society, the public as conceived and understood by him. The public may be a phantom public and need have no counterpart in reality. Consider for example the attempted control of a small boy's behavior by means of Santa Claus or the "bogeyman."

Social distance, a sociological concept, refers to the differences between the mores or the ideals of individuals in groups and implies tensions or crises inherent in different sets of mores and ideals. Social distance exists between management and labor, rich and poor, the younger generation and the older, one nationality or racial group and another. Strikes, lynchings, race riots, and even wars are the reflections in large part of the social distance between groups of human beings. In so far as such distance persists we shall have failed to achieve the "brotherhood of man." The reduction of social distance between groups and the evaluation of the individual on his own merits are major parts of the democratic ideal, and in studying and working with social distances we are again concerned in the main with attitudes.

Character has ethical connotations sufficiently unambiguous to require little analysis here. The person of character is the moral person as defined in terms of attitudes. He behaves in accordance with individual ideals that are socially approved.

This brief and sketchy exploration of the meanings of related terms is perhaps sufficient to show the central nature of the concept of attitudes. Further elaboration of the concept in all its varied aspects is contained in Dewey's classic *Human Nature and Conduct* (*11*) and in the writings of the Allports (*1, 2*), who attempt to relate the concept to the structure and functions of the nervous system as "neuromuscular sets."

THE ORGANIZATION OF ATTITUDES

In the field of attitudes, as in the field of mental ability, questions concerning organization are concerned mainly with the degree of specificity or generality, or of the size of the organizational units to be observed in an individual's personality or behavior, that is, whether attitudes are organized into large structures or small ones, into "cobblestones" or "grains of sand." For example, are we justified in calling a person

"liberal" or "conservative" and from this general label infer-
ing his attitude toward a large number of more specific atti-
ude objects, such as races, nationalities, internationalism,
abor, income taxes, and so on? Similarly, are we justified in
abeling a person "honest" or "dishonest" and thereby inferring whether he will exhibit honest or dishonest behavior in
a wide variety of situations, such as taking an examination,
returning excess change to a grocer, voluntarily confessing a
rule violation in athletic competition, and so on?

These questions concerning the generality or specificity of
attitudinal organization have not been answered in the same
way by various researches and experiments which have been
concerned with them. Some researches have drawn conclusions
in favor of specificity and some in favor of generality. Perhaps
the most influential of the researches supporting the doctrine
of specificity have been the studies of Hartshorne and May (21).

Concerning the traits and attitudes of honesty, service, and
self-control, their conclusions, broadly stated, are that we are
unjustified in considering these traits and their related attitudes as general characteristics of children, but rather that
they are a function of the specific situation in which the child
is placed, and that an individual behaves similarly in different
situations only in so far as these situations are alike. For example, although it is possible to state that the child who
cheated in one classroom situation would cheat in another,
the same child might be scrupulously honest in athletics, party
games, etc. Stealing money these writers find unrelated to stealing answers on examinations. Consequently, the traits and
attitudes centering around the concept of honesty were considered to be highly specific.

Other studies, however, have shown very different conclusions concerning the organization and interrelationships of
attitudes. Cantril (10) examined the responses of a sample of
college students to a series of terms, statements, personality
sketches, and the Allport-Vernon *Study of Personal Values*.
He found evidence for generality of some sort in mental life

which is independent of specific content. Similarly, Herrick (24) employed a group of mental tests, rating devices, autobiographical sketches and interviews, and also drew conclusions in favor of the existence of general attitudes of a college student group concerning certain social issues and matters of conduct.

Further evidence in favor of some generalization of attitudes within individuals is found in the significantly greater than zero correlations which have been found between various attitudes such as those toward pacifism, communism, and the church. Radicalism-conservatism has been found to be a general attitude enabling prediction of more specific attitudes toward races, national ideals, imperialism, militarism, international good will, birth control, religion, etc. Even in the field of character traits and attitudes, Herrick, in the study cited above, was able by the method of factorial analysis to show that the data of Hartshorne and May contained certain "group factors" or clusters of character traits and attitudes, a finding in sharp disagreement with the extreme specificity inferred by those authors.

In a series of "Studies of Social Intolerance," Gough (20) comes to such conclusions as the following.

. . . It appears that the more anti-Semitic students are on the average less liberal in social outlook, less tolerant of other races and groups, less internationally minded, more nationalistic, more cynical concerning the ideals of democracy, less impressed by the record of achievement in securing human rights and privileges in this country, less tolerant and trusting of others in a general way, less magnanimous, less respectful of others' integrity, less able to overlook and ignore minor irritations and frustrations, less concerned with resolving and rectifying problems once they do arise in interpersonal interaction and are less sociable. In respect to socioeconomic status, the more prejudiced students come from poorer homes, and tend to exhibit characteristic fears, insecurities, and doubts which are often associated with such backgrounds. The prejudiced subjects are clearly less intelligent, and, as would now be expected on the basis of previous data, show the attitudes and beliefs which the California group designated as "antidemocratic."

In another paragraph he summarizes as follows.

If a brief review is attempted of the factors which seemed to characterize the more anti-Semitic subjects in the several samples, it seems that the following impressions emerged: (1) lower intellectual level; (2) disadvantaged economic background; (3) less sociability, and participation in school activities; (4) inferior academic performance; (5) greater uneasiness and discomfort in social situations; (6) greater tendency to complain of personal dissatisfactions, problems, and annoyances; (7) narrowness of outlook in regard to national and international affairs; (8) debunking attitude toward questions of political-social ideals and goals; (9) antagonism toward many out-groups, not just some particular out-groups; (10) emphasis on nationalism, chauvinism, and conservatism; (11) feelings of victimization and exploitation.

All of these factors are similar to those observed in other studies and seem to justify the conclusion that there is a discoverable and identifiable network of attitudes and beliefs, into which the specified ethnic opinions are characteristically integrated.

The differences in the conclusions concerning generality and specificity may at least in part be due to the differences in the ages of the group studied since generality of mental organization may become greater as age increases. The integration and self-consistency of attitudes would thus be a function of the amount of time during which an individual has been under the influence of the socially organized sets of attitude patterns by which his own consistency was judged. The studies of Hartshorne and May were concerned with elementary school children, and those of Gough with high school seniors. It may well be that high school pupils will be less consistent than college students, but more consistent, integrated, and predictable from situation to situation, from one attitude to another, than elementary school pupils.

Another factor determining the degree of generality found is the narrowness or breadth of the attitude considered. The more narrowly we define an attitude, the more closely it is related to other similarly narrowly defined attitudes and the higher the degree of generality which we will infer. For example, if we consider attitudes toward the prohibition of wines and beer as one attitude, and attitudes toward prohibition of whiskey and brandy as another distinct attitude, we shall find these two attitudes highly correlated, and conclude that we have evidence for a general attitude toward the prohibition of alcoholic beverages. But this illustrates merely the procedure used in constructing instruments to measure attitudes whereby a group of closely knit, internally consistent statements of attitudes are assembled so as to provide a statistically reliable test. If this is the case, what should be our criterion or basis for distinguishing between single, unitary attitude entities and attitudes which should be considered not as units or entities in themselves but merely as components or elements of attitudes? Where should we stop in our breakdown of attitudes? There is, of course, no absolute rule in this matter. Attitudes, or the attitude object of reference by which they are more conveniently denoted, should be defined or considered as entities separate from other attitude objects in terms of the practical reasons for our concern with attitudes. Another quotation is in point here (*31*:1029).

The needed caution is simply that *no* attitudes as measured are genuine entities in the sense that there is anything "absolute" about them. For practical purposes any set of verbal responses which is statistically reliable is considered an entity and given an appropriate name. Any measured attitude, no matter how reliable, might conceivably be broken down into two or more different attitudes with slightly different labels. A single label implies nothing concerning singleness of attitudes. Indeed, the concept of singleness has meaning only in regard to the object of reference. If the attitude measured has reference to a custom, person, or institution commonly accepted as an isolable phenomenon and is reliably measured, it may be regarded as an entity.

In summary then, the generality or specificity of attitudes

may be considered to be a function of (1) the degree to which attitude objects or attitudes themselves are organized into sets of related clusters by the society in which an individual lives; (2) the degree to which an individual has absorbed the structure or organization of the society in which he lives, which in turn is the function of his age, maturity, and sensitivity to social forces; and (3) the narrowness with which an attitude is defined, broader, more inclusive attitudes being more likely to be independent, self-contained, and "specific" than attitudes more narrowly conceived.

THE DETERMINERS OF ATTITUDES

Why does a given individual have a certain attitude? Where shall we look for the causes or origins of a person's attitude? How do people become different in attitudes, that is, why are some liberal and some conservative, religious or atheistic, favorable or unfavorable toward a given teacher, a given subject, vocation, or any other attitude object? One answer to these questions has been provided by G. W. Allport (2:810-811). He points out four ways in which attitudes are developed. They may be labeled (1) integration, (2) differentiation, (3) shock, and (4) adoption. Integration is the development of an attitude through accumulation of a large number of experiences over a long period of time all of which influence the individual in a given direction. Thus, long continued failure in solving arithmetic problems will be integrated by a pupil into an unfavorable attitude toward arithmetic. Development of an attitude by differentiation may be described as a splitting off of a specific attitude from a more general one, as when an individual has an unfavorable attitude toward arithmetic as a result of his unfavorable attitude toward *all* school subjects. Attitude development by shock is due to an unusual, violent, or painful experience. A child's attitude toward dentists may thus be quickly and forcefully molded by the experience of having a tooth pulled. Finally, an attitude may be developed by adoption, in that the individual merely follows the example of friends, teachers, parents, newspapers, and other opinion-molding agencies. The son who is a Republican merely because his father is a Republican illustrates this way of developing an attitude.

Another point of view in regard to the determiners of attitudes is exihibited in the classification of related variables by Newcomb (*31*:912-1046). He deals with the relationship between attitude and (1) individual characteristics, (2) experimental variables, (3) life experience, and (4) other attitudes.

Under *individual characteristics* are included sex, age, intelligence, and such nonintellectual characteristics as muscle coördination, suggestibility, persistence, susceptibility to majority influence, ability to break long-established habits, speed of reaction time, tendency to sacrifice accuracy to speed, ability to think in unusual terms, neurotic tendency, ascendance–submission, and other personality variables.

Under *experimental modification,* Newcomb deals with investigations in which attitudes have been measured before and after the introduction of some experience to modify them. These experiences may in turn be classified as those occurring within the classroom and those occurring as extraschool experiences. The school experiences are chiefly those due to particular curricular material, especially in the social sciences, and those due to specific teachers, usually either liberal or conservative with respect to broader issues. The extraschool experiences include motion pictures, radio programs, concerts, speeches, and other forms of propaganda.

Under the heading of *life experiences* as determiners of attitudes, Newcomb includes the more "normal," everyday kind of experiences. Typical of these are such factors as educational level reached or amount of education received, college military training in the ROTC, the experience of college fraternity life, familiarity in contacts with races and nationalities, continued experiences of association with a particular family, allegiance to particular religious groups, racial or national background, socioeconomic status, residence in rural or urban environment or in different national or cultural areas. Newcomb summarizes the influences of these "natural" experiences as follows.

(*a*) Few generalizations are justifiable concerning experiences which are more or less individual rather than being associated with a particular group or a particular locality. (*b*) Experiences which are regularly associated with family, race, or church groups enable better prediction of attitude. (*c*) Experiences shared by large communities geographically defined enable practically no prediction of attitude, except for urban-rural differences in racial prejudice and superstitious beliefs for sectional differences within this country in regard to Negroes and Orientals.

Under the heading of *interrelationships of attitudes,* Newcomb deals with the question of generality and specificity which has already been discussed in this chapter. We may conclude our discussion of determiners of attitudes with a reference to the two most broadly conceived classifications of such determiners: personality differences on the one hand, and conformity-enforcing agencies or social institutions on the other. The first of these will tend to produce variability within groups and the second produces differences between groups. In considering attitudes for purposes of education, training, or personal analysis, one should look to these two kinds of factors for an explanation of the attitude.

THE RATIONALE OF CONSTRUCTING SUMMATED ATTITUDE QUESTIONNAIRES

The practical reasons for concern with attitudes that we indicated as a criterion for deciding which attitudes or their objects of reference should be treated as separate entities, has led to the production of a very large number and variety of measuring devices. For purposes of discussion, we shall group them under five rather general headings: (1) personality inventories, (2) interest inventories, (3) problem inventories, (4) occupational attitudes, and (5) social attitudes. Even on their face there is some overlapping in these categories, and future research will no doubt clarify the kind and amount of over-lapping as well as sharpen the distinction among them. (These different kinds of summated questionnaires will be discussed in the next section.)

The investigator begins with reasonable hypotheses as to the kinds of questions that will elicit responses which, when combined into a single score or a group of subscores, will tend to be a measure of the "entity" or "entities" that he has in mind—neurotic personality, vocational interest, occupational attitudes, social attitudes defined with respect to social issues, groups, actions, or whatever. Guidelines for selecting and formulating the items will be psychological theory, clinical reports, survey of the relevant literature as it relates to the purpose in question, and the insights and judgments of specialists in the area under consideration. Frequently when a suitable pool of items has in the judgment of the investigator been assembled, they will be submitted to a jury of specialists for criticism as to content, wording, and a decision on the best answers for the items.

At this point, the investigator may decide to retain only those items upon which a predetermined majority of his "expert" jury agree, or he may retain all the items for tryout with a defined population sample with a view to statistical validation of the items in terms of (1) an external criterion, or (2) an internal criterion (usually the total score on the questionnaire or such parts as are to receive part scores), or (3) both of these procedures. Those items which survive this analysis as being valid are then retained for the final form or forms of the instrument. The instrument is then, or should be, administered to another suitable population sample for determining the usual statistics relevant to questions of reliability and validity of the instrument as a whole.

It will be noted that the general procedure is in no way different in principle from the construction of a standardized so-called achievement test in academic subjects. Further refinements are, of course, possible beyond those already described.

Theoretically, at least, it is possible and desirable to compute the intercorrelations of the items in the instrument, to factor-analyze the resulting matrix of zero-order correlations, and to determine the minimum number of "dimensions" or factors that need to be postulated as being measured by the items in the instrument.

By way of a concrete illustration we shall review the construction of a widely used instrument, the *SRA Youth Inventory*, designed to obtain a measure of the problems of teen-agers as they see them (*32*).

The *SRA* Youth Inventory is a check list of 298 questions that has been designed as a tool to help teachers, counselors, and school administrators to identify quickly the problems that young people say worry them most.

The Inventory was constructed under the auspices of the Purdue Opinion Panel, with the coöperation of more than a hundred high schools and over 15,000 teen-agers throughout the country. The questions were developed by asking hundreds of students to state anonymously in their own words what things bothered them most. These hundreds of essays were carefully analyzed and checked against the results of previous youth surveys. In addition, the literature on adolescent psychology was reviewed as a basis for additional items.

All these ideas were sifted and the items were prepared, using the terminology of the young people themselves to cover as wide a range of problems as possible. These items were then administered via the mechanism of the Purdue Opinion Panel to thousands of high school students in every section of the country. The statistical data upon which the Inventory is based were obtained from a stratified sample of this group. Table 3 gives the composition of this sample. The results of this study constitute the first systematic country-wide analysis of what young people consider to be their most important problems.

Because the influence of anonymity of response was not known, a "split sample" technique was used to determine its influence. Half the schools participating in the Panel received instructions to have their pupils sign their names, while the other half responded in the usual anonymous fashion. While a good many items showed statistically reliable differences, the actual magnitude of these differences was so slight as to make

TABLE 3. Composition of Stratified Sample of High School Students
Used in Making Analysis
(All Ballots Were Signed)

Classifications	Number of Cases[a]	Percent in Sample	Percent in Population (Approx.)
Total sample	2500	100	100
Boys	1194	48	50
Girls	1306	52	50
9th grade	818	33	32
10th grade	680	27	28
11th grade	528	21	21
12th grade	474	19	19
East	519	21	28
Midwest	1535	62	32
South	239	10	28
Mt. Pacific	162	7	12
Rural (less than 2500 pop.)	1209	48	42
Urban (more than 2500 pop.)	1291	52	58
Protestant	1655	66	70
Catholic	544	22	20
Jewish	150	6	6
Other or none	150	6	4
Low economic group	1809	74	No data
High economic group	646	26	available

a Classification data were missing on some cards, hence in some groupings there are slightly fewer than 2500 cases.

them practically negligible. No difference in excess of 6 percent was found for any of the items.

Before the items were administered, they were categorized by two trained psychologists, working independently, into eight categories which were named as follows: (1) My School, (2) After High School, (3) About Myself, (4) Getting Along with Others, (5) My Home and Family, (6) Boy Meets Girl, (7) Health, and (8) Things in General.

Also, before the items were administered, it was decided to test the hypothesis that certain of the items might be separately scored to constitute a "basic difficulty" index or a "personality" inventory. To this end, seven trained psychologists were asked to judge which items if checked as problems would indicate such basic difficulties. They agreed substantially on 102 of the original 298 items.

The Inventory thus yields ten different scores: a total problems score, a score for each of the eight areas, and a "basic difficulty" score.

To ascertain whether or not items had been properly assigned to their respective categories, a biserial coefficient of correlation was computed between each item and the total score in each of the eight areas, using a sample of a thousand ballot cards drawn from the national sample. Thus a total of 2400 biserial r's were computed.

In computing the biserial r's, each item was correlated with the total score of the area in which it was itself included. To ascertain by how much the coefficients of correlation were increased by this overlap of the item with its part score, a series of empirical checks were made which in effect partialed out the spurious correlation. In general, the corrections ranged from a low of 0.03 to a high of 0.10 in the items where the correlation was recomputed.

Since the upper limit of 0.10 appeared to be a generous index of the maximum amount of spurious correlation, each item was examined for reallocation after this correlation had been subtracted. On the basis of all the item analysis data, twenty-seven items were reassigned from their original categories to new categories in which they had higher validity. An inspection of the validity coefficients in each area after "purification" indicates that there is sound reason to believe on grounds of both face validity and the statistical criterion that the eight categories are now fairly homogeneous, and that a total score derived by summing the items checked in each area has psychological meaning.

Reliabilities for each of the eight problem areas were computed for the sample of 1000 used in the item analysis by means of the Kuder-Richardson Case II formula (28). Table 4 below gives these reliabilities.

The reliability of the basic difficulty scale was computed for the total norm sample with the Kuder-Richardson Case III formula (28).

TABLE 4.   Reliability Coefficients for Eight Problem Areas

Area	Reliability
1. My School	0.84
2. After High School	0.90
3. About Myself	0.88
4. Getting Along with Others	0.88
5. My Home and Family	0.94
6. Boy Meets Girl	0.87
7. Health	0.75
8. Things in General	0.89

These reliabilities indicate clearly that scores on these categories constitute psychological "entities" in the sense discussed earlier in this chapter.

What of the validity of this instrument? When the term validity is used in connection with an aptitude or achievement test, it usually refers to the accuracy with which the test measures what it is supposed to measure. Validity is preferably determined against an outside criterion, such as grades in school or how long it takes to learn a task of some sort.

The *SRA Youth Inventory* is supposed to provide an indication of what a student *thinks* are his problems. For this there is no obvious or readily available outside criterion. The items which an individual checks have validity for that individual. As long as a student thinks that certain things bother him, it makes little difference whether the problems are real or whether he is unconsciously exaggerating their importance. The measure of validity becomes in a sense the reliability coefficient.[1]

A measure of the validity of the individual item may be obtained from a summary of the results of item analysis. In computing the biserial coefficients of correlation, it will be recalled, each item was correlated with the total score of the category to which it had been assigned. A total score, when used in this way, is often known as a *criterion of internal consistency*.

TABLE 5. Median Biserial Correlation Coefficients Between Each Item and Area Total Score
($N = 1000$)

Area	1	2	3	4	5	6	7	8
No. of items	33	37	44	40	53	32	25	34
Median r	0.54	0.57	0.50	0.53	0.70	0.58	0.51	0.58

As a test of the relative psychological independence of these eight areas of problems, the scores for a random 1000 individuals on each of the parts or areas were intercorrelated, yielding the results shown in Table 6.

TABLE 6. Intercorrelations of Total Scores on Eight Problem Areas
($N = 1000$)

Area	1	2	3	4	5	6	7	8
1. My School	(0.84)	0.40	0.55	0.45	0.42	0.35	0.34	0.20
2. After High School		(0.90)	0.46	0.58	0.33	0.46	0.36	0.39
3. About Myself			(0.88)	0.67	0.50	0.45	0.47	0.35
4. Getting Along with Others				(0.88)	0.46	0.59	0.51	0.48
5. My Home and Family					(0.94)	0.46	0.47	0.32
6. Boy Meets Girl						(0.87)	0.50	0.48
7. Health							(0.75)	0.46
8. Things in General								(0.89)

These intercorrelations of the total scores for the eight problem categories clearly indicate the relative psychological inde-

---

[1] In statistical logic the validity of the instrument could on this argument be as high as the square root of the coefficient of reliability. In general, however, a test cannot be more valid than it is reliable.

pendence of the areas. The highest correlation (0.67) is that between scores on "About Myself" and "Getting Along with Others." The lowest (0.20) is between "My School" and "Things in General." Only six of the twenty-eight intercorrelations exceed 0.50. In other words, the amount of variance which any two tests have in common is in most cases less than 25 percent. This is not an unreasonable amount of overlap, for we should hardly expect an individual with problems in one area not to have related problems in other areas as well.

The problem of the validity of the basic difficulty score can be further studied in terms of the "extreme group" technique, i.e., of having trained clinical psychologists or counselors designate the maladjusted pupils and the well-adjusted pupils in a school population on the basis of clinical diagnosis and independent of scores on the Youth Inventory. These clinical judgments can then be used as an outside criterion for the Inventory would, on the basis of this criterion, have validity if it, too, separated these two groups on the basis of the basic difficulty score. Other criteria that might be used are dropping out of school for assigned reasons, a study of school disciplinary cases, and, of course, a longitudinal follow-up study of groups with extreme scores in terms of their subsequent school and life histories.

It should also be mentioned that to ensure validity in terms of the pupils' understanding of the questions, a study of the vocabulary difficulty and of the readability of the content was made (*17, 18, 35*).

This somewhat lengthy detour by way of describing the highlights of the construction of a summated questionnaire will perhaps make clear the general procedure widely applicable to the construction of such instruments. It should be said in passing that this inventory could hardly have been constructed were it not for the fact that modern punched-card machinery was used throughout. The pupils recorded their answers on IBM Mark-Sensing cards, and these responses were then translated into punched holes by means of a machine for this purpose. Sorting and tabulating by means of other IBM machines were then done to obtain all of the statistics, including a set of sixteen different norms, one set for each sex and grade, and for urban and rural groups separately. (See *Examiner Manual* for the *SRA Youth Inventory*.)

KINDS OF SUMMATED QUESTIONNAIRES

Let us now rather briefly examine a variety of kinds of summated questionnaires that have been devised to serve many different kinds of practical purposes.

Personality Inventories

The instruments that have been devised and published under this or similar titles have as a primary aim the measurement of personal social-emotional adjustments. Most of these "personality tests" consist of undisguised attempts to ask the individual a list of highly personal questions concerning his inner life, peculiarities, mistakes, and faults. There are, therefore, a number of difficulties and hazards inherent in this type of measuring device.

The first of these difficulties is that of obtaining frank responses. Adjustment is an *emotional* matter, something at which people cannot look in the light of pure reason alone. In contemplating their own adjustment they are more likely to become biased, prejudiced, secretive, and deceitful of others and of self, than when contemplating their achievement in geometry, their physical health, or even their mental ability. Adjustment is also a *social* matter that deals with relationships to other people, so there is a stronger desire for social acceptability in terms of adjustment than with other individual attributes. For these reasons it is more difficult to elicit truthful responses.

The individual is likely to conceal responses to questions concerning modes of behavior whose social acceptability or unacceptability is obvious or suspected, and this is where the majority of these instruments are weakest.

A second difficulty inheres in the fact that valid answers to many such questions are not given not only because individuals are dishonest, but also because they simply do not know the truth about themselves concerning many questions of emotional and social adjustment. For example, individuals may be unaware that a "yes" answer to the question "Do you daydream frequently?" would be true for them. They may often daydream without being aware of it. Similarly, they may differ widely in their interpretation of "frequently," some interpreting it as once a week, others as once a day.

Similar lack of insight or understanding may invalidate responses to such questions as "Do you frequently have spells of the blues?" or "Does your ambition need occasional stimulation through contact with successful people?" The objection to such questions on these grounds may be answered by saying that it is not the truth of his answer that determines whether an individual is adjusted but rather the way he feels about the subject. This defense is at least partially rebutted by the fact that answers to such questions are usually interpreted in one way, regardless of the significance of the question to the individual or of his unique understanding or lack of understanding of it.

A third set of difficulties in evaluating adjustment centers around the problem of the organization of personality and its analysis into the attitudinal traits or dimensions by which it may be described and understood. Allport and Odbert (3) give a list of 17,953 "trait" names for describing behavioral characteristics. Constructing a test and giving it a name like "neuroticism" or "introversion" is of course not sufficient to set up that trait as a genuine dimension of personality. To be so considered it must satisfy certain logical statistical requirements, such as relative independence of other traits.

Further, the trait must be consistent within itself so that various measures of it (items on the personality questionnaire, for example) correlate much more highly with one another than they do with measures of other supposed traits, and, finally, the instrument must yield a reliable measure of the trait.

In another sense, however, the need for unique traits is perhaps not so great in the field of adjustment evaluation if the devices used are considered not as precise "measuring instruments" but rather as rough aids to understanding the individual. When used in this way, and in the hands of a clinical psychologist or psychiatrist, such devices may assist in indicating some individuals whose maladjustment is sufficiently serious to warrant investigation by more refined techniques. At any rate, the desirability of some categorization of the areas in which adjustment can occur has been increasingly recognized by personality test builders.

Thus the technique of factor analysis has been applied to personality traits and adjustment evaluation devices. Flanagan (16) applied it to the *Bernreuter Personality Inventory*. From this analysis of the correlations among the responses to 125 questions, two independent and internally consistent traits emerged—self-confidence and sociability.

At the stage of the analysis where the clusters of questions, tests, or measurement instruments must be interpreted in psychologically significant fashion, the process becomes subjective, as does any process of "armchair psychologizing." Here the results of factor analysis must interact with theories of personality structure, of the nature of society, and of the human organism. The value of the results of the factor-analytical method of determining traits also depends upon the validity of the measures of psychological behavior which compose the original battery of tests analyzed. Inasmuch as the original measures which entered into the factor analysis of Flanagan were made up of highly personal, undisguised, direct questions, the test retains the disadvantages of this approach; the questions are merely scorable in such a way as to yield relatively independent, uncorrelated subscores whose validity remains to be determined.

A fourth difficulty with most adjustment evaluation techniques of this sort is that they provide for the interpretation of a given response or bit of evidence in the same way for all personalities. In doing so they disregard the principle that a given fact about a person reveals his adjustment primarily by reason of the way he feels about that fact. Adjustment depends on the satisfaction of motives or the satisfactory solution of problems or overcoming of obstacles. Hence, the objectively like response for two individuals may mean maladjustment for the one and good adjustment for the other.

Thus an answer to an item on an adjustment questionnaire should not be, although it usually is, scored in the same way for all individuals. For example, the individual's response to the question "Do you make new friends easily?" is frequently interpreted with respect to his social adjustment without regard for his feeling about the desirability of making new friends easily, his satisfaction or dissatisfaction with his ability in this respect, his attitude toward others' opinion of his ability, or the relationship of this attitude to other attitudes. The full meaning of the individual's response to such a question depends upon all such associated attitudes, interpretations, and individualized meanings.

Similar difficulties arise in interpreting the answers to most of the other questions on "personality tests." How does the individual feel about his response? Does he consider it desirable or undesirable? Does it lower or raise his self-respect? Does he consider his response that of the average person, of the people he admires, of the ideal person? Is it reasonable to assume with respect to a given individual that he wants to be like the average person in a particular trait or like persons he admires or like his concept of the ideal person? The significance for adjustment or maladjustment of any given bit of evidence, of any behavior item, or of the answer to any specific question depends upon all such associated considerations.

The *Personal Data Sheet,* an instrument devised by Woodworth during World War I (*37*), is the intellectual forebear of a very large proportion of the personality inventories that have been developed since. It consists of 116 yes-no questions such as "Do you usually feel strong and well?" "Do you feel tired most of the time?" "Does it make you uneasy to go into a tunnel or subway?" "Do your interests change quickly?" "Has any of your family committed suicide?" The score is the total number of neurotic answers, with expert opinion as the criterion of such answers.

Another widely used inventory is the *Bernreuter Personality* Inventory (6). This instrument was designed to measure (1) neurotic tendencies, (2) self-sufficiency, (3) introversion-extroversion, and (4) dominance-submission. It consists of 125 questions taken in large part from other already existing inventories by Woodworth, Thurstone, Laird, Allport, and others. The constant alternatives for the items are "yes, no, and ?." The reliabilities for the four scales as determined for 128 college students are reported as ranging from 0.85 to 0.88.

One final and more recent example of personality inventory that we shall briefly mention is the *Minnesota Multiphasic Personality Inventory* (23). This instrument is available and can be administered in either an individual or a group form, and consists of 566 items. At this writing the comparability of the individual and the group forms is not too well established. There is already an extensive published research literature concerning this instrument, but limitations of space prohibit examining or citing this literature in detail here. Suffice it to say that greater clinical and statistical sophistication has probably gone into the construction and the research than is true of most other instruments of this kind.

Ellis (12) has exhaustively and critically reviewed the technical literature with reference to the validity of personality summated questionnaires. The reader interested in this problem is referred to his review of 360 studies and to a somewhat more recent review by Ellis and Conrad (13). Table 7 is based upon data presented by Ellis (12).

TABLE 7. Data on Validity of Personality Inventories
(Derived from Ellis (12))

r	Behavior Problems Diagnosis	Diagnosis of Delinquency	Psychiatric or Psychological Diagnosis	Rating Diagnosis	Test Intercorrelations	Over-rating[a]	Indiv. Administration[b]	Totals
0.70 to 1.00	2	15	36	12	9	6	10	90
0.40 to 0.69	1	6	9	10	18	.	3	47
0 to 0.39	6	13	30	22	28	36	2	137
Totals	9	34	75	44	55	42	15	274

[a] This column is not based on correlations but on results of self-ratings against inventory results. Since Ellis defines validity as "negative," "mainly negative," etc., and applies these descriptions to these studies, they are tabulated here *as if* they were correlational.

[b] It is obvious that "overrating" and "individual administration" are not validity criteria in the same sense as are the other column headings.

186

From this summary it is clear that such instruments are to be used with caution and require for their use and interpretation adequately trained personnel.

A quotation from Ellis and Conrad (*13*:419) is in point by way of a general evaluation: "Military applications of personality inventories have yielded enough favorable results to command attention. In contrast, personality inventories in civilian practice have generally proved disappointing." And again (*13*:421): "In conclusion it appears, while the experimental or statistical shortcomings of many of the military studies justify a cautious attitude toward the results obtained, the fact cannot be ignored that the inventories usually did make some definite contribution to psychiatric screening. The success of the inventories in the military situation encourages the hope that similar inventories may prove equally useful in civilian practice."

Interest Inventories

The reader will recall that earlier in this chapter we equated the concept of *interest* with the more general concept of *attitude*. Those interested in the applications of psychology to human affairs have devised a variety of summated questionnaires designed to measure interests in more or less well-defined areas such as vocations, school subjects, play, reading, mechanical activities, social activities, and the like. Fryer (*19*) describes the following attempts to evaluate interest by means of information tests.

1. *Agricultural Engineering Test* (Burtt)
2. *Children's Play Interests* (Terman)
3. *Children's Reading* (Wissler)
4. *College Women's Occupational Interests* (McHale)
5. *Girl's General Trade Interests* (Toops)
6. *Men's General Trade Interests* (O'Rourke and Toops)
7. *Men's Mechanical Interest* (O'Rourke)
8. *Social Interests* (Ream)

But in surveying the correlations of these tests of interests with other estimates of interests and with measures of ability and achievement, he concludes (*19*:290):

There is no valid evidence that something different to ability is measured by information tests. What is thought to be an evidence of interest in these measures of information may be but a measure of the extent to which these tests are measures of the same abilities. The safest conclusion, as already stated, is that information tests measure information. But the theory persists that in achievement, as evidenced in the acquisition of information, there is present an effect of interest as well as of abilities.

Some more recent measuring devices in this general area are as follows.

1. Van Allyn, K., *Basic Interest Questionnaire: For Selecting Your Vocation or Avocation,* 1938-1939.
2. Brainard, Paul P., and Brainard, Ralph T., *Brainard Occupational Preference Inventory,* 1945.
3. Cleeton, Glen U., *Cleeton Vocational Interest Inventory,* rev. ed., 1937-1943.
4. Gregory, W. S., *Gregory Academic Interest Inventory,* 1946.
5. Garretson, O. K., and Symonds, Percival M., *Interest Questionnaire for High School Students,* 1942 ed.
6. Kobal, A., Wrightstone, J. W., and Kunze, K. R., *Inventory of Vocational Interests,* Acorne National Aptitude Tests.
7. Van Allyn, K., *Job Qualification Inventory,* 1945-1947.
8. Kuder, G. F., *Kuder Preference Record.*
9. Manson, Grace E., *Occupational Interest Blank for Women,* 1931.
10. Lee, E. A., and Thorpe, L. P., *Occupational Interest Inventory,* 1944-1946.
11. Cardall, A. J., Jr., *Primary Business Interests Tests,* 1942.
12. Strong, E. K., Jr., *Vocational Interest Blank for Men,* rev., 1927-1938.
13. Strong, E. K., Jr., *Vocational Interest Blank for Women,* rev., 1933-1947.

More could be added to this list, but for a more exhaustive list the reader is referred to the *Mental Measurements Yearbooks* (*9*). In the yearbooks the reader will also find bibliographies of published research studies concerning these instruments, and critical reviews of the instruments by specialists in the field of measurement. Evaluation of these instruments by the specialists ranges from such a comment as: "Any resemblance between this scale and a scientific instrument is purely coincidental" to "Is one of the best tools available . . . to determine objectively . . . vocational interest."

The rationale of the construction and validation of such instruments must obviously be understood by the counselor, director of personnel, or whoever uses such instruments, for this rationale must carry the burden of confidence in the use of such instruments. Despite their limitations, all competent specialists agree that the better ones constitute decidedly important and useful tools in the armamentarium of the applied psychologist.

Problem Inventories

We have already reviewed in some detail the construction of the *SRA Youth Inventory,* which, with its geographically broad coverage, and its sixteen sets of norms, is at this writing probably the first instrument of its kind to be based upon a carefully selected nationally stratified sample of the population for which it is designed. In its Basic Difficulty Index, it obviously overlaps and serves the same purposes as do personality inventories.

For purposes of illustration we shall describe a few other similar instruments. *The Mooney Problem Check List (29)* has been designed for three levels—junior high school, senior high school, and college. While rather similar in item content to the Youth Inventory, the Mooney Check List differs from it sharply in its conceptualization, in that the former has been processed and evaluated in accordance with the usual concepts of validity and reliability applied in test technology generally. Mooney, however, maintains that his check list is not to be thought of as a test, and that the traditional concepts of reliability and validity are not appropriately applied to it. Doubtless the checking or nonchecking of individual items will tell the skillful counselor much, but to deny that one is attempting to measure psychological dimensions to which the concepts of psychological measurement apply appears to us invalid. Two adaptations of *The Mooney Problem Check List* have been published *(4, 30)*.

An instrument designed to give a basis for recreational guidance *(36)* is designed to serve both survey and individual guidance functions.

The reader is again referred to the *Mental Measurements Yearbook* for exhaustive coverage bibliographically of instruments of this sort, as well as for critical reviews by specialists. In passing we may observe that the classificatory scheme we are following here is obviously arbitrary—but so would any other scheme for classification be. It is interesting to note in this connection that the *Dunlap Academic Preference Blank* is in the *1949 Mental Measurements Yearbook* listed under "Character and Personality," while such instruments as the *Kuder Preference Record* and the *Strong Vocational Interest Blank* are listed under vocations. Ordering these instruments to the general concept of attitudes and to the rationale underlying their construction gives, in our judgment, as rational a basis for classification as any and better than most.

Occupational Attitudes

Under the heading of occupational attitudes it is obviously reasonable to include the entire large area of occupational morale. In the light of our earlier discussion, the relevant attitudes here will obviously be concerned with the emotional integration of the individual within a group with reference to attitude objects judged to be of vital concern to the group. A later chapter will deal with this more in detail.

In this section we shall review occupational attitudes of a somewhat different sort as exemplified in such instruments as *How I Teach* (27), *How Supervise?* (14, 15), *How I Counsel*

(5), *How Teach and Learn in College* (22), and *How Bring Up a Child* (33).

These measuring instruments are grouped together here because the rationale of their construction is basically the same and consists of the following steps.

1. Each item is selected from the literature, from experts, and/or from a sample of the population to which the final instrument is to be applied, on the hypothesis that the item is functionally related to the attitude or attitudes complex that it is desired to measure.

2. The assembled pool of items is then submitted to a jury of specialists in the area concerned for critical evaluation of the items as being relevant and for a judgment as to which of the three or five agree-disagree alternatives is the best answer. The answers on which this jury substantially agree then provide a first approximation to a scoring key for the instrument. We have found our colleagues in other institutions very cooperative in this kind of critical evaluation, but have also found that a check for 5 or 10 dollars attached to the covering letter is highly correlated with the percentage of returns. In fact by this device, it is not difficult to get 100 percent cooperation!

3. The items that survive step 2, plus any that the investigators may choose as promising, in spite of disagreement among the experts, are then included in an experimental form of the instrument and administered to a sample of the population for whom the instrument is intended.

4. The results of step 3 are now processed in accordance with the standard procedures for determining validity in terms of the criterion of the total score on the test. If items were included on which the jury of specialists were not agreed, they are not included in determining the total score but are validated individually and independently. All items that discriminate significantly are retained for the final form or forms of the test.

5. Two forms of the test are now selected from the items that have qualified in terms of both the experts' judgment and their validity in terms of the total score. This is done by selecting items judged to be similar in content and as nearly as possible equal

in "difficulty" and discriminating power as between the upper and lower tails of a distribution on the total score (this is usually the upper and lower 27 percent).

6. The two forms are now administered to yet another relevant population sample and the reliability of form against form is determined.

The instrument is now ready for use and further validation against such criteria as may be available. For the test *How Supervise?*, for example, it has been shown that the test discriminated successfully between forty-six successful supervisors and fourteen nonsupervisors in an office machine manufacturing company, where the average percentile test scores were 75 and 23, respectively. In a second study in a surgical supply manufacturing concern two groups selected by the testing supervisor as being superior and inferior supervisors, respectively. The critical ratio of the difference in scores was 4.4. A third study in a large laundry had divided sixteen supervisors into five groups from "superior" to those with "most limited supervisory responsibilities," this having been done in advance of administering the test. The raw scores for these groups were 54.7, 49.7, 44.7, 40.0, and 32.0 respectively. Two "before and after" tests, one in a supervisory training course (*26*), the other in a class of university students in a course in applied psychology (*25*), yielded highly significant gains in scores.

The interested student will be able to think of other external criteria against which to test the validity of such instruments as are here under consideration. It is obvious that such instruments are not the ideally pure, unidimensional kinds of instruments that pure theory would desire. Doubtless, we shall make progress toward such unidimensional instruments with further research. In the meantime, however, it must be noted that the external criteria that are the practical concern of those who must deal with these problems in practical situations are also complex and multidimensional, and in the practical situation, half a loaf is better than no bread in measuring the relevant attitudes and being able to predict better than chance on some external criterion.

Social Attitudes

The last two or three decades particularly have produced an enormously large psychological literature concerned with attitudes toward a bewildering variety of attitude objects, toward minority groups, social institutions, proposed social actions, and the like. At the present writing this literature is still growing in what appears to be a geometric progression. Out of this literature is emerging a body of scientifically grounded theory concerning particularly the structure of personality in our culture, and along with this, or frequently in advance of valid theory, more or less sound practice in all areas of organized human social activity—in industry, in education, in the armed forces, in penology, and in clinical diagnosis and therapy generally. We shall deal with some of these matters in more detail later.

SUMMARY

This chapter has been concerned with the summated attitude questionnaire. A variety of synonyms and near-synonyms of the concept of attitudes have been equated with it, and we have examined the problems of specificity versus generality of the organization of attitudes and their organization in the personality. Five kinds of summated questionnaires and the methodology of their construction have been reviewed.

Questions

1. How do *mores, morality* and *morale* agree? How do they differ? How could you test, empirically, the synonymity of these and similar terms?
2. How is a motive related to an attitude?
3. In Gough's "Studies of Social Intolerance," he lists a number of impressions which characterize the more anti-Semitic subjects: "(1) lower intellectual level . . . (3) less sociability . . . (9) antagonism toward many out-groups," and others. Would

you say that they could all be attributed to lower economic status?

4. From the description of the high school sample as described in the Purdue Opinion Panel, would you feel justified in generalizing to the United States high school population? Defend your answer.

5. Could an interest inventory be used as a preliminary clinical aid in discovering maladjustments? If yes, how? If no, why not?

6. Is it possible to answer question 5 through experiment? If so, outline the design of such an experiment.

7. An industrialist says that the morale of the workers in his organization is very low. The president of the local labor union says concerning the same group of workers that their morale is very high. Can both be right? Explain.

8. How could one determine whether generality versus specificity of an attitude is a function of age?

9. Are all attitudes learned?

10. Does the conscious analysis of one's own attitudes change them?

11. Will an individual with membership in several social groups of conflicting ideologies tend to become more liberal than others with more limited exposure to various attitudes?

12. What is a "liberal education" as related to attitudes?

Bibliography

1. Allport, F. H., *Social Psychology*, Boston: Houghton Mifflin Company, 1924.

2. Allport, G. W., "Attitudes." In Murchison, Carl (ed.), *Handbook of Social Psychology*, Worcester, Mass.: Clark University Press, 1935.

3. Allport, G. W., and Odbert, H. S., *Trait-Names; A Psycho-Lexical Study: A Study from the Harvard Psychological Laboratory*, Princeton, N.J.: Psychological Review Company, 1936.

4. Bender, R. E., *Problem Check List: Form for Rural Young People,* Columbus: Ohio State University Press, 1946.

5. Benz, Stanley, "An Investigation of the Attributes and Techniques of High-School Counselors," *Purdue University Studies in Higher Education; Further Studies in Attitudes Series* XII, 1948, no. 64.

6. Bernreuter, R. G., *Personality Inventory,* Stanford, Calif.: Stanford University Press, 1931.

7. Bingham, W. V., *Aptitudes and Aptitude Testing,* New York: Harper & Brothers, 1937.

8. Briggs, Thomas H., *Secondary Education,* New York: The Macmillan Company, 1933.

9. Buros, Oscar K. (ed.), *Mental Measurement Yearbooks,* New Brunswick, N.J.: Rutgers University Press, 1938, 1945, 1949, and 1953; 4 vols.

10. Cantril, H., "Generalized and Specific Attitudes," *Psychol. Monogr.,* 1932, *42*(no. 192).

11. Dewey, John, *Human Nature and Conduct,* New York: Henry Holt and Company, Inc., 1922.

12. Ellis, Albert, "The Validity of Personality Questionnaires," *Psychol. Bull.,* 1946, *43*(no. 5):385-440.

13. Ellis, Albert, and Conrad, Herbert S., "The Validity of Personality Inventories in Military Practice," *Psychol. Bull.,* 1948, *45*(no. 5):385-427.

14. File, Q. W., "The Measurement of Supervisory Quality in Industry," *J. appl. Psychol.,* 1945, *29*:323-337.

15. File, Q. W., and Remmers, H. H., "Studies in Supervisory Evaluation," *J. appl. Psychol.,* 1946, *30*:421-425.

16. Flanagan, J. C., *Factor Analysis in the Study of Personalities,* Stanford University, Calif.: Stanford University Press, 1935.

17. Flesch, R., *The Art of Plain Talk,* New York: Harper & Brothers, 1946.

18. Flesch, R., "A New Readability Yardstick," *J. appl. Psychol.,* 1948, *32*(no. 3):221-233.

19. Fryer, Douglas, *The Measurement of Interest,* New York: Henry Holt and Company, Inc., 1931.

20. Gough, H. G., "Studies of Social Intolerance: I. Some Psychological and Sociological Correlates of Anti-Semitism; II. A Personality Scale for Anti-Semitism; III. Relationship of the Pr Scale to Other Variables; IV. Related Social Attitudes;" *J. soc. Psychol.,* 1951, *33*:237-246, 247-256, 257-262, 263-269.

21. Hartshorne, H., and May, M., *Studies in the Nature of Character,* New York: The Macmillan Company, 1928-1930, vols. I-III.

22. Harvey, Lucy Jean, "The Mental Hygiene of Higher Learning

as the Student Sees It," *Purdue University Studies in Higher Education,* 1945, no. 53.

23. Hathaway, Starke, and McKinley, J. Charnley, *The Minnesota Multiphasic Personality Inventory,* New York: Psychological Corporation, 1943.

24. Herrick, V. E., "The Generality and Specificity of Attitudes," Unpublished Ph.D. Thesis, University of Wisconsin Library; referred to in Young, Kimball, *Personality and Problems of Adjustment,* New York: F. S. Crofts & Co., 1940.

25. Karn, H. W., "Performance on the File-Remmers Test, How Supervise? Before and After a Course in Psychology," *J. appl. Psychol.,* 1949, *33*(no. 6):534-539.

26. Katzell, R. A., "Testing a Training Program in Human Relations," *Person. Psychol.,* 1948, *1*:319-329.

27. Kelly, Ida B., and Perkins, K. J., "An Investigation of Teacher Knowledge of and Attitude Toward Child and Adolescent Behavior in Everyday School Situation," *Purdue University Studies in Higher Education: Further Studies in Attitudes Series* IV, 1941, no. 42.

28. Kuder, G. Frederick, and Richardson, M. W., "The Theory of the Estimation of Test Reliability," *Psychometrika,* 1937, *2*: 151-160.

29. Mooney, Ross L., *The Mooney Problem Check List,* Columbus: Ohio State University Press, 1941-1947.

30. Morison, Luella J., *Problem Check List: Form for Schools of Nursing,* Columbus: Ohio State University Press, 1945.

31. Murphy, G., Murphy, L. B., and Newcomb, T. M., *Experimental Social Psychology,* New York: Harper & Brothers, 1937.

32. Remmers, H. H., and Shimberg, Benjamin, *SRA Youth Inventory and Manual,* Chicago: Science Research Associates, 1949.

33. Stedman, Louise, A., "An Investigation of Knowledge of and Attitudes Toward Child Behavior," *Purdue University Studies in Higher Education,* 1948, no. 62.

34. Sumner, W. G., *Folkways,* Boston: Ginn & Company, 1906.

35. Thorndike, E. L., *Teachers' Word Book,* New York: Teachers College, Columbia University, rev. ed., 1944.

36. Wilkinson, Richard, and Tessy, S. L., *Recreation Inquiry,* New York: Psychological Corporation.

37. Woodworth, R. S., *Personal Data Sheet,* Chicago: C. H. Stoelting Company, 1917.

CHAPTER VII

· · ● · ● · ● · ● · · ·

Less Direct Measures of Attitudes

INTRODUCTION

The preceding chapters have discussed various methods for measuring attitudes usually thought of as direct methods. They are called direct in the sense that the purpose of requesting a response is usually obvious to the subject. This obviousness of intent has been the basis for a frequent objection to such techniques. An individual easily recognizes that his personality is being evaluated and in some situations it may not be to his advantage to have this done. Hence, he can easily distort his answers in the direction which he deems advisable in view of the circumstances.

The methods to be discussed in this chapter have attempted to circumvent this difficulty by employing techniques which measure attitudes indirectly. Here the individual is presented with a relatively unstructured stimulus or situation in which the real purpose of the measurement, that of determining his attitude, is not apparent to him. Included here also are those techniques which sample the individual's behavior and determine his attitude from the known or assumed relationship existing between this behavior and the attitude being measured.

A point which should be kept in mind during the evaluation of indirect methods is that theoretically any sample of behavior will yield some knowledge about the subject. Thus all of these techniques are of value in that they tell us something about the subject. The difficulties and criticisms that are encountered are practical ones. We are interested in obtaining as much dependable knowledge about an individual as possible and to do so with the minimum expenditure of time and effort. Consequently, our evaluation should be in terms of how adequately a particular technique fulfills this requirement.

WORD ASSOCIATION AND RELATED TECHNIQUES

Word Association Techniques

Since attitudes are to be considered as predisposing the individual to certain unique forms of action under certain varying conditions, we may tap these attitudes by observation of the forms of action the individual uses under specific conditions and in specific situations set up by the experimenter. One technique for tapping these attitudes is the method of word association. This is one of the earliest and most common methods of discovering the tendencies of the individual to give unique and characteristic responses to specific stimuli.

In the method of word association, developed from the original work of Galton (50), the subject is requested to respond with a word that comes to mind when the experimenter supplies a word. The word supplied by the experimenter may be a key word of importance or a control word which is used to set the general pattern of the situation and supply a body of words to surround the key words. The response word may be any word that the subject desires to give, or he may be restricted to a specific type of word (a similar or opposite word in meaning, for example). Significant characteristics of the response are the particular response word and its relation to the stimulus word, the time of delay between response and stimulus, the overt behavior of the subject during the test situation, and any other factors which might indicate that the subject has reacted to the stimulus with an emotional or intense reaction. It becomes apparent that the significant responses are those that tap the deepest and most intense attitudes of the subject, those attitudes which play the greatest part in directing the individual's personality and behavior.

Considerable work has been done in the field in order to discover the validity of the word association method in disclosing personality structure. The unique value of most recent work with word association is the provision of a hypothetical rationale for its method and interpretation. Writing in 1931, Symonds (*123*) believed that the potential fertility of the method had been largely ignored. Pretested word lists are now available, designed to disclose information related to specific areas of personality, including emotional security, parental attitudes, sexual attitudes, religious concepts, etc. The majority of studies of word associations have been descriptive in nature. While descriptive study is necessary to the development of a technique, theoretical and quantitative approaches may be more desirable. At present it appears that the methods of attack on attitude structure become more descriptive as they attempt measurement by increasing indirect and subjective means. This may be an inherent limitation to the general indirect approach.

Sentence Completion Techniques

The sentence completion test is a modification of the original by Payne (*96*). This method is designed to permit a more verbal outlet in response to the controlled stimulus. Here the subject is requested to complete a partially formed sentence and the direction, length, and nature of the completion serves to supply clues to latent attitudes of the subject. Again there is an inherent difficulty in quantification of the results.

The open-ended polling question is an apparent outgrowth of the sentence completion test. The population under examination is permitted free comment upon a general question, and the answer tends to disclose more complex attitude factors, including conflict, ignorance, indecision, etc., than a simple yes-no response to a fixed question (*57*).

An interesting characteristic of the sentence completion test and the word association test is the relatively structured nature of the stimulus and the availability of a practically unlimited number of responses. The structured nature of the stimulus is also present in the other related techniques.

Completion Techniques

The completion technique, which is also known as a story-telling technique, provides a basic theme for elaboration. Studies of this particular method are very limited, but apparently it has been used with some degree of success with both children and adults. At present we must view completion methods as being in the experimental stages.

Tautophone Test

A novel technique which removes the structuring of the stimulus was developed in 1936 by Skinner (*118*) and is named the Tautophone Test. Here the individual is subjected to a series of recorded vowel patterns of low intensity. The decreased intensity permits a certain amount of confusion and indecision on the part of the subject as to the exact nature of the sounds heard. The experimenter indicates that the low-level sound is conversation and asks the subject to repeat what he is hearing. The response, resulting as it does from a non-conversion stimulus, serves as an indication of the subject's inherent tendencies. Grings (*52*) has found that the test is better as a diagnostic instrument for certain classes or groups than for individuals. The greatest difficulty seems to stem from the time-consuming nature of the test and the difficulties in scoring and interpreting.

VISUAL STIMULUS TECHNIQUES

One of the characteristics that sets visual stimulus techniques together is their stress upon a nonverbal and yet visual form of stimulus. The stimulus can be classified as being simply a picture, a fairly realistic picture in some cases, and a vague and abstract picture in others. Some of the most common of these techniques include the Rorschach, Cloud Pictures, Thematic Apperception Test, Picture Frustration Method, and the Szondi Test.

The Rorschach Test

The efforts of a Swiss psychiatrist, Hermann Rorschach, resulted in our present Rorschach Test. His work was made public in 1921 (*110*), and even though this was one of the earliest of the so-called "projective techniques," it remains one of the most popular. The subject is presented with a series of ten ink blots, some in color, and is asked to describe what he sees. An analysis of the response is based upon the location of the response in relation to the area of the ink blot; the characteristics of the ink blot used (including use of form, shading, color, and movement properties); the content of the responses; and its popularity as a response. Each of these general areas of investigation leads the examiner to certain specific insights concerning the subject's personality. For example, a purely color-based response is an indication of a rather infantile affectivity.

Certain deviations from the original Rorschach technique are necessary for use of the test in group situations. The original test, upon which most of the large body of normative information has been obtained, was strictly controlled and individualistic. Four general group methods have been attempted with more or less success. Harrower-Erickson and Steiner (*55*) projected the ink blots upon a screen. They also used a method where a series of multiple-choice answers were presented. A slightly different method was used by Eysenck (*43*) which called for the ranking of a series of multiple-choice answers. This approach leads to a tendency toward greater reliability of response than simple multiple choice. The fourth general method calls for the self-administration of the Rorschach.

One of the best evidences of the interest in the Rorschach Test lies in the voluminous mass of literature that has accrued about it. Bell (9) lists 798 references in his bibliography. The criticism has been leveled at Rorschach workers that they disregard scientific technique and use a sort of magic to gain the results they report. The quality of the literature is evidence that the approaches of science have not been entirely disregarded even though traditional methods have been modified and new methods have been applied. The distinct impression is gained that the best critics of the Rorschach technique are found among its exponents. It is regarded generally, by those who use it, as a method which still needs much development and must, even in its present state, be used with caution as well as enthusiasm.

The interpretation of a Rorschach record is an artistic achievement depending upon the ability of the examiner to interrelate a multiple number of variables, a process aided but not accomplished by scoring. With a technique such as a Rorschach the measuring of validity and reliability is a critical issue. The exact measure of these qualities is difficult to ascertain, and as yet the studies that have set out to evaluate the method in these terms are few. They have reported conflicting results.

Lord (75) indicates that repetition of the Rorschach Test produces significant differences in response. These differences in response are largely assigned, however, to differences in examiner techniques. Variations in rapport are also considered to produce important changes in response.

The Thematic Apperception Test

The second best known of the "projective techniques" is the Thematic Apperception Test (TAT) as developed by Morgan and Murray (86). The subject is presented with a series of pictures composed of people in certain situations. The situations are not clearly defined and the subject is requested to make up a story around the picture. The test is based on the theory that in the constructing of stories around ambiguous picture stimuli the individual organizes material from his own personal experiences, partly the immediate perceptions of the stimuli and partly the associations to those perceptions selected from the conscious and preconscious imagery. In achieving these fantasies the conscious and preconscious impulses, the defenses, and the conflicts of the individual are expressed, permitting the interpreter to discover the content of such characteristics of the personality. The specificity of the responses is both an asset and a liability in practice. It prevents simple generalizations but it handicaps those who are competent to use the method by introducing such complexities that the standardization of procedure and the comparisons of results between investigators is difficult to achieve.

There have been several modifications of the Thematic Apperception Test. Generally they have been of the following types:

1. Reduction of number of pictures
2. Administration of the test under frustrating conditions
3. Combination of the TAT pictures with other pictures
4. Allowing the selection of pictures
5. The securing of written responses in group situations
6. Presentation of possible multiple-choice responses

The first three methods, adaptations for individual administration, have been frequently used and have been supported by a fair amount of research. The method of selection of pictures was first advocated by Oppenheimer (95), but considerable research remains to be accomplished before its value can be objectively demonstrated. At present it appears doubtful whether the method of multiple-choice responses will ever be of great value but the writing of responses in a group situation shows apparent promise especially with intelligent subjects.

The TAT may well be of value in the measurement of attitudes after more study has been accomplished. It is a diagnostic instrument in the sense that it gives an understanding of the individual in his own life setting (42).

Other Picture Techniques

Various other picture methods have been attempted during the past 30 years and some psychologists have written glowing reports of the possibilities of them (88). Proshansky (100) used the picture method in an attitude study. In his group test of attitudes toward labor he used a series of seventeen antilabor and eighteen prolabor pictures. Later Morgan and Murray (86) studied sentiments toward war, religion, sex, and parents partially by the means of a picture selection test made up of 225 pictures depicting forty-five foci of sentiments. Pickford (98) recently developed a binocular apparatus arranged so that the subject could look through a window into a box and view a picture 2 meters away. The picture was illuminated but a glare was thrown into the eyes of the subject so that the picture was invisible. The glare could be decreased in steps and the subject was asked to report what he saw at each interval. In his original experiment using fifteen pictures and ten subjects, Pickford found that the subject's conscious reaction type was usually revealed. Verville (130) used incomplete pictures in her study of the effect of set toward the test situation upon the behavior in the situation.

Rosenzweig Picture Frustration Study

Rosenzweig (111) developed a test made up of twenty-four pictures resembling incomplete cartoons which he called the Picture-Association Study for Assessing Reaction to Frustration. The pictures are made up of two figures involving some degree of frustration. The subject is requested to write in the appropriate response to the situation. The test, though somewhat immature, has already proved a useful supplement to personality tests in clinical situations as shown by reports of Shakow, Rodnick, and Lebeaux (115).

The Szondi Test

A Hungarian psychologist, Lipot Szondi, began developing

the Szondi Test in 1930 and has since given it to over 5000 subjects. The bibliography at present is very limited but if the test results are confirmed it should prove to be a most useful instrument. The test proper consists of forty-eight photographs of different faces in six sets. The subject is requested to choose the two pictures most liked and the two pictures least liked. The ease of administration and evaluation should make it an instrument of great utility.

EXPRESSIVE MOVEMENT AND RELATED TECHNIQUES

Expressive movement has been defined by Allport and Vernon (3) as "those aspects of movement which are distinctive enough to differentiate one individual from another." Such things as how an individual walks or what his facial expression may be probably are unique to him. The problems investigated by Allport and Vernon were those of how consistent such forms of expression are and how we can obtain an objecjective measure of them. Their studies on these problems and those of Wolff (135, 136, 137) represent the most comprehensive research that has been done in this area.

Wolff directed most of his work toward the determination of how these various forms of movement and expression are related to the attitudes and personality characteristics of the individual. He was further interested in the impression these movements make on others. For example, in one of his early experiments (135) Wolff recorded the voices of his subjects pronouncing the same sentence and also photographed their hands without their knowledge. He found that judges could match voices and photographs of the hands with better than chance expectancy. He also found that subjects could recognize the voices of persons they knew, but failed to recognize their own. He explained this resistance to self-recognition as due to unconscious emotional involvement of the subject when he is attempting to characterize his own personality.

It must be recognized that, as yet, only tentative exploration of this difficult field of expressive movement has been under-taken and that much research must be accomplished before these methods yield information that will contribute significantly to personality diagnosis.

The Analysis of Handwriting

Graphology is now generally accepted as a projective technique. One of the important factors in bringing about this change of attitude in America has been the arrival in this country of so many displaced European research workers who brought with them a favorable attitude toward graphology. Until recently most of the work in this area was done by the European workers. Binet (15) demonstrated the expression of personality in handwriting when he asked judges to distinguish men and women, honest and dishonest persons, from specimens of handwriting. He obtained positive results which were statistically significant.

An American study along these lines was made by Downey (34) who obtained agreements of judgments based on gait, gesture, and handwriting in about 70 percent of the cases against the 50 percent of chance expectation.

But instead of these positive results, only negative results were achieved by other psychologists, such as Hull and Montgomery (61), who tried to verify correlation by certain graphologists between specific elements of handwriting and character traits. They obtained as many positive as negative correlations, the average of all being -0.016. Thus there was a hypercritical rejection of graphology by American psychologists until 1933 when the studies of Allport and Vernon (3) marked a turning point. This does not mean that graphology has managed to overcome the widespread suspicion that has surrounded it or has reached a stage of development that merits uncritical acceptance of its findings. It has, however, begun to emerge as a highly legitimate field of psychological experimentation and research.

Mira Myokinetic Psychodiagnosis

Emilia Mira, of Buenos Aires, has proposed and made preliminary investigations of a projective device based upon the theory that each subject must have, in a given moment, a particular set of movements more capable of being elicited than all others. This theory is an inference from the observation of Cheuvreuil in 1828 that merely the image of a "pendulum" is sufficient to start that movement in the body unconsciously. Therefore, if we discover certain individual trends toward movement in a subject we may presume that there is some idea motivating that movement. If such movements are found to be constant in a person, then the differences between individuals might be regarded as habitual attitudes of reactions. Since this test takes only a short time to administer (30 minutes on the average), and the equipment needed is easy to procure, it is a very practical technique for diagnostic use. At the present time, however, its results are so tentative that it cannot be applied immediately to discriminate clinical groups or to analyze the structure of the personality in individual cases. Standardized experiments with the technique should be relatively easy to develop, and since the results are primarily objectively analyzed, comparison of its use by various experimenters should be possible.

Visual-Motor Tests

While the tests to be discussed here are not new, their use in personality testing is of recent origin. The first personality test to be based upon visual-motor methods was developed by Bender (10), and has become known as the Bender Visual-Motor Gestalt Test. Bender used figures first suggested by Wertheimer (134) as the material for her test. Her use of these figures as a test procedure was based upon extensive research into the ability of children and adults with various personality disorders to reproduce these figures.

Bender used both full exposure and tachistoscopic exposure during drawing in her experiments. The evaluation of the drawings was made on the basis of the movements involved, the perceptions implied by the figures drawn, the characteristics of the drawings themselves, and associated behavior. The potential advantages of these methods are (1) their rapidity, (2) their tapping of two major aspects of the personality, the perceptual capacities and the motor activity, and (3) their similarity to test procedures now in common use in psychological diagnosis, permitting inclusion of these methods within other tests in a natural and nondisrupting fashion. Their weakness is in the limited evidence of validity and reliability as yet accumulated.

Drawing, Painting, and Other Arts

There has been a great variety of experiments on the relationship between personality and various forms of art. Some of the earliest volumes of psychological and educational journals contained articles dealing with children's art. These background studies contributed a foundation upon which art has developed as a projective technique.

The methods for securing art samples have ranged from spontaneous artistic activity with a wide range of materials, through combining such free art with more controlled tasks, to rather rigid methods of limiting the projects, the materials, and the circumstances under which the art is produced. The primary aspects of art which have been analyzed are the use of the medium, the form elements, and the general performance of the individual.

One technique particularly adapted to children is finger painting, developed by Shaw (*116*) in 1930. The most thorough and systematic analysis of this method has been developed by Napoli (*91*), who has set forth many hypotheses about the meaning of its different characteristics. His interpretation is based on study of the total behavior of the individual from the beginning to the end of the painting act. Since much of the interpretation in its present application lacks objectivity, investigators have not been able to relate particular attitudes or personality characteristics to the quantitative aspects of the drawing. Whether or not future research accomplishes this objective, finger painting will remain as a technique with unusual recreational, personal release, and artistic values, which of themselves make it important in the clinical situation.

A somewhat different approach has been the method of completing pictures. Probably the first use of this type of test for the diagnosis of personality was by Sanders, application of whose test was reported by Berger (12). This measure calls for the completion in crayon of six barely suggested line drawings. The productions were judged in terms of position, content, coloring, integration, and various other characteristics. Sanford developed a picture completion test for personality diagnosis (113), which was used by Murray in his extensive investigation of fantasy (89, 90). The most systematic proposal for a test based on completing pictures has been presented by Hellersberg (56), in what she calls the Horn-Hellersberg Test. Although the test has been suggested and its merits explored to a certain extent by the author, it is, at the moment, still in the introductory stages, as is the case with most projective devices.

The Mosaic Test

A test originating with Löwenfeld in 1929 (76), this test has not been extensively used in the United States, but it has become part of the regular battery of personality tests in many British clinics. The Mosaic Test bears a relationship to Löwenfeld's World Test like that of the Rorschach to the TAT. The Mosaic Test reveals more the personality structure; the World Test, more the content of disturbing complexes. Löwenfeld's materials for the test consisted of 465 small wooden blocks in various colors and shapes. Diamond and Schmale (32) used similar materials and such simple instructions as "Make anything you like out of the pieces." Time, while recorded, was not limited.

This test satisfies so many of the criteria of a good projective technique that it would seem to merit much further development. Its present usefulness is impaired by the lack of extensive research studies with various clinical groups of subjects and by the absence of standardized methods of interpretation, which are, however, difficulties that enthusiastic clinical psychologists, with a bent for research, may in time overcome.

Voice and Speech

It is surprising that our most important means of communication, the voice, which in everyday life enters so strongly into our judgments of others, should have been used so infrequently in a controlled scientific manner for the determination of personality characteristics. Pear (97) has stated that since speech is a form of action, it is natural that some persons' speech style should reflect their general behavior. Also Allport and Cantril (2) have demonstrated that the voice does convey correct information concerning outer and inner characteristics of the personality. A possible explanation of why so little research has been done in this area is the difficulty of separating the voice and speech. We need only observe the profound influence a speaker may have even though his words are almost meaningless to realize that there is a difference between voice and speech. But whatever future developments may reveal, it appears at present that studying voice and speech is primarily useful as a supplemental technique which may provide us with important insights into the individual's attitudes.

PLAY, DRAMA, AND RELATED TECHNIQUES

The measurement of attitudes, a difficult task at best, is further complicated when the subject is unwilling to enter into the highly artificial situation imposed by certain attitude scales, or is unable to verbalize his emotions as so frequently is true with children. For this reason play, drama, and their related techniques have proved very valuable in the measurement of attitudes, especially with children.

In this area we shall consider directed play, the World Test, psychodramas, and sociodramas together as one type of research tool which is available to the investigator whose concern is with the measurement of attitudes. It may be interpolated that while these techniques are frequently used for catharsis (the release of emotional tension achieved by permitting the subject to relive unpleasant experiences either directly or vicariously) they are equally valuable as devices for identifying and quantifying attitudes.

Play

The reader who is familiar with children will readily appreciate the fact that an adult will frequently meet with frustration when he attempts to discover, through direct questioning, the attitudes which underpin the overt behavior of a child. When asked, "Why did you hit your friend?" the child will often say, "I don't know." This response, while it cannot always be taken at face value, gives some indication of the child's inability to rationalize or explain his conduct, even under direct questioning. How can this "block" be circumvented?

One of the earliest and still most effective techniques for measuring children's attitudes was devised by David Levy (69), who used dolls to represent various members of a family. The child usually reveals those attitudes he holds toward his own family by projecting his emotions into the dramatic situations which he creates with his doll family. Attitudes such as "hostility," Levy has pointed out, are revealed by the unique behavioral and emotional patterns demonstrated by the child in the play situation.

In addition to Levy's work, other investigators have used less structured materials such as clay, dough, finger paints, and coloring materials as media through which the child gives tangible evidence of his attitudes. While these media have the advantage of being comparatively less structured than the doll family, and consequently give reader freedom of expression to the child, the resulting activity may be more difficult to analyze and interpret since the end product of the child's activity (a finger painting, etc.) may reveal no clearly defined relationships to the attitudes which motivated the child's efforts. The reader will doubtless notice much similarity between this technique and the "expressive movement technique" used with adults and described earlier in this chapter. Much of the theoretical framework is the same.

We may summarize by saying that play is primarily of value in investigating attitudes of children but also has demonstrated worth for adults. With very young children, play is, and will probably remain, the most valuable and productive diagnostic technique.

The World Test

A technique which, in some respects, is similar to the play techniques described previously is the World Test. Instead of dolls (or other materials such as clay or finger paints) the subject is given replicas of the major component parts of a world community such as hospitals, schools, armies, modes of transportation, homes, churches, and so forth, in miniature. The subject is then asked to create a "world." This highly unique method for measuring attitudes was devised at the London Institute of Child Psychology by Löwenfeld (76) in 1929. The suggestion for the test came from the author H. G. Wells in a book entitled *Floor Games*, published in 1911. The primary uses of the test have been as a diagnostic instrument and as a medium of communication in child therapy. Its present state of development owes much to C. Bühler, who visited the Löwenfeld Institute in May, 1934, and began the study of normal children with the test. This research resulted in the standardization of procedures, and in the publication with Kelly (21), in 1941, of uniform test materials, a manual, and record forms.

In a small study by Dubin (*38*), toys of four special types were used in the building of "worlds" as a means of determining attitudes. Six women students of Barnard College, and four men students of Columbia College, were asked to construct a dramatic scene, or "the world as you see it today," and also, "the world as you would like it to be." They were provided with eighty toys representing the four functional groups: (1) war, (2) public service, (3) labor, and (4) travel and entertainment. An interview was held with each subject, when he interpreted the worlds he had made. Three graduate students in psychology were given pictures of the worlds and asked to predict on a five-point scale the responses of the students on "A Survey of Opinions," modeled after Murphy and Likert's *Public Opinion and the Individual* (*87*).

Although there was considerable variability among the judges' predictions in individual cases, the mean coefficient of correlation was plus 0.49, which would indicate that the building of "worlds" is likely to have considerable validity as an attitude measuring device, if such results were to hold up on experimentation with different groups, and with different opinion scales. As in so many other projective techniques, the World Test shows promise, but it needs validation by extensive research to increase its usefulness as a diagnostic tool. Its chief value will probably remain in its suitability as a means of communication in therapy.

The Psychodrama and the Sociodrama

Two closely related techniques which have gained wide use in the area of attitude measurement are the psychodrama and the sociodrama. Because of their similarity we shall treat them together. These techniques lend themselves even more readily to use with adult groups (in the case of the sociodrama), and with adults (when considered individually) in the psychodrama. In these situations, the subject(s) may be given a specific role in a dramatic situation and asked to respond to that role as he thinks it appropriate to do so. A less definitely structured situation can be created by merely instructing the individual to act out any fantasy that may occur to him. The first official psychodramatic situation took place on April 1, 1921, at the Komoedien Haus, a theater for the drama, in Vienna. Then, as now, its guiding spirit was J. L. Moreno. For the reader who may wish to learn more about these techniques, three references are suggested: (1) *The Theatre of Spontaneity (82)*. This volume of 113 pages was originally written by Gustav Kiepenheuer Verlag, Potsdam, Germany, in 1923. The manuscript establishes the spontaneity theory of play and dramatic techniques. This book may be considered a forerunner of most of the literature which has subsequently appeared. (2) A second article (*85*) includes Moreno's definition of the term "psychodrama" and its relation to sociometry. (3) A final reference (*80*) published in three volumes is, perhaps, the most comprehensive statement available regarding the theory and practice of the psychodrama and sociodrama as tools for the practicing psychologist.

Two major criticisms of these techniques have been made. One is the serious lack of standardization with respect to initiating and interpreting the end product of these methods. While Moreno has made some suggestions in this area, they are not yet sufficiently comprehensive or scientific to warrant their uncritical acceptance. A second, and equally important, consideration lies in the fact that, while the psychodrama does permit expression of behavior, a measure of its validity is needed. In spite of the claims that psychodrama circumvents the necessity of validation, such studies are essential. Serious research into the relation of the behavior on the psychodrama stage and the more realistic life behavior of the individual must be undertaken.

Despite these, and other limitations, the psychodrama may be accepted rather readily as a projective technique of considerable ingenuity and worth.

The *sociodrama*, in reality, is but a variation of the psychodrama, but we may differentiate the terms by defining the sociodrama as a technique which explores *intergroup relations* and deals with *collective ideologies* as opposed to the inter-personal relations and private ideologies dealt with by the psychodrama.

INTRAGROUP ATTITUDE MEASUREMENT

The attitudes of the members of a group are of considerable importance in determining the functioning of the group. Of the many attitudes possessed by group members, those attitudes concerned with the presence of the other members are the most significant in relation to the smooth working of the group itself. If the members of a group are displeased with their comrades, conflict, disunity, and discontent usually result. Since man exists, works, plays, and dies surrounded by a social framework of other individuals, and since man is constantly a member of a group, intragroup attitudes take on an impor-tant meaning for the social psychologist and student of atti-tudes.

The field of sociometry has developed around a series of simple and effective techniques designed to tap, among other things, the intragroup attitudes of individuals. Does John Jones want Bill Smith as a roommate? Will Fred increase his production rate if his work partners are changed? Is Sally too restricted in her circle of friends to become happy in her cot-tage? These become questions in need of answers. They are the questions whose answers may lead to increased group effi-ciency, increased pleasure, and increased happiness on the part of the group members and the community at large.

Sociometry is largely the result of the striking insights of J. L. Moreno. Moreno's *Who Shall Survive?* (79) disclosed a number of worthy group measurement techniques around which sociometry has grown. *Who Shall Survive?* is the central work in the field, and *Sociometry* serves as the main publica-tion journal for those doing work on intragroup structure and attitudes.

The individual who tends to classify himself strictly as a

sociometrist may often reject many techniques not originally developed by Moreno or his followers. These techniques are classified as "pure-sociometric" methods. The individual who tends to classify himself as a social psychologist or social scientist is more inclined to look upon the original sociometric techniques as introductory wedges into the complex field of intragroup attitudes, where some of the newer methods developed outside the restricted field of sociometry may show greater value or possibilities. Caution must often be used in evaluation of many sociometric claims as being perhaps too comprehensive for small-sample, restricted research (74).

In the present discussion, the term sociometry will be used in its broadest sense to cover many techniques, some developed by Moreno and the pure-sociometrists, others by near-sociometrists and men in other fields. All are designed to tap intragroup attitudes.

The Sociometric Test

The most popular and most commonly used technique is Moreno's Sociometric Test (79, 83). In this test all the members of a group are questioned. They are asked to choose other members of the group with whom they would like to do something. They may be choosing roommates, work-group members, dining-room tablemates, "buddies" in the armed forces, etc. They may be asked for an unlimited number of choices or may be restricted to a certain number. In addition to asking for choices of those acceptable, there may also be a request to indicate which members are unacceptable or rejected. In a true sociometric test, the "something" is always specifically indicated; it may be a roommate, playmate, etc., but not just a "friend." Another characteristic of the true sociometric test (94) is that the group members must be motivated by the knowledge that their choices will actually serve to alter the group structure. The use of the sociometric test is not necessarily for research but often for social action (79). There is, implicit in this requirement, a recognition of the importance of motivation in determining the accuracy of expression to latent attitude structures. However, the greatest body of sociometric information available to date is research. Some question has risen as to the exact differences resulting from the motivation for group change and the motivation of coöperation with a research project.

Since, to alter the group structure properly, the name of the person doing the choosing must be known, work done without revealing the name of the chooser is often rejected by pure-sociometrists. A number of studies have been done omitting this information, however, in order to reduce the ego involvement of the choice indicator (*28, 114*).

The Spontaneity Test

A more intense insight into intragroup attitudes is obtained by use of the Spontaneity Test, also developed by Moreno (*79*). Here two individuals who are sociometrically related are brought together. They may have accepted or rejected each other, or one may have accepted or rejected the other. In any case, they have formed some connection by a prior sociometric test. A scene is set by indicating to one member that he is to attempt to raise a certain emotion in the other individual. The emotion may be rage, fear, fondness, etc. The experimenter specifies the exact emotion, but the subject is permitted free use of verbal tools to produce it. Various factors are recorded in the spontaneous situation that results. The success or failure to raise the emotion, the type of mechanism used, the effect, the verbal output of the members, and the emotional states of both members, all serve as useful attitude clues. For example, a high verbal output in attempting to produce rage and a low output in attempting to produce fondness may indicate a latent tendency toward antisocial interaction between the two members. Usually both members of the pair are subjected to the test alternately; both attempt to produce certain emotions in the other. In all cases the emotion is set by the experimenter and is unknown to the individual who is to be made emotional. In addition to other factors, the test serves mainly to disclose some of the basic attitude factors that lead to the original sociometric relationships found in the Sociometric Test.

Interaction Testing and Process Analysis

Both interaction testing (*82*) and process analysis (*7, 79*) may be applied under controlled or uncontrolled situations. The control may be present in the form of "scene setting" or "situation setting." In these cases the individuals to be analyzed are brought together and asked to act out a certain problem or situation. This may serve as a form of psychodrama or sociodrama. Otherwise the work may be done in a normal situation not deliberately set up for the test. Individuals may be observed in a home or a nursery school, for example.

In interaction testing many systems can be used, but the basis of the technique is more or less the same. The observers attempt to record the exact time at which each member of the group starts to work, talk, or act with another member. This is the starting time of a contact. The time is recorded when the contact ends, and the time for pauses between contacts is noted. As a result, the complete patterns of friendship interactions, as a function of time, are obtained. Frequency and length of contact tend to indicate patterns of friendships and possible lines of communication. It should be noted that this does not directly disclose intragroup attitudes, but it does give certain insights based on the patterns of contacts.

Process analysis probes deeper into the interaction patterns of a group. Here the entire conversation of the group is recorded and the result is subjected to content analysis, study of time delays, emotionality, and interaction patterns. This, of course, serves to result in deeper investigation than interaction testing. The results may prove more valid and hold greater insights. Validation of the results has not been attempted to any great extent (*74*).

Sociometric data obtained from nearly all forms of socio-metric testing is still largely descriptive. Data from the Socio-metric Test may be indicated in the form of an individual index showing number of acceptances and rejections, accepta-bilities and rejectabilities, number of choices and times chosen

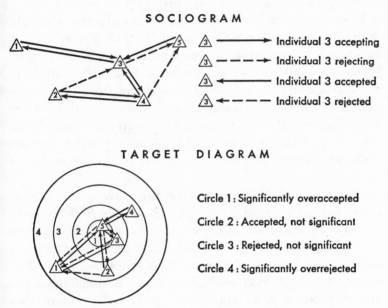

FIGURE 10.   Typical Sociogram and Target Diagram.

by others. A more disclosing method of representation calls for a sociogram.

The sociogram is a diagram on which each member of the group is represented by a circle or triangle. Connecting lines between triangles indicate acceptances or rejections, with arrowheads indicating who accepts or rejects whom (79, 83, 84). This method was developed by Moreno and is still strongly defended by him. Northway (93) uses a target diagram that incorporates both sociogram and index. The target diagram is a sociogram except that the triangles are not placed on the diagram indiscriminately. A number of concentric circles are drawn and the triangles are located in respect to the bull's-eye target of concentric circles. Each circle represents a probability level of chance deviation. Those individuals who are significantly overchosen as acceptable are located close to the center; those significantly overrejected, furthest from the center.

Another descriptive form of representation calls for indicating the results of the Sociometric Test on a matrix. Each member of the group is represented horizontally and vertically. When individual A chooses individual B, a mark is made in the matrix along the horizontal form A and along the vertical form B. Thus horizontal scanning indicates patterns of choosing while vertical scanning indicates patterns of being chosen (46, 63, 71). Moreno offers criticism of this method as opposed to the sociogram (81), believing that it is less productive of insights.

Attempts to quantify sociometric data have been made by Bronfenbrenner (20) and Criswell (27, 29, 30). Both use techniques designed to determine whether the number of choices received by an individual is significantly greater than can be expected on the basis of chance. Bronfenbrenner applies the binominal distribution and Criswell uses the method of chi square. Both methods retain some questionable assumptions when applied to choice situations in sociometry and both have been criticized (74). However, they demonstrate an attempt toward quantification that tends to indicate a felt need in the growth and maturity of the science. Use of Fisher's "analysis of variance" by Seeman (28, 114) demonstrates a technique that may prove highly fruitful in sociometry.

Sociometric techniques in general, and variations of the Sociometric Test in particular, have been applied to a large variety of problems in group attitudes. Sociometric patterns can disclose the effects of social stratification on friendship patterns (73, 119). The effect of stratification on patterns of family visits has also been successfully investigated (71).

Studies in friendship and social acceptance among children as well as studies in leadership and isolation have been significantly completed (47, 62).

When sociometric work is done on a large scale, the use of total populations often is impossible and problems of sampling appear. Where friendships cut across an entire community, sociometric and social patterns may be successfully obtained by a sample of about 20 percent. Evidence is available to indicate that samples as large as 50 percent are necessary where the friendship bonds are in small clusters, as in a large city (121). Here is a noticeable drawback of the method in the analysis of communities of great size. Smaller samples often miss complete clusters of friends with an accompanying distortion of results. As in other surveys, a distortion will result from a failure to call back on individuals who were not present when first contacted. Certain types of families tend to be away from home more than others, and class or occupational biases may result. Area control is often indicated to reduce overlap and conflict between investigators (121). Stewart and Stewart discuss these problems, as well as the problems of the individual interviewer, at great length (121, 122).

Although no great emphasis has been placed upon determination of reliabilities for sociometric work (74), the little that has been done tends to indicate that the results of the Sociometric Test are quite stable. However, stability as represented by test-retest reliability may demonstrate a lack of sensitivity in a test, thus failure to measure actual changes. Memory may also serve to increase these reliabilities in sociometric testing. Jennings (62) obtained coefficients of test-retest reliability as high as 0.95 and as low as 0.65.

A highly significant study by Eng and French (41) indicates the relationship between the Sociometric Test and the more conventional methods of measuring attraction-rejection patterns of attitudes. The intercorrelations of results obtained through an unlimited choice Sociometric Test, mean ranks from rank-order arrangement, and the method of paired comparisons are indicated below.

	Mean Ranks	Unlimited Sociometric Test
Paired comparison	0.90	0.90
Mean ranks (rank order)	—	0.89

The very high intercorrelations between unlimited sociometric results, paired comparison results, and mean ranks may lead to the conclusions that for many applications the simple rank-order method of determining a continuum may prove both efficient and economical (*41*). This may also be an indication that the sociometric test as such may not tap areas unique and unaccessible to other forms of attitude testing.

THE USE OF RATING SCALES (OTHER THAN SELF-RATINGS) IN THE INDIRECT MEASUREMENT OF ATTITUDES

One example of indirect measurement of attitudes is found where a person is asked to rate the attitudes, traits, or behavior of persons that he knows. Following are some examples of situations in which this kind of rating is commonly done.

1. Ratings of subordinates by supervisors or executives in a business or industry. Here the results are used as a basis for employee retention or discharge, salary or wage adjustments, promotion or advancement, and for employee counseling (*14, 35, 49*).
2. Service ratings (similar to the above) of civil service employees by superiors, sometimes required by statute (*8, 101*).
3. Rating of job applicants by employment interviewers (*22, 124*).
4. Rating of teachers by school or university students (*102, 104*).
5. Rating of salesman performance by professional shoppers—raters who pose as customers (*33, 67*).

What items of attitude, trait, or behavior are such persons called on to rate? Following are some representative examples.

1. Personal appearance
2. Quality of an employee's work
3. Speed or quantity of an employee's work

4. Coöperativeness
5. Tact
6. Potential for advancement
7. Aggressiveness
8. Initiative
9. Overall efficiency of an employee

General Purpose of Ratings

The purpose of ratings is generally conceived to be that of measuring the characteristics of the persons being rated. The use of ratings usually implies that an objective measure of the trait being rated is not available, or at least not easily or inexpensively available. Thus, even a short-form intelligence test is likely to be superior to an employment interviewer's ratings in the measurement of intelligence of job applicants. Or, it would be considerably better to use data from employee's clock cards as a measure of employee absenteeism and tardiness rather than a supervisor's rating.

Rating By-Products—Rater Attitudes

The rater also reveals many of his own attitudes in his ratings. There has been a surprising general lack of adequate study of this aspect of the rating process, particularly in the field of industrial merit rating of employees. However, some investigators, including Adams (1), Argelander (5), Conrad (26), and Greene (51), have studied or observed the dynamics of raters' attitudes as they affect the rating process.

For instance, a rater who, when rating his subordinates on coöperativeness or ability to get along with others, rates nearly all of them low, is perhaps suggesting that he himself is hard to get along with. The rater who (as frequently) rates all of his subordinates high on most or all traits of a descriptive rating system, reveals, perhaps, a sense of loyalty to his workers—but also a lack of inclination or ability to discriminate among them as realistically as would be needed to serve the ends of the rating system.

RATING METHODS

Rating methods may be generally classified under two main headings: (1) *relative ratings,* where the results should indicate which of the persons in a group are relatively higher (or lower) than others in a group on the trait being considered; (2) *descriptive or absolute ratings,* where the primary emphasis is on describing how high or how low each person is considered to be on the trait in question.

Relative Methods

Ranking (53). For example, let us suppose that a person is given a list of ten names of persons that he knows and asked to rate them on aggressiveness. In ranking them he would first select the name of the person he considered to be the most aggressive as number one—the next most aggressive person, number two—and so on down to the least aggressive person (in his opinion) as number ten. Using the trait of aggressiveness in this example illustrates how persons being rated as demonstrating the *most* of a given trait may not necessarily be given the most desirable rating. Note also, that nothing is said about *how aggressive* any of the persons in the group are. If the ten persons being rated were a group of salesmen in a high-pressure sales campaign, the least aggressive person might still be described as "very aggressive." On the other hand, a group of ten Sunday School teachers rated in the same way might (but not necessarily) all be relatively low in aggressiveness.

Paired Comparison (53). Using a paired comparison rating method, each of the subjects to be rated is paired once with each other subject to be rated. For simplicity's sake let us take a paired comparison rating list for four persons:

A vs. B	A vs. C
B vs. C	D vs. B
C vs. D	A vs. D

In this case, the rater has been asked to consider only two persons at a time and to underline the one subject of the pair who rates highest on the trait. Each subject's name appears three times in being paired with the other subjects. The subject's rating is equal to the number of times his name was underlined in the example above: C = 3 highest; B = 2; D = 1; A = 0 lowest.

This method becomes somewhat cumbersome when the number of subjects to be rated is large, since the number of pairs to be considered equals N (number of subjects) multiplied by $\frac{1}{2}$ $(N - 1)$. Rating twenty subjects by this method would require $20 \times 19 \times \frac{1}{2}$ or, to express it another way, 190 pairs of names.

Multidimensional Psychophysical Method (104).   Another method, known by this imposing title, has recently shown considerable promise. Under this method successive groups of three names are presented to the rater, instead of successive pairs as in paired comparison. The rater is asked only to select which two of each three names are "most alike" in terms of the trait being considered. After he has treated each of the three-name groups in this way, he is asked to indicate which one person in the group is at the "most" extreme of the trait and which one person at the "least" extreme. With this information, the statistical technician can rather easily resolve out a rating for each of the subjects relative to the others in the group. This method has the advantage of concealing the rating significance of the separate decisions from the rater to a certain degree, and of mitigating the burden on the rater of identifying directly those persons who rate low on the trait (with, of course, the exception of the one or two who are at the low extremes).

Descriptive Rating Methods

Graphic Scales (54).   The following example illustrates a graphic rating scale:

TACT

/	/	/	/	/
No tact	Little tact	Average	Tactful	Extremely tactful

With a rating scale such as this a rater may rate one or several subjects. By contrast, the relative rating methods require more than one rating subject—and within reasonable limits the larger the group of ratings, the better the results (at least in terms of interpretation). Descriptions of trait degrees may be in abstract terms such as "poor, fair, average, good, and excellent," or in specific descriptive behavioral terms.

The Check List Method.   Another method of descriptive ratings consists of a whole series of random descriptive terms. One of the original check list rating systems was developed by Probst (*99*). The rater is asked to go through the list of terms, checking those which are applicable to the person being rated. In the developmental phase of a check list, the results of the ratings are somewhat difficult to interpret beyond the qualitative descriptiveness inherent in the group of words and terms used to describe any one person. However, study of the individual check list items compared with widespread criterion groups can result in a check list instrument which can be scored by weighted items just as a test.

Forced Choice Rating Method (117).   Under this method each of a series of rating items consists of three or four descriptive words or phrases. The rater is asked to select two phrases from each item—the one which is most descriptive of the subject, and the one which is least descriptive. The composition of the phrases in the various items may be varied so that some of the items contain all complimentary phrases and some of the items contain all derogatory phrases. With this method, interpretation of the rating results must be based on a pre-validation of the choice alternatives against an intensive criterion study or a widespread group criterion. Originally developed for evaluation of officers in the armed services, this technique is finding ever-increasing acceptance in other situations and shows much promise. By concealing the true import of the various evaluations from the rater, it helps to avoid the typical rating problems of "halo" effect and lenient tendency described below.

Narrative Description. As implied by the title, the rater is asked to write a free narrative description of the ratee. For instance, a supervisor might be told that one of his men was being considered for promotional transfer to another job and department. Either orally, or in written form, the supervisor might be asked to report "what he thinks of this man—his attitudes and abilities."

Difficulties Inherent in Ratings as Measurements

Ideally the rater should act as an objective, impartial judge, considering separately and distinctly each of the ratee traits to be measured. Actually, raters often fail to meet this ideal for two similar reasons: (1) If the rater's overall impression of the ratee is high (or low) he may be influenced to rate most of all traits accordingly in a nondiagnostic manner. (2) If the rater considers one trait as of paramount importance, he may tend to rate the other traits at about the same level as this one trait.

In either of these cases, the rater is, essentially, performing just one rating rather than the several separate trait ratings desired. This difficulty is known as the "halo effect" (*16*).

Another difficulty of rating systems specific to the descriptive methods is the reluctance of raters in general to rate a reasonable proportion of people in the lower descriptive categories. Often raters will rate all persons at and above the midpoint of a descriptive scale. This difficulty has been named "lenient tendency." Efforts to avoid lenient tendency, such as forced distribution (for instance, requiring raters to rate 10-20-40-20-10 percent respectively at each of the degrees on a five-point scale), merely result in what is essentially a relative and not a descriptive method.

The Spearman-Brown Prophecy Formula

The saying, "Two heads are better than one," or the saying, "There is safety in numbers," seems to express a kind of logic applicable to ratings. Considering the fallibility of ratings discussed above, it would seem unwarranted to conclude very much about a person from one rater's judgments of that person. If, however, two or more individuals have rated the person in question, then comparisons can be made to determine how closely the raters agree. If the raters agree with each other, the person interpreting the ratings will have more confidence in the ratings. If the raters disagree, the rating score which best expresses a single evaluation of the ratee is the arithmetic average of the several ratings.

The amount of confidence which can be placed in the rating results is, then, considerably increased when several raters are used rather than one or two. This makes sense when it is considered that biases of individual raters tend to be canceled out when averaging several ratings, and that such an average would be the best possible single score to express a person's "true" score.

The amount of agreement in ratings is usually expressed as a correlational coefficient of reliability. A general expression of the amount of agreement between raters may be obtained by taking various pairs of raters who have rated the same men and correlating their ratings. The general expression of reliability of the rating of one rater would then be obtained by taking an average of these coefficients.

The Spearman-Brown formula implements mathematically the observation made above that the mean rating of a group of raters will be more reliable than a single rating. Using the average correlation between two individual raters, the Spearman-Brown formula makes it possible to predict rather accurately the correlation between the average ratings of two groups of raters of any given size. Empirical tests of this formula have been made by predicting the reliability of the average ratings of a group of raters—then actually having two groups of raters rate the subjects and correlating the average ratings of the two groups (*65, 103, 108*). These studies lead to the conclusion that the reliability of averaged judgments increases directly with the number of judges according to the Spearman-Brown formula, assuming only that the added judges are comparable to the original judges in terms of ability to rate.

RATINGS IN PRACTICE

Teacher Ratings by Students

An example serving to illustrate the use of rating scales is found in the series of studies of teacher effectiveness via ratings by students, under Remmers. Since it generally is agreed that the learner's attitudes are of primary importance in the effective learning of skills, knowledge interests, and ideals in school, these and other similar studies become of considerable importance in exploring the attitude dynamics of the teaching situation.

Most frequently, graphic scales were used in the measurements of attitudes. For instance, in the Purdue Rating Scale for Instruction ten scales are used to measure the classroom characteristics of the instructor.

1. Interest in subject
2. Sympathetic attitude toward students
3. Fairness in grading
4. Liberal and progressive attitude
5. Presentation of subject matter
6. Sense of proportion and humor
7. Self-reliance and confidence
8. Personal peculiarities
9. Personal appearance
10. Stimulating intellectual curiosity

Sixteen additional items measure attitudes toward other aspects of the learning situation, such as:

11. Suitability of the method or methods by which subject matter of the course is presented
12. Suitability of the size of the class
13. The degree to which the objectives of the course were clarified and discussed
14. The agreement between the announced objectives of the course and what was actually taught
15. Suitability of the reference materials available for the course
16. Suitability of the laboratory facilities available for the course
17. Suitability of the assigned textbook
18. The use made of tests as aids to learning
19. Amount of freedom allowed students in the selection of the materials to be studied
20. How the course is fulfilling your needs
21. Range of ability in the class
22. Suitability of the amount and type of assigned outside work
23. The weight given to tests in determining the final grade for the course
24. Coördination of the tests with the major objectives of the course
25. Frequency of tests
26. The overall rating of the instructor

Findings in several of these studies illustrate the value of the rating approach. One of the early studies (104) demonstrates that students' judgments are quite stable and reliable. Another study (36) throws light on an old controversy by demonstrating that ratings of instructors do not vary significantly as between alumni (with their more mature perspective) and current students. Still another study (102) finds that the grades of individual students have little influence on their ratings of the instructor. Teachers are found to be able to improve their teaching and consequently their ratings by students as a result of their studying student ratings of themselves (131). Findings in one study (40) suggest that certain teachers are likely to be more successful with classes of high ability level students, and that other teachers are likely to be more successful with lower ability level students—viewed both in light of student ratings and student achievement.

Thus, ratings are illustrated as a method contributing to the study of the dynamics of situations and also as contributing suggestions and supporting evidence for corrective practice in those situations. The reader will not find it difficult to draw parallels between these studies and other situations in which similar techniques might be used beneficially, such as evaluations of supervisors by employees, ratings of salesmen by shoppers or customers, and so on.

A point worthy of note regarding the rating of superiors by subordinates is that usually a fairly large number of persons may be used to rate each person being evaluated. This fact contributes in large part to the very satisfactory reliabilities of mean ratings reported in these studies.

With respect to our consideration of rating scales, it is interesting and significant to note that one of the first rating scales devised to measure the competence of academic administrators in terms of subordinates' judgments ("a worm's-eye view," in the words of the Editorial Foreword) can be described as being both authoritative and exhaustive. "Some Psychological Dimensions of Academic Administrators" (58), an unpublished doctoral thesis at Purdue University which concerns itself with this problem, has been condensed and published (59) by the Division of Educational Reference of Purdue University. This study may be summarized as follows.

A rating scale was prepared which enables subordinates to evaluate administrators in the following areas: (1) intellectual balance, (2) emotional balance, (3) administrative leadership, (4) administrative planning, (5) use of funds, (6) capacity for work, (7) accomplishment, (8) relationship with subordinates, (9) public relations, and (10) social responsibility.

This scale was first tested on administrators in many of Indiana's institutions of higher learning, and the obtained data was found to be statistically reliable and valid. The scale establishes norms whereby an administrator may discover not only his own relative strengths and weaknesses, but also his status with respect to his peers.

The writer concludes that while the instrument was not designed as a device for correcting administrative weaknesses, it is highly useful for discovering and identifying them. The fact that it can be used in almost any situation where an appraisal of administrators by subordinates is desirable suggests that its potentiality as a tool for upgrading administrative services is large. In addition to the other results three central factors (59) within the scale were revealed by a factor analysis.

Rupe (112) undertook a study to measure the effectiveness of business and industrial executives as judged by their immediate subordinates. This information about himself could be used by the executive for self-improvement or for the improvement of understanding between himself and his employees. The Purdue Rating Scale for Executives was used to measure this effectiveness, and the findings were compared with a prior study by Hobson (58) with academic administrators.

Two factors common to various traits of business and industrial executives, as determined by this study, were (1) social responsibility to subordinates and society and (2) executive achievement. Although the factors found by Rupe and by Hobson (59) have been named differently by the two writers, similarities of factor patterns are striking. The similarities between business and industrial executives and academic administrators were found to be much greater than their dissimilarities, thus making it possible to use the same subordinate-executive rating scale for both groups.

This scale does not give all the answers that might be desired concerning executive ability. It does provide an executive who wishes it an honest and anonymous appraisal of his effectiveness as seen by his subordinates. It permits him to compare these appraisals with those of other executives and provides a means of arriving at information which will highlight areas of strength and weakness which are difficult to survey in any other way.

Kirk (*66*) applied the scale constructed by Remmers and Hobson to a national sample of eighty-eight elementary and secondary school administrators, who were rated by 1153 of their subordinates. He used the Horst (*60*) method of summing averages to determine the reliability which proved to be 0.66. The single-item reliabilities ranged from 0.399 to 0.799. From this study, he concluded that this scale was less reliable for public school administrators than for college administrators. The distributions of the ratings were significantly skewed to the left, and there were several statistically significant differences in variability in ratings on items when compared to Hobson's (*58*) findings.

Use of Rating Scales—Summary

Rating scales and rating systems, after all, are only processes of systematizing human judgments, and are not measuring instruments in themselves. Rather, the rater becomes the measuring instrument. The results of ratings can be no better than the ability and inclination of the rater to make accurately discriminatory judgments. Thus the training and motivation of the raters (*5, 37*) is an integral part of a successful system of rating.

Since ratings are a mixture of measurement of ratee traits with the projection of rater attitudes and biases the results are somewhat difficult to interpret. If, for example, a number of raters agree that a certain ratee is very coöperative, then the best conclusion is that the ratings are accurately descriptive of the ratee. If, however, the raters do not agree, then two possibilities may account for the disagreement: (1) That some of the raters have projected themselves into the rating, thus erring in their appraisals (this is the most frequent assumption, although not necessarily the most logical one); (2) that the ratees actually evidence different degrees of a trait in different situations and in working with different people.

Since typical rating systems exhibit considerable disagreement among raters, the difficulty of explaining this disagreement or of interpreting the results acts often as a deterrent to effective use of rating plans. When, however, the traits to be measured are of great importance and no other measurements are available, the use of systematic ratings is almost always to be preferred to the resort to random unsystematic judgments.

EMPATHY

What Is Empathy?

The concept of empathy is not a new one, but it has within perhaps the last decade gained the attention of scholars as a highly important attitude and personality factor. The concept is believed to have had its scientific origin with Lipps (70) who, in his studies in aesthetic appreciation, proposed the systematic theory of *Einfühlung*. Although the scientific concept has its origin coinciding with the beginning of the twentieth century, many of our great men of literature, art, music, and the theater have given expression to the ideas underlying the concept in the centuries long past. Mozart, in his beloved music, emphasized the feeling of the court in his stately minuets with only an underlying pathètique of the man himself.

> "Oh wad some power the giftie gie us
> To see oursilves as ithers see us!
> It wad frae mony a blunder free us
> And foolish notion."

Robert Burns calls for the "giftie," the secret of which may well lie within the study and development of the concept of empathy. It seems fitting that the scientific concept of empathy had its birth in the study of aesthetic appreciation.

Empathy is the ability to place oneself in the place of another individual so as to be in a position to predict and become aware of the other's attitudes, behavioral characteristics, and emotionality. Empathy appears to be the ability to perceive cues related to another's basic attitude structure. Webster's *Dictionary* gives this definition "Empathy: Imaginative projection of one's own consciousness into another being." Warren's *Dictionary of Psychology* defines it: "1. (esth.) The imaginal or mental projection of oneself into the elements of a work of art or into a natural object; 2. (psychoan.) a mental state in which one identifies or feels himself in the same state of mind as another person or group."

Projection and Empathy

Projection, a word used in both definitions quoted, is usually defined in introductory textbooks in psychology as the felt need for and process of blaming one's own shortcomings on persons or agencies outside of and beyond the control of oneself. The veteran student tends to justify his failure on an examination because of time lost in school while in the service of his country. The adolescent girl tends to blame her lack of popularity on the parental restrictions placed on her. These are examples of "projection" in this sense. Another use of the word, with a different theoretical frame of reference, is apparent in "projective techniques."

In order for both terms, empathy and projection, to be useful semantic referents, it becomes necessary to discriminate operationally between them. Where does empathy end and projection begin in the sense of attributing to others characteristics which they may or may not actually possess? Remmers (*105*) proposes an operational, quantitative index that will discriminate between them and provide more precise semantic referents for each. "Let us use the term 'empathy' when the individual's or group's measured position on one or more defined psychological dimensions is (within allowable error of measurement) the same as that estimated for the individual or group by another individual or group. Let us use the term 'projection' when there is a really significant difference between the measurement and the estimate, so that we know that two different mental functions are operating."

Studies in Empathy

Experiments by Travers (*125, 126, 127*) in the ability of individuals to judge group opinions, experiments on "faking" vocational-interest test scores (*11, 18, 72*) and scores on "personality" tests or adjustment inventories (*77, 120*) are obviously studies to determine an individual's ability to predict another individual's or group's response or score, where these responses or scores are defined, or are later defined, by a score key or norms for the instruments in question.

In a study by Northaker (*92*) testing the teachers' ability to predict the response of high school pupils to a variety of items in the Purdue Opinion Poll for Young People, she sets the ground work for testing the hypothesis suggested by Remmers (*105*), "Teachers' ability to empathize with their pupils, especially in the interpersonal areas freighted with attitudes, when measured will be found to be an important factor in the teachers' influence upon personality development of pupils." Evidence pointing in this direction may be found in studies by Carter (*24*) and Remmers (*109*). If this hypothesis can be substantiated, it should provide an important basis for training, selection, placement, and guidance of teachers.

A technique of measuring reciprocal empathy was developed by Remmers (*105*) while working on an experimental design to test procedures for reducing the "gap" between management and labor. Using the same technique a number of students (*31, 109, 120*) at Purdue University have completed studies concerning reciprocal empathy in widely separated problems. The technique suggested by Remmers (*105*) and used in this group of studies consists in having an individual or group, *A*, answer a set of relevant attitude questions. *A* is then asked to give the response that he would expect from another individual or group, *B*. *A* is asked to respond a third time to this same set of questions as he would expect *B* to predict *A*'s response to these questions. *B* is then subjected to the same procedures.

In the studies referred to here, only the first two responses were required.

Anikeeff (4), working with a national high school sample, obtained results indicating that empathy was greatest in the relationship between attitudes ascribed to a group by (1) an out-group and (2) the group itself. Since the study was concerned with groups in social conflict, it was concluded that a standard stereotype of attitude classification was being used. This stereotype tended to cut across group-conflict boundaries within the culture.

In a study in industrial empathy by Remmers and Remmers (109), devised to arrive at a comparison of labors' and managements' attitudes toward supervision, a copy of *How Supervise?* (45), together with a Personal Data Sheet and an explanatory letter, was mailed to 150 labor leaders. The response was excellent, the ultimate returns amounting to two-thirds of the original list. No compensation was offered other than a promise to send each subject his score if desired, so response was entirely voluntary.

For the second part of the study the 100 labor leaders who participated were requested to fill out an additional copy of *How Supervise?* as they felt a "typical company man" would do so. No remuneration was offered, and forty-two of the original 100 responded. A later study of management was planned to follow.

From this study it was concluded that understanding of the psychologically "best" supervisory methods in industry is greater among union leaders than among industrial management. The younger labor leaders tended to have the higher scores in *How Supervise?* These scores did not seem to be related to formal education, or to supervisory experience in industry. Labor leaders tended to stereotype management and regarded management as possessing relatively less understanding of good supervisory attitudes and methods than it actually does. Labor leaders scored significantly higher than they scored management.

A subsequent study by Miller and Remmers (*78*) was the obverse of the one just discussed. The attitudes of a sample of management were measured, as well as their estimates of how labor leaders and rank-and-file workers would answer items of the test. The procedure resolved itself into three parts: (1) Each subject was given two sets of the same form of *How Supervise?* with instructions to take the first test using his own opinion. (2) The subject was asked to mark an "x" over the answer on the second test which he felt a typical labor leader would give, and (3) to encircle the answer which he thought a typical member of the labor rank and file would give.

Analysis of the data indicated that management on the average tended to overestimate labor leaders' scores on the test or, in other words, the average person in management attributed better supervisory attitudes to labor leaders than the available facts warrant. Furthermore labor leaders on the average tended to underestimate management's scores on the test—they attributed worse supervisory attitudes to management than the available facts justify. Since there was a lack of norms on the test for labor rank-and-file members, it was only possible to infer that management on the average does not underestimate laborer's attitudes, but this inference will require further experimental verification.

These studies clearly illustrate that here we have a method for providing additional insight into the nature of labor-management, or any other tension situation conflicts.

A similar technique for the measurement of the ability to empathize has been developed by Dymond (*39*). Her measure of empathy becomes a measure of how close an individual can predict another individual's self-rating. It is also a measure of how close an individual can predict how another individual will rate him. These two abilities to predict serve as measures of empathy, either indicated by accurate prediction or by extent of deviation or error in prediction. The ratings are done on six scales of five points each. These scales are on extent of feeling superior, friendly, leader tendency, shyness, sympathy, and security. Both members of the pair complete these ratings. Dymond points out the close relationship between the ability to empathize optimism, outgoing personality structure, and warm emotionality.

Empathy in general, and reciprocal empathy in particular, may provide clues to the important central element in social facilitation and/or conflict. This may well hold every promise of being the "giftie" of Robert Burns: "to see oursilves as ithers see us!"

ERROR-CHOICE OR DIRECTION OF PERCEPTION

Another promising indirect attitude measurement technique is that of error-choice (54, 132, 133) or the direction of perception technique (13). Hammond (54) suggested that attitudes can be indirectly measured by the bias shown in answering a mixture of factual and nonfactual questions concerning a given topic or issue. In so far as the respondent is unaware of the true intent of the questions, they provide a structured projective technique that, like other projective techniques, minimizes attitude test set. Examples of "nonfactual" items from Hammond's "Information" Test follow.

Financial reports show that out of every dollar (1) 16¢, (2) 3¢, is profit.
Man-days lost because of strikes from January to June, 1946, were (1) 34.5 million, (2) 98.6 million.
Most unions have fees (1) over, (2) under, $35.
There (1) is, (2) is not, freedom of religion in Russia.

Wechsler (132) constructed an error-choice inventory under the guise of an information test on labor-management relations with certain errors designed to elicit constant errors due to known bias. Its administration to 186 university students yielded results as hypothesized. Income, political preference, and labor affiliation were related to inventory scores, but age and sex were not.

In a subsequent study Wechsler (*133*) administered a revised form of the Labor Relations Information Test to a group of advanced university students and a sample of management people, labor union officials and members, and labor mediators. He points out that error-choice, when applied to labor-management problems, while a good attitude measurement technique, would have to be constantly revised to take cognizance of the latest developments in labor relations. He includes suggestions for avoiding methodological mistakes in further error-choice measurement.

Sample questions from Wechsler's "Labor Relations Information Inventory" follow.

1. *Factual Information Items.*
   In 1948, the majority of strikes were caused by issues over (*a*) collective bargaining terms of existing agreements, (*b*) union recognition.
2. *Nonfactual Error-Choice Items.*
   During April of 1948, the coal and meat strikes increased the number of workdays lost through voluntary stoppage to (*a*) 10 million workdays, (*b*) 6 million workdays.
   Correct answer: 8 million workdays.
   During the strike wave of April, 1948, the percent of estimated working time lost was (*a*) 1.1%, (*b*) 2.2%.
   Correct answer: 1.6%.
   The 1948 increases in the price of steel were: (*a*) proportional to the union's wage gains, (*b*) comparatively greater than the union's wage gains.
   Correct answer: Not accessible.

GENERAL CLASSIFICATION AND METHODS

An interesting classification of indirect approaches to the measurement of attitudes has been devised by Campbell (*23*).

1. Nondisguised-structured: the classic direct attitude tests of Thurstone, Likert, *et al.*
2. Nondisguised-nonstructured: the free-response interview and questionnaire approaches the biographical and essay studies.
3. Disguised-nonstructured: the typical projective techniques.

4. Disguised-structured: tests which approximate the objective testing of attitudes.

Further, Campbell suggests that any number of methods
of indirect measurement of attitudes may be developed by
following the general procedure below:

First, take *a plausible task:*
a. which your respondents will all strive to do well.
b. which is sufficiently difficult or ambiguous to allow individual
differences in response.
c. which can be loaded with content relative to the attitude which
you seek to measure.
Next, test the responses of individuals for persistent selectivity
in performance, for correlated or nonrandom errors.

Measurements conforming to this developmental approach
should be useful in the analysis of attitudes.

The generality of Campbell's requirements may suggest to
the reader the wide scope of the field of possible attitude measurement techniques.

SUMMARY

In this chapter we have reviewed the techniques which have
been devised to effect the relatively indirect measurement of
attitudes. Seven areas have been explored: (1) word association, a method which utilizes the subject's response to a
selected list of key words or phrases; (2) visual stimulus, which,
as the term implies uses pictures or diagrams to secure emotionally toned responses from the subject; (3) expressive
movement, a technique predicated upon the assumption that
attitudes are revealed and may be analyzed from overt behavior
of the subject (such as handwriting, gait, etc.); (4) play, drama,
and related techniques which permit and encourage the subject to project his emotional predisposition into a situation
where the subject's emotions may be more readily identified
and analyzed either by the examiner or the subject, or both;
(5) intragroup attitude measurement, a fairly comprehensive

area of research in itself, concerned with measuring attitudes by requiring the individual to choose other individuals within his functioning social groups either as desirable or undesirable members of that group with respect to certain criteria; (6) rating scales, one of the earlier and still widely used tools for measuring attitudes of the individual, which are based upon some variation of a continuum of values; and (7) other techniques which have been developed to achieve the same purposes as previously described procedures, but which, for one reason or another, could not readily be classified under one of the preceding headings.

Despite this seeming wealth of methodology which has been and is being devised to measure attitudes, the reader is cautioned against the unwarranted assumption that the indirect measurement of attitudes is now an exact science. While it is true that an excellent beginning has been made, existing techniques must be refined, standardized, and elaborated before the practicing psychologist can, with any degree of assurance, answer the basic question which underlies all research in psychology, "Why do we behave as we do?"

Questions

1. Can you think of any way of measuring the amount of halo effect in ratings?
2. Is the criticism valid that the Rorschach results cannot be statistically analyzed? If so, does it rule out the method as a valid aid in diagnosing maladjustments?
3. What is it that is projected in projective techniques?
4. What are the psychoanalytic concepts that are the foundation for projective techniques?
5. For a child who cannot verbally respond to a situation is it reasonable to hypothesize that relatively unstructured projective techniques are more valid as attitude measurements than are structured situations?
6. How would you operationally differentiate among the concepts of empathy, identification, and projection?
7. In a rating experiment the intercorrelations of the "traits" were

not significantly lower than the reliabilities (self-correlations) of the traits. What can you conclude from this?

8. Construct a sociometric device to measure who of a group of fifty would work best together as a committee of five.

Bibliography

1. Adams, H. F., "The Good Judge of Personality," *J. abnorm. soc. Psychol.*, 1927, *22*:172-181.
2. Allport, G. W., and Cantril, H., "Judging Personality from the Voice," *J. soc. Psychol.*, 1934, *5*:37-55.
3. Allport, G. W., and Vernon, P. E., *Studies in Expressive Movement*, New York: The Macmillan Company, 1933.
4. Anikeeff, A. M., "Reciprocal Empathy: Mutual Understanding Among Conflict Groups," *Purdue University Studies in Higher Education*, 1951, no. 77:11-48.
5. Argelander, A., "The Personal Factor in Judging Human Character," *Character & Pers.*, 1937, *5*:285-295.
6. Armstrong, R. O., "Talking Your Ratings," *Personnel*, 1943, *20*:112-115.
7. Bales, R. F., *Interaction Process Analysis*, Cambridge: Addison-Wesley, 1950.
8. Belinski, H. S., "Developing Effective Service Ratings," *Person. Admin.* 1940, *3*:5-10.
9. Bell, J. E., *Projective Techniques: A Dynamic Approach to the Study of Personality*, New York: Longmans, Green & Co., Inc., 1948.
10. Bender, L., "A Visual-Motor Gestalt Test and Its Clinical Use," *Res. Monogr. Amer. orthopsychiat. Ass.*, 1938, *3*.
11. Benton, A. L., and Kornhauser, G. I., "A Study of 'Score Taking' on a Mechanical Interest Test," *J. Amer. Med. Coll.*, 1948, *23*:57-60.
12. Berger, E., "Der Sandersche Phantasietest im Rahmen der psychologischen Eignungs-Untersuchung Jugendlicher," *Arch. ges. Psychol.*, 1907, *14*:137-207.
13. Bernberg, R. E., "The Direction of Perception Technique of Attitude Measurement," *Int. J. opin. attit. Res.*, 1951, 5(no. 3):397-406.
14. Bills, M. A., "A Method for Classifying the Jobs and Rating

the Efficiency of Clerical Workers," *J. Person. Res.*, December-January, 1922-1923, *1*:384-393.

15. Binet, A., *Les Revelations de l'ecriture d'apres une controle scientifique*, Paris: F. Alcan, 1906.

16. Bingham, W. V., "Halo, Invalid and Valid," *J. appl. Psychol.*, 1939, *23*:221-228.

17. Bingham, W. V., and Moore, B. V., *How to Interview*, New York: Harper & Brothers, 1941.

18. Bordin, E. S., "A Theory of Vocational Interests as Dynamic Phenomena," *Educ. & psychol. Meas.*, 1943, *3*:49-65.

19. Boring, E. G., *A History of Experimental Psychology*, New York: Appleton-Century-Crofts, Inc., 1929, 441.

20. Bronfenbrenner, U., "The Graphic Presentation of Sociometric Data," *Sociometry*, 1944, 7:283-289.

21. Bühler, C., and Kelley, G., *The World Test. A Measurement of Emotional Disturbance*, New York: Psychological Corporation, 1941.

22. Burtt, H. E., *Principles of Employment Psychology*, New York: Harper & Brothers, 1942, 450-474.

23. Campbell, D. T., "The Indirect Assessment of Social Attitudes," *Psychol. Bull.*, 1950, *47*(no. 1):15-38.

24. Carter, Gerald Clayton, "Student Personalities as Instructors See Them," *Purdue University Studies in Higher Education*, 1945, no. 54.

25. Charters, W. W., and Waples, D., *The Commonwealth Teacher Training Study*, Chicago: University of Chicago Press, 1929.

26. Conrad, H. S., "The Personal Equation in Ratings: A Systematic Evaluation," *J. educ. Psychol.*, 1933, *24*:39-46.

27. Criswell, Joan H., "Sociometric Methods of Measuring Group Preferences," *Sociometry*, 1943, *6*:398-408.

28. Criswell, Joan H., "Note on Seeman's Approach to Intra-Group Negro Attitudes," *Sociometry*, 1946, *9*:207-209.

29. Criswell, Joan H., "The Measurement of Group Interaction," *Sociometry*, 1947, *10*:259-267.

30. Criswell, Joan H., "Foundations of Sociometric Measurement," *Sociometry*, 1949, *9*:7-13.

31. Davidoff, M. D., "A Study of Empathy and Correlates of

Prejudice Toward a Minority Group," Unpublished Ph.D. Thesis, Purdue University, 1948.

32. Diamond, B. L., and Schmale, H. T., "The Mosaic Test: 1. An Evaluation of Its Clinical Application," *Amer. J. Orthopsychiat.*, 1944, *14*:237-250.

33. Dorcus, Roy M., "Methods of Evaluating the Efficiency of Door-to-Door Salesmen of Bakery Products," *J. appl. Psychol.*, 1940, *24*:587-594.

34. Downey, J. E., *Graphology and the Psychology of Handwriting*, Baltimore: Warwick & York, 1919.

35. Driver, R. S., "Training as a Means of Improving Employee Performance Rating," *Personnel*, May, 1942, *18*:364-370.

36. Drucker, A. J., and Remmers, H. H., "Do Alumni and Students Differ in Their Attitudes?" *Purdue University Studies in Higher Education: Further Studies in Attitudes Series* XV, 1950, no. 71:62-74.

37. Drury, Lynn B., "Selecting Employees for Advancement," *Person. J.*, 1941, *20*:166-171.

38. Dubin, S. S., "Verbal Attitude Scores Predicted from Responses in a Projective Technique," *Sociometry*, 1940, *3*:24-48.

39. Dymond, R. F., "Personality and Empathy," *J. consult. Psychol.*, 1950, *14*(no. 5):343-350.

40. Elliott, D. N., and Remmers, H. H., "Characteristics and Relationships of Various Criteria of College and University Teaching," *Purdue University Studies in Higher Education: Further Studies in Attitudes Series* XV, 1950, no. 70:5-61.

41. Eng, Erling, and French, R. L., "The Determination of Sociometric Status," *Sociometry*, 1948, *11*:368-371.

42. Eron, L. D., "A Normative Study of the Thematic Apperception Test," *Psychol. Monogr.*, 1950, *64*:1-48.

43. Eysenck, H. J., "A Comparative Study of Four Screening Tests for Neurotics," *Psychol. Bull.*, 1945, *42*:659-662.

44. Fear, R. A., and Jordan, B., *Employee Evaluation Manual for Interviewers*, New York: Psychological Corporation, 1943.

45. File, Q. W., "The Measurement of Supervisory Quality in Industry," *J. appl. Psychol.*, 1945, *29*:323-337.

46. Forsyth, E., and Katz, L., "A Matrix Approach to the Analysis of Sociometric Data," *Sociometry*, 1946, *9*:340-347.

47. Frankel, E. B., and Potashin, R., "A Survey of Sociometric Literature on Friendship and Social Acceptance Among Children," *Sociometry*, 1944, 7:422-431.

48. Freyd, M., "A Graphic Rating Scale for Teachers," *J. educ. Res.*, 1923, 8:433-439.

49. Fuller, S. E., "Goodyear Aircraft Employee Counseling," *Person. J.*, October, 1944, 23:145-153; November, 1944, 23:176-185.

50. Galton, F., *Inquiries into Human Faculty and Its Development*, London: Macmillan & Co., Ltd., 1885, 182-302.

51. Greene, E. B., *Measurement of Human Behavior*, New York: The Odyssey Press, Inc., 1941, 691-713.

52. Grings, W. W., "The Verbal Summator Technique and Abnormal Mental States," *J. abnorm. soc. Psychol.*, 1942, 37:529-545.

53. Guilford, J. P., *Psychometric Methods*, New York: McGraw-Hill Book Company, Inc., 1936.

54. Hammond, K. R., "Measuring Attitudes by Error-Choice: An Indirect Method," *J. abnorm. soc. Psychol.*, 1948, 43:38-48.

55. Harrower-Erickson, M. R., and Steiner, M. E., "Modification of the Rorschach Method for Use as a Group Test," *Rorschach Res. Exch.*, 1941, 5:130-144.

56. Hellersberg, E. F., "The Horn-Hellersberg Test and Adjustment to Reality," *Amer. J. Orthopsychiat.*, 1945, 15:690-710.

57. Herzog, Elizabeth G., "Pending Perfection: A Qualitative Complement to Quantitative Methods," *Int. J. opin. attit. Res.*, 1947, 1:31-48.

58. Hobson, Robert L., "Some Psychological Dimensions of Academic Administrators," unpublished Ph.D. Thesis, Purdue University, 1948.

59. Hobson, Robert L., "Some Psychological Dimensions of Academic Administrators." Published with Rupe, Jesse C., "Some Psychological Dimensions of Business and Industrial Executives," *Purdue University Studies in Higher Education*, 1950, no. 73.

60. Horst, P., "A Generalized Expression for the Reliability of Measures," *Psychometrika*, 1949, 14(no. 1):21-31.

61. Hull, C. L., and Montgomery, R. P., "Experimental Investi-

gation of Certain Alleged Relations Between Character and Handwriting," *Psychol. Rev.*, 1919, *26*:63-74.

62. Jennings, H. H., *Leadership and Isolation*, New York: Longmans, Green & Co., Inc., 1947.

63. Katz, L., "On the Metric Analysis of Sociometric Data," *Sociometry*, 1947, *10*:233-241.

64. Kelley, T. L., "The Applicability of the Spearman-Brown Formula for the Measurement of Reliability," *J. educ. Psychol.*, 1931, *22*:66-71.

65. Kelley, E. L., Miles, C. C., and Terman, L. M., "Ability to Influence One's Score on a Typical Pencil and Paper Test of Personality," *Character & Pers.*, 1936, *4*:206-215.

66. Kirk, R. B., "A Study of Subordinates' Attitudes Toward Public School Administrators," Unpublished Master's Thesis, Purdue University, 1950.

67. Kneeland, Natalie, "That Lenient Tendency in Rating," *Person. J.*, 1929, *7*:356-366.

68. Knight, F. B., "Qualities Related to Success in Teaching," *Teach. Coll. Contr. Educ.*, 1922, no. 120:68.

69. Levy, David M., "Hostility Patterns in Sibling Rivalry Experiments," *Amer. J. Orthopsychiat.*, 1936, *6*:183-258.

70. Lipps, Theodor, "Das Wissen von Fremden Ichen," *Psychologische Untersuchungen*, 1907, *1*:694-722.

71. Longmore, T. W., "A Matrix Approach to the Analysis of Rank and Status in a Community in Peru," *Sociometry*, 1948, *11*:192-206.

72. Longstaff, H. P., "Fakability of the Strong Interest Blank and the Kuder Preference Record," *J. appl. Psychol.*, 1948, *32*(no. 4):360-369.

73. Loomis, C. P., "Ethnic Cleavages in the Southwest as Reflected in Two High Schools," *Sociometry*, 1943, *6*:7-26.

74. Loomis, C. P., and Pepinsky, H. B., "Sociometry 1937-1947: Theory and Methods," *Sociom. Monogr.*, 1949, *20*:1-27.

75. Lord, Edith, "Experimentally Induced Variations in Rorschach Performance," *Psychol. Monogr.*, 1950, *64*:1-31.

76. Löwenfeld, M., "The World Pictures of Children," *Brit. J. med. Psychol.*, 1939, *18*:65-101.

77. Meehl, P. E., and Hathaway, S. R., "The *D* Factor as a

Suppressor Variable in the Minnesota Multiphasic Inventory," *J. appl. Psychol.*, 1946, *30*:525-564.

78. Miller, F. G., and Remmers, H. H., "Studies in Industrial Empathy: II. Managements' Attitudes Toward Industrial Supervision and Their Estimates of Labor Attitudes," *Person. Psychol.*, 1950, *3*:33-40.

79. Moreno, J. L., *Who Shall Survive? A New Approach to the Problem of Human Inter-Relations*, Washington, D.C.: Nervous and Mental Disease Publishing Co., 1934.

80. Moreno, J. L., *Psychodrama*, New York: Beacon House, Inc., 1946, vols. I–III.

81. Moreno, J. L., "Sociogram and Sociomatrix, A Note to the Paper by Forsyth," *Sociometry*, 1946, *9*:348-349.

82. Moreno, J. L., *The Theatre of Spontaneity*, New York: Beacon House, Inc., 1947.

83. Moreno, J. L., and Jennings, H. H., "Sociometric Measurement of Social Configurations," *Sociom. Monogr.*, 1945, *3*.

84. Moreno, J. L., and Jennings, H. H., "Time as a Measure of Inter-Personal Relations," *Sociom. Monogr.* 1947, *13*.

85. Moreno, J. L., and others, "Discussion of Sociometry: Symposium," *Sociometry*, 1943, *6*:197-344.

86. Morgan, C. D., and Murray, H. A., "A Method for Investigating Phantasies, the Thematic Apperception Test," *Arch. Neurol. Psychiat.*, 1935, *34*:289-306.

87. Murphy, G., and Likert, R., *Public Opinion and the Individual*, New York: Harper & Brothers, 1938.

88. Murphy, L. B., *Social Behavior and Child Personality*, New York: Columbia University Press, 1937.

89. Murray, H. A., "Techniques for Systematic Investigation of Fantasy," *J. Psychol.*, 1937, *3*:115-143.

90. Murray, H. A., *Explorations in Personality*, New York: Oxford University Press, 1938.

91. Napoli, P. J., "Finger Painting and Personality Diagnosis," *Genet. Psychol. Monogr.*, 1946, *34*:129-231.

92. Northaker, Patricia, "Attitudinal Empathy of a Defined Population I," Unpublished Master's Thesis, Purdue University, 1949.

93. Northway, M. L., "A Method for Depicting Social Relation-

ships Obtained by Sociometric Testing," *Sociometry*, 1940, *3*:144-150.

94. Northway, M. L., and Potashin, R., "Instructions for Using the Sociometric Test," *Sociometry*, 1946, *9*:242-248.

95. Oppenheimer, F. Pamela, "A Case Study in Status Symbols," *J. abnorm. soc. Psychol.*, 1945, *40*:187-194.

96. Payne, H. F., *Sentence Completions*, New York: New York Guidance Clinic, 1928.

97. Pear, T. H., *Voice and Personality*, London: Chapman & Hall, 1931.

98. Pickford, R. W., "Personality and the Interpretation of Pictures: A New Projection Technique," *J. Personality*, 1949, *17*:211-220.

99. Probst, J. B., *Service Ratings*, Chicago: Bureau of Public Personnel Administration and the Civil Service Assembly of U.S. and Canada, 1931.

100. Proshansky, H. M., "A Projective Method for the Study of Attitudes," *J. abnorm. soc. Psychol.*, 1943, *38*:393-395.

101. *Public Personnel Studies, Service Ratings*, Washington, D.C.: Bureau of Public Personnel Administration, Personnel Research Project, June, 1941, *10*:17-18.

102. Remmers, H. H., "To What Extent Do Grades Influence Student Ratings of Instructors?" *J. educ. Res.*, 1930, *21*:314-317.

103. Remmers, H. H., "The Equivalence of Judgments to Test Items in the Sense of the Spearman-Brown Formula," *J. educ. Psychol.*, 1931, *22*:66-71.

104. Remmers, H. H., "Reliability and Halo Effect of High School and College Students' Judgments of Their Teachers," *J. appl. Psychol.*, 1934, *18*:619-631.

105. Remmers, H. H., "A Quantitative Index of Social-Psychological Empathy," *Amer. J. Orthopsychiat.*, 1950, *20*:161-165.

106. Remmers, H. H., Series of Unpublished Lectures at Purdue University, 1950.

107. Remmers, H. H., "The College Professor as the Student Sees Him," *Purdue University Studies in Higher Education*, 1927, No. 11.

108. Remmers, H. H., Schock, N. W., and Kelley, E. L., "An Em-

pirical Study of the Validity of the Spearman-Brown Formula as Applied to the Purdue Rating Scale," *J. educ. Psychol.*, 1927, *18*:187-195.

109. Remmers, Lois J., and Remmers, H. H., "Labor Leaders' Attitudes Toward Industrial Supervision and Their Estimates of Managements' Attitude," *Person. Psychol.*, 1949, *2*:427-436.

110. Rorschach, H., *Psychodiagnostics* (trans. by P. Lemkau and B. Kronenburg), Bern: Huber, 1942.

111. Rosenzweig, S., *Rosenzweig P-F Study*, Pittsburgh: Western State Psychiatric Hospital, 1944.

112. Rupe, J. C., "Some Psychological Dimensions of Business and Industrial Executives," *Purdue University Studies in Higher Education*, 1950, no. 73.

113. Sanford, R. N., *Physique, Personality and Scholarship*, Washington, D.C.: National Research Council, 1943.

114. Seeman, M., "A Situational Approach to Intra-Group Negro Attitudes," *Sociometry*, 1946, *9*:199-206.

115. Shakow, D., Rodnick, E. H., and Lebeaux, T., "A Psychological Study of a Schizophrenic: Exemplification of a Method," *J. abnorm. soc. Psychol.*, 1945, *40*:154-175.

116. Shaw, R. F., *Finger Painting*, Boston: Little, Brown & Company, 1934.

117. Sisson, D. E., "Forced Choice—The New Army Rating," *Person. Psychol.*, 1948, *1*:365-381.

118. Skinner, B. F., "The Verbal Summator and a Method for the Study of Latent Speech," *J. Psychol.*, 1936, *2*:71-108.

119. Sower, C., "Social Stratification in Suburban Communities," *Sociometry*, 1948, *11*:235-243.

120. Steinmetz, Harry C., "A Study of the Ability to Predict Test Responses," Unpublished Ph.D. Thesis, Purdue University, 1947.

121. Stewart, F. A., "Some Sampling Problems in Sociometric Surveys," *Sociometry*, 1948, *11*:301-307.

122. Stewart, F. A., "An Interviewer's Report on Adult Sociometric Study," *Sociometry*, 1948, *11*:308-319.

123. Symonds, P. M., *Diagnosing Personality and Conduct*, New York: Appleton-Century-Crofts, Inc., 1931.

124. Tiffin, J. A., *Industrial Psychology,* New York: Prentice-Hall, Inc., 1947, 23-26.

125. Travers, R. M. W., "A Study in Judging the Opinions of Groups," *Arch. Psychol.,* New York, 1941, *266*:1-73.

126. Travers, R. M. W., "The General Ability to Judge Group Knowledge," *Amer. J. Psychol.,* 1943, *56*:95-99.

127. Travers, R. M. W., "A Study of the Ability to Judge Group Knowledge," *Amer. J. Psychol.,* 1943, *56*:54-65.

128. Uhrbrock, R. S., "Analysis of Employment Interviews," *Person. J.,* 1933, *12*:98-101.

129. U. S. Civil Service Commission, *Efficiency Rating Manual,* Washington, D.C.: Personnel Classification Division, Efficiency Ratings Administration Section, 1944.

130. Verville, F., "The Effect of Emotional and Motivational Sets in the Perception of Incomplete Pictures," *J. genet. Psychol.,* 1946, *69*:133-145.

131. Ward, W. D., and Remmers, H. H., "The Training of Teacher Personality by Means of Student Ratings," *Sch. & Sci.,* 1941, *53*:189-193.

132. Wechsler, I. R., "An Investigation of Attitudes Toward Labor and Management by Means of the Error-Choice Method: I," *J. soc. Psychol.,* 1950, *32*:51-62.

133. Wechsler, I. R., "A Follow-Up Study on the Measurement of Attitudes Toward Labor and Management by Means of the Error-Choice Method," *J. soc. Psychol.,* 1950, *32*:63-69.

134. Wertheimer, M., "Studies in the Theory of Gestalt Psychology," *Psychol. Forsch.,* 1923, *4*:300-350.

135. Wolff, W., "The Experimental Study of Forms of Expression," *Character & Pers.,* 1933, *2*:168-176.

136. Wolff, W., *The Expression of Personality,* New York: Harper & Brothers, 1943.

137. Wolff, W., "Involuntary Self-Expression in Gait and other Movements: An Experimental Study," *Character & Pers.,* 1935, *3*:327-344.

PART TWO

· · · • • • · ·

Applications of Opinion
and Attitude Measurement

CHAPTER VIII

...••●•...

Applications in Business

INTRODUCTION

In a competitive economy, the businessman is dependent upon the good will of the consumer. If the public attitude toward the company or its product is unfavorable, the company may find itself in the red. Few industries can be sure of their markets for an indefinite period. The businessman cannot afford merely to keep abreast of the times. If he is to be successful, he must anticipate the attitudes and wants of his customers; he must study his markets, his customers, and his competitors.

Business has been applying the techniques of attitude research to many of it problems for several decades. The field of advertising probably best exemplifies the most extensive application of psychological techniques to business. Copy research has endeavored to analyze the consumer, locate his weaknesses, and prepare advertising copy that will not only sell the product, but will keep customers buying a particular brand despite the enticements of competitors. Copy research has been concerned with what to say, how to say it, and the selection of the most effective media for reaching the consumer.

In recent years the application of psychological techniques in business has gone far beyond the limited sphere of copy research. A thriving industry known as market research has offered its services to business to help sell more goods to more customers. Its secret weapons have been techniques for finding out people's attitudes—what they want, how much they are willing to pay, and how extensive the market may be. Before a manufacturer invests his capital in a new product, he can make sure that it is an item that will sell. Before he builds up an inventory, or tries to distribute the product over a wide area, he makes use of the know-how of the market researcher to ascertain whether the product meets with public acceptance. The same know-how enables him to learn what changes the public wants, to what new uses the product may be put, where potential customers may be found.

The threat of competition makes it imperative that the businessman know how the public feels about his product and about his company. He must know whether he is gaining or losing ground in relation to his competitors. He must keep an eye to the future in order to know what people will want the day after tomorrow. If he has a heavy investment in radio, magazine, or direct mail advertising, he can't afford to base his advertising policy on guesswork. He wants to know whether his ads are being read or heard, by whom, and especially whether the ads really influence people to buy.

PRODUCT DEVELOPMENT

In our capitalist economy, profits are considered the reward for risking capital on new ventures. The businessman who opens a hot-dog stand and the man who thinks he has a better mousetrap seldom know in advance how the public will respond to their offerings. They may strike it rich or they may find that their venture is bankrupt.

To reduce the risk involved in new enterprises, many business firms have used market research to figure the odds before placing a heavy bet on some new product or service. Product development has become a special field of research, intended to ascertain in advance consumer attitudes, what specifications must be met, and whether the product that is finally offered is acceptable to the consumer.

Discovering needs is not always easy. The consumer's behavior must be studied closely to find out what items he is likely to buy. Researchers usually rely on interviews to ferret out product ideas. They talk to prospective customers, to users of competing products, and to people who have discontinued using the product. They try to find out what people like and what they do not like, what they would like to have if they could write their own specifications. This type of interviewing calls for special techniques and a special skill in guiding the respondent from general description, to negative criticism, and then on to positive, constructive criticism. The interviewer tries to learn what problems the consumer faces and what he thinks can be done about them. A housewife, for example, might be asked to describe in detail her daily routine. The interviewer may then probe to find out what the housewife considers difficult or distasteful about each task. It is from such raw materials that emerge the ideas for many of the kitchen gadgets that brighten the housewife's day.

To make sure of user acceptance of a new product, business has found it wise to subject the items to ordinary use by ordinary users. Frequently, merely showing the item to people is sufficient to find out whether it meets with general approval. More often, however, leaving the new product and one of its competing brands on the pantry shelf will give a more definitive answer. Callbacks will show which product the housewife likes best by noting the rate at which each box is consumed. At the end of the test period, the interviewer may offer to give the housewife another box of whichever brand she prefers. This method forces a choice between the two brands and shows their relative strength. The interviewer then tries to learn the reasons why the housewife preferred one brand over the other. He tries to ascertain the strong and weak points of the new product. He may discover, for example, that children are more favorable toward the new product than adults, or that women object to the package because it shows fingerprints too readily.

The attitudes expressed in such interviews provide the businessman or sales manager with important clues which will enable them to make revisions in the product design before they build up a large inventory. Such revisions may give the new product a competitive advantage. They know in advance what people like and do not like about the product and they have a rough idea of how it measures up against competing brands. In other words, the entrepreneur is in a much better position to launch full-scale production than he would otherwise have been.

COPY RESEARCH

The major goal of copy research is to discover the advertising appeals that are most effective in selling a product or bringing about some attitude change in the public. Advertisers spend more than a billion dollars a year to reach the public with a message about their wares or about their organization. It is not surprising, then, that advertisers want their copy tried out beforehand to make sure that it will meet with popular approval. They want to know whether people see their ads, whether they know the trade name of their product, and whether they have learned to associate the product or trade name with a particular slogan.

A relatively simple way of finding out what people think of an ad is to show it to a group of laymen while it is still in a rough stage. Consumer juries, as these groups are called, are some times shown a number of different layouts and asked to select the one that appeals most to them. To facilitate such judgment, the method of paired comparisons may be used. In this way, each ad is matched with every ad and the one most frequently chosen emerges as the "best" ad. Sometimes specific parts of an ad are rated separately. The judges may be asked which illustration they like best, which text is most readable, which headline is most effective.

The consumer jury method gives the advertiser a basis for selecting the ad which seems to have the greatest appeal. It is a relatively inexpensive method, since the layouts can be presented to the jury in rough form, just as they come from the artist's drawing board.

The advertiser is rarely satisfied with merely pretesting his advertising copy. He wants to know whether people read it after it has been printed in magazines or newspapers. At first, this looked like a fairly easy problem. All one needed to do was interview people who had read the magazine or newspaper and ask them whether they had seen the ad. One might go through a magazine with a reader, asking him to point out all the ads he remembered having read. The proportion of the total group saying they had read the ad would then, presumably, be an index of the ad's drawing power.

The inadequacy of this method soon became apparent as experimenters discovered various possible sources of error. Lucas (*19*), for example, was one of the first to demonstrate that the number of readers reporting that they had seen an ad might readily be inflated in the following ways.

1. False identification due to confusion with another ad.
2. Deliberate false identification to be accommodating or for prestige reasons.
3. Confusion due to familiar adjacent material.

Lucas pioneered in developing methods to correct for confusion and falsification in order to arrive at more accurate estimates of readership. One of his techniques was the use of a "dummy" magazine in loose-leaf notebook form. The "dummy" edition contained advertising from the current issue as well as advertising from a forthcoming issue. Persons who said they had seen the current issue were asked to point out the ads they remembered having looked at. An adjusted score was then computed which corrected for the inflationary factor introduced by people reporting that they had seen ads that had not yet been published. Lucas has shown how unreliable gross percentages may be. For example, two ads may have been pointed out as having been seen in the current issue by 40 percent and 55 percent of the readers, respectively. Yet, when correction is made for the degree of confusion and false identification, the corrected score for both ads turns out to be just about the same, 33 percent and 32 percent, respectively. Additional techniques for dealing with this problem will be discussed in the section dealing with readership studies.

The use of a number of other devices such as "dummy" magazines has helped solve some of the problems resulting from confusion, but many unanswered questions still remain. What kinds of ads catch reader interest? What parts of an ad are read most often? Do cartoons on the same page distract the reader's attention from the ad?

Karslake (*13*) developed an eye camera which records the eye movements of a person reading a magazine. By studying the film record, experimenters could ascertain accurately what parts of an ad attracted attention and how long a person spent on each ad. However, these studies have usually been conducted under laboratory conditions and have been criticized as somewhat artificial.

Recently, Brandt (*4*) reported on an extension of this technique. His method enables readers to be studied without their knowledge, thus eliminating the artificiality of the laboratory situation. Cameras were concealed on hair dryers in beauty parlors to obtain a real-life picture of what advertising and reading material attracted and held the attention of women as they leafed through the magazine. One-way screens were also used to observe the reading behavior of patients in doctors' and dentists' waiting rooms and of customers in barbershops. This type of direct observation is believed to give a more reliable picture of what interests readers than relying on their verbal statements.

Merely knowing that his advertisement has been seen will not satisfy the advertiser unless he is also assured that a positive impression has been made on the reader. Does he remember the trade name of the product or the name of the manufacturer? The identification test attempts to answer this question by using a specially prepared notebook in which the trade name, slogan, and manufacturer's name have been blocked out of the advertisements. The reader attempts to identify the advertiser from the remaining portions of the advertising copy. Presumably, advertising that really registers will be correctly identified, while that which does not will be missed.

The total impact of an advertising campaign is frequently measured by the strength of the impression that advertising via all media has made on consumers. This is a test not so much of a specific ad, but of an advertising theme or slogan that the company wishes to impress on the public. Open-ended interviewing is sometimes used to get the answer to this type of problem. Consumers are asked such questions as, "What brand of toothpaste have you seen or heard advertised lately?" The respondent is then asked what the advertising said. From these responses, it is possible to ascertain what brands are successfully making an impression on the reader and what features of the advertising message are most effective in "stamping in" an association between the product and its trade name.

Link (14) has pioneered in testing advertising by the method of "triple associates." This method is appropriate when a company has established a slogan or used a central theme in its advertising message. According to Link, the main objective of such advertising is to establish a strong association between a product and the brand name. The slogan or advertising theme is believed to help reinforce this association. Thus, when a customer approaches a cigarette counter, the idea of a cigarette should bring Chesterfield to mind because "They Satisfy."

In using the triple-associates method, the interviewer may ask, "What cigarette advertises 'They Satisfy'?" The first associate is *cigarette,* the second is *"They Satisfy,"* and the third is *Chesterfield.* If the campaign has been successful, the mention of the first two associates should elicit the third. This technique may be especially useful when a new advertising theme is being tried out. Link reports that in 6 weeks Lux impressed the slogan, "Use Lux to cut down runs," on 43 percent of all women (14).

Coupons and free offers are frequently used to test the pulling power of advertising copy. By coding the coupons appearing in different magazines, an advertiser may learn which media are most effective. In one study (3), the Walnut Growers Association offered a free recipe book to readers sending in a coupon. A number of different advertising themes were tried in several magazines. The cost per inquiry ranged from 70 dollars to 33 cents each. Analysis of this type of data furnished information for planning future promotional campaigns.

The elaborate devices used by advertisers to improve the effectiveness of advertising copy has roused the ire of consumer groups seeking reforms in advertising. C. E. Ware, President of Consumer's Union, has expressed the opinion that market research and copy research do not serve the consumer's interest (5). He made a telling point when he asked, "What chance has the consumer got when the sellers have studied his whims, caprices, and fears, and are able to take advantage of his technical ignorance?"

PUBLIC RELATIONS RESEARCH

Industrial management has not been content with merely studying the attitude of the public toward its product or the effectiveness of a particular advertising message. Millions of dollars are spent annually on institutional advertising to create favorable attitudes toward the organization which makes or sells the product. Such advertising is intended to improve public relations by convincing the public that the company is making an important contribution to the economic and social welfare of the nation or community. The themes used in institutional advertising stress such things as the dependability of the product, the extensive research conducted to improve the product, and the integrity and honesty of the manufacturer.

One of the most extensive measurements of public attitudes toward large companies is carried on by the Psychological Corporation as part of its Brand Barometer surveys. This program is supported by eight of the nation's leading corporations

(15). Four times a year, 10,000 people in 147 cities and towns are asked how they feel about the "policies" of each of the sponsoring companies. They are also asked their attitude toward specific aspects of policy, such as the "labor policy" of the companies in question.

In this way, the business leaders are able to observe any change in public attitude and to note the trend of public feeling. Analysis may reveal that certain groups or certain areas have unfavorable attitudes toward a company. This information enables management to review its policies to ascertain the causes of unfavorable attitude and also to design propaganda which will help bring about a more favorable attitude.

The attitudes of specific groups are sometimes made the subject of special investigations by the public relations executives. It may be important to know the attitudes of stockholders toward certain company policies; or a company may wish to know what type of retirement plan its employees would like to have without letting the workers know that the survey is being made by management. Sometimes, the company may wish to check on how its dealers feel about its product or some feature of its selling policy; it may wish to know how the attitude of sales clerks toward its product compares with the attitude they have toward competing lines.

BUYING BEHAVIOR

Favorable attitudes resulting from persuasive advertising and good public relations presumably show themselves in terms of actual sales. Some manufacturers are content with the gross sales figures tabulated by the sales department. Others want to know not only how many units of the product were sold, but who bought them. They also want to know how their sales compare with their competitors' figures. Information of this type enables businessmen to plan selling campaigns to reach people who are not at present customers and to gauge the inroads they may be making into a competitor's market.

Market research has developed several techniques for studying attitudes evinced as buying behavior. Direct observation of customers as they shop for goods often reveals the brand preferences among economic groups. Observers can note the relative frequency with which each brand of a certain type of commodity is selected. Interviews are often conducted to ascertain the reasons that a customer preferred a particular brand. This technique has many ramifications, since it may be applied at the time of purchase or at a later date. The interviewer, in any case, would try to find out what the customer says he likes about the brand he bought, how he happened to start using it, why he discontinued his previous brand. Data of this sort are invaluable in planning sales campaigns and in improving the product to meet with greater consumer acceptance.

Direct observation cannot always be used. According to Barton (1), chain stores like A&P, Kroger, and Safeway do not permit ". . . commercial researchers to enter their stores for the purpose of estimating their sales." Since these stores account for a large portion of retail sales, and since many of them have their own brands, any survey which did not take account of chain store sales would give a misleading picture of the market.

The Psychological Corporation's Brand Barometer has already been described briefly in connection with public relations research. The most important aspect of the Barometer surveys is the information they collect about the buying behavior of the American public. Psychologists associated with the Marketing Research Division of the Psychological Corporation supervise staffs of interviewers in 147 American cities and towns. The sample used in the surveys is stratified by economic groups within a given community. Thus, a family with an income of $5000 in one community might find itself in the highest category, class A, while in another community that income level might be typical of the upper middle class, called class B in the survey. Ten percent of the interviews are conducted in homes of the highest income group (group A), 30 percent in B-group homes, 40 percent in C-group homes, and 20 percent in *D*-group homes. The first half of the interview is always with the housewife or some other adult female in the household. To obtain a sex comparison on certain items, the second half of the interview is obtained from women in half the homes and from men in the other half.

A wide variety of household commodities are covered in the questions answered by women. These include items like mayonnaise, margarine, coffee, tea, and beer. The questions answered by both men and women deal with cigarettes, hand lotion, and toilet soap. Men answer only questions about shaving cream, while the women answer questions about shampoos, face creams, and face powders. In each case, the respondent is asked about the last item that he purchased or used, for example, "What brand of coffee did you buy last?" or "What brand of soap did you use last for washing dishes?"

The questions are not aimed at measuring sales, but customers. Their purpose is to find out whether more or fewer *people* are buying a given product and to compare the standing of each brand is relation to competing brands. A manufacturer can tell from the Barometer whether he is gaining or losing customers and whether his competitors are making inroads into his market. The brand preferences of various economic groups may also be studied to learn among what groups potential customers may be found. Freiberg (*8*) gives an illustration of how brand preferences may shift. In 1941, 22 percent of the highest economic group used Maxwell House Coffee but only 11 percent of the lowest economic group. In 1944, the Barometer showed that just about the same proportion of people in each income group were using this brand. Its use among the wealthiest group had declined a bit, but the drop was more than offset by the increase in use among the other groups.

The reliability and validity of the Brand Barometer "last purchase" questions were investigated by Jenkins and his associates in 1938. Interviewers called on 150 *B*-group homes and asked twenty-six questions, nineteen of which were of the "last purchase" type. The sheets were coded so that the respondent could be identified. Forty-eight hours later the same interviewer returned to the same house and attempted to reinterview the original respondent, explaining that the sheets had been lost. Most of the respondents consented to be reinterviewed. A comparison of the answers to each item on the first and second interview showed high consistency of response. The percent naming the same brand both times ranged between 97 percent for beer (most people denied using any) to 87 percent for hand lotion. The percent consistency for tires dropped to 85 percent, but this was attributed to the confusion between Goodrich and Goodyear.

The validity of the Brand Barometer was investigated by Jenkins and Corbin (*12*). A check was made of the verbal report of last purchase against the sales slips of seventy respondents who shopped at the same grocery. The percent agreement between the interview statement and the sales-slip record ranged from 100 percent for bread to 62 percent for flour. The average agreement was 78 percent. Of the thirteen commodities studied, ten showed validity indices above 70 percent. None fell below 60 percent.

CONSUMER PANELS

The consumer panel is an attempt to go beyond the questionnaire method in studying buying behavior and consumer attitudes toward certain products. The National Consumer's Panel is operated by the Industrial Survey Company. Four thousand selected families, representing about 10,000 individuals, participate in the panel. The sample rotates 25 percent each year, giving a complete turnover every 4 years.

Unlike the Brand Barometer, the consumer panel uses the same individuals over a long period of time. Detailed personal data are available about the income, educational level, and occupation of each member of the Panel family. These facts permit analyzing buying behavior in greater detail than is possible with the questionnaire method.

Participants are trained to keep a careful daily record of

their purchases, reading, and radio listening. The diary calls for information as to the brand purchased, the color or flavor, size of package, number of units, price, place of purchase, and person doing the buying. Diaries are collected weekly and the participants are usually rewarded in points which entitle them to select premiums from a gift catalogue.

Diary entries are punched into Hollerith cards and analyzed according to various personal data breakdowns. Since the record is available for the same family for several years, comparisons can be made of the family's buying from period to period. In this way trends may be charted to ascertain how a given brand is holding up in competition. Subscribers to the Panel may learn among what groups their brand may be slipping and they may obtain valuable information about package, color, and size preferences.

Buying may also be related to the kinds and amount of advertising to which the consumers were exposed. Since a record is kept of the magazines and newspapers received in the home and the radio programs that were heard, the effectiveness of various media may be charted. Families may be subdivided according to the amount of the commodity they purchased during the year. Then the amount of use can be compared with the amount of advertising which reached them.

The Industrial Survey Company operates two types of panels. One is continuous and deals chiefly with foods, drugs, and various media of communication. A second panel is repetitive, but not continuous. It collects information about new products, how products are used, and consumer opinion of various products.

One of the unanswered questions about the consumer panel is how representative its members are once they become brand conscious. The use of rotation attempts to reduce this source of bias. The validity of consumer panel measurements is said to be very high. Barton (1) reports that the panel technique has been validated by comparing the manufacturer's record of yearly sales with panel estimates of consumers. The panel technique's estimate comes within 6 to 10 percent on individual brands, according to Barton.

Panels are also used by several national magazines to get reader reactions to advertised products and to the editorial content of the magazine. These panels are primarily adjuncts of the advertising department and provide information which is useful in demonstrating to advertisers that it is a desirable medium through which to reach people who will buy the product.

THE MERCHANT'S VIEWPOINT

The attitudes of the merchant have long been overlooked as a source of valuable information about many aspects of marketing. The alert manufacturer wants to know how dealers feel about his merchandising policies. Dealers often know which are the best media for reaching customers, which sales appeal is most effective, which type of special offer gets the best results.

Organizations which try to create good will over a wide territory may wish to maintain a check on the practices of individual units, knowing that one rotten apple may spoil the barrel. Checking on the effectiveness of training programs is another purpose to which dealership surveys may be applied.

Haring (9) reports a survey of gas stations to ascertain the effectiveness of a service-station-attendant training program and to compare the service among several competing chains. It was hoped that the survey would reveal to its sponsor points in the training program that needed additional attention so that service could be further improved.

The method of observation used was ingenious and tailor-made for the situation. The interviewer, usually accompanied by his wife, followed a definite set of instructions in preparing his car before entering a service station. His gas supply was not to exceed 5 gallons; his oil supply was to be obviously low; his windshield was to be dirty (even if he had to spray it with muddy water to make it that way); and the rear tire nearest the gas tank was to be noticeably deflated. When entering a gas station, the interviewer was instructed to park midway between the "regular" and the "premium" pumps and to say to the attendant, "Put in 5 gallons, please."

The interviewer and his wife noted exactly what the attendant said and what he did. They discovered, for example, that the attendants often made no effort to get the customer to use the premium fuel; he would merely assume that the customer wanted "regular." They also found that many of the attendants did not even suggest that the customer might want more than 5 gallons. More than half of the attendants did not bother to check the air in the soft tire. Before leaving the station, the interviewer and his wife would check the condition of the rest rooms and observe the items on display in the "store" window.

This type of survey yields a mountain of information about the serviceman's attitude toward the customer and toward his job. It points out the effectiveness of selection and training programs and suggests ways for improving training-program content.

When an industry has a national association to promote the general welfare of the industry, surveys may be used to collect information that will be of value to all members. This viewpoint is relatively new. Heretofore, market research has been conducted mainly to gain a competitive advantage for one organization or brand. Industry-wide surveys are intended to assist the whole industry in planning for the future.

One such survey was sponsored by the book industry. It was conducted jointly by the Book Manufacturers Institute and the Marketing Research Division of the Psychological Corporation. In addition to questioning a nation-wide sample of readers, interviewers also questioned book dealers to obtain their opinions about book buying trends and desirable changes in merchandising and advertising.

READERSHIP STUDIES

The techniques used to estimate how many people read an advertisement have already been described. Many of the advertiser's questions, however, may still be unanswered. He may want to know how much duplication there is between the readers of magazines *A* and *B*. He may ask how many people read each magazine, who they are, whether they are potential customers. These questions pose research problems that must be answered by the magazine.

Editors and business managers, too, are interested in knowing who their readers are. The editor can use such information in determining editorial content; the business manager can use it to lure new advertising to his publication.

The published circulation figures do not give a reliable picture of readership. It is important, for example, that advertisers know whether a magazine reaches upper-, middle-, or lower-income-level homes; whether men as well as women read the magazine; whether readers own their own homes, have cars, or play golf. It is to answer questions like these that research has been undertaken to find out who reads various magazines.

Who Reads the Magazine?

When magazines are sold mainly through subscriptions, its readers may be studied in several ways. One of the most obvious is the reader panel. These are subscribers who have been invited to comment on the magazine. This group is usually willing to fill out questionnaires about their attitudes, their likes and dislikes in the magazine's bill of fare. They will also consent to divulge, without much prodding, personal data about themselves. It is thus possible for a magazine to learn about the income level of its readers, home ownership, what appliances they own, what things they plan to buy, how they spend their leisure time, etc. Such information can obviously be very useful to advertisers.

Unless precautions are taken, it is easy to get an unrepresentative sample of readers in the panel. Those from the higher-income level and those who are most interested in the magazine will be more willing to participate. There is also a tendency for the more articulate readers to serve on voluntary panels. The results are thus distorted and do not give a true picture of the people who get the magazine.

When magazines are sold chiefly from newsstands, it is more difficult to obtain a description of readers. The pulp magazines in particular pose a challenge to investigators, since many people who regularly read them will deny doing so for reasons of prestige. House-to-house interviewing usually gives a distorted picture of reading habits. When people are asked what magazines they usually read, respondents tend to name "prestige" periodicals and to deny reading anything that might be considered "lowbrow."

When interviewers attempt to make actual magazine inventories in the home, they find that readers of popular magazines will usually coöperate, while nonreaders or readers of pulps will find excuses for not permitting the inventory to be made.

Some investigators have successfully disguised their purpose by posing as magazine collectors for some charity. Persons in the upper-income group are usually willing to donate magazines to a worthy cause and are not likely to suspect the real purpose of the solicitation. The investigator is then able to determine what magazines are actually in the home. He often finds considerable disparity between the verbal report and the physical inventory.

Sometimes the investigator poses as a buyer of back issues of magazines. He offers to pay the original sale price for back issues of certain magazines. In this way the thrifty housewife can often be induced to part with magazines she would deny having if the question had been asked directly.

The Research Department of the Crowell-Collier Publishing Company (*31*) engaged the Psychological Corporation to conduct a survey that would reveal the kind of people that buy or subscribe to *Collier's*. It was not a readership survey in the usual sense, since it did not attempt to find out whether the magazine was read. The study merely attempted to establish whether the magazine was present in the home.

Block sampling was used in the investigation; the resulting sample correlated closely with census data. Interviewers sought to ascertain the following things:

1. Composition of the household by age, sex, income, education, marital status, and employment
2. Type and size of home
3. Ownership or rental of home
4. Stability of residence
5. Number and type of household appliances
6. Automobile ownership

To avoid bias, the interviewers were not told who was sponsoring the survey. It was merely called "An Appliance and Magazine Survey." The questionnaire did not specify which magazines were of particular interest. A total of 8000 homes in cities of over 50,000 population were visited. Of these, 1246 were found to possess *Collier's*. The *Collier's* families were then compared with non-*Collier's* families. The survey showed that *Collier's* homes were above average in size, that the family was larger than the average, and that the educational level of the *Collier's* group was above the average of the non-*Collier's* group. A similar analysis was made for each of the breakdowns. No data are given for other magazines covered in the survey. This, of course, is understandable, since the purpose of the study was to gather data useful to *Collier's* in selling advertising. Market research in general is characterized by self-interest and it is seldom that sponsors of this type of research will make public information that might prove useful to competitors or to applied psychology in general.

Studying Reader Interests

The editorial side of magazine and newspaper research is conducted along lines quite similar to those already described under the heading of copy research. While advertisers seek evidence that people read their ads, the editor wants to know what articles people have read and what type of material interests them the most.

Here the interviewer faces the same inflationary factors that are met in copy research and in other readership surveys. Ways must be found to counteract the respondent's tendency to give answers that he thinks are expected or those which will show him in a more favorable light to the interviewer.

The usual methods of confusion control, such as showing advance copies of the magazine, may be used to adjust spuriously high readership figures. The *Life* Continuing Study of Magazine Audiences has experimented with various techniques to meet this problem. They think that they finally have an answer. Their secret lies in setting up a situation where the person being interviewed does not feel ego-involved, where his prestige is not at stake. To accomplish this, a special interview technique has been developed. The respondent is shown six magazines, only three of which are being studied. He is asked to indicate which of them he has looked at during the past 6 months. Before inquiring about specific articles, the interviewer gives the person a chance to tell him what types of articles he likes best and which recent articles he can remember. The interviewer points out the possibility of confusing articles in one magazine with those in another and he asks the respondent whether he has noticed this himself. This period of preparation usually places the respondent at ease and makes him feel he has already made a positive contribution. It avoids the negativism and the defensive reaction which is aroused when an interviewer begins by asking questions about a magazine which the person hasn't seen. To save face, he may fabricate responses which will place him in a favorable light.

Instead of asking directly which articles the respondent has seen, the interviewer invites him to look through a magazine, pointing out that it may be an issue that the respondent has not yet seen. He asks the respondent to point out the articles that look interesting. After each item he asks, "Does it look interesting?" "Is this the first time you have seen it?" In this way the interviewer may quickly establish whether or not the person has seen that issue. If he hasn't seen the issue, the interviewer continues to ask only whether articles are of interest. If he has seen that issue, the second question is repeated after each article. Research by the *Life* investigators has shown that this technique eliminates practically all confusion and yields highly reliable results.

Two types of information are obtained from the *Life*-type interview. First, the editorial staff learns which articles people like to read; and second, they learn what types of articles are of interest to both readers and nonreaders. This information may be useful in shaping future policy.

Industry-Sponsored Research

While most market research may be considered an investment in attitude research that will pay off to a single company, there are instances of such research sponsored by an entire industry for the benefit of all its members. The book industry survey, mentioned earlier, is an example of this type of research.

The book industry as a whole wanted to know whether the wartime boom in books would continue after the war ended. There were many questions that book publishers wanted answered. What type of books do people want to buy? What prices are people willing to pay? Where do people get books? Do they read them? Do those who read more buy more? What is the relationship between educational level and readership? What differences are found by sex, economic status, and religious background? What is the influence of book reviewers? Do people have plans that include more or less space, time, or inclination for books?

To answer questions like these, Link of the Psychological Corporation and Hopf of the Book Manufacturers Institute

(*17*) undertook a nation-wide survey to ascertain attitudes and reading behavior of the American adult. After eight preliminary questionnaires had been tried out, a final sixty-three-item questionnaire was administered to a cross section of adults in 106 cities and towns by 235 interviewers, using a quota sampling technique.

The interviewers asked each respondent about the extent of his book reading, newspaper reading, magazine reading, radio listening, and movie attendance yesterday, i.e., the day preceding the interview. One third of the interviews were conducted away from homes—in places of amusement, in bus and railroad terminals, and in shopping centers—to avoid a bias which would be present if only stay-at-home adults were included.

The interviewers soon discovered that two sources of bias could not be eliminated: (1) Readers were proud of being readers and were willing to talk, while nonreaders resisted the questions. Hence, the interviewers tended to get people who were interested in books. (2) The better educated were more articulate and were more willing to coöperate, while the poorly educated would not coöperate. A third possible source of bias, not mentioned by the authors, was the failure to include a sample of men in the armed forces.

Some of the highlights of the survey may be listed briefly to illustrate the wealth of material which the survey uncovered for its sponsors. It showed that 70 percent of the books are read by 21 percent of the population, about 90 percent by half the population. Fifty-seven percent of the books are borrowed, 31 percent are bought, 11 percent are gifts. The lower-income group buys as often as the highest in proportion to the amount of reading each does. Fiction is read by 58 percent, nonfiction by 31 percent. Only 4 percent of the population reported having read the Bible on the previous day.

Formal education was found to be the major factor in inducing people to read. The higher the educational level, the higher the readership rate. All signs pointed to a long-range increase in reading with bookstores, book clubs, and department stores being the major sources of books. More than one-third of the population was found to have purchased sets of books at one time and most of these people said they were well satisfied with their investment.

The investigators reached the conclusion that some of the risk could be taken out of publishing by more extensive use of sampling techniques. Sampling could help the publisher determine the price at which he could sell the most copies. But more important, perhaps, would be pretesting of books on selected samples to find out whether they were likely to meet with popular approval. By submitting the manuscript or selected sections to a panel of representative readers and using the proper techniques for recording their reactions, the probable success of a book could be gauged with considerable accuracy.

RADIO RESEARCH

Radio research shares many of the problems faced by the magazine and newspaper survey, but many of its problems are unique; they have challenged the ingenuity of scores of investigators.

The unique feature of radio research is the narrow time span within which program research must be done. Attitudes toward a radio program must be ascertained during the program or shortly after it is heard; next week is usually too late. Even the matter of counting listeners is usually done while the program is on the air or within a short time after it has been broadcast. However, Roper has shown that this need not necessarily be so. Radio researchers have adapted the techniques of opinion polling and market research to catch the elusive listener before the impression of a program fades.

Radio advertisers ask practically the same questions as magazine advertisers: How many people listen to my program? Who are they? Do they know who sponsors the program and what is being sold? Does the program help sell the product?

Those on the production end of radio ask questions that sound a great deal like the ones a magazine or newspaper editor might ask: What programs do people like best? How may programs be improved? What programs appeal to different age groups and to different economic levels? How can radio render greater service to the community?

How Many Listeners?

One of the primary concerns of both program sponsors and radio executives is the determination of how many people listen to a given program. To the advertiser, this information is probably more important than the quality of the program; unless people tune in to his program, they will not hear the advertising, no matter how good the program may be in a technical sense. As a result of this emphasis on the size of program audiences, terms like "Hooper rating" have become part of the American jargon. A high audience rating enables a program to command a large income and advertisers vie with one another to "buy" the show. The mere fact that the program has many listeners seems to have a snowball effect; new listeners are attracted because they want to follow the crowd.

There are four major techniques for estimating the number of listeners to a given program. Historically, the earliest method is that of the telephone recall. It was introduced by the Coöperative Analysis of Broadcasting (CAB) in 1931, but it has since given way to the coincidental method developed by Hooper in 1934. The telephone recall method interviewed radio listeners by telephone during a stated period after each program. Interviewers tried to find out what programs had been heard during that period. The coincidental method also utilizes the telephone interview, but limits itself to the period during which the program is on the air.

In 1941, The Pulse, Inc., in New York City, introduced a personal interview roster method which asks people about their listening during a given period on the same day or preceding evening. The fourth method was introduced by Nielsen in 1942. Nielsen utilizes a mechanical device which is attached to the radio receiving sets in selected homes. The apparatus records the stations to which the set is tuned, how long it remains tuned to a given station, and what pattern was followed in selecting a station.

Advocates of the telephone coincidental method, popularly known as Hooper rating, contend that it is best because it is an actual interview with a listener at the time the program is on the air. Data are thus obtained from a respondent who is qualified to report on his own listening and who can tell the interviewer who else may be listening. The Hooper-type interview asks the following questions.

1. Were you listening to the radio just now?
2. To what program were you listening?
3. What station, please?
4. What is advertised?
5. How many men, women, and children in your home were actually listening?

These questions give the program sponsor a picture of the size and composition of his audience and an index of their awareness of the advertising message.

The coincidental method has been criticized on several counts. It is limited to telephone homes, except in rural areas where it is supplemented by a diary method. Since 90 percent of American homes have radios and only 50 percent have telephones, the telephone sample is likely to be biased by a higher proportion of higher-income homes. The sampling technique has also been criticized for its failure to control the composition of the listening group that is called from one 15-minute period to the next. Since names are randomly selected from the telephone directory, there is no assurance that the samples are comparable for each quarter-hour program.

Another limitation of the method is the relatively small number of calls that can be made in a 15-minute period. This, together with the fact that nontelephone homes are missed altogether, may seriously diminish the accuracy of the Hooper technique. Furthermore, the brief interview does not permit the interviewer to obtain such personal data as the age, socio-economic status, education, occupation, or nationality of the respondent. Hence, no adequate description or analysis of the sample is possible.

The roster method seeks to overcome these difficulties by relying on personal interviews, made about a half-day after the program is broadcast. For example, beginning at noon, people are asked about the programs of the preceding morning. Those interviewed in the morning respond to questions about the programs of the preceding evening.

The interviewer carefully sets the stage before asking each respondent what programs he or she heard. For example, if the interview is with a housewife, she is first led to reconstruct in her mind the activities of the morning. She is asked at what time she got up, who was at home, what time the family had breakfast, and at what time she turned on the radio. When the interviewer has clearly established the time that the listening began and ended, he shows the roster to the housewife. The roster lists all programs broadcast in that area during each 15-minute period. The housewife is shown only the roster for the period she has indicated that she was listening to the radio. She indicates on the roster what programs she heard during each 15-minute period. Thus, in a single interview, listening for a definite time period is established and the pattern of listening behavior may be discerned.

The roster method enables the interviewer to obtain the relevant personal data from each respondent so that analysis can be made by age, sex, socioeconomic status, etc.

Comparison of the results obtained by the roster method and the coincidental method show high agreement. Roslow (22) reports a remarkably high agreement in the popularity ranking of both stations and specific programs. He points out that the roster method makes it possible for a small number of roster interviews to do the work of many times that number of coincidental telephone interviews. Roslow states that in New York, for example, the 6300 roster interviews are adequate to give a reliable picture of listening over a 24-hour period. To obtain the same information by the coincidental method would require 151,000 telephone calls.

The roster method has sometimes been improperly used by inexperienced research workers or by persons desiring to load the results in favor of certain programs. A respondent might be asked, for example, to answer a question like this: "To which of the following programs do you listen frequently?" The programs listed may not be equally popular and may not come at the same time. This approach may be useful as a screening question to find out what people listen to a specific program so they may be interviewed about the program. But it does not give a reliable measure of the size of the listening audience. Only when the list of programs is limited to a specific time interval and includes all programs broadcast during the time interval can the results be interpreted as a reliable indication of a program's relative popularity.

The Nielsen meter method of audience measurement has the advantage of providing a continuous record of the listening behavior in a family. The meter is attached to the radio set and shows not only what stations were tuned in, but also the point at which they were tuned out.

Critics of the meter method point out that there is no assurance that anyone is listening to a program even though it may be tuned in on a set. People frequently turn on the radio and then go off to another part of the house. The method also fails to provide any information as to the composition of the listening group. Although the socioeconomic status and the number of members in the family may be known, there is no record of how many people were listening to a particular program or who they were.

Since the meter is fairly expensive, its use is limited. Permission must be obtained from set owners to install the meter and this factor limits its use to homes where people are willing to coöperate. Critics have pointed out that the pattern of listening may be affected by the family's awareness that a record is being made of their listening.

Effectiveness of Radio Advertising

The techniques for measuring the effectiveness of radio advertising bear a strong resemblance to those used to test the effectiveness of magazine advertising. Some are almost identical, while others are new, devised especially for radio.

Premium offers are frequently used to gauge the pulling power of a program. Sometimes special sales offers are made only over the air. One store offered nylon hose at a reduced price to listeners who mentioned that they heard the offer on the radio; others paid the regular price. Buick owners in the Chicago area were once offered free lubrication service if they told the dealer that they had heard the offer on the air. These offers bring customers to the store or service station and also enable the sponsor to find out whether his advertising message gets attention. However, it does not enable a sponsor to learn the extent of his audience or the impression his message has made on people who do not bother to accept his special offers.

The Brand Barometer studies of the Psychological Corporation enable the advertiser to learn the effectiveness of his radio advertising by comparing the buying habits of listeners and nonlisteners. By means of the triple-associates question, he may learn whether there are differences between the people who know his advertising slogan and those who do not. Since the Brand Barometer studies are conducted several times each year, shifts in buying of a product may be studied in relation to changes in the program or the advertising theme. Such information is often of value to advertisers in planning promotional campaigns.

While the Brand Barometer studies are sponsored by certain corporations wishing to use the information to competitive advantage, somewhat similar studies are carried on by the major networks to collect data that will help them to sell advertising time.

In 1940, the Columbia Broadcasting System (*30*) engaged Elmo Roper to measure the extent of listening to forty evening programs broadcast regularly over CBS and to determine the sales impact of each of these programs. The questions Roper set out to answer were stated in this way:

1. *What is my net effective audience?* How many actual listeners do I reach with my sales message—often enough to sell goods?
2. *What is my program's net sales impact?* How many additional customers is the program making for me—customers I would not otherwise be selling?

To answer these questions, the Roper organization conducted 10,000 personal interviews on a stratified sample of adults. The questions about products were asked first and were followed by questions about the frequency of listening to the forty CBS programs. The validity of the product-use questions were checked by visits to 212 homes for the purpose of ascertaining what brand of product the respondent actually had on the shelf. The resulting inventory showed that the answers were 90 percent correct or the respondent claimed that he was "just out" of the item.

Unlike the coincidental method or the roster method which provide an estimate of how many people heard a given program, the method used by Roper sought to ascertain how many times a month each program was heard by the people interviewed. Respondents were classified as 0-, 1-, 2-, 3-, or 4-times-a-month listeners. This information enabled Roper to study the relationship between the frequency of program listening and product use. He found that about 50 percent of those interviewed listened to the forty programs, on the average, three or four times a month. About 25 percent listened one or two times a month, while the remaining 25 percent listened less than once a month.

The Roper study shows that it is not only the size of the audience that counts, but also the frequency with which people listen to the program. People who listen once or twice a month buy 43 percent more of the product than nonlisteners, while those who listen three or four times a month buy 57 percent more of the product than nonlisteners. Even the occasional listener who tunes in less than once a month is found to buy 31 percent more of the product than those who do not listen at all.

These figures are interpreted by CBS as evidence that radio advertising is responsible for additional customers and that there is a definite relationship between the frequency of listening to a program and the use of the products advertised. This conclusion seems reasonable, since the stratified sample held other factors such as age, sex, socioeconomic status, region, and size of community constant. Listeners and nonlisteners were presumably exposed to similar amounts of advertising by other media. Hence, the differences found in their use of the various products does appear to be related to radio listening. We must remember, however, that an untested assumption underlies this conclusion. Until it has been demonstrated that listeners and nonlisteners are alike in all other respects and that they are exposed to equal amounts of advertising by other media, we cannot be sure that radio listening is the only variable involved.

Both the Psychological Corporation and the National Broadcasting Company have made surveys among dealers to find out which advertising media were most effective in promoting sales of toilet goods, groceries, and gasoline. The studies were conducted one year apart, yet they show close agreement.

Approximately 3000 dealers were asked to name three of their best-selling nationally advertised brands. They were then asked, for each brand name, "What kind of advertising has helped these sales most?" The 400 brands most frequently mentioned were analyzed. Link and Corby (*16*) report that the results agreed closely with the known facts about the specific advertising campaigns that were being conducted in connection with the brands mentioned. Radio advertising was mentioned most frequently by all three groups of dealers.

Advertising Media	Druggists		Grocers		Gasoline Dealers	
	Psych. Corp. %	NBC, %	Psych. Corp. %	NBC, %	Psych. Corp. %	NBC, %
Radio	65.0	70.3	58.3	62.3	69.4	63.2
Magazines	6.9	7.1	6.8	8.1	4.8	7.9
Newspapers	24.6	20.3	31.3	27.2	14.5	14.1
Billboards	0.6	1.0	1.3	2.0	6.7	12.8

Program Analysis

The people who prepare radio programs face the same problem that magazine and newspaper editors face. They want to know whether people like their program and what parts are liked better than others. Unfortunately, the radio editor cannot very readily send out interviewers with copies of the program in a brief case to buttonhole people to get their reaction to various parts of the program. Such a procedure would be both costly and time-consuming.

For lack of more precise methods, broadcasters for many years relied on fan mail and the reaction of studio audiences to supplement the judgment of experts.

Frank Stanton, now President of CBS, and Paul Lazarsfeld, Director of the Office of Radio Research at Columbia University, developed the Program Analyzer to remove some of the guesswork from program analysis. The Program Analyzer is a modified polygraph. The listener's seat is provided with two buttons. The right hand button is green and indicates "like." The left hand one is red and stands for "dislike." Listeners are told to hold down one or the other of the buttons to indicate their reaction to what they are hearing on the radio. Indifference is indicated by not pressing either button. The reliability of the Program Analyzer was studied by

Schwerin (24). He had two groups of nineteen subjects indicate whether they were interested or not interested in the items of a newscast. The agreement between the two groups was found to be $r = 0.89$ for items which were of interest. This hardly seems like an adequate measure of the reliability of the instrument, but it is the only reference to its reliability that could be found in the literature.

The subjects used with the Program Analyzer are usually studio audiences although any group could be brought together for the purpose of listening to the program being studied. Subjects are first given detailed instructions about the apparatus and are given a chance to practice and to ask questions. After the program is over, the parts marked "like" or "dislike" by each subject are located on the recording and played back during an interview. In this way, the reasons for the expressed attitude may be probed while the recollection of the program is still relatively fresh.

It is also possible to summate the likes and dislikes of all the subjects to obtain a quantitative indication of the extent to which a program was liked or disliked.

Peterman (20) describes an analysis of a public affairs program dealing with the topic of civil rights. Forty-seven women and five men participated. The polygraph records showed wide variation in the individual response to the program; but despite the variation, a clear pattern of likes and dislikes appeared in the summary. The audience liked best the parts in which the narrator spoke. Those parts where he made short, simple, direct statements were liked better than the involved and abstruse commentaries. The audience disliked the weird organ effects, parts of the chorus, and the dramatization of a near-riot. Interviews revealed that the main reason for liking parts was the subject matter presented, while the main reason for disliking parts was the medium through which the part was presented.

The Program Analyzer also makes possible the study of

group differences—for example, what parts of a program children or old people like best. The technique also makes possible controlled experimentation. One factor at a time, such as content or manner of presentation, may be varied while other factors remain unchanged.

Radio Panels. Radio panels are also used for program analysis. In 1936 H. P. Longstaff organized a panel of 100 housewives who were paid to listen to a program carefully and regularly for a period of 6 weeks. The panel was selected not from housewives who were already listeners, but from among those who were not listeners or who had listened for a few days and then stopped. The object of the study was to discover the reasons for the failure of this program to reach a larger audience and to obtain clues which might enable it to be improved. As a result of the study, the program was radically changed.

The Psychological Corporation conducts most of its radio panels by personal interview, although some panels have been conducted by mail questionnaire. Panel directors find it very important to maintain close contact with panel members in order to get maximum benefits. They have found such panels very helpful in strengthening the best points of the program, eliminating the weak points, improving the selling message, and working out the kinks.

SUMMARY

In this chapter we have presented the applications of opinion and attitude research to business—advertising and selling. Product development, advertising copy, public relations, buying behavior as a criterion, consumer panels, dealer surveys, readership of magazines and books, and radio research have been reviewed as to techniques and methods. At this writing it is scarcely possible to include anything of consequence on the new giant of mass communication, television. Hence, this chapter will soon fail to be, to the extent of this omission, complete.

Questions

1. Suggest ways of keeping a consumer panel from becoming biased.
2. Are sales increases or decreases necessarily a valid index of consumers' attitudes toward a product?
3. List the advantages and disadvantages of the roster method, the recall method, and the meter method as techniques for sampling the composition of a radio or television audience.
4. Could the "dummy" technique be used in radio and television research?
5. Can you think of cases in which there may have been *negative* correlation between advertising and sales?
6. Would a random sample of addresses yield a representative sample of radio listeners?
7. How do you explain the apparently greater percentage of effective advertising done by radio as compared with other media?
8. Do you agree or disagree with the president of Consumers' Union that market research and copy research are not in the consumers' interest?
9. How does television compare with other media in terms of effective advertising?

Bibliography

1. Barton, S. G., "Movement of Branded Goods to the Consumer." In Blankenship, A. (ed.), *How to Conduct Consumer and Opinion Research,* New York: Harper & Brothers, 1946, pp. 58-70.
2. Beville, H. H., Jr., "The ABC's of Radio Audiences," *Publ. Opin. Quart.,* 1940, *4:*195-206.
3. Borden, N. H., *The Economic Effects of Advertising,* Chicago: Richard D. Irwin, Inc., 1942.
4. Brandt, H. F., "A Scientific Approach to the Study of Magazine Readership," *Program, 20th Annual Meeting of the Midwestern Psychological Association,* May, 1948.
5. Churchman, C. W., Ackoff, R. L., and Wax, M., *Measurement of Consumer Interest,* Philadelphia: University of Pennsylvania Press, 1947.

6. DuBois, C., "How Many Readers?" In Blankenship, A. (ed.), *How to Conduct Consumer and Opinion Research,* New York: Harper & Brothers, 1946, pp. 209-221.

7. Freiberg, A. D., "Copy Testing." In Blankenship, A. (ed.), *How to Conduct Consumer and Opinion Research,* New York: Harper & Brothers, 1946, pp. 118-136.

8. Freiberg, A. D., "Psychological Brand Barometer." In Blankenship, A. (ed.), *How to Conduct Consumer and Opinion Research,* New York: Harper & Brothers, 1946, pp. 71-85.

9. Haring, C. E., "The Last Three Feet." In Blankenship, A. (ed.), *How to Conduct Consumer and Opinion Research,* New York: Harper & Brothers, 1946, pp. 232-240.

10. Hooper, C. E., "The Coincidental Method of Measuring Radio Audience Size." In Blankenship, A. (ed.), *How to Conduct Consumer and Opinion Research,* New York: Harper & Brothers, 1946, pp. 156-171.

11. Jenkins, J. G., "Dependability of Psychological Brand Barometers: I. The Problem of Reliability," *J. appl. Psychol.,* 1938, 22:1-7.

12. Jenkins, J. G., and Corbin, H. H., "Dependability of Psychological Brand Barometers: II. The Problem of Validity," *J. appl. Psychol.,* 1938, 22:252-260.

13. Karslake, J. S., "The Purdue Eye Camera; A Practical Apparatus for Studying the Attention Value of Advertisements," *J. appl. Psychol.,* 1940, 24:417-440.

14. Link, H. C., "A New Method for Testing Advertising and a Psychological Sales Barometer," *J. appl. Psychol.,* 1934, 18:1-26.

15. Link, H. C., "The Ninety-Fourth Issue of the Psychological Barometer and a Note on its Fifteenth Anniversary," *J. appl. Psychol.,* 1948, 32:105-117.

16. Link, H. C., and Corby, P. G., "Studies in Radio Effectiveness by the Psychological Corporation," *J. appl. Psychol.,* 1940, 24:749-757.

17. Link, H. C., and Hopf, H. A., *People and Books,* New York: Book Manufacturers Institute, 1946.

18. Lockley, L. C., "Market Description—Quantitative and Qualitative." In Blankenship, A. (ed.), *How to Conduct Consumer and Opinion Research,* New York: Harper & Brothers, 1946, pp. 11-28.

19. Lucas, D. B., "A rigid Technique for Measuring the Impression Value of Specific Magazine Advertisements," *J. appl. Psychol.*, 1940, *24*:778-790.
20. Peterman, J. N., "The 'Program Analyzer': A New Technique in Studying Liked and Disliked Items in Radio Programs," *J. appl. Psychol.*, 1940, *24*:728-741.
21. Robinson, R. A., "Use of the Panel in Opinion and Attitude Research," *Int. J. opin. attit. Res.*, 1947, *1*:83-86.
22. Roslow, S., "Measuring the Radio Audience by the Personal Interview Roster Method," *J. appl. Psychol.*, 1943, *27*:526-534.
23. Roslow, S., and Kelly, N., "The Personal Interview-Roster Method of Radio Measurement and its Application." In Blankenship, A. (ed.), *How to Conduct Consumer and Opinion Research*, New York: Harper & Brothers, 1946, pp. 172-180.
24. Schwerin, H., "An Exploratory Study of the Reliability of the 'Program Analyzer,'" *J. appl. Psychol.*, 1940, *24*:742-748.
25. Stonborough, T. H. W., "The Continuous Consumer Panel; A New Sampling Device in Consumer Research," *Appl. Anthrop.*, 1942, *1*(no. 2):37-41.
26. Welch, A. C., "Consumer Research in the Development of Advertising Copy." In Blankenship, A. (ed.), *How to Conduct Consumer and Opinion Research*, New York: Harper & Brothers, 1946, pp. 96-117.
27. White, P., and White, M., "Research for Product Development." In Blankenship, A. (ed.), *How to Conduct Consumer and Opinion Research*, New York: Harper & Brothers, 1946, pp. 29-42.
28. Wulfeck, W. H., "Public Relations Research." In Blankenship, A. (ed.), *How to Conduct Consumer and Opinion Research*, New York: Harper & Brothers, 1946, pp. 86-95.
29. Advertising Research Foundation, *Copy Testing*, New York: The Ronald Press Company, 1939.
30. Columbia Broadcasting System, *Roper Counts Customers*, New York: Columbia Broadcasting System, 1941.
31. Crowell-Collier Publishing Company, *The Collier's Market: A Qualitative Survey by the Psychological Corporation*, New York: Crowell-Collier Publishing Company, 1946.

CHAPTER IX

· · · · ● · · ·

Applications in Government

INTRODUCTION

Since this chapter deals with the uses made of attitude studies by the government, it seems appropriate to discuss briefly at the beginning how attitude and opinion studies fit into the framework of democratic government. Our conception of the best government is the government serving its people in accordance with their wishes and desires. The expression of their wishes, attitudes, biases, feelings, etc., is certainly an integral part of a functioning democracy, and the recording and making known of such feelings can be done, in part, through attitude and opinion surveys.

Attitudes Toward Governmental Use of Attitude Measurement

It has been suggested by a good many persons that broader use of public opinion polls would be a cure for a great many governmental ills. Legislators, it has been suggested, would be placed in a better position to vote in accordance with their constituents' feelings; the undue influence of vociferous minorities could be counteracted; undesirable attitudes and areas of misinformation could be discovered and steps taken to correct them; legislators could be called to account for flagrant disregard of their constituents' opinions; administrators could use the polls as guides in planning and implementing programs of action; top-group control of political party nominations could be fought. These and other arguments have been set forth in favor of attitude and opinion measurement in government.

On the other hand there are many persons who have pointed out that "government by polls" is an exceedingly dangerous development. "Is 'public opinion' or the 'voice of the people' infallible," they ask, "and should it be followed in blind obedience by legislators?" Critics like Walter Lippmann would maintain that the large mass of people has neither the time nor sources of information available to make wise decisions on governmental policy possible. Such decisions, it is held, should be the duty of the legislator who presumably has the ability and resources necessary to permit his making the correct decisions. It should also be his duty to "lead" his constituents and to guide them in forming their opinions rather than to follow their expressed opinions uncritically. The point has also been made (1) that too literal acceptance of poll results can lead to a subversion of the democratic process, for the traditional procedure of the accommodation and adjustment of differences will be replaced by a blanket acceptance of majority opinion—even when the majority may consist of only 51 percent of the people.

Attitude Study as a Tool of Government

Certainly this chapter is not the place to develop the above arguments fully. It is sufficient here to recognize that attitude and opinion studies are undoubtedly useful as *tools* of government in the hands of both legislators and administrators. How far the use of such studies should extend in the formation of broad public policy and—here there would be little argument—in ascertaining public opinion with the idea of viewing it as *one* of the factors in the total situation to be considered in planning any governmental action is not our concern here. But while there is certainly no universal agreement as to the infallibility of public opinion, the fact that certain opinions are held about certain issues is one factor to take into account in deciding how to deal with those issues.[1]

Let us take a concrete example of how attitude studies can be so used. In 1940 the Forest Service of the United States Department of Agriculture experienced considerable difficulty with the local inhabitants in the neighborhood of its national forests in Louisiana. Several fires were discovered which had obviously been set, one of them resulting in the burning over of a very large tract of forest land. In addition, wire cutting of the preserve fences, which had been put up to restrict cattle and keep out hogs, was prevalent. As a result of these difficulties, the Division of Program Surveys in the Department of Agriculture—an agency set up to measure attitudes—was asked to investigate the situation with a view toward determining first, the causes of the friction between the Forest Service and the local people, and second, methods of reducing it. An attitude study was undertaken and the results led to the conclusion that the Forest Service had failed to consider adequately the effects of its policies upon the local economy and traditions. The Service was concentrating on the raising of trees, thus reducing the amount of grazing land which the local inhabitants felt was needed. In addition it was found that the Service had been inept at times in its contact with the public. As a result of this study, the Forest Service began to consider more carefully local socioeconomic factors in its program planning, and, in addition, a training program of forest supervisors and rangers was instituted which included considerations of good public relations in dealing with local inhabitants (21).

What does the legislator and administrator think of public opinion polls? Kreisberg (12) in 1944 sought to determine the attitudes of a sample of federal legislators and policy-making administrators toward the polls. He found governmental administrators more favorable than the congressmen. In fact,

---

[1] Hartman (6) has observed that there is a big functional difference between the *mandatory* and *advisory* implications of any expression of group opinion.

appreciably less than half of the congressmen thought that ". . . public opinion polling is helpful . . . to the working of democratic government," though they did agree that the polls influenced their colleagues. Hartman (6) questioned New York State legislators in 1942 and found that they used the polls wherever relevant and that they voted according to the expressed public opinion unless very strongly motivated otherwise. It would thus appear on the basis of these two studies that, while a good proportion of our lawmakers may not be too strongly in favor of polls, most of them believe the poll results have had an influence on legislative behavior.

Governmental vs. Private Agencies

A distinction might well be made at this point between opinion and attitude measuring agencies outside of the government (such as the American Institute of Public Opinion and the *Fortune* Poll) and those within the government. This distinction is by no means absolute, and some overlapping does occur. In general, however, the two types of agencies can be considered separately. Usually the outside agencies have based the major portion of their studies upon issues of national interest, many, of course, having a bearing upon major governmental policies. Examples are the questions of the European Recovery Plan and the United Nations Charter. The public findings on such questions as these undoubtedly do have an effect on legislative (and probably administrative) actions, yet such polling lies outside of governmental jurisdiction, and there would be little argument that this is the proper situation.

If the government conducted such polls, they would be in constant danger of being prostituted to selfish governmental or partisan political ends. As the situation now exists, however, the published information of such polls (which often acts to inform governmental officials of existing opinion) are directed not specifically toward those persons in government but toward the general public and social scientists. Thus, many issues studied may have very little importance for governmental functions while others may be quite intimately connected, and while government may be vitally interested in certain of the data published by the polling agencies, its interest does not, and probably will not, lead to governmental participation in such polling.

The government has, however, made extensive use of attitude and opinion polling through various agencies of the executive branch. At the present time, such work is much reduced, but immediately before and during World War II the use of attitude measurement was extensive. In general, governmental opinion studies have been oriented differently from those of the extra-governmental agencies. While the outside agencies have been generally interested in polling on issues of public interest per se, the government studies have been usually conducted with some specific and fairly immediate functional objective in mind.

Most of the studies have been undertaken to answer administrative problems related to the planning or implementation of governmental action. Thus, one study measured public acceptance of war bond drives, another the feelings toward rationing. Proposed programs were sometimes pretested on small representative samples to determine, first, whether they would be accepted and, second, if changes should be made. Morale studies were made to determine the general feelings of certain segments of the population toward the war and war efforts. The armed services studied the attitudes of their personnel toward various phases of their training. This list of studies could be continued, but those mentioned here serve to show that attitude and opinion studies by the government usually have been conducted with quite definite functional objectives in mind.

The distinctions made here between governmental and non-governmental attitude studies are not rigidly valid, but in general this difference in orientation can be kept in mind. Where most attitude studies done by the government have been means to ends and have been controlled by those ends, the published attitude studies done by independent agencies outside of the government have very often been ends in themselves. Actually, a great many of the governmental studies could be compared to private market research. Here, however, the product is governmental action rather than soap or cigarettes or hair tonic. It is with such studies conducted by governmental agencies that this chapter will deal.

EXTENT AND METHODS OF GOVERNMENTAL ATTITUDE MEASUREMENT

Division of Program Surveys

Probably the first extensive and organized effort to set up an attitude measuring agency in the government took place in 1939. In that year the United States Department of Agriculture created the Division of Program Surveys under Rensis Likert. This agency was created after the value of attitude measurement had been demonstrated by a small group of interviewers who moved around the country and interviewed farm people with respect to their feelings toward some of the Department's programs. The purpose of the agency was to measure attitudes, usually in respect to some departmental program in operation or in the planning stage. Actually, the Division not only undertook such studies for agencies within the Department of Agriculture but also for governmental agencies outside of that Department (2).

It was probably not by chance that the Department of Agriculture was a leader in governmental study of attitudes. In some respects it is quite unique among governmental agencies. Many of its activities are of a service nature. It comes into intimate contact with a large proportion of the farming population and under such circumstances has to be constantly alert to its public relations and to what is expected of it by the farmers. Serving farmers with many different problems and under many different circumstances as it does, successful procedures in one area of the country often prove relatively inapplicable in others. As Tolman and Likert have pointed out (23:67), "a major [problem] is that these [farm] programs, like all relatively general and standardized measures, are not equally fitted to the specific needs of each of the many local situations or population groups to which they are applied." Thus it can be seen that attitude measurement offered an answer to many functional problems. While most of its studies have had direct applicability, some have not. Studies have been undertaken which dealt with such problems as morale or what the farmers expected of the postwar era. Information concerning these areas, while not of immediate use, is undoubtedly of great value in overall, long-range governmental planning.

A partial list of the studies conducted by the Division is given here in order to provide an idea of the scope of the various studies and the uses to which they could be put.

Attitudes of farmers toward various aspects of the Agricultural Adjustment Authority

Attitudes of rural people toward their radio service

Public response to a war loan drive

Consumer acceptance of dried milk

Consumer attitudes toward shortages and rationing

Factory workers' knowledge of nutrition and the effect of informational campaigns concerning nutrition

Effect of a campaign to increase home storage of potatoes during an overstocked period

What farmers thought the major postwar problems would be

Marketing research to learn the practicability of new marketing techniques for farm products

Extent of home gardening and canning

Attitudes of farmers toward buying and selling farm land—whether they thought land values would rise or fall

Factors motivating farmers in the production and marketing of certain farm commodities.

A great deal of space could be spent on how such studies as those listed might fit into a functioning governmental department's operations and the implications of the utilization of such studies. In this chapter dealing with applications, however, we shall limit ourselves quite stringently. Most of the studies listed above were obviously investigated as the result of the need for answers to immediate problems or for answers to constantly recurring problems. While some of the information so obtained might have had far-reaching implications, the important purpose for the studies was probably the immediate and direct use to be made of their results.

There was, for example, the study of consumer acceptance of dried milk (4). While its findings might indicate the extent to which dried milk would be used in the postwar period and so suggest changes in governmental policy concerning the dairy industry, the survey would hardly have been approved on such grounds alone. Rather, at the time the study was made, an immediate need was felt for learning how this new and war-necessitated product was being accepted and how successful its retail distribution might be expected to become. Since increased use of dried milk would alter the demand for fresh and condensed milk, knowledge of the degree of its acceptance was important.

An example of an attitude study directed toward less immediate objectives is one concerned with factors—particularly noneconomic ones—which motivated farmers in the production and marketing of hogs (25). Here is a problem having implications not only for the Department of Agriculture but the field of economics in general. No administrative decision pertaining directly and specifically to hog raising and marketing could be expected to result from the study, but its findings might well give economists a better understanding in general of the reasons behind farmers' decisions concerning production and marketing of their products. More generally still, the study might be useful to psychologists in their quest for a better understanding of motivation.

One other feature of the studies listed above might be mentioned. Several of them did not deal solely with expressed attitudes. They were also concerned with the respondents' knowledge. In the study of the effectiveness of a program to stimulate home storage of potatoes (26), for example, the respondents were asked questions on the actual amount of potatoes they had stored and the type of campaign material with which they had come in contact; in addition they were asked such attitudinal questions as "why" they had stored potatoes and "how" they thought the campaign might have been improved and made more effective. Here we see a complementary relationship between factual and attitudinal questions, each one adding to the total understanding.

The Division of Program Surveys has used an extensive field staff in its studies and has developed a highly efficient area sampling technique. In general, the following procedure was used in conducting surveys. After the usual development and pretesting, the questionnaire was sent to the field staff. This staff contained full-time interviewers with educational backgrounds in psychology, anthropology, sociology, or economics. They followed the question schedule from memory in asking the questions which were generally open-ended. Respondent's answers were recorded as nearly verbatim as possible, and after terminating the interview the interviewers "wrote-up" the interview in its entirety. In addition, they scored the answers on a three- or five-point scale of favorableness.

In a central office the written reports were analyzed. Types of arguments, reasonings, and rationalizations were tabulated, as were the relationships between types of answers and arguments. In addition, relationships were determined between such factual items as size of farm, type of farm, geographical location, economic level, and the respondent's attitudinal responses. As mentioned above, questions were open-ended, emphasis being placed upon getting at the reasoning behind the respondents' answers. Interviewers used nondirective probing and in general the interviews were quite intensive (2, 20, 21, 23).

It will be worthwhile to mention the area sampling technique evolved by the Bureau of the Census, the Bureau of

Agricultural Economics (under which the Division of Program Surveys was founded), and the Statistical Laboratory of Iowa State College. It is called the "master sample of agriculture," and with its help it is possible to determine, with relative ease, the small sampling areas in which subsampling can be carried out.

This master sample of agriculture consists of large-scale county maps, each showing the boundaries of small sampling areas (averaging 2.5 square miles in size). On these maps is given information useful for drawing samples, such as the expected numbers of farms and dwellings for each of the small geographical areas, together with their cumulated totals. There are available with these maps listings of all towns, villages, cities, and densely populated places having an estimated population of 100 or more. Such a collection of data as this is a tremendous undertaking, but once accomplished it serves to facilitate area sampling throughout the country (*8, 11*). It is obvious, of course, that periodic revision of such data will be necessary.

Other Governmental Attitude-Measuring Agencies

The Division of Program Surveys, while probably the largest and most extensive single governmental agency engaged in attitude measurement, has by no means been alone in the field. It has been considered first and in some detail because the work of the Division made possible reference to several examples of attitude measurement. We shall now list briefly some of the other agencies which have engaged in attitude and opinion measurement, noting the methods they have used.

Office of Government Reports. This agency did not use any of the techniques we commonly associate with opinion and attitude measurement. Its purpose was to keep the President and certain governmental agencies informed as to current public opinion on various topics. The agency's reports were based on the periodic reports of its "state directors" who also reported on special issues as requested. These state directors obtained their information by interviewing community leaders and officials expected to be well informed concerning the local status of public opinion. Such men as journalists, educators, civic officials, and lower federal officials were thus interviewed. From these interviews the state directors gained an impression of current public opinion which they passed on to the Office of Government Reports which in turn grouped the reports for presentation to the various governmental agencies served (20).

Such a technique as this would certainly not pass the rigid inspection of most social scientists. Personal biases might color the reports of the state directors, as might pressure from above. In addition there could be only the roughest of checks on the validity of the reports. In favor of the method, however, is the fact that it allowed fairly rapid and pliable investigations which, if interpreted in the light of previous experience with its validity, might prove to be useful in indicating the general tenor of public feeling and regional variations in feeling.

Press Intelligence Service.   This section was set up under the Office of Government Reports. As the name implies, the duties of the Service were to keep abreast of current press content. It prepared each day a classified and annotated bibliography of both editorial and news items about governmental affairs. It also prepared a digest of magazine articles on public affairs. Press clippings were made available to those persons and agencies in the federal government that requested them (20).

This service, while not in itself an attitude measuring agency, did facilitate the dissemination of press comment throughout the government, and though press comment could not be thought of as validly indicating public opinion, it is certainly one of the major factors in the formation and expression of public opinion. Knowledge of its content placed government officials in a favorable position to understand, plan for, and meet public reactions as they occurred.

Bureau of Public Relations, Research and Analysis Branch,

United States Army. This bureau served the Army in somewhat the same manner that the Press Intelligence Service served the governmental agencies. It carried on an analysis of press items related to national defense. This analysis was both of a continuing nature (covering general topics of importance to the army) and of a specialized nature (when intensive research was desired upon special topics). The analysis, in general, consisted of rating the press items on a scale of favorableness and tabulating the major ideas and idea sequences (*20*).

Division of Farm Population and Rural Welfare. This Division in the Department of Agriculture has used both attitude studies and sociometric techniques in several resettlement communities. This information has been desired, not so much for its pertinence to public opinion polling, as for its information concerning community interrelations and problems (*20*).

Sociological Research Project. This project, with the cooperation of the United States Navy, War Relocation Authority, and the United States Indian Service, investigated the use of public opinion polling techniques as an aid to the administration of a dislocated community. This information was desired because it was felt that the experience and knowledge so gained might be applied to problems encountered in the occupation of enemy countries (*14*).

United States Strategic Bombing Mission. Upon occupation of both Germany and Japan a full-scale investigation was made of the effect of the bombing upon these enemy countries. One phase of these investigations was the study of the effect of the bombing upon civilian morale. This was done by means of interviews.

Two types of interviews were used: a cross section of the civilian population, and national and local community leaders. In the first case the respondents were questioned concerning the effect of the bombings upon themselves. From the community leaders, information was sought which would *explain* the data obtained from the interviews of the cross-section sample. In addition to the interviews, government reports and documents were examined for supplementary information to clarify the respondent's reports. One of the controls in the selection of the cross-section sample was extent and type of bombing experienced and the resulting morale (27, 28).

In such a study as this, the immediate purpose was the determination of the effect of bombing upon morale. For social scientists, however, this need not have been the only use made of the findings, for they might also have served to give additional understanding of the effect of catastrophic events and extended strain upon human beings, individually and collectively.

Research Branch, Information and Education Division, War Department.   This agency polled the soldiers on a wide variety of subjects. The procedure involved was relatively simple, so far as selection and contact of the sample was concerned. Serial numbers lent themselves to random selection of respondents, and the respondent's presence and coöperation in answering the questionnaire was easily arranged. The respondent's attitudes were obtained by use of anonymous paper-and-pencil questionnaires filled out under the supervision of noncommissioned officers. Here are a few of the topics investigated.

Attitudes of infantrymen toward their branch of the service
Attitudes concerning training received
Attitudes of both white and Negro soldiers toward segregation
How movies altered attitudes
Pride in outfit
Type of junior officer preferred by Negroes
Postwar plans
Interest in various types of movies

The work done by this organization has been published in four volumes (22). This monumental project is a landmark in the development of social psychology.

Investigation of interest in various types of movies was studied by means of a Program Analyzer. Like the instrument for use in the radio audiences this was an apparatus which allowed each man viewing the movie to press one of two buttons as he watched the movie. One button indicated dislike for a particular portion of the movie, while the other button indicated liking. These responses could be electrically recorded and cumulated to indicate portions of the movie liked and disliked, while subsequent interviews brought out the reasons for such likes and dislikes (*29*).

Army Air Forces Aviation Psychological Program. This program involved studies of attitudes toward a wide range of topics, such as the attitude of returned combat flyers toward a second tour of aerial combat, or the attitudes of convalescing air force patients toward their hospitals and activities therein (*13, 18*).

Bureau of Naval Personnel. This Bureau conducted opinion surveys for numerous purposes. It measured the opinions toward their training of the men who had had actual experience, and asked for suggestions on how to improve that training. It determined attitudes toward the availability of news and orientation education. In addition, the Bureau conducted a study among the amphibious forces personnel to determine their feelings toward their assignment in those forces (*17*).

Civilian Surveys Division, Office of Civilian Requirements. This Division was set up during the war to determine the needs of civilians. It used, after some preliminary studies, a national sample developed by the Bureau of the Census. This sample consisted of 5000 households which were polled to find out what shortages were causing the greatest difficulty among consumers. A survey was also made concerning purchases. The information thus obtained was used to determine the shortage of various items, price lines of items in greatest demand, and probable future demand for household items and appliances. In addition to the surveys of consumers, information was obtained periodically from selected mail-order houses, and chain and department stores. Such information served as a check on the varying levels of shortages (*16*).

Surveys Division, Office of War Information. One of the principal objectives of the Office of War Information was to publicize certain war measures and to urge participation in them. The Surveys Division was set up to evaluate by means of public opinion surveys the effectiveness with which these objectives were reached.

The Division pretested the understanding of information materials, such as trial forms of instructions for the Office of Price Administration rationing booklet. It evaluated the effectiveness of informational campaigns by trend studies of popular understanding, support of, and participation in various wartime programs. It sought to determine the public's more basic feelings and attitudes with a view toward general, long-range guidance for wartime programs in general. It also conducted special researches aimed at specific problems. Among these was a study of industrial absenteeism and morale which will be discussed more fully later (*9*).

Correspondence Panels. This agency was initiated by the Office of Facts and Figures and was subsequently transferred to other governmental agencies. It used the panel technique and found that such a procedure permitted a maximum of depth and validity with a minimum of time and expense. Six panels of correspondents were included. These were small businessmen, editors, housewives, social workers, labor spokesmen, and clergymen. A panel of veterans was added toward the close of the war. The persons composing these various panels were located in sample areas worked out by the Bureau of the Census so that the various sizes and types of communities were correctly represented.

The correspondents were volunteers and served without compensation. They made two types of reports. First, they wrote monthly letters covering the topics, and opinion concerning them, most discussed in the preceding month. Second, from time to time they wrote special reports in answer to open-ended questions on specific topics. These monthly letters and special reports were supposed to contain the views most often expressed by the people with whom the correspondents came into contact.

The obvious shortcoming of such a technique is the inability to obtain exact percentages of persons holding various attitudes. In addition, correspondent bias is a factor which must be considered, though persons who were acquainted with the panels claimed that with experience each correspondent's viewpoint could be learned and taken into consideration in evaluating his reports. The evaluation itself was a qualitative matter, and as such is possibly subject to the charge of lack of objectivity. On the other hand, the technique was relatively rapid and inexpensive, and the fact that the Correspondence Panels were in operation for over 4 years suggests that they were found to be valuable (7).

Committee on Food Habits, National Research Council. Here is an example of a private agency subsidized by the government and working with various governmental agencies. The Committee was made up of both *executive* members and *liaison* members. The executive members consisted of scientists and scholars in food habits who had no connection with the government; the liaison members were governmental employees whose duty it was to maintain contact between various governmental agencies interested in the Committee's work and the Committee itself (5).

This agency studied food habits and folkways during the war with the object of learning how best to improve the nutrition of the country's population as a whole. It used a variety of techniques, one of which will be described briefly here. Called "qualitative attitude analysis," this method consisted essentially in the analysis of verbatim records of responses to open-ended questions. By use of a check list, a record of each separate idea supplied by each respondent was kept; in addition, the relationship between the various ideas was noted. Such an analysis was done first on a community basis and then community responses were drawn together. Under this analysis, it was frequently found that the ideas expressed fell into definite patterns. For example, the ideas labeled *A*, *B*, *C*, and *D* might generally be found to be expressed together, while the ideas labeled as *E*, *F*, and *G* might also be generally found together. When such patterns of ideas had been determined, the results of the studies were expressed by composite statements, each statement representing all of the ideas falling into a single pattern.

An analysis of this kind is of course open to the criticism of lack of objectivity. It does, however, allow evaluation of a higher order than the mere tabulation of ideas without any regard for their interrelationships (*15*).

Surveys Conducted by Nonspecialized Agencies

The foregoing list of agencies should give the reader an appreciation not only of the scope of the techniques utilized in ascertaining attitudes and opinions, but of the wide variety of purposes served by the various agencies. One should not, however, draw the conclusion that these were the only agencies concerned with attitude studies. Quite often a governmental agency not specifically interested in attitude studies might become involved in a problem which required the investigation of attitudes, and in such a situation it might set up and conduct the study itself. A good example of this in practice is the study done by the Veterans Administration to investigate the effects of wage ceilings set for on-the-job trainees, and the attitudes of these trainees toward the ceilings. An attitude study was initiated and carried through by the Veterans Administration for its special purposes (*19*).

TWO EXAMPLES

In the previous section we have discussed quite briefly some of the governmental agencies which have been interested in attitude measurement. We shall now discuss in more detail studies carried out by two of these agencies. These are significant, not only for the results they obtained, but for the techniques used.

Industrial Morale Study

At various times during World War II the question of excessive absenteeism of industrial workers came up. The Office of War Information, in its capacity as the governmental information agency, was naturally interested in whether it was in a position to combat this problem. Rather than embarking precipitately upon a publicity campaign to reduce industrial absenteeism on the assumption that it could and should be reduced, the OWI wisely decided first to investigate the situation in a number of industrial plants in order to learn whether it needed remedying, and if so, what the best approach would be. It was for these purposes, then, that a morale study was initiated.

Three distinguishing features may be noted in this study. In the first place, it was quite extensive, covering eighteen industrial plants which represented six war industries. This extensive coverage allowed comparison of attitudes in the light of varying conditions. Most studies under private auspices could probably not have afforded such a coverage. In the second place, the study was undertaken with a very definite objective in mind upon which practical action could be taken. Many morale studies, on the other hand, have either had the information concerning morale as an end in itself, with little practical action contemplated, or at best have resulted in relatively little action. Here, however, the objective was not information concerning morale for its own sake, but information upon which to base an administrative decision and possibly definite action. In the third place, factual information as well as attitudinal information was sought, the two supplementing each other. These three factors are by no means characteristic of governmental attitude studies only, but the first two at least indicate differences which quite often appear between privately sponsored studies and government studies.

Interviews covered workers from eighteen industrial plants representing six war industries. Community leaders in the areas in which these plants were located also were interviewed. The six war industries represented were shipbuilding, electrical equipment, nonelectrical machinery, aircraft, ordnance, and nonferrous metals. From each of the eighteen plants 100 workers were selected at random. Each was interviewed and the absentee record of each was obtained. Information elicited from these respondents included factual data such as number of dependents, marital status, employment history, and wage rate. Attitudinal data were also obtained concerning the respondent's feelings toward the community, the plant, and his job. From the attitudes expressed a morale index was determined. In addition to these randomly selected workers, certain of the workers most recently absent were also interviewed to find the causes of absence.

Community leaders, such as newspapermen, educators, and plant officials were interviewed intensively with respect to community conditions such as transportation facilities, housing, etc. Information was also sought concerning the plant—its history, treatment of absenteeism, personnel policies, health and safety record, size, etc.

The factual data including the absentee record and attitudinal data were then studied in relation to each other and in relation to the community and plant situations. On this basis the absentee problem was evaluated in terms of whether it was caused by slackness or poor worker morale. If such were felt to be the situation, then a publicity campaign could be put into operation which would attempt to motivate the workers to feel more responsibility and so improve their work attendance. Actually, however, the decision reached on the basis of the study was that the absenteeism was due mainly to conditions beyond the workers' control and that a campaign would be ill-advised (*10*).

In this example we see illustrated the very practical use made of an attitude survey in determining what sort of administrative action should be taken. We shall give next a brief description of another attitude study conducted by the government.

This study required a technique to enable the prediction of the financial conduct of the public during a period in which such knowledge was extremely important but relatively unpredictable from past experience.

Postwar Financial Survey

At the close of World War II, a financial situation existed which caused a good deal of alarm among economists. During the war years a number of financial changes had occurred. First, savings had increased tremendously; many lower-income persons who had never saved before had built up appreciable savings accounts. Second, the makeup of the wage-earning public had altered considerably during the war years due to the unprecedented demand for workers. As a result, there was little information on the exact composition of the wage-earning population or on the proportions of various levels of wage earners. Finally, there was a constantly increasing demand for scarce goods. These factors, then, made the prediction of the spending and saving behavior of the American public an extremely unsure thing. Yet, though the prediction of such behavior was difficult, it was very important, if the economy of the country were to be maintained on an even keel.

Information in three areas was sought by the government: the distribution of liquid holdings, expectations as to disposition of accumulated savings, and expectations as to continuance of savings. If these could be determined, and if the attitudes expressed were valid indicators of future financial action, then plans could be made for the financial behavior of the public. The Federal Reserve System therefore requested the Division of Program Surveys to conduct a survey of liquid holdings and expected spending.

The survey used area sampling. The eleven major metropolitan areas were automatically included in the survey. The counties outside of these areas were then stratified according to degree of urbanization, percent of industrialization, previous sales of savings bonds, average farm size, and percent of native white inhabitants. Within these strata counties were selected randomly, and within the selected counties "spending units" were selected at random, a "spending unit" being defined as all persons in the same dwelling, belonging to the same family, who pooled their incomes to meet living expenses. In all, 3000 "spending units" were studied in the spring of 1946 by means of hour-long interviews. From the data so obtained, prediction was made as to what to expect in the way of spending and saving by the public.

Since the technique—so far as it applied to economic behavior—was relatively new, and since it dealt with a subject upon which respondents might be inclined to give invalid or evasive answers, it was felt that the results obtained should be verified in so far as possible by comparing them with outside data. This comparison was made for the estimates which were arrived at concerning total personal holdings of liquid assets and the total of individual incomes. These estimates were compared with other estimates made by different agencies based upon different data, and were found to agree within the limits allowed by sampling error. The prediction, based upon the study, that savings would fall during 1946, was also subsequently proved to be correct.

The actual techniques involved in the study were usual enough, using area sampling and intensive interviewing. The subject investigated, however, was of such a nature that the study, aside from its significance as a useful tool for economists, has two interesting features.

First, let us consider the sampling involved. Data were wanted upon the financial behavior of the public as a whole. This necessitated the use of a representative sample which would include, in proper proportions, all economic levels of the population. This requirement could be met by area sampling, yet such a technique, unless modified, might lead to unreliable results. The reason for this seeming paradox is that the financial behavior of high-income persons is disproportionate to their numbers. Thus, in the sample of 3000, relatively few higher-income persons would be interviewed and results obtained from them would, correspondingly, be relatively unreliable. The importance of their financial behavior in terms of the overall picture, however, would be quite great, and the relatively small numbers of such persons in a straight area sample might lead to invalid results. Because of this, therefore, the higher-income group was "oversampled" so that results based upon this group would be more reliable. Final figures, of course, were determined by the proper weighting— in terms of the total population—of the results obtained from the various income levels of the sample.

The second significant feature of this study is the complementary manner in which the factual and attitudinal data worked together. Both types of data when considered in conjunction with each other led to conclusions which could not have been obtained by the use of only one type of data. As an example of this, consider the prediction of savings. To the question of whether they expected to save more or less in the coming year, about the same proportion of people said that they expected to save more as there were who said they expected to save less. Upon this data alone, one would have expected savings to continue at about the same rate. Yet when the income level of the respondents was correlated with expectations of increased or decreased savings, the conclusion was that savings would actually decrease, since the income levels of the persons expecting to save more were higher than the level of those expecting to save less. This higher-income group could be expected, of course, to decrease the amount of their savings more than the lower-income group could be expected to raise theirs, and so the overall result would be a decrease in savings (3, 24).

SUMMARY

In this chapter we have dealt relatively briefly with the implications of attitude studies in government. Most of the studies are seen to have been a result of practical problems encountered in planning and implementing governmental action. They have, in general, been more in the manner of market surveys than in the manner of the public opinion polls of Roper and Gallup; they have dealt more often with specific issues than with broad generalities, for it is with specific issues that most functional problems, be they in government or not, arise. As a result, the studies have not had, in the main, general legislative implications and have not dealt with problems of broad governmental policies. While there is no doubt much to be said for and against governmentally operated polls dealing with public issues having legislative implications, the attitude studies which have been conducted to aid in the *functioning* of the executive branch of government would appear to have much more in favor of them than against them.

Questions

1. Is there danger that polling can lead to a subversion of the democratic process?
2. Discuss: "A dictatorship does not need and would not use any attitude studies."
3. Was the expense of polling a justifiable part of the government's program during World War II?
4. What criteria could be used in judging the value of an opinion survey on legislative issues?
5. Would it benefit a political party to conduct a poll concerning the major political issues and then write its platform accordingly?
6. If opinion polling became sufficiently acceptable to the general public to impel legislators to comply with its findings, is it possible that minority and pressure groups would attempt to influence the reports on poll results?
7. Could a polling agency be formed in the government that would not be under political influence and control? If so, how?
8. What evidence can you find concerning the "band-wagon" effect, i.e., the alleged tendency of voters to get on the apparently winning side?
9. Suppose that legislation is proposed whereby the federal gov-

ernment would supervise or control all public opinion surveys. What arguments pro and con could you make?

10. A one percent sample of voters in a national election will have less sampling error than the preëlection polls have typically shown. Why not avoid the tremendous expense of national elections, as now carried out, by a carefully designed, scientific sample?

11. Why are governmental administrators apparently more favorable to public opinion polls than are members of Congress?

12. How can the results of the United States Census help in attitude surveys?

13. Hypothesize some results of "government by polls." How would you test your hypotheses?

14. Can you see any areas of application for government polls other than those discussed in this chapter?

15. This chapter discusses the need to oversample the high-income group in a study of savings. How would you proceed to get the proper "weights" in the end result of the survey?

16. Could studies of attitudes become an instrument in the cause of international peace? Discuss.

Bibliography

1. Bernays, E. L., "Attitude Polls—Servants or Masters?" *Publ. Opin. Quart.*, 1945, *9:*264-268*b.*

2. Campbell, A., "Attitude Surveying in the Department of Agriculture." In Blankenship, A. (ed.), *How to Conduct Consumer and Opinion Research,* New York: Harper & Brothers, 1946, pp. 274-285.

3. Campbell, A., and Katona, G., "A National Survey of Wartime Savings," *Publ. Opin. Quart.*, 1946, *10:*373-381.

4. Cook, H. L., and Koecker, R. W., "Retail Distribution and Consumer Acceptance of Dried Milk in Houston, Texas," Washington, D.C.: Bureau of Agricultural Economics, U.S. Department of Agriculture, 1945.

5. Guthe, C. E., "History of the Committee on Food Habits," *Bull. Natl. Res. Coun.*, 1943, no. 108:9-19.

6. Hartman, G. W., "Judgments of State Legislators Concerning Public Opinion," *J. soc. Psychol.*, 1945, *21:*105-114.

7. Herzog, Elizabeth G., "Pending Perfection: A Qualitativ Complement to Quantitative Methods," *Int. J. opin. atti. Res.*, 1947, *1*:31-48.

8. Jessen, R. J., "The Master Sample of Agriculture: II. Design, *J. Amer. statis. Ass.*, 1945, *40*(no. 229):46-56.

9. Katz, D., "The Surveys Division of OWI: Governmental Us of Research for Informational Problems." In Blankenship, A (ed.), *How to Conduct Consumer and Opinion Research*, Nev York: Harper & Brothers, 1946, pp. 241-250.

10. Katz, D., and Hyman, H., "Industrial Morale and Publi Opinion Methods," *Int. J. opin. attit. Res.*, 1947, *1*:13-30.

11. King, A. J., "The Master Sample of Agriculture: I. Develop ment and Use," *J. Amer. statis. Ass.*, 1945, *40*(no. 229):38-45

12. Kreisberg, M., "What Congressmen and Administrators Thinl of the Polls," *Publ. Opin. Quart.*, 1945, *9*:333-337.

13. Lawrence, D. H., and Leving, A. S., "Attitude Studies." In Bijou, S. W. (ed.), *The Psychological Problems in AAF Con valescent Hospitals*, Washington, D.C.: Government Printing Office, 1947, pp. 79-91.

14. Leighton, A. H., and others, "Assessing Public Opinion in a Dislocated Community," *Publ. Opin. Quart.*, 1943, *7*:652-668

15. Metraux, Rhoda, "Qualitative Attitude Analysis—A Tech nique for the Study of Verbal Behavior," *Bull. Natl. Res Coun.*, 1943, no. 108:86-94.

16. Noyes, C. E., and Hilgard, E. R., "Surveys of Consumer Re quirements." In Blankenship, A. (ed.), *How to Conduct Con sumer and Opinion Research*, New York: Harper & Brothers 1946, pp. 259-273.

17. Pace, C. R., "Information Surveys as Evaluative Devices." In Stuit, D. B. (ed.), *Personnel Research and Test Development in the Bureau of Naval Personnel*, Princeton, N.J.: Princeton University Press, 1947, pp. 410-432.

18. Shaffer, L. F., and Pearson, R., "Attitudes and Preferences of Returned Personnel." In Wickert, F. (ed.), *Psychological Research on Problems of Redistribution*, Washington, D.C.: Government Printing Office, Report no. 14, 1947.

19. Shapiro, S., and Eberhart, J. C., "Interviewer Differences in an Intensive Interview Survey," *Int. J. opin. attit. Res.*, 1947, *1*:1-17.

20. Shils, E. A., "A Note on Governmental Research on Attitude and Morale," *Amer. J. Sociol.,* 1941, *47:*472-480.

21. Skott, H. E., "Attitude Research in the Department of Agriculture," *Publ. Opin. Quart.,* 1943, *7:*280-292.

22. Stouffer, S., and others, *The American Soldier,* Princeton, N.J.: Princeton University Press, 1949-1950, vols. I-IV.

23. Tolman, R., and Likert, R., "Psychologists' Services in the Field of Agriculture," *J. consult. Psychol.,* 1942, *6:*65-68.

24. Villard, H. V., "A National Survey of Liquid Assets," *Fed. Reserve Bull.,* 1946, *32:*574-580, 716-722.

25. *An Exploration of Factors Motivating Hog Farmers in Their Production and Marketing,* Washington, D.C.: Bureau of Agricultural Economics, U.S. Department of Agriculture, 1947.

26. *The Potato Storage Campaign in Pittsburgh—Its Publicity and Effectiveness,* Washington, D.C.: Bureau of Agricultural Economics, U.S. Department of Agriculture, *Program Surveys Division Study* 84-I, 1944.

27. *The Effects of Strategic Bombing on Japanese Morale,* Washington, D.C.: Morale Division, U.S. Strategic Bombing Survey, 1947.

28. *The United States Strategic Bombing Survey Over-All Report,* Washington, D.C.: U.S. Strategic Bombing Survey, 1945.

29. *What the Soldier Thinks,* Washington, D.C.: Research Branch, Special Service Division, Army Service Forces, 1943.

CHAPTER X

· · · ● ● ● · · ·

Applications in Industry

INTRODUCTION

The effectiveness of labor-management relations is reflected by individual manager and worker attitudes and opinions. It is the improvement of attitudes that constitutes a prime objective of management to the end of securing effective work and reduced labor costs. Production losses stemming from industrial strife, absenteeism, labor turnover, slowdowns, etc., are usually traceable to undesirable attitudes. The way men feel about their jobs and their employers is what chiefly differentiates them from the machines with which they work, and this fact is unquestionably a most crucial production factor.

It is of prime importance to recognize that the worker is also a man of other roles in society. He is a citizen, father, church-goer, a union man, member of a political party, and so on, *ad infinitum*. The roles the worker plays outside the plant cannot be completely disregarded, for they may seriously affect his strictly occupational activities and duties.

The causes of absenteeism, labor turnover, excessive fatigue, slowdowns, and other problems of industrial production often lie outside the plant.

The British (*49*) support this viewpoint, having profited by their wartime experience with production efficiency: "Industrial output depends first of all on the health, efficiency, and enthusiasm of the workers. The workers, on their side, can give of their best only when conditions of work and management in the factories, of life in their homes, and of transport to and from their work are such as to make it possible for them to keep in good health and spirits."

The plant is in itself a society, sometimes well organized, sometimes not. The social structure and society of the plant is not divorced from society as a whole. It is a part of society, a truly vital part.

Industrial strife, morale, and attitudes are responses which men make to their working conditions, and they directly influence the way in which labor will work and coöperate with management. The worker's adjustment to his job is determined only in part by his skill and aptitude. The worker's attitude toward his job is determined, in very large measure, by his relations with his fellow workers and with his foreman. If he fits in with the gang and gets along with his boss, he is inclined to be satisfied with his job. If he doesn't get along with fellow workers or foreman, then he very likely doesn't like his job.

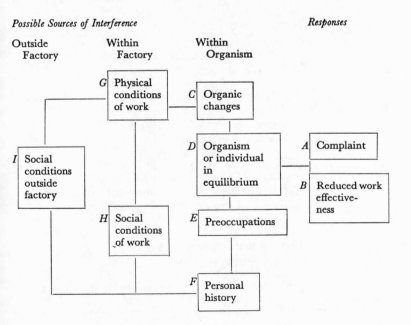

Possible Sources of Interference   *Responses*

The possible sources of interference with production have been charted by Roethlisberger, Dickson and Wright (*64:328*), both outside and within the plant. (See chart, p. 317.)

In examining interference with production from the point of view of types of waste of labor resources and some social values which demand or encourage waste in our society, Moore (*52:263*) has employed the following table.

Major Types of Waste	Subtypes and Examples	Social Values at Issue
Number	Nonemployment: Institutionally restricted: Age, sex, financial independence	Ascribed status and roles; stability and functions of family
	Quasi-institutionally restricted: Caste, citizenship, criminal conviction	In-group and upper-group dominance; "free labor," "right" (and obligation) to work; business and technological vs. "human" interests
	Unemployment: Marginal employability Seasonal Technological Business cycle	
Time	Workdays and weeks Legally or contractually restricted hours	"Spread the work"
	Voluntary absenteeism	Leisure
	Lost-time accidents and sickness	Health
	Work year Seasonal and other short-term employment	
	Strikes	
	Layoffs	Right to strike
	Labor turnover	Business interests
	Serious accidents and diseases	Free mobility
	Work span Shortened life expectancy Incapacitating and fatal accidents and diseases	
	"Superannuation"	Presumed superiority of youth

Major Types of Waste	Subtypes and Examples	Social Values at Issue
Speed or rate of work	Inefficient organization and supervision Inadequate incentives Voluntary restriction of output	"Fair reward"; health (fatigue and monotony); "spread the work"
Skill	Inadequate training Erroneous prediction of requirements Errors in classification Failure to promote or "upgrade" Irrelevant grounds for selection	Free occupational choice Reward for ability; equality of opportunity

Advantages of Studying Employee Attitudes

To provide management with an adequate communications channel with labor for the transmission of worker attitudes and opinions, various surveying methods have been devised. Irwin (28) lists seven major benefits of such studies.

1. They have provided measurements of the trends of employee thought and knowledge about the company. Thus they indicate the strengths and weaknesses in the company's program of closer relationship.
2. They have increased the pride and confidence of the employee in his company. These qualities have been greatly augmented by quick action on the company's part in remedying unsatisfactory conditions.
3. They have stimulated employee suggestions for more improvement.
4. They have strengthened training programs. Frequently a program has certain aspects which, in theory, sound fine but in practice are wide of the target. More realistic training is now possible.
5. They have put supervision on its toes. Supervisors have taken new account of human relations and are getting to know their people better.
6. They have assisted management and union to know one another

better and to appreciate the fact that the other group is just as desirous as themselves of building a sounder industrial commonwealth.

7. They have produced better working conditions. Not only do these spell greater efficiency, but by removing a major cause for discontent they lessen the possibility of strikes and costly slowdowns.

Kornhauser (*40, 41*) writes that attitude studies do the following:

1. They give management a measure of how well it is doing its job of leadership, how well morale is being maintained. It is a rating of management's efficiency in personnel matters.
2. Attention is called to specific problems and sources of irritation that need attention—conditions of work, supervision, personal problems, etc. Often the employees have specific constructive suggestions to offer.
3. Workers are given an opportunity to unburden themselves—to get things off their chests and to feel that the company is really interested in them and their problems. The mere talking makes them feel better.
4. A mine of specific concrete cases is opened, to be used—anonymously—in instructing supervisors in better methods of dealing with their men.

Kornhauser further points out that management derives pertinent information from attitude surveys that pertain to:

1. The general level of employee satisfaction or morale. Management obtains a clear impression as to whether the mental health of the organization as a whole is reasonably good or shows disturbing weaknesses.
2. Comparisons within the organization. For example, it is discovered that certain of the company's plants, divisions, departments, or occupational groups are decidedly lower in morale than are other parts of the organization and hence are places which require special attention.
3. Differences in satisfaction among individuals. Almost always, even when morale as a whole is good, a number of employees are found to have decidedly unfavorable feelings and to reflect

considerable hostility or dissatisfaction. While the identity of these persons is not known, their presence does call management's attention sharply to the need for improved methods of selection, placement, and individualized treatment in order to keep trouble from so-called "problem-employees" at a minimum.

4. Attitudes regarding particular matters: the direction of satisfaction and dissatisfaction. Whether morale is high or low, there are bound to be great differences in satisfaction with respect to different aspects of work relationships. Widely varying amounts of dissatisfaction may be expressed regarding, for example, wage rates or the methods by which they are established, treatment by supervisors and specific supervisory procedures, physical conditions of work, adequacy of equipment, and so on through the long list of points toward which attitudes are expressed. The most definite outcome of employee attitude surveys is usually management's determination to do something about these matters where the greatest amounts of dissatisfaction are manifested.

Kolstad (39) has set up three requirements for an attitude study so that it may be of value to management. The study should provide for:

1. A measure of overall general job morale.
2. The opportunity on the part of the employee to express his attitude on a large number of specific points concerning his job, working conditions, his relationship to his fellow workers, his relationship to his supervisors, his understanding of managerial policies, and so on.
3. An evaluation of the specific attitudes and beliefs in terms of their correlation with general morale.

In addition to other techniques, the exit interview is often employed and has been found to be an excellent source of information. Drake (17) maintains that other methods for ascertaining attitudes only give a cross section or static, rather than dynamic, view of the situation, whereas the attitudes being investigated are constantly changing. The exit interview is a continuous process and provides day-to-day information that reflects the changes occurring within the employee group, especially with regard to dissatisfactions about which management may be able to take constructive action. A further advantage of the exit interview arises from the fact that comments frequently made in the face-to-face situation would not be written, even anonymously.

In recent years, the industrial counselor, bearing such varied titles as personnel interviewer, industrial relations interviewer, in-plant counselor, has been increasingly used. The purpose of an in-plant counseling service is to deal with personal problems of workers which affect rates of turnover, and absenteeism, worker-management relations, and rates of production. A counseling service gives the worker a chance to talk over personal matters with someone able to assist him. It helps management to recognize the importance of human factors in production problems. It provides management with information on conditions which, as they affect the worker, impede production.

Difficulties in Measuring Employee Attitudes

Five areas of problems and difficulties in ascertaining employee attitudes are readily discernible. They are: (1) employee coöperation; (2) ability to reveal attitudes with no language handicap on the part of the workers; (3) the ability of the investigators to report and interpret attitudes; (4) the adequacy of the attitude measurements in terms of a complete or rounded picture; and (5) the possibly unrealistic view attained from attitude measurement. On this last point, Kornhauser says (40): "Attitudes as they occur in their natural state have most complicated interconnections. What we call one attitude is usually one aspect of a tangled network. What we get in our measurements is a one-dimension description—simply an index of how favorable or unfavorable the feeling is toward an object. For practical purposes we usually want to know far more."

In the attempt to uncover attitudes in industry, two types of work have been prominent. The first is the measurement of employee attitudes. The second seeks to discover and reveal factors which determine employee attitudes. In seeking to determine the factors in operation, investigations have been carried out for practically all attitude objects in the work life of an employee.

INDUSTRIAL MORALE

Industry is concerned with not only individual worker attitudes but group attitudes. These group attitudes are usually spoken of as morale. Industrial morale may be said to be a condition in which individuals and groups are willing to subordinate personal goals to further employer objectives. McMurry (46) claims that job satisfaction is an important aspect of morale, and that worker dissatisfaction derives principally from (1) personalities of top management as revealed in company policies and practices, and (2) personalities of executives and supervisors with whom workers come into contact. The latter come to symbolize the company. To the extent that this is true, morale is evidently a matter of interpersonal attitudes. In a survey made by Cherington and Roper for the National Association of Manufacturers, 42.9 percent of the employees named the foreman when asked to define management.

Morale and Attitude

Hull and Kolstad (27) have made the assumption that morale is a function of the worker's general attitude toward his job and company. This general attitude is influenced by attitudes on specific points such as pay, hours, working conditions, supervision, and personnel policies, and morale is largely a composite of such specific attitudes. Their study of "Morale on the Job" yielded results that fail to show any high relationship between morale scores and types of work done, nor does there seem to be any significant correlation between morale and general wage level. The results do suggest, however, that there is some relationship between skill and morale, that is, that a cross section of workers in highly skilled trades would give somewhat higher scores than a cross section of unskilled labor.

There is a definite pattern in the relationship between tenure of employment and morale. In general, employees with less than 1 year's service had relatively higher average scores than have those with from 1 to 5 years of service. The trend then reverses at about the 5-year point, with employees of more than 5 or 10 years' service having scores somewhat above the average for the entire group. Since length of service and age are highly associated, the same general pattern obtains when age alone is considered, but there is a general tendency for morale to increase with age when length of service is held constant.

Department managers, foremen, and other supervisors usually can be expected to have higher scores than those of rank-and-file employees; usually, indeed, the average morale score increases with the amount of responsibility involved.

Hull and Kolstad conclude that industrial morale is not singly determined by material considerations of pay, working conditions, vacations, and company benefit plans. Equally important is employee satisfaction derived from the recognition of, and respect for, his personality. The persons having direct supervision over workers, such as foremen and department managers, play a vital role in the determination of employee morale. The quality of this immediate supervision appears to create a mental set which influences attitudes on factors of the job situation outside the realm of supervision.

Requirements of a Morale Study

Blankenship (*10*) says that any effective system of measuring morale should yield more than the status of morale alone. Subordinate requirements that should be met include:

1. Information about attitudes of employees and their working conditions.

    a. Opportunity for the employee to express his feelings on a large number of specific points (i.e., his relations to other employees, supervisors, hours, pay, etc.)

b. Determination of the relation of these specific feelings to morale

c. Calling attention to specific "sore spots"; both in the plant and in specific situations

2. The opening of a wealth of material for the use of scientists, training of supervisors, etc.

3. Production of a healthy, cathartic effect upon the individuals studied.

FACTORS IN MORALE

The question may be posed as to what are the basic factors underlying morale and what are its determinants. Aside from the widely publicized factors of wages, hours, and general working conditions usually accepted as the subjects for most labor-management disputes are the many trivial irritations in the daily work scene. Such things as poor toilet facilities, warm drinking water, inconvenient location of time clocks, a grouchy supervisor, inadequate instruction on job changes, etc., when experienced daily and linked together, often culminate in strong feelings of dissatisfaction which may crop out in violent uprisings out of all proportion to the immediate situation precipitating the outbreak. These trivial matters are often so covered and hidden from the eyes of management that they go unnoticed as the basic causes of much employee discontent. Such minor irritations become so much a part of the daily work life, that often even the employee fails to recognize consciously these conditions as the underlying reasons for his dissatisfaction.

Management must know the basic causes of employee dissatisfaction in order to attain efficient production and industrial peace. Attitude studies, if properly conducted, furnish management with an effective means of gaining insight into its labor relations problems. Such studies have already shown management many of the causative factors underlying employee attitudes and morale.

A field study of worker morale and the factors related to it was made in five shipyards by Katz and Hyman (*30, 31*) through intensive interviews with representative samples of workers, through background interviews with key informants representing management and labor, and through observations by field workers. Worker morale varied from shipyard to shipyard and was correlated with the productivity of the yards. Katz and Hyman draw the following conclusions from the data.

1. Like other social processes, there is a circular causal relation between morale and production. Good production gives men a feeling of accomplishment and leads to increased effort. Low production reduces motivation which in turn leads to reduced productivity. Instead of a one-way causal relation, most social processes show this circular interaction.

2. Worker morale is most directly related to its immediate physical and psychological context. The factors associated with the job itself are of primary importance in keeping the worker well motivated at his work. If production is going well, if his supervisor treats him fairly, if promotional opportunities are good, if earnings are satisfactory, if the health and safety conditions in the factory are superior, then job satisfaction will be high. Moreover, under such circumstances, most individuals can absorb considerable punishment on the outside and still keep up their work morale. The inference should not be drawn, of course, that management has no stake in good living conditions for workers in the community. Rather the implication of the findings is that management should put its first emphasis upon making the job itself remunerative and psychologically rewarding.

3. In addition to generalizations which apply to more than one worker-morale situation, the significance of any factor for worker motivation needs to be understood in relation to its specific plant and community background. Remedial programs, especially, should take into account the meaning of specific conditions and measures as they relate to the existing context or field of forces.

The Survey Research Center at the University of Michigan

as made a number of significant attitude studies of differences etween high-producing and low-producing work groups, particularly as to the characteristics of supervisors. They find that n the high-producing sections the supervisors are significantly nore likely to give general rather than close supervision, to ike the amount of authority and responsibility they have in heir jobs, to spend more time in supervision, and to be mployee, rather than production or management, oriented 32, 58).

In a study of industrial empathy by Remmers and Remmers 63), 100 labor leaders' attitudes were measured by means of he test *How Supervise?*[1] A representative sample ($N = 42$) of hese labor leaders also responded to another form of the test is they thought a typical representative of management would answer it. The conclusions drawn from this study are given below. They must, of course, be interpreted in light of the fact that the sample was a self-selected one—only those who wished to coöperate did so.

1. As measured by the test, *How Supervise?*, understanding of the psychologically "best" supervisory methods in industry is slightly but not reliably greater among union leaders than among industrial management.

2. Labor leaders' scores on *How Supervise?* are related to age, union experience, and working experience in industry, in that the younger, less experienced men obtain the higher scores, and the older, more experienced men, the lower scores. There is a strong presumption that this negative relationship does not hold for management.

3. Labor leaders' scores on *How Supervise?* are not related to degree of formal education, position in the labor hierarchy, number of people represented in past and present union jobs, or supervisory experience in industry.

4. In terms of the items on *How Supervise?*, labor leaders show a tendency to stereotype management, in that management is

[1] Q. W. File and H. H. Remmers. The Test in three forms and the *Manual* published by the Psychological Corporation, New York.

regarded as possessing relatively less understanding of good supervisory attitudes and methods than it actually does.

5. Labor leaders score significantly higher on the test when taking it as themselves than they score as management.

6. There are no significant relationships between the scores attributed to management by labor and the personal history variables—i.e., education, age, union experience, plant experience, position in the union hierarchy, number of people represented in past and present union jobs, and supervisory experience.

A second study (*51*) reversed the procedure by measuring a sample ($N = 150$) of management on the test *How Supervise?* and asking them also to answer on another form of the test (1) how the respondents thought typical labor leaders would answer the test items and (2) how rank-and-file labor would answer them. The conclusions, again to be interpreted in light of the sampling limitations, follow.

1. Management on the average tends to *overestimate* labor leaders' scores on the test or, in other words, the average person in management attributed better supervisory attitudes to labor leaders than the available facts warrant.

2. Labor leaders on the average tend to *underestimate* management's scores on the test—they attribute worse supervisory attitudes to management than the available facts warrant.

3. In view of the absence of norms on the test for labor rank-and-file members and in view of the substantial equality· of management's projected scores for labor leaders and rank-and-file laborers, it may be inferred that management on the average does not underestimate laborers' attitudes as they would be if obtained. Obviously this inference requires experimental verification.

4. Management has moved significantly nearer the position of experts in mental hygiene and industrial relations in its supervisory attitudes—it has improved significantly in a few years.

5. There is a low but significant positive relationship between

management's supervisory attitudes and years of formal education ($r = 0.238$, S.E.$_r = 0.09$).

6. There is a low but not quite reliable positive relationship between management's years of education and the attitudes it attributes to labor leaders ($r = 0.17$, S.E.$_r = 0.09$).

7. There is a low but rather reliable correlation between management's years of education and the attitudes it attributes to labor rank and file ($r = 0.22$, S.E.$_r = 0.09$).

8. There is no appreciable relationship between management's attitudes and the number of persons supervised ($r = 0.16$, S.E.$_r = 0.09$).

9. There is no appreciable relationship between the number of men supervised and the attitudes attributed by management to labor leaders ($r = 0.09$, S.E.$_r = 0.10$).

10. There is no appreciable correlation between years of formal education and number of men supervised ($r = 0.02$, S.E.$_r = 0.10$).

11. Having had a supervisory training course has no appreciable effect on management's own attitudes ($r = 0.16$), those it attributes to labor leaders ($r = 0.14$), or to labor rank and file ($r = 0.03$).

12. Management's attitudes are reliably positively related to those it attributes to labor leaders ($r = 0.49$, S.E.$_r = 0.06$) and to labor rank and file ($r = 0.49$, S.E.$_r = 0.06$).

13. The attitudes attributed by management to labor leaders and rank and file are reliably more similar ($r = 0.78$, S.E.$_r = 0.06$) than management's attitudes and those they attribute to labor leaders and labor rank and file. In other words, the differences between an r of 0.78 on the one hand and of 0.41 and 0.49 on the other are reliable.

I have elsewhere (62) differentially defined empathy and projection: When A's estimate of B's responses on any psychological dimension (in this case, test items in *How Supervise?*) coincide with the actual measurement of B on this dimension (within allowable error of measurement) then empathy is established. A has successfully "put himself in the other fellow's shoes." To the extent, however, that the null hypothesis must be rejected as between these two measures, there is present projection on the part of *A*, since what he professes to see in *B* is not actually there, but is the product of *A*'s own personality.

By this definition it is clear that labor leaders empathize less and project much more than does management, assuming that the samples of labor leaders and of management are at all representative. It would be highly desirable to repeat these experiments on a much broader statistical base.

Job Satisfaction

Some years ago Hoppock (*23*) interviewed the small community of New Hope, Pennsylvania. Six percent of the population was unemployed and of the 357 employed adults, 309 or 88 percent answered the questions. The results showed that 15 percent did not like their jobs; 15 percent felt satisfied with their jobs less than half the time; 24 percent would have liked to change both their jobs and their occupations; 10 percent disliked their jobs more than they thought other people disliked theirs; 9 percent were indifferent; and the remainder, 21 percent; indicated various degrees of liking or satisfaction.

When the subjects were invited to take their choice of all the jobs in the world, 36 percent indicated that they would leave their present occupation; 16 percent indicated that they would leave their present job but remain in the same occupation; while 48 percent would remain in the same job and occupation. Sixty-six percent of the subjects got more satisfaction from their jobs than from the things they did in their spare time.

On the basis of these data Hoppock (*23*:7) concludes: "The most logical inference from available data is that the persons actively or consciously dissatisfied with their jobs are a minority group representing probably one-third or less of the employed adult population."

Hoppock, comparing his findings with others, found satisfaction apparently increasing with age: Thorndike found the same; Fryer and Kornhauser and Sharp found no relationship; Strong found older workers liking fewer occupations but retaining the same order of preference among them. Hoppock found no significant differences between the best and least educated; Fryer and Kornhauser and Sharp found the same. Hoppock found an apparent relationship between dissatisfaction and neurotic tendency, agreeing with Kornhauser and Sharp, while McMurry found it in some cases but not in others and Pintner found no relationship. Hoppock found no sex differences, but Thorndike and Uhrbrock found women better satisfied than men. Hoppock also found supervision apparently affecting satisfaction, which was agreed with by Bressenden, Frankel, and Kornhauser and Sharp. Hoppock found an apparent relationship between satisfaction and occupational status and Thorndike and Uhrbrock found the same.

In conclusion, Hoppock comments:

Job satisfaction is related to a good many things besides financial return. Some of these factors are relative status of the individual within the social and economic group with which he identifies himself, relations with superiors and associates on the job, nature of the work, earnings, hours of work, opportunities for advancement, variety, freedom from close supervision, visible results, the satisfaction of doing good work, opportunities for service to others, environment, freedom to live where one chooses, responsibility, vacation, excitement, opportunity for self-expression, competition, religion, opportunity for or necessity of traveling, fatigue, appreciation, or criticism, security, and ability to adjust oneself to unpleasant circumstances.

Super (76) investigated the job satisfaction of 273 employed men aged 20 to 68, and found that slightly over 60 percent were satisfied with their jobs. There was a significant, but not linear, relationship between occupational level and job satisfaction. Two occupational scales were found to exist: one of white-collar workers and the other of manual workers. Professional occupations were highest in job satisfaction, managerial next, and commercial least, in the white-collar scale. Skilled occupations ranked highest in the manual scale. The amount of change of occupational level had little effect on job satisfaction, while direction of change had considerable effect. The nature of the work itself appeared as the most frequent reason for disliking a job. Economic reasons ranked second. Managerial policies were ranked third. Job satisfaction was found to develop cyclically; older adolescents from 20 to 24 tended to be satisfied with their jobs; young men from 25 to 34 tended to be dissatisfied; older men tended to be satisfied.

One instrument designed to measure job satisfaction is the "Tear Ballot," a summated questionnaire so arranged that the respondent indicates his responses to the item alternatives by tearing the edge of the sheet at appropriate points. The originator, Kerr (34) and his students have studied and reported on the validity of this instrument. Reliability for 12 employee groups was shown to have a range of 0.65 to 0.88 and an average of 0.83. For 98 New Orleans wage earners Kerr obtained a validity coefficient of 0.36 when each item was weighted according to its own correlation with job tenure (turnover reversed) (35).

Another study (82) by Van Zelst yielded a coefficient of 0.82 against the criterion of mutual-averaged ratings on desirability as working partners of 66 building-trades workers—34 carpenters and 32 bricklayers all of whom had been working together for at least 3 months. Van Zelst cautions, however: "The high correlation (0.82) between mean interpersonal desirability of workers and job satisfaction may be somewhat overestimated. The occupations studied here are currently in high demand on the labor market and, with a limited supply of these skills, the worker has a wide range of jobs to choose from. With wages fixed, his choice of job therefore probably depends on other factors . . ." including presumably attitudes toward co-workers and other factors included in the Tear Ballot.

With the criterion of responses to a union ballot designed

to measure attitude toward the union, its machinery, the shop steward and union achievement, Gottlieb and Kerr (22) obtained a validity coefficient of 0.74 with scores on the Tear Ballot for 467 workers in a jewelry and plastic-goods manufacturing concern.

Empathetic ability as a criterion (36) for the Tear Ballot yielded a validity coefficient of 0.44 when both measures were administered to 125 skilled industrial workers by Van Zelst (83). The same author in a very interesting and well-controlled sociometric regrouping experiment with two groups of building-trades workers found, after an interval of 3 months, that the average for the thirty-six experimentally regrouped workers had a significantly higher average score on the Tear Ballot—44.8 as against an initial score of 38.5. The control group of thirty-six men showed no significant change—39.6 and 39.3, respectively. More important, labor turnover and production costs were significantly lower for the experimental group than for the control group (84).

Speroff (74), for thirty-six employees in two different plants, obtained a correlation of −0.76 between Tear Ballot scores and the frequency of worker-initiated, worker-manager interviews, thus strongly supporting his hypothesis that grievance and "catharsis" sessions were negatively correlated.

Incentives. Management has been handicapped, Whyte (87) believes, by the acceptance of an oversimplified theory of human motivation. It has been assumed that the worker is motivated primarily, if not exclusively, by a desire for material reward. Therefore, if a man is offered good wages and reasonable economic security, he should be satisfied.

While economic incentives are still given primary emphasis in industry, their limitations are becoming more apparent. But, in many cases, this has only led management off in vain pursuit of some other simple factors that will solve morale problems.

A questionnaire employing the paired comparison technique was distributed to determine employee attitudes toward five incentives by Blum and Ross (11). They found that advancement and security were considered more important than salary, and that the attitudes of employees depend on such major classifications as sex, marital status, and age.

PUBLIC OPINION POLLS

Roper (65, 66, 67) has used polling methods in the field of worker opinion and has reported as follows:

Question: "Which one or two things would you say gives a person the best chance to advance at the place where you work?"

	Total	Prof. and Exec.	Salaried Employees	Factory Workers	Union Workers
The quality of his work	47.0	63.7	50.6	43.4	35.4
His energy and willingness	44.5	55.7	41.5	42.3	39.1
How well he gets on personally with his immediate bosses	17.5	12.1	16.6	18.7	21.2
Whether he is a friend or relative of a high official	5.6	3.4	6.6	7.6	9.7
How long he has been with the company	11.9	5.4	10.9	16.6	19.4
How good a politician he is	5.4	6.0	7.0	3.5	6.6
Don't know	10.4	6.0	5.2	10.5	11.1

Question: "Do you feel personally that if you work harder on your job than the others around you this will pay off in promotion or advancement for you, or wouldn't it make much difference?"

	Total	Prof. and Exec.	Salaried Employees	Factory Workers	Union Workers
Will pay off	47.0	58.3	49.3	39.9	37.8
Will not pay off	40.5	30.2	39.7	49.3	51.7
Don't know	12.5	11.5	11.0	10.8	10.5

From the answers to both questions two generalizations can be made: (1) While the absolute percentages differ for the four groups, the relative ranks of these percentages tended to be the same and (2) the attitude patterns of professional and technical personnel as compared with "factory workers" and "union workers" differed significantly.

Undesirable Features of a Job. There have been various approaches to the problem of determining what factors, hidden or otherwise, might be discovered by soliciting opinions and attitudes from employees. One novel approach was used by Fraser and others (*20*) in asking employees what were the "main strains of their particular jobs." It was reasoned that the main strain might arise from the nature of the job, or from the conditions under which it was performed, and at the same time, it might be any unpleasant or otherwise undesirable feature, irrespective of whether it was a strain in the strict sense of the term.

OPINION OF THE WORKERS CONCERNING THE MAIN STRAIN OR UNDESIRABLE
FEATURES (IF ANY) OF THEIR JOBS

| | Percentages holding the opinion | |
Cause of Main Strain of Job	Among 817 Men	Among 873 Women
Physical environmental conditions:		
General to the shop	38.6	37.7
Special to the job	12.7	14.2
Nervous or mental strain:		
Boredom or monotony	21.7	37.2
Eyestrain	22.3	27.8
Demand for accuracy or memory	12.4	8.6
Technical or supervisory responsibility	9.8	0.9
The personal relationship involved	6.0	3.3
Pressure for speed	5.3	9.9
Physical strain from:		
The exertion required	22.8	17.0
Postural requirement	3.7	5.5
Production or maintenance difficulties	10.3	2.4

It would appear from this analysis that a worker's satisfaction with his job might be increased by attention to its physical environmental conditions. Fraser indicates particularly those possible improvements general to the shop, such as diminution of the sources of mental strain, and avoidance of unduly heavy work—probably in that order of importance. Clearly both the last two aspects in part concern the appropriateness of the job to the worker concerned. Under physical environmental conditions were classified strains relating to such aspects as ventilation, lighting, and cleanliness. It is clear that the two most frequent types of nervous or mental strain noted were boredom or monotony and eyestrain.

Attitude and Intelligence

The data available permitted examination of another condition which Fraser thought might contribute to the worker's attitude toward his job—the appropriateness of his abilities to those required for the job. His evidence showed that there is some association between attitude toward the job and its appropriateness to the worker's intelligence.

Morale Factors Rated

In an extensive study of the factors affecting employee morale, Raube (*61*) found that job security was selected by the largest number of employees in each of six companies as the foremost among seventy-one morale factors affecting their attitude toward work and the company. Raube investigated the first factor in importance in addition to ratings of the five most important factors. Following are his tabulations.

FIRST FACTOR IN IMPORTANCE

Factor	Percent
Job security—employment stabilization	30.6
Compensation (base pay)	8.7
Type of work	7.2
Opportunities in the company for advancement	4.7
Profit-sharing plans (excluding employee-saving plans)	3.8
Supervisors' temperament and personality	3.5
Practice of informing you of your job status (both of your successes and failures)	3.1
Physical working conditions (on the job)	3.1
Employee merit or performance rating (an organized and systematic method of appraising your performance)	2.5
Company's attitude toward employees (its interpretation of policies whether liberal or conservative)	2.3

TOTAL, FIVE MOST IMPORTANT FACTORS

Factor	Percent
Job security—employment stabilization	44.7
Opportunities in the company for advancement	30.7
Compensation (base pay)	27.9
Employee financial benefits, such as group life insurance, sickness insurance, and pensions	24.4
Practice of informing you of your job status (both of your success and failure)	19.2
Type of work	18.5
Vacation and holiday practices	16.4
Supervisors' temperament and personality	16.3
Profit-sharing plans (excluding employee-savings plans)	15.7
Physical working conditions (on the job)	14.4
Company's attitude twoard employees (its interpretation of policies whether liberal or conservative)	13.6

Raube (61) also reports the work done by other surveys to determine the relative importance of a limited number of morale factors. One study consisted of employees' rating factors as "How Much Each Factor Means to Me" in three gradations: "a whole lot, quite a little, practically nothing." Following are the results of an inquiry into 250 employees' ratings.

Factor	A Whole Lot	Percent Quite a Little	Practically Nothing
How am I doing on my job—good, fair, not so good	88	12	..
My vacation and holiday privileges	85	14	1
Extra pay (such as bonuses)	84	12	4
My job rate	81	18	1
How my supervisor treats me	79	19	2
How my company treats me	77	22	1
Physical working conditions on my job	72	24	4
Quality of supervision on my job	72	25	3
Is my job secure	71	24	5
Special benefits (insurance)	70	19	11
Job evaluation as applied to my job	70	25	5
Attention given my grievances	63	28	9
My opportunities here for advancement	62	18	20

Factor	A Whole Lot	Percent Quite a Little	Practically Nothing
Approximately 1200 employees ranked twelve factors submitted to them as follows:			
Job security	74	17	9
How my supervisor treats me	72	22	6
Physical working conditions on my job	68	22	10
How my company treats me	67	21	12
My job rate	66	22	12
Quality of supervision on my job	65	22	17
Being told how well I am doing on my job	64	17	19
Extra pay (such as bonuses, incentives, etc.)	64	11	25
Special benefits (insurance)	61	20	19
Attention given complaints	58	23	19
My opportunities here for advancement	56	21	24
Opportunities to make suggestions	55	24	21

To indicate that rank positions of factors are not universally true for the whole population of workers, Maier (*44*) cites a survey in which department-store workers, miscellaneous workers, factory workers, and union and nonunion workers are compared. Little relationship if any was shown between the ranking of ten factors by factory workers as compared with department store and miscellaneous workers.

Music. There have been many studies of individual factors thought to be of importance in affecting attitude, morale, and productivity. One of the areas most recently rather extensively investigated has been in music. Among the foremost of the investigators in this area are Kerr (*33, 34*), Kirkpatrick (*37, 38*), Smith (*72*), and Spears (*73*).

Kerr (*33*) reports that a group of 229 electrical workers express an overwhelming confidence in certain psychological powers of music.

64% think it improves their feelings toward associates.
93% believe it helps them when tired.
79% say it soothes their nerves.
48% think it helps their digestion.

89% believe it helps them in performing a wearisome, monotonous task.

77% say it helps make them forget their worries.

The influence of an industrial music program, which systematically varied the amount, type, and distribution of music played, was studied in a plant of approximately 1000 employees over a 3-month period by Smith (72). An effort was made to determine effects of music on employee attitudes, piecework production, and industrial accidents.

Prior to the music program, 98 percent of the employees thought that music during working hours would be at least "mildly pleasant" and 74 percent thought it would be "extremely pleasant." The intensity of interest in music decreased somewhat with age. At the end of the music program, there were no decreases in the desire for music while working.

As for production, increases were statistically significant in addition to being large enough to be of economic importance; under varying conditions of music, it increased from 4 to 25 percent. The more an employee wanted music, the more music tended to increase his output; the more the employee's job permitted conversation while working, the more music tended to increase production.

Analysis of music programs in their relation to individual accident records, none of which showed statistically significant differences, indicated that there was no difference between the number of accidents on music days and on nonmusic days, and that accidents tended to decrease with music in the earlier part of the shift, but to increase with music in the latter part.

A particularly interesting factor is management's attitude toward the effects of music on employees. Spears (72) says that management's concern centers around abstract benefits derived from music rather than on any possible ensuing material profit.

OTHER INDUSTRIAL ATTITUDES

Although the individual worker is the most common source of information on attitudes in industry, various studies have been conducted among union leaders and employers which indicate that they are not cognizant of how workers feel on many issues.

The Union

Houser (25) questions the accuracy of union spokesmen's interpretations of their members' needs. He claims that management cannot learn its workers' real desires from the union demands.

THE UNION ASSERTION	THE FACTS
1. "We want better salaries"	Pay ranked 25th in importance out of 34 items
2. "We want opportunity for advancement"	56% do not want promotions, but prefer development on their present job. The opportunity for promotion ranked 20th out of 34 items
3. "We want security on the job"	83% say they are fairly sure of holding their jobs as long as they do good work. 26% are very sure
4. "We want better medical service"	81% approve the quality of the medical service but its rank is 31st in importance
5. "We don't want conflicting orders from our superiors"	Only 17% say they get conflicting orders. It ranks 11th in importance
6. "We want improvement in the Mutual Benefit Association"	87% approve the Association as it is. Its rank is 27th in importance

Houser then lists the first ten employee attitudes in this organization in their descending order of importance with the percentage of dissatisfaction.

Attitude	Importance	Dissatis-faction, %
Knowing whether work is improving	1	13
Fairness of promotional practice	2	78
Encouragement to offer new ideas and try out better methods	3	66
Understanding difficulties of job by supervisors	4	84
Sufficient help to get results expected	5	21
Grievances—assurances of fair hearing and a square deal	6	27
Freedom to seek advice in new problems	7	54
Invitation to offer suggestions when plans are being considered	8	61
Being given reasons for changes ordered in work	9	51
Assurance of pay increases when desired	10	59

Houser concludes that the dynamics of employee psychology seems to be at least as much of a closed book to union leadership as to executives.

The Employer

Watson (85) reports rankings assigned eight factors in morale by employers and employees. A rank order coefficient of +0.1 shows that the two rankings have no better than chance agreement with each other.

Benge (5) reports rankings of employees in a department store and the executives of the stores. Here again the relationship turned out to be +0.1, not significantly greater than zero.

SIGNIFICANCE OF EMPLOYEE ATTITUDES

Studies have been carried out on the relationship of attitudes to all phases relating to production efficiency. A series of studies by the Western Electric Company in its Hawthorne plant (64) effectively demonstrates the importance of worker attitudes and morale in an industrial organization. The grievances of employees, the expression of dissatisfaction and discontent through absenteeism, turnover, slowdowns, etc., should be viewed by management as behavioral indicators of discontent. Disregard of such expressions can only lead to poor labor relations culminating in eventual work stoppages or slowdowns.

Management must know what the worker thinks about his job and his company for purposes of self-defense in the role of an operating industrial organization which is trying to maintain efficient production. The worker, seeking an outlet for expressions of discontent to release feelings of aggression, may in part use attitude surveys as his release valve. This method of release is preferable to industrial strife. If constructive management action based on the attitude survey follows, morale will be improved.

Surveys of industrial morale show that employee attitudes vary significantly from one department to another and between plants and companies. Such attitude variations may serve as a gauge of labor relations. Significant differences in employee attitudes are usually found between large and small companies. A survey (6) showed the morale in the smaller companies to be rather consistently better than in the larger companies.

EMPLOYEE ATTITUDES AND CONDUCT

Roethlisberger, Dickson, and Wright (64) at the Hawthorne plant of the Western Electric Company, have investigated employee attitudes in regard to such factors as rest pauses, increased output, increased earnings, authority, shorter working day, shorter hours, and toward one another in the working group. Perhaps the most interesting was the attitude of the individual worker toward the way he should conduct himself. These sentiments, which were connected chiefly with output, may be summarized as follows.

1. You should not turn out too much. If you do, you are a "rate-buster."
2. You should not turn out too little work. If you do, you are a "chiseler."
3. You should not tell a supervisor anything that will react to the detriment of an associate. If you do, you are a "squealer."

4. You should not attempt to maintain social distance or act officious. If you are an inspector, for example, you should not act like one.

It may be concluded that the individual's position in the group was in large part determined by the extent to which his behavior was in accord with these sentiments.

WASTE AND EFFICIENCY

Scientific management strives to eliminate waste, increase efficiency, reduce costs, and increase quality, at the same time giving each of the factors of production its just share of the fruits of production. Much time, effort, and money is expended to this end. Yet there is probably no phase of the industrial program in which there is more "wishful thinking" than that indulged in by management as to the attitudes of its employees toward the company.

The very costly problems of labor turnover, absenteeism, accidents, work slowdowns, fatigue, boredom, and monotony, are largely the result of unsatisfactory worker attitudes.

Boredom, Monotony, and Fatigue

Maladjusted employees—the dissatisfied, the disgruntled—will very likely be bored by, and "tired" of, their work. These and other evidences of negative attitudes will generally result in lowered output. Such feelings of tiredness are not very closely if at all related to output of physiological energy. They reflect, rather, basic dissatisfaction, for pay increases alone are probably rarely if ever the remedy.

The signs of fatigue and boredom have been summarized as follows (49).

1. Lowered output. Acute boredom, which makes the worker dislike even the idea of starting work, is often shown by low output at the start and then a gradual rise as the end of the work approaches.
2. Lowered quality of work. Fatigue and boredom often cause the quality and quantity of work to suffer.

3. Increased number of accidents. It is well known that fatigue results in an increase of accidents since it lessens the power to control movements, to concentrate, and to remember precautions. It is not so widely realized that boredom, which makes workers inattentive and slow, has a similar effect.
4. The behavior of the worker. Individuals vary considerably in the way in which they behave when bored or tired. Usually a bored person is discontented, and apt to complain about working conditions; he often attaches excessive importance to opportunities for promotion and for using his own ideas. On the other hand, he may "daydream" and be uninterested in his work and surroundings. He may be either more fault-finding or more apathetic than a worker who is interested in his job.

The effects of fatigue are shown to vary. Some, when overtired, are listless and quiet, while others become depressed, irritable, or obstinate. The bodily symptoms of excessive fatigue frequently are indigestion, headache, eyestrain, muscular pain, and loss of appetite. A bored person often feels some of these symptoms and thinks that he is tired. However, if he is given more interesting work—or when work is over—his symptoms, unlike those of a fatigued person, will usually disappear.

The study quoted above continues with the causes of fatigue and boredom and considers hours of work, nature of the job, working conditions, and attitude of the worker. Particularly interesting is the importance attached to rest pauses, and to early stages of fatigue in skilled workers—shown by the way in which they work and not by the quality or quantity of their work. In the attitude of the worker, both boredom and fatigue are much more likely to arise if there are no strong incentives to work. Few workers are given the opportunity to understand fully the importance and function of the articles they help to make and their relation to the final product.

Lack of opportunity for promotion, and payment by time rather than by results, also tend to decrease interest and energy. Unreasonable inequalities in payment, and unjust or unsympathetic treatment by foremen or management, have the same effect. Dissatisfaction, feelings of antagonism, and anxiety all use up mental energy and increase fatigue. Any conditions which do not stimulate or which frustrate the normal impulses and needs of men and women tend to increase boredom. Loneliness or isolation at work makes most people, after a time, feel depressed, bored, or tired. The pleasures of companionship and—especially on dull jobs—the interest of talking to fellow workers do much to prevent or relieve boredom. In fact, many workers feel this social life in the factory is a real compensation for dull jobs.

Taylor, Thompson, and Spassoff (78) make the following generalizations.

1. Under ordinary working conditions there is an inverse relationship between amount of work produced and reported feelings of tiredness and boredness.
2. The same observation holds true in respect to observable boredness and tiredness, as rated by the experimenters.
3. The greater the amount of work done, the greater is the amount of intragroup variability in production rate.
4. The introduction of rewards such as rest pauses and bonuses, facilitates production markedly, but has little effect on reported feelings of tiredness and boredness.
5. Knowledge that a rest pause is imminent retards production for the period immediately preceding the pause.
6. Indulgence in activities such as talking or laughing tends to objectify the working situation and also tends to inhibit to some extent reports of tiredness and boredness.
7. The group working situation has little effect on reported or observed feelings of tiredness and boredness.

Absenteeism

Noland's (54) study of the relationships between expressed attitudes and absenteeism among workers shows the significance of employee attitudes as a production factor. Items concerning the worker's satisfaction with the job were, taken collectively, most closely associated with absenteeism. The most promising of these items, as points of attack on the problem, were degree of satisfaction with the job, extent of being bothered by varying work, and fairness and kindliness of treatment by fellow workers.

The workers' opinions regarding the efficiency of management were next most closely associated with absenteeism records. The important considerations turned out to be the foreman's display of appreciation of good work and needless shifting of workers from job to job.

Katz and Hyman (*30*) report the industrial morale in war plants as follows.

1. Overall plant rates of absenteeism showed a moderate correlation with the nature of community conditions. But, in-plant conditions were more important than community conditions.

Plants with High Absenteeism Were Plants with	Correlation
Serious transportation difficulties	0.46
Serious housing problems	0.48
Poor physical working conditions	0.73

2. Individual rates of absences were related to dissatisfaction with in-plant conditions. When we arbitrarily defined an absentee for purposes of comparison as a worker who had been away from work for more than 3 percent of the time over a 3-month period, it was found that specific aspects of worker morale were related to absence.

Morale Components	% of Each Group Who Were Absentees
Workers disliking job	44
Workers liking job	36
Workers disliking plant as place of work	50
Workers liking plant	37
Workers objecting to plant health conditions	43
Workers finding plant a healthy place	36
Workers objecting to plant safety conditions	45
Workers satisfied with safety conditions	37

Morale Components	% of Each Group Who Were Absentees
Workers dissatisfied with promotional policy	40
Workers satisfied with promotional policy	34
Workers lacking confidence in management	45
Workers with confidence in management	37

Absenteeism has been viewed as an aggressive act on the part of the worker striving for recognition and status. If the worker thinks that management is not too concerned about him as an individual, he "fights back" at this frustrating situation by not appearing on the job. His logic is that management, not recognizing him when on the job, will feel his absence. This has been exemplified by the work of Fox and Scott (19) who found that "absenteeism is a symptom of a worker's attitude; and his attitude is conditioned in very large measure by the quality of attention that management pays to his problem, both technical and human."

The conditions affecting absenteeism which exist in the general work situation are, according to Kushnick (43), placement of workers, management policy and attitude, and physical working conditions. Kushnick asserts that proper job placement is fundamental to job satisfaction. Having a person perform that work for which he is suited best by temperament, aptitude, and intelligence is an important part of personnel management. Only in this way can the worker be made to feel the challenge of his work, and to derive the intangible satisfactions that come from a job well done.

Investigating the causes of absenteeism of 550 employees in eight departments, Jackson (29) lists his results as follows.

1. Poor work habits indicated by trouble and fighting with other workers or foremen, laziness, tardiness, horseplay and bad previous work records   6%
2. Personal maladjustment, indicated by separation, divorce, fam-

ily quarrels, symptoms of psychoneurosis, unstable personal life, drinking, breach of peace, etc. 9%

3. Dissatisfaction with work, indicated by many transfers, complaints about work, machines, or men, complaints about pay or working conditions, lack of interest . . . complaints about the management 16%

4. Irresponsibility, indicated by unexplained absenteeism, incapability of being left on own resources, not working the job but thinking leisure activities more important, no loyalty to the company or the job 17%

5. Outside difficulties, indicated by outside business or shopping problems, home responsibilities, transportation and housing difficulties, moving visits to out-of-state homes 17%

6. Sickness or fatigue, indicated by evidence of sickness, doctor's or hospital care, accidents resulting in lost time, and complaints about health, fatigue, etc. 35%

Bixler (9), reporting for the National Safety Council, describes 4800 individual cases of personal causes of accidents.

1. 50% were caused by improper attitude. This included such things as willful disregard of instructions, recklessness, violent temper, absent-mindedness. . . .

2. 30% were caused by lack of knowledge or skills. . . .

3. Only 2% were caused by bodily defects. . . .

Selling (71) presents the psychiatrist's point of view by saying that there is a relationship between nutrition and industrial accidents. There is also a connection between absenteeism, frequent job changes, and accidents. The most important reason for accident proneness is faulty attitude. The individual causes for accident proneness seem to be physical inadequacy, psychological inadequacy, mental deficiency and neuroses, preoccupation with other problems, dissatisfaction with a part of the whole of the plant's setup, and a bad safety attitude which may include recklessness, indifference, or antagonism to law and order.

On the matter of preoccupation with other problems, Speroff and Kerr (75) obtained interesting and significant results in an investigation of the relationship between a sociometric measurement with accident rate. Each of ninety men (44 Negroes and 46 Spanish-speaking workers) was requested to name the other workers whom he "would most like to work with" and also whom he "would least like to work with." These men worked in nine teams, from four to six men to a team. The correlation between the obtained "interpersonal desirability value" for these men and their 3-year accident record was —0.54, statistically very reliably above zero. The authors hypothesize that interpersonal rejection is a major factor in causing worry, hence preoccupation with this social situation and hence greater liability to accidents.

MINORITIES

The question of minorities in industry is of such scope that at best it can be touched upon only briefly in this chapter. Minority groups in industry include such individuals as the Negro worker, the Mexican worker, the Jewish worker, the Chinese worker, and many other national and religious groups. In a special minority category is the woman worker.

As we have seen, the industrial plant is not an organization isolated from the total social scene, but is an integral part of society. The people who make up the plant's "social structure," from the rank-and-file worker to the top executive, play a variety of roles outside the plant which directly influence their in-plant behavior and attitudes. Biases of caste, color, religion, and many other varieties of social pressure and indoctrination to which the individual is subjected from childhood, cannot be shaken off by the mere act of punching a time clock. This is most evident in both labor and management's reaction to the Negro in industry, an attitude which is carried over to a lesser or equal degree in the treatment of other minorities.

The Negro population in the United States offers a greater potential labor force to industry than any other single minority group. Yet, the Negro worker is the "last to be hired and the first to be fired." Management has in the past, and continues in many cases, to refuse consideration of the Negro for any type of employment. More often than not, when accepted, he is accepted for a menial job. Though it may not be conscious of doing so, management is, in this way, denying to itself a large segment of the labor market which could be used to help bring about the productive capacity required for a stable economy.

On the whole, the white worker has not been too disposed toward accepting the Negro as an associate. His stereotyped conception of the Negro as an individual and member of a "race" and his feelings of economic insecurity present serious obstacles to acceptance of the Negro worker on an equal basis in such plants where management has attempted to do so. This attitude was translated into overt action during World War II, for example—when the Negroes had made their greatest advances in industry—in such incidents as the Harlem and Detroit race riots and in numerous "wildcat" strikes carried on to protest the hiring of Negroes for skilled jobs or for upgrading a Negro worker.

O'Connor (55) found, in a survey of 402 companies, that before the defense emergency 73.4 percent either did not employ Negroes at all or used them only for janitor service and unskilled labor, and 26.6 percent used them for skilled or semi-skilled work. Only 27 of these companies were in the south; 13 used skilled Negroes, 14 did not. Of 108 plants employing Negroes, 61 reported that their white employees did not object much to working with Negroes; 10, that there was "no definite objection"; 4, "some complaint"; and 4, "serious objection." Women employees, it seems, "react more violently than do men employees." In 52 plants, labor unions either approved the employment of Negroes or did not discriminate; only 8 were prejudiced against them.

Many companies reported that the white employees did not object to the Negroes who had been employed for some time, but did object to the introduction of Negroes in a department traditionally white, or to an increase in the ratio of Negro employees. There is little objection to Negroes in common labor jobs "but those in the semiskilled trades and on up the line show an increasing amount of resentment. . . . This attitude may be fostered by the active opposition of some of the unions covering skilled labor." Interestingly enough, the greatest objection to Negro workers was not found in the South but in the Border States. White workers most often objected to sharing sanitary and locker equipment with Negroes or to participating jointly in the use of recreational facilities.

The plants surveyed were asked to compare Negro and white workers on the basis of ability, production, regularity in attendance, accident record, and intelligence. On all but the last point the overwhelming majority ranked Negroes as equal to white workers, with a few indicating in each case that they were superior. On the last point they were evenly divided except for one which reported "better than whites."

Gardner (21) points out that the position of Negroes in our society and the generally accepted attitudes toward them produce serious problems in their introduction into a factory or work group. Parts of the whole caste system in which he is kept separate and subordinate are the common, irrational beliefs in the uncleanliness and disease of the Negro. Concurrent with these attitudes are the refusals on the part of white workers to share washrooms, locker rooms, and eating facilities with Negroes. These attitudes actually are expressions of the social processes by means of which Negroes are kept at a distance.

These attitudes of the white worker are not only apparent in his actions in the plant, but are carried over to his trade union. Discriminatory policies appear to be carried on principally by the American Federation of Labor's craft unions where status and skill are given more importance than in the industrial-type union. However, many local and independent national unions still evidence reluctance to admit Negroes on an equal basis with their white members—a result of the Negro's role as a scab and strike breaker in periods of vicious antiunion activity, a fact which unions find it hard to forget.

MANAGEMENT VIEWS ATTITUDE STUDIES

Modern management in its effort to improve production should look favorably upon attitude studies as a means of improving the human element in production. But experience has shown that often the greatest opposition to such studies has come from members of management.

This situation casts light on the attitudes of management itself. From the reasons given for opposition to attitude surveys it becomes evident that much insecurity is felt by executives, and they fear what attitude studies might reveal about their effectiveness as managers.

Typical of the conditions a poll is apt to reveal are: (1) poor operating methods; (2) undesirable working conditions; (3) weaknesses in supervision; (4) inconsistencies and inequalities in company policies; and (5) hostilities toward top management. Inasmuch as many of these reflect directly on management's competence, it is obvious that many executives are not eager to have them brought to light.

In one case reported by McMurry (48), a CIO local requested an employee opinion poll to aid in the settlement of a labor-management dispute and agreed to abide by the findings. Management flatly refused to permit such a poll, though the polling was to be done by an independent outside organization.

Management's Rationalizations

Some of the reasons offered by management for its resistance to attitude studies are as follows: The poll will "suggest" dissatisfaction and thus create poor morale and ill will toward the company. Although in some situations this claim may prove to be valid, in many studies it has been proved false in two ways. In the first place, if the poll itself caused the dissatisfaction, such discontent should be rather evenly expressed among departments; yet most attitude studies show wide variations in the kind and degree of dissatisfaction expressed in the various departments of a company. Second, further investigations of dissatisfaction voiced on polls usually show the unsatisfactory conditions actually to exist.

A second claim often made against attitude studies by management is that polls will upset employees emotionally, distract them from their work, and result in much discussion of these matters both on and off the job, causing direct and indirect losses of production time. In reply to this argument, it might be stated that polls generally require no longer than 30 minutes. The release of emotional tension through polls usually facilitates production, and employee discussion has not been found to disrupt production routine significantly. As pointed out by McMurry (48), the motives of executives who claim losses in production time and fail to see the long-range gains are rather transparent, particularly when one watches costly plant equipment being bought for the very same argument of future productivity.

Another argument given by management for rejecting attitude surveys is that many employees will either refuse to answer the questions or give silly or irrelevant responses. The success in gaining employee coöperation lies mainly in the adequacy of the presentation of the study to the workers. When the project is carefully planned so as to make certain that the employees understand thoroughly its purpose, the number of irrelevant responses is negligible, and seldom do employees ever refuse to answer.

A fourth, and strongly emphasized, complaint of management against attitude studies and polling is that the bringing out into the open of the issues they cover gives unions ammunition with which to attack the company. This may be a serious potential threat, but there are no cases to date to support this claim. Rather, in companies where strikes may be imminent, attitude surveys facilitate the settlement of disputes.

Opinion polls, conducted by an outside, independent organization, are often not discussed with the union in advance of their administration. This is naturally often resented by the unions; but little reluctance is encountered on the part of the union members to answer the questions.

In short, if the labor organization has confidence in the integrity of the company, there is little reason to anticipate trouble of any kind.

Allaying Management's Fears

Common sense offers four methods for allaying management's fears for its own security.

1. Referring management to executives of other companies which have conducted these polls successfully.
2. Making it clear to management that the findings will be handled confidentially.
3. Where the poll is recommended by an outside consultant, he can accept the responsibility for the effect of the poll upon the employees.
4. Sometimes management will consent to the trial of a poll in one department on a pilot basis. Later reassured, it will go ahead with the entire organization.

It might be said that the greatest impending danger associated with the use of employee attitude surveys and opinion polls is the failure of management to help correct conditions in need of adjustment as revealed by the studies. Negligence or refusal to take action may add employee distrust of management to the existing dissatisfaction. The result is more hostile feelings and tension.

Some unions may resent the surveying of employee opinions and attitudes if they are indoctrinated with fear that this is another management tool with which to combat the union. However, if the study is conducted in an unbiased, scientifically controlled manner and members of the union are protected from reprisals from management, it is difficult for union officials to oppose such studies. There are some unions that recognize the good that can come from such studies and frequently, attitude surveys have been conducted under a joint management-union sponsorship.

Employees as individuals are usually favorably disposed to attitude studies. A typical report of a study made by Bergen (7), revealed that 74 percent of the employees favored such studies, 22 percent were neutral, 3 percent were unfavorably disposed to such studies and 1 percent did not answer.

SUMMARY

The importance of the human factor in industry is becoming increasingly apparent. Good labor-management relations are essential for efficient production. One of the greatest needs of modern industry is an adequate two-way communications system between labor and management. Without such means, good industrial relations are virtually impossible.

The status of labor-management relations in any organization is reflected by employee attitudes and opinions. Poor labor attitudes lead to breakdowns in the production organization in the form of accidents, absenteeism, scrappage, etc. Thus, it is vitally important that industrial management know the attitudes of its employees, and, upon discovering these attitudes, take definite action to build good morale. However, because of many fears and prejudices, both management and unions have generally opposed systematic attitude surveys. Management itself has been the most reluctant in accepting these studies; yet it stands to gain much from such research.

Basic to all attitude studies are the problems inherent in gaining adequate management and labor confidence and support. All studies of attitudes must be conducted on as objective and free-from-bias basis as possible, with adequate provisions for the protection of individuals from damaging retaliations.

The role of attitude studies in industry is that of an instrument for the procurement of high production efficiency and the attainment of greater satisfaction and social welfare for industrial workers. Employee attitudes are an integral factor of production and must be identified and properly reckoned with in personnel and production policies and practices. Attitude studies must be so designed as to evaluate properly each individual industrial setting.

Irrational attitudes of both management and labor toward members of minorities hinder industrial as well as community harmony.

Questions

1. Discuss the statement, "Management's interest in employee attitudes arises from the belief that attitudes are important determinants of efficiency." Is efficiency the only justification for attitude studies, or can they be justified on other grounds?

2. Would it be reasonable to state that some attitude studies achieve therapeutic purposes as well as measurement purposes? If you accept this statement, give examples of studies which you feel achieve this dual purpose.

3. Would it be possible to have a high degree of job satisfaction among the workers in a plant and at the same time a low rate of production? Give reasons for your answer.

4. Design a study to test this hypothesis: "In the average industrial plant more workers are in jobs below their intelligence level than in jobs above their intelligence level."

5. Spears says that management's concern centers around abstract benefits derived from music rather than in any possible ensuing material benefit. Is this a rationalization on the part of management?

6. If workers generally look upon foremen as representatives of management, why do labor organizations tend to look upon them as members of labor?

7. What methods may be used to change the attitudes of white workers toward Negroes and of Negroes toward whites?

8. Does accident proneness exist? If so, how are attitudes related to this phenomenon?

9. What hypotheses have you to account for the higher morale of older workers? How could you test such a hypothesis?

10. What advantages and disadvantages are there in having a morale study in an industrial organization conducted by an outside agency?

11. What are some of the possible advantages and disadvantages of using the results from an employee opinion poll to aid in the settlement of a labor-management dispute?

12. To what extent should management make attitude surveys related to the home situation, community situation, interpersonal relations in the plant, etc.?

13. From the studies cited in this chapter do you conclude that the amount of pay is the chief factor in job satisfaction? What are other large factors?

14. Attack or defend: "There should be more emphasis on continual, periodic 'feeling of the industrial pulse.'"

15. To whom does the counselor in industry owe his loyalty?

16. Is music desirable for all classes of jobs? How would you test this?

17. It has been said that pay and working conditions are frequently poorer in small firms than in large ones. If this is so, why should morale tend to be higher in small firms, as has been alleged? Outline an investigation to determine the relevant facts.

18. It has been said that women workers are more aware of mental strain than their men co-workers. If so, why is this? Could you find out? How?

Bibliography

1. Allport, G. W., "The Nature of Democratic Morale." In Watson, G. (ed.), *Civilian Morale,* Boston: Houghton Mifflin Company, 1942.

2. Arvensberg, C. M., and McGregor, D., "Determination of Morale in an Industrial Company," *Appl. Anthrop.,* 1943, *1*(no. 2):12-34.

3. Aspley, J. C., and Whitmore, E. (eds.), *The Hand Book of Industrial Relations,* Chicago: Dartnell Corporation, 1943.

4. Baruch, D. W., "Why They Terminate," *J. consult. Psychol.,* 1944, *8*(no. 1):35-46.

5. Benge, E. J., *How to Make a Morale Survey,* New York: National Foremen's Institute, Inc., 1941.

6. Benge, E. J., "How to Learn What Workers Think of Job and Boss," *Fact. Mgmt. Maint.,* 1944, *102*(no. 5):101-104.

7. Bergen, H. B., "Measuring Wartime Attitudes and Morale," *Person. J.,* 1942, *21*(no. 1):2-9.

8. Bingham, W. V. D., and Moore, B. V., *How to Interview,* New York: Harper & Brothers, 1931.

9. Bixler, H. R., "Emotional Factors in Safety," *Person. J.,* 1946, *25*(no. 1):9-14.

10. Blankenship, A., "Methods of Measuring Industrial Morale." In Hartmann, G. W., and Newcomb, T. M. (eds.), *Industrial Conflict: A Psychological Interpretation,* New York: The Cordon Company, Inc., 1939.

11. Blum, M. L., and Ross, J. J., "A Study of Employee Attitudes Toward Various Incentives," *Personnel,* 1942, *19*(no. 1): 438-444.

12. Burtt, H. E., *Psychology and Industrial Efficiency,* New York: Appleton-Century-Crofts, Inc., 1929.

13. Cathcart, E. P. (chairman), "Industrial Health in War," *Med. Res. Coun., Industr. Hlth. Res. Bd. Emergency Rep.,* March, 1940 (no. 1).

14. Collier, H. E., "The Mental Manifestation of Some Industrial Illnesses," *Occup. Psychol.,* 1939, *13*:89-97.

15. Cooper, A. M., "Developing Morale or Creating Hysteria," *Personnel,* 1944, *20*(no. 5):266-269.

16. Daugherty, C. R., *Labor Problems in American Industry,* Boston: Houghton Mifflin Company, 5th ed., 1941.

17. Drake, C. A., "The Exit Interview as a Tool of Management," *Personnel,* 1941, *18*(no. 1):346-350.

18. Eisemberg, P., and Lazarsfeld, P. F., "The Psychological Effects of Unemployment," *Psychol. Bull.,* 1938, *35*(no. 6):358-390.

19. Fox, J. B., and Scott, J. F., "Management Causes Absenteeism," *Person. J.,* 1944, *22*(no. 9):326-329.

20. Fraser, R., and others, "The Incidence of Neurosis Among Factory Workers," *Med. Res. Coun., Industr. Hlth Res. Bd. Rep.,* May, 1947, no. 90:1-66.

21. Gardner, B. B., *Human Relations in Industry,* Chicago: Richard D. Irwin, Inc., 1947.

22. Gottlieb, B., and Kerr, W. A., "An Experiment in Industrial Harmony," *Person. Psychol.,* 1950, *3*:445-453.

23. Hoppock, R., *Job Satisfaction,* New York: Harper & Brothers, 1935.

24. Hoslett, S. D. (ed.), *Human Factors in Management*, Parkville, Mo.: Park College Press, 1946, p. 205.

25. Houser, J. D., *What People Want from Business*, New York: McGraw-Hill Book Company, Inc., 1938.

26. Hughes, E. C., "Race Relations in Industry." In Whyte, W. F. (ed.), *Industry and Society*, New York: McGraw-Hill Book Company, Inc., 1946.

27. Hull, R. L., and Kolstad, A., "Morale on the Job." In Watson, G. (ed.), *Civilian Morale*, Boston: Houghton Mifflin Company, 1942.

28. Irwin, J. W., "Sampling Workers' Opinions," *Mgmt. Rev.*, 1946, *35*:118-119.

29. Jackson, J. H., "Factors Involved in Absenteeism," *Person. J.*, 1944, *22*(no. 8):289-295.

30. Katz, D., and Hyman, H., "Industrial Morale and Public Opinion Methods," *Int. J. Opin. Attit. Res.*, 1947, *1*(no. 3): 13-30.

31. Katz, D., and Hyman, H., "Morale in War Industry." In Newcomb, T. M., and Hartley, E. L. (eds.), *Readings in Social Psychology*, New York: Henry Holt and Company, Inc., 1947.

32. Katz, D., Maccoby, N., and Morse, Nancy C., *Productivity, Supervision and Morale in an Office Situation*, Ann Arbor: Survey Research Center, Institute for Social Research, University of Michigan, 1950.

33. Kerr, W. A., "Factor Analysis of 229 Electrical Workers' Beliefs in the Effects of Music," *Psychol. Rec.*, 1942, *5*(no. 7): 213-221.

34. Kerr W. A., "Where They Like to Work; Work Place Preference of 228 Electrical Workers in Terms of Music," *J. appl. Psychol.*, 1943, *27*:438-442.

35. Kerr, W. A., "On the Validity and Reliability of the Job Satisfaction Tear Ballot," *J. appl. Psychol.*, 1948, *32*:275-281.

36. Kerr, W. A., and Speroff, B. J., *The Empathy Test*, Chicago: Psychometric Affiliates, 1951.

37. Kirkpatrick, F. H., "Music and the Factory Worker," *Psychol. Rec.*, 1942, *5*(no. 7):197-204.

38. Kirkpatrick, F. H., "Music in Industry," *J. appl. Psychol.*, 1943, *27*:268-274.

39. Kolstad, A., "Employee Attitudes in a Department Store," *J. appl. Psychol.*, 1938, *22*:470-479.

40. Kornhauser, A. W., "The Technique of Measuring Employee Attitudes," *Personnel*, 1933, *9*(no. 4):99-110.

41. Kornhauser, A. W., "Psychological Studies of Employee Attitudes," *J. consult. Psychol.*, 1944, *8*(no. 3):127-143.

42. Kornhauser, A. W., and Sharp, A. A., "Employee Attitudes," *Person. J.*, 1932, *10*(no. 6):393-404.

43. Kushnick, W. H., "The Role of Psychology in Absenteeism." In Gafafee, W. M. (chairman), *More Manpower Through Reduction of Absences*, Proceedings, 17th Annual Meeting of the Industrial Hygiene Foundation, November, 1942, p. 39.

44. Maier, N. R. F. *Psychology in Industry*, Boston: Houghton Mifflin Company, 1946.

45. McGregor, D., "Conditions of Effective Leadership in the Industrial Organization." In Hoslett, S. D. (ed.), *Human Factors in Management*, Parkville, Mo.: Park College Press, 1946.

46. McMurry, R. N., "Management Mentalities and Worker Reactions," *Adv. Mgmt.*, 1942, *7*(no. 4):165-172.

47. McMurry, R. N., "Opinion Poll, Follow-Up Interview, and Exit Interview as Morale Builders in Industry," *Amer. J. Orthopsychiat.*, 1945, *15*:348-350.

48. McMurry, R. N., "Management's Reaction to Employee Opinion Polls," *J. appl. Psychol.*, 1946, *30*(no. 3):212-219.

49. *Medical Research Council, Industrial Health Research Board,* "Conditions for Industrial Health and Efficiency—Absence from Work and Prevention of Fatigue," *Pamphlet No. 2,* 1944.

50. Miles, G. H., "Effectiveness of Labour Incentives," *Hum. Factor,* London, 1932, *6*(no. 2):53-58.

51. Miller, F. G., and Remmers, H. H., "Studies in Industrial Empathy: II. Managements' Attitudes Toward Industrial Supervision and Their Estimate of Labor Attitudes," *Person. Psychol.*, 1950, *3*:33-40.

52. Moore, W. E., *Industrial Relations and the Social Order,* New York: The Macmillan Company, 1946.

53. Noland, E. W., "Worker Attitudes and Absenteeism," *Amer. sociol. Rev.*, 1945, *10*:503-510.

54. Noland, E. W., "Why Do Workers Stay Away," *Fact. Mgmt. Maint.*, 1946, *104*(no. 1):131-132.

55. O'Connor, W. B., "The Use of Colored Persons in Skilled Occupations," *Conf. Bd. Mgmt. Rec.*, 1941, *III*(no. 12):156-158.

56. Pennock, G. A., "Industrial Research at Hawthorne," *Person. J.*, 1930, *8*(no. 4):296-313.

57. Pennock, G. A., and Putnam, M. L., "Growth of an Employee Relations Research Study," *Person. J.*, 1930, *9*(no. 1):82-85.

58. *Productivity, Supervision and Employee Morale*, Ann Arbor: Survey Research Center, Institute for Social Research, University of Michigan, *Human Relations Series* I, *Report* I, 1948.

59. Putnam, M. L., "Improving Employee Relations," *Person. J.*, 1930, *8*(no. 5):314-325.

60. Raube, S. A., "Factors Affecting Employee Morale," *Conf. Bd. Mgmt. Rec.*, 1944, *6*(no. 12):351-353.

61. Raube, S. A., "Factors Affecting Employee Morale," *Conference Board Reports, Studies in Personnel Policy*, 1947, (no. 85).

62. Remmers, H. H., "A Quantitative Index of Social-Psychological Empathy," *Amer. J. Orthopsychiat.*, 1950, *20*(no. 1):161-165.

63. Remmers, Lois J., and Remmers, H. H., "Studies in Industrial Empathy: I. Labor Leaders' Attitudes Toward Indusitrial Supervision and Their Estimate of Managements' Attitudes," *Person. Psychol.*, 1949, *2*:427-436.

64. Roethlisberger, F. J., Dickson, W. J., and Wright, H. A., *Management and the Worker*, Cambridge, Mass.: Harvard University Press, 1940.

65. Roper, E., "The Fortune Survey," *Fortune*, 1947, *35*(no. 1): 5-16.

66. Roper, E., "The Fortune Survey," *Fortune*, 1947, *35*(no. 5): 5-12.

67. Roper, E., "The Fortune Survey," *Fortune*, 1947, *35*(no. 6): 5-10.

68. Schenet, N. G., "An Analysis of Absenteeism in One War Plant," *J. appl. Psychol.*, 1945, *29*:27-39.

69. Schultz, R. S., "Psychology in Industry," *Person. J.*, 1937, *16*(no. 6):220-223.

70. Seidman, J. E., "Dissatisfaction in Work," *J. soc. Psychol.*, 1943, *17*:93-97.

71. Selling, L. S., "Psychiatry in Industrial Accidents," *Adv. Mgmt.*, 1945, *10*(no. 2):70-75.

72. Smith, H. C., "Music in Relation to Employee Attitudes, Piece-Work Production, and Industrial Accidents," *Appl. psychol. Monogr.*, 1947(no. 14):7-59.

73. Spears, E. M., "Music in Industry," *Conference Board Reports, Studies in Personnel Policy*, 1947 (no. 78).

74. Speroff, B. J., "Job Satisfaction Study of Two Small Indiana Plants," unpublished manuscript, 1951.

75. Speroff, B. J., and Kerr, W. A., "Steel Mill 'Hot Strip' Accidents and Interpersonal Desirability Values," *J. clin. Psychol.*, 1952, *8*:89-91.

76. Super, D. E., "Occupational Level and Job Satisfaction," *J. appl. Psychol.*, 1939, *23*:547-564.

77. Taft, R., and Mullins, A., "Who Quits and Why," *Person. J.*, 1946, *24*(no. 8):300-307.

78. Taylor, J. H., Thompson, G. E., and Spassoff, D., "The Effect of Conditions of Work and Various Suggested Attitudes on Production and Reported Feeling of Tiredness and Boredness," *J. appl. Psychol.*, 1937, *21*:431-450.

79. Thompson, L. A., "Measuring Susceptibility to Monotony," *Person. J.*, 1930, *8*(no. 3):172-196.

80. Tiffin, J., *Industrial Psychology*, New York: Prentice-Hall, Inc., 1942.

81. Uhrbrock, R. S., "Attitudes of 4430 Employees," *J. soc. Psychol.*, 1944, *5*:365-377.

82. Van Zelst, R. H., "Worker Popularity and Job Satisfaction," *Person. Psychol.*, 1951, *4*:405-412.

83. Van Zelst, R. H., "Validation Evidence on the Empathy Test," unpublished manuscript, 1951.

84. Van Zelst, R. H., "Validation of a Sociometric Regrouping Procedure," *Appl. psychol. Monogr.* (in press).

85. Watson, G., "Work Satisfaction." In Hartmann, G. W., and Newcomb, G. T. (eds.), *Industrial Conflict: A Psychological Interpretation*, New York: The Cordon Company, Inc., 1939.

86. Watson, G., "Morale During Unemployment." In Watson, G.

(ed.), *Civilian Morale*, Boston: Houghton Mifflin Company, 1942.

87. Whyte, W. F., *Industry and Society*, New York: McGraw-Hill Book Company, Inc., 1946, chap. 10.

88. Woods, W. A., "Employee Attitudes and Their Relation to Morale," *J. appl. Psychol.*, 1944, *28*:285-301.

CHAPTER XI

· · · · ● · · ·

Applications in Community
Interrelations

INTRODUCTION

From the point of view of attitude research, relations among
members of a community is a field as broad as it is challenging.
This is especially true when one chooses to include in the
concept of "community" all units of human organization, from
the family to the community of nations, and when one desig-
nates as falling within these wide boundaries attitudes toward
government, toward socioeconomic problems, toward racial
and ethnic groups, toward crime and delinquency, toward
marriage, morals, and the church, toward ideologies, foreign
and native—toward, in short, all ideas, institutions, and groups
that constitute the social order under which we live.

Because social scientists have interpreted and defined the
field of community interrelations in just such a fashion, the
relevant literature is so all-inclusive as to prohibit anything
but superficial coverage in this chapter. An attempt will be
made here merely to acquaint the reader with applications of
the more important techniques employed in research of this
kind with some of the findings which have accrued. To this
end, it seems desirable to discuss the literature in terms of
research methods, presenting each technique in connection

with a few of the studies in which it was used. Included in this chapter, then, is a brief survey of each of the following techniques: (1) The interview; (2) paper-and-pencil scales; (3) social distance; (4) social action; (5) historical analysis. A brief review of research on the development of social attitudes concludes the discussion.

THE INTERVIEW

The interview, one of the earliest methods to develop for investigating intergroup attitudes, remains among the most widely employed in social-scientific research. It is the technique most often used by public opinion polling agencies, by market researchers, by man-on-the-street radio commentators. It has the advantage of directness and wide flexibility, and the disadvantage that its data may be distorted by interviewee reaction to the interviewer and by the interviewer. For these reasons it is often used in conjunction with other, less personalized techniques—observation, paper-and-pencil questionnaires, etc. In the following paragraphs, studies in which the interview method predominated are briefly discussed, in order to familiarize the reader with the wide range of social attitudes to the study of which this method is appropriate.

During World War II, Kornhauser (*32*) undertook an ambitious project, involving a prolonged investigation of the attitudes of Chicago residents toward war problems and policies. Over a one-year period, he and his assistants conducted personal interviews with Chicagoans from all racial, occupational, and economic groups, discussing with them such propositions as war and peace aims, and the possibility or desirability of a negotiated peace. He found a majority in favor of fighting the war to the finish, although a greater proportion of Negroes than whites favored an immediate negotiated peace. A majority stated themselves "mildly willing" to sacrifice for the war effort, with Negroes less willing than whites. Most of Kornhauser's subjects were antiwar, but felt it "inevitable"; and a majority regarded World War II as primarily a defensive struggle, on the part of the United States, to prevent domination from abroad.

In an attempt to determine tenant reactions to a wartime federal housing project, McPherson and McPherson (*39*) interviewed families of fifty-four shipyard workers employed at the Mare Island Navy Yard, Vallejo, California, and living in a government housing project called Chalbot Terrace. The families were divided into two groups, group *A* including thirty-seven families with children of preschool age, and group *B* composed of seventeen families with children in school. Inquiries were made as to how the tenants made friends under war housing conditions; how children were cared for while parents worked; how leisure hours were occupied; how often parents were able to "go out"; how present associates compared with friends and associates "back home"; how whites and Negroes felt about each other as neighbors and co-workers; what constituted the tenants' major complaints about the housing project; and how they regarded the state of their health, since moving to the Terrace.

In 1943, Link (*37*) conducted a nation-wide survey in order to study the attitudes of three large groups toward important social issues of the time. The interviewers used questionnaires uniform in content, and 7000 personal interviews with farmers, urban dwellers, and college students were conducted. The groups were measured and compared as to their attitudes toward possible postwar economic conditions, the growing power and prestige of organized labor, the modern tendency toward greater centralization of government and enlarged federal control of business, and their own personal postwar aspirations.

By means of lengthy interviews, Sargent (*48*) investigated attitudes toward war and peace of twenty-five town dwellers and twenty-five farmers in a Midwestern agricultural community. He found high morale in both groups with respect to expectation of victory and willingness to sacrifice, but low morale with respect to anticipated postwar conditions. Attitudes toward allies were generally favorable, and in spite of a widespread belief that brutal atrocities were committed by enemy armies, there was a decided lack of animosity toward the peoples of enemy nations. Three-fourths of the subjects favored United States participation in an international league, but few anticipated lasting peace. The author reported finding no correlation of attitudes with age, sex, occupation, political affiliation, or degree of formal education of the subjects.

During the depression of the 1930's, when talk of "class consciousness" and the "class struggle" ran high, Kornhauser (31) conducted a series of interviews in an effort to determine the extent to which such socioeconomic class feelings actually existed. His subjects were several thousand men and women in a representative sample drawn from different sections of the city of Chicago. He found that awareness of class differences existed strongly only among the very wealthy and the very poor, and among major business executives and labor union officials. He found, also, that various personal factors—sex, age, race, education, religion, foreign birth, unemployment, change in income level, newspapers read, presidential vote, and satisfaction with job—were related to the extent of class awareness in the twenty economic groups surveyed.

Hayes studied the political attitudes of 8500 voters, in relation to consistency of attitudes (20), some general factors in political issues, and party regularity of the voters (21). Interviewers were volunteers from the League of Women Voters, who questioned subjects on issues in the 1932 presidential campaign. Among the findings which resulted from this study are the following: (1) Consistency of attitude varied with the issue involved, and with the political affiliation of the subject, the Socialists displaying the greatest consistency, Democrats least. (2) Logically unrelated attitudes were related in voters' minds—i.e., government ownership of industry was related to recognition of the USSR, cancellation of war debts and progressive taxation of the rich. (3) "Bolting" from one political party to another was closely related to differences on specific issues, and there was little evidence of "voting for the man," "protest voting," or "band-wagon voting."

Of a somewhat different nature was a study conducted by Zawadzki and Lazarsfeld (60) concerning the psychological consequences of unemployment during the last depression. In this case, fifty-seven autobiographies of unemployed residents of Warsaw, Poland, were compiled by interviewers from the Institute of Social Economy, and analyzed from the point of view of emotional disturbances engendered by a long period of depression and unemployment. In order to study the same general problem, Forsyth (17) investigated attitudes toward public relief of residents of a rural community in Minnesota, by means of observation, interviews, scales to measure morale and general adjustment, and a Likert-type scale measuring attitude toward relief.

By means of single-question interviews, Lapiere (34) studied race prejudice in France and England. In France, 428 people were asked the question, "Would you let a good Negro live at your home?" Among those living in rural areas, 181 out of 227 replied affirmatively to the question; among urban dwellers, 106 out of 201 said "yes." Thirty-one hotel managers were asked if they admitted Negroes, and it was found that only seven of the hotels drew the color line, those seven being tourist hotels catering largely to American and British trade. In England the author found a different situation; of the 315 people interviewed, 254 admitted that they held a prejudice, and only four out of twenty hotels did not discriminate against Negroes.

In another study of antiminority prejudice, Kingsley and Carbone (29) investigated attitudes toward discrimination on grounds of nationality. They asked more than 150 Italians and Italian-Americans if they had ever experienced discrimination of this kind; when they had experienced it; what form the discrimination generally took; whether or not they had retaliated, and if so, how; whether or not they resented such prejudice and how intensely; and how well they liked Americans in general.

Very shortly after the Harlem race riot of 1943, Clark (9) questioned Harlem residents on their attitudes toward group violence, in an attempt to establish a tentative pattern of its acceptance and rejection. Although the author found no general attitudinal pattern, the results are of considerable interest and social importance. Of the sixty-seven Negroes interviewed, 60 percent condemned the riots and 30 percent condoned them, the latter group containing the greater proportion of males and a higher age level than the former. The condoners appeared to be more highly educated than the condemners, were outspoken in opposition to the Hearst press and much of the Negro press, and were largely concerned with the bare facts of race prejudice, rather than with ethical or moral considerations with respect to violence. The author found little relationship of attitude toward group violence with church attendance or place of birth.

Along similar lines, a study inspired by the Los Angeles "zoot suit" riots was conducted by Humphrey (25) in Detroit, a city which contains a large group of Mexican-Americans. The purpose of the investigation was to compare the popular stereotype of Mexican-American youths with the social types actually existing. On the basis of both observation and interviews, the writer found that the concept of the Mexican-American youths as flashy, antisocial, and law-breaking did not accurately describe any of her subjects, and that they were far more likely to be characterized by docility, submission to parents, generosity toward siblings, friends, and relatives, and courtesy and modesty in most situations. The greatest antisocial aggression appeared in those young people who had been brought to the United States in early infancy and had become most "Americanized." Her conclusion was that Mexican-American youths, like all others, are molded by the social-cultural forces with which they come into contact.

In a study of anti-Semitism, Robinson and Rohde (*45*) compared the results obtained from two interview methods and two kinds of interviewers. A random sample of New York City residents were interviewed with respect to their attitudes toward Jews by both Jewish and non-Jewish interviewers using, alternatively, the direct and indirect approach. It was found that respondents more readily expressed anti-Semitic views to non-Jewish-appearing interviewers, and that anti-Semitic responses were most numerous to direct questions.

PAPER-AND-PENCIL SCALES

Paper-and-pencil attitude scales have appeared, and continue to appear, in many and varied forms. One of these is the so-called preference questionnaire, in which the subject is required to rank in order or compare by pairs various attitude objects of a like nature—i.e., racial or ethnic groups, religious groups, occupations, presidential candidates, etc. Another is the stereotype questionnaire, in which subjects are asked to choose a given number of characteristics on the basis of which they identify social-cultural groups. Another is the situational questionnaire, wherein hypothetical real-life situations are presented and the subject is asked to indicate his probable response to such situations. Perhaps the most commonly used type of paper-and-pencil scale is the one in which subjects endorse or reject certain statements about one or more social groups or institutions. Because of ease of administration to large groups, the paper-and-pencil questionnaire has been very widely used in social-scientific research; for this reason considerable space in this chapter is given studies making use of this technique.

Bernard (*2*) administered to 500 students at the University of Colorado a questionnaire designed to measure their attitudes toward marriage, sex, and family. The subjects were asked to indicate their views on sex liberty for engaged and unengaged couples; marriage versus a career for women; degree of intelligence desired in the husband or wife; desirability of marriages which cut across class lines; infidelity; birth control; sex education for children; divorce; and the importance of sex relations in marriage.

Just prior to the outbreak of World War II, Stagner, Brown, Gundlach, and White (54) administered to about 180 social scientists a detailed questionnaire on which subjects indicated their views with respect to prevention of war. While the experts disagreed sharply on the desirability of such short-run policies as neutrality legislation, they were found to be in essential agreement on a long-range program of internationalism: freedom from economic nationalism, education directed toward understanding other nations and ideologies, breakdown of narrow patriotism, etc.

At about the same time, Stagner (52) designed a new scale of attitude toward war, administering it to a randomly selected sample of the population, in an effort to discover relationships between attitude toward war and certain other factors. He found that men under forty were stronger in opposition to war than men over forty, and that of the two sexes, women were most pacifistic. He found also that military training, membership in veterans' organizations, and a conservative political orientation were positively correlated with a militaristic attitude, and that labor and professional men were significantly more antiwar than clerical workers and businessmen. Military preparedness and neutrality laws were favored as war prevention measures by the militaristic respondents, while the pacifistically inclined favored "taking the profits out of war."

Katzoff and Gilliland (27), by means of a Thurstone-type scale, measured college students' attitudes toward the world conflict over a one-year period preceding United States entry into World War II. Almost 1500 students in nine colleges were tested and comparisons made of colleges and regions. Students from the coastal and Rocky Mountain regions were found to be most interventionist, those from the Midwest and Southwest most isolationist, and falling in the middle were Negroes from West Virginia State College and industrial workers at Akron, Ohio.

Fay and Middleton investigated factors related to liberal and conservative attitudes among college students by a study divided in three parts. More than 500 DePauw University students filled out the Thurstone scales of attitudes toward communism, patriotism, the United States Constitution, law, and censorship. They were required, also, to fill out personal information questionnaires. In the last part of the study (13), the subjects' attitudes on all five issues were correlated against parental membership in such organizations as the American Legion, Veterans of Foreign Wars, Daughters of the American Revolution, and various fraternal orders. In part one of the study (14), attitudes were related to fathers' occupations and size of home towns. And in part two (15), relationships were sought between attitudes and fathers' political preferences.

Lentz (35) studied personage admiration and other correlates of conservatism-radicalism, using as subjects adults with a median age of twenty-two. He found that conservatives in his sample tended most to admire religious and military leaders, jazz-type entertainers, and athletes, while radicals admired scientists, inventors, authors, and classical-type entertainers. Radicals reported more engagement in skilled or professional work, a higher degree of education, more books in homes, wider traveling experience, and less participation in sports and church activities than conservatives. Conservatives were found to be more opposed to change than radicals, more prudish in in regard to sex matters, less sympathetic toward the underdog, more "capitalistic" despite lower economic status, more militaristic and nationalistic, and more prejudiced against minority groups.

In a mid-depression year, 1937, Whisler and Remmers (59) studied the relationships among liberalism, optimism, group morale, and intelligence. A group of 300 Purdue University students filled out the Harper Liberalism-Conservatism Scale, a scale to measure optimism-pessimism, and a third scale measuring general morale. Little relationship was found between judgments of "goodness of life" and liberalism, but liberalism was found to be correlated +0.32 with intelligence. Comparison of this group's liberalism-conservatism scores with the scores of groups measured in earlier depression years showed the students to be insignificantly less liberal than those tested in 1933-1934, but significantly more liberal than those tested in 1931-1932.

Edwards (*12*), by means of an unlabeled fascist attitude scale, investigated college students' reactions to actual fascist principles as contrasted with their unstinting rejection of the fascist label. He found that while none of his groups tested markedly profascist, they were inclined more in that direction than their dislike for the label would lead one to expect. Similarly, Katz and Cantril (*26*) investigated attitudes of Princeton University students toward fascism and communism, in terms both of labels and the principles involved in the two doctrines. They found that while students rejected both labels, the term "communism" carried the greater stigma; that knowledge of the terms' definitions was little related to intensity of opposition; that, from the point of view of acceptance of principles, one-third of the students were for fascism; and that more communist than fascist principles were accepted, except with respect to property rights, in which case fascist principles were the more acceptable.

In a very interesting experiment over twenty-five years ago, Davis (*11*) compared Russian school children's rankings of forty-five occupations with rankings of the same occupations by American school children. He found that while American children ranked "banking" first and "ditch-digging" last, Russian children rated "peasant" first and "banker" among the last. Results of further investigation of three different Russian groups indicated that they invariably ranked banking and the priesthood at or near the bottom.

In a study of the church as a socializing agency, Horton (*24*) measured attitudes of 300 college students toward Christianity and the church. An original scale was devised, containing such propositions as: "To me, the word (Christianity-Church) suggests such ideas as (*a*) a beautiful and inspiring ideal . . . (*f*) a program for social justice . . . (*1*) an unpleasant duty"; "I think that the churches today find most of their followers among . . . (*b*) devout believers who want to worship God . . . (*h*) people who are behind the times in their thinking"; and others of that nature. Subjects were found to be generally favorable toward both the church and Christianity, but more favorable toward Christianity than toward the church.

During World War II, Morgan (*41*) studied attitudes of college students toward the Japanese, administering a fifty-item scale to 170 students at Northwestern University. Four issues were emphasized in the scale: (1) assimilability of the Japanese into American society; (2) eye inferiority; (3) trustworthiness; (4) cruelty. He found a slight tendency to reject the statement, "Japanese are not assimilable," complete disbelief that the Japanese's eyes are inferior, a general feeling that Japanese are not trustworthy, and an avoidance of direct judgment as to their cruelty.

Patrick (*44*) investigated attitudes with respect to women as executives in government positions. Three groups were measured—women executives themselves, men executives, and nonexecutive women. The author found evidence of definite stereotyped attitudes in all three groups. In addition, the women executives filled out detailed questionnaires concerning personal factors, which the author compared with the stereotyped attitudes toward them. He found the majority of women executives to be self-supporting, with some supporting other relatives; one-third were married, a large proportion having children; most of the marriages were of long duration, with only a small percentage of divorce, which, the author states, supports the assertion that women's jobs do not necessarily interfere with their marriages. The women jobholders stated that the greatest career handicap they had experienced was general prejudice against them in executive positions.

Crespi (*10*) conducted a wartime survey of public opinion toward conscientious objectors, using as subjects a stratified random sample of 1184 people, and measuring opinion by means of a paper-and-pencil ballot together with interviews. He found that, in conflict with the popular "scapegoat" hypothesis, public approval of conscientious objectors actually increased with continuance of the war. Those who had experienced the greatest frustration as a result of the war displayed the most favorable attitudes toward objectors. Crespi also found that the public supported, three to one, conscientious objectors' efforts to reform selective service and secure benefits under it.

Smith (*50*) constructed a twelve-item, Likert-type scale to appraise the generalized attitude of Americans toward the verbal symbol, "Soviet Russia." He administered the scale to five groups—white university students, Negro university students, Catholic college girls, adults, and high school students—and found that the attitude of all groups at the time (early 1944) was slightly pro-Russian. In an additional study (*51*), Smith administered the scale to 300 college students and compared the most highly favorable 25 percent with the least favorable 25 percent on the basis of attitudes toward such issues as possible postwar Russian expansion and United State domestic policies, and with respect to political party affiliation, religion, and books read about Russia.

In a study of the impact of war on the nationalistic frame of reference, Stagner and Osgood (*55*) measured attitudes of a repeated sample of college students during the period from April, 1940, to March, 1942, and a sample of adults in the earlier year. Subjects judged such concepts as "100 percent Americanism," "dictatorship," and "pacifists" on the basis of eight qualitative gradients—e.g., weak-strong, noble-bestial. The student and adult populations were found to be quite similar in attitude, despite differences in age, experience, economic status, etc. According to these authors' data, nationalistic concepts reached a peak of approval just prior to Pearl Harbor, with military concepts making much the greatest gain thereafter. There was evidence of stereotypes breaking down during the period of shifting attitudes; evidence, also, of culture patterns coercing individual frames of reference into uniformity.

Newcomb (43) investigated attitudes of college students toward the Spanish Civil War, in a study of the influence of attitude climate on the acquisition of information pertinent to the attitude object. Students at Bennington College, Catholic University of America, and Williams College were measured. Bennington students were found to be generally pro-Loyalist, with Williams students neutral. At both Bennington and Catholic University, a high relationship existed between information and attitude, when information was favorable to locally approved opinion. Correlations with unfavorable information were close to zero. From these data, the author concluded that attitude and acquisition of information were codetermined by the prevailing attitude climate of the community.

In an attempt to formulate a more rigorous definition of the phenomenon of ethnocentrism, Levinson (36) constructed an ethnocentrism (E) scale containing three subscales—Negroes, other minorities, patriotism—and administered it together with a previously constructed anti-Semitism scale. He found ethnocentrism, as measured by his scale, to be highly correlated with anti-Semitism. Further investigation showed politico-economic conservatism and moralism-conventionalism to be correlated $+0.50$ with ethnocentrism. The author concluded that the ethnocentric attitude is based on a rigid in-group-out-group frame of reference, involving stereotyped negative imagery with respect to the outgroup, and positive imagery and submissive attitudes toward the ingroup.

Another approach to the ethnocentric attitude was evolved

by Rokeach (*46*). He hypothesized that ethnocentrism is characterized by a general mental rigidity factor which also manifests itself in solving nonsocial intellectual problems. On the basis of this hypothesis, Rokeach measured ethnocentrism by means of the United States Public Opinion Study Ethnocentrism Scale, and selected the upper and lower halves. Rigidity was measured by requiring the subjects to obtain various quantities of water by manipulating three jars of given capacity. To establish set, several problems were presented, solvable by only one complicated method. Then more problems were given, solvable by other, simpler methods and also by the original complex method. He found definite differences between the two groups in approach to the problem solving. The highly prejudiced group gave more complicated solutions than the less prejudiced group, used more scratch paper and verbalized more solutions.

Interested in the question of the intensity of social attitudes, Cantril (*8*) administered to a representative, nation-wide sample of adult whites scales measuring attitude toward Negroes, government, and business. In addition, he obtained measures of the intensity of the attitudes, plus certain personal information. He found that (1) more extreme attitudes were more intensely held; (2) greatest intensity existed in those subjects defensively opposed to change in the old norms; (3) older, better educated, more economically secure people held attitudes more intense than did their inferiors in those respects; and (4) the greatest extremes of intensity occurred with respect to attitude toward Negroes. Cantril suggests that a more reliable index of opinion than knowledge of direction of attitude alone is knowledge of both direction and intensity.

Britt and Menefee (*7*) investigated the influence upon public opinion of wide publicity about a social issue, the issue in this case being the Dies Un-American Activities Committee. A Gallup Poll of December 11, 1938, indicated that 74 percent of the people who had heard of it wanted the Dies Committee to continue. During this period, the work of Dies and his committee members received perhaps its widest publicity. The authors wished to discover whether or not the organizations condemned and condoned by Dies were similarly condemned and condoned by their subjects. Four groups of college students were given questionnaires on which they encircled the names of organizations of which they approved, most of these organizations having received recent publicity by the Dies Committee. Differing conditions prevailed in the experiment, some of the subjects reading and hearing only pro opinions, some only con opinions, and some both pro and con. The authors' results indicate that the effect of Dies Committee publicity was less than might be supposed, although the "Communist" label was shown to be quite effective.

Walsh (57) analyzed a survey of public opinion toward Russia conducted during the war years by the Office of Public Opinion Research. From his findings, he concluded that Americans dislike communism, but are reconciled to Soviet Russia's permanency in the community of nations; that about one out of three Americans strongly distrusted Russia's motives; that only one American in ten was even reasonably well informed about Russia; and that the decisive factor in United States opinion toward Russia was kind and amount of information, rather than economic status, religious preference, or political affiliation.

Attitudes of soldiers were measured during World War II by the Information and Education Division of the Army Service Forces (United States War Department) (58). Specialists from the Research Branch prepared questionnaires and administered them to the men on a group basis. By this means, enlisted men were able to indicate their views on such day-to-day considerations as recreational facilities, occupation of leisure time, what to do with savings. They also expressed their attitudes toward such major problems as race relations under military conditions, relations with allies, and relations between officers and enlisted men.

SOCIAL DISTANCE (A SOCIOMETRIC APPROACH)

In this section attention is directed chiefly to the concept of social distance between groups, a generalized kind of sociometric measurement originated in the 1920's by Bogardus. Considerable work has been done with the social distance scales, but in the interest of conserving space, only a few studies are cited here.

Bogardus (5) first used the social distance concept and scale in 1925, at which time he was regional director for the Pacific Coast Race Relations Survey. His purpose then was to measure the degree of intimacy, or nearness, which one racial group would allow another in daily relationships. Since that time, however, the social distance scale has been put to work to measure not only racial distance but also distance between parent and child, husband and wife, occupational groups, fraternity brothers, and business partners, to mention only a few.

A neat description of Bogardus' basic scale is contained in his 1933 report of the revised edition (4). Sixty statements, all expressing some degree of social nearness or farness, were rated by 100 judges as to the amount of social distance separating them. By the Thurstone method, the original sixty were reduced to seven equidistant statements, on the basis of which subjects rate racial, ethnic, occupational, and religious groups. The seven statements are, in order, as follows.

1. Would marry
2. Would have as regular friends
3. Would work beside in an office
4. Would have several families in my neighborhood
5. Would have merely as speaking acquaintances
6. Would have live outside my neighborhood
7. Would have live outside my country

Subjects are presented with forty racial or ethnic groups, thirty occupations, and thirty religions to rate. From the scale, a "racial distance quotient" is obtained by adding the numbers of the statements checked and dividing by the number of races presented. The same procedure is followed in obtaining an "occupational distance quotient" and a "religious distance quotient." Finally, a general "social distance quotient" is computed by simply averaging the values of the subquotients.

By means of this technique, Hamren (*18*) attempted to measure the degree of social nearness or farness existing between members of the American Federation of Labor and members of the Congress of Industrial Organizations. Rank-and-file members of local unions from each of the two organizations were asked the following questions:

1. Would you have an AFL (CIO) member for an acquaintance?
2. Would you have an AFL (CIO) member for a friend?
3. Would you scab on an AFL (CIO) member?
4. Would you work on a job with an AFL (CIO) member?

Hamren found that, contrary to popular opinion based on the widely publicized bickering of high union officials, the rank and file have no feeling of distance on grounds of international affiliation. He noted a slight tendency toward greater tolerance on the part of CIO members.

SOCIAL ACTION

The main purpose of the action program as a method for measuring social attitudes—a purpose which constitutes its major advantage—is to simulate as nearly as possible, under experimental conditions, the real-life situation with which people come into frequent contact, and with which they must, of necessity, cope. Such organizations as the Committee on Racial Equality and the Committee on Community Interrelations of the American Jewish Congress have made frequent use of the action technique, and a few illustrative studies are cited below.

Over an extended period of time, Mowrer (*42*) studied authoritarianism versus self-government in the management of children's aggressive reactions. His subjects were twenty-odd preadolescent "problem children" between the ages of three and twelve, at the New Haven Children's Center. Alternating one year of autocratic adult discipline with one year of self-government, he noted that more rapid adjustmental progress accompanied the latter condition, which was also the one preferred by the children. Hypothesizing broadly from his results, Mowrer suggests that pupil self-government in schools constitutes the best training for citizenship in a democracy, and that in the authoritarian system of child management lie the roots of fascist orientation.

An experiment by Smith (*49*) proposed to modify the attitudes of white college students toward Negroes. Forty-six graduate students at Columbia University, after recording their attitudes toward Negroes on a paper-and-pencil scale, spent two week-ends in Harlem, where they attended parties and teas, heard speeches by Negro leaders, and visited homes. A control group of equal size did not participate in the Harlem week-ends. Smith found that attitudes of the forty-six subjects in the experimental group shifted radically in the direction of favorableness toward Negroes, a gain which was still reliable 11 months later.

Harding, Citron, and Selltiz (*19*) investigated anti-Semitism from the point of view of the effectiveness of various types of answers to anti-Semitic remarks. The subjects—1139 New York City adults, 92 Newark, New Jersey, adults, and 67 Peoria, Illinois, adults—were assembled in groups of from fifteen to thirty individuals. The groups were then presented with dramatizations of situations in which an anti-Semitic remark was made. The remark was answered by the various "actors" in two or more different ways: (1) by emphasizing the American tradition of fair play and equal treatment of individuals; (2) by stressing the concept of individual differences and the danger and inaccuracy of generalizations about groups; (3) by making no reply at all. Each answer was presented calmly or in a militant fashion, in order to test subjects' reactions to those two approaches. Following the skit, subjects indicated on a ballot which type of answer they preferred. It was found that the quiet answer was preferred to the militant one, regardless of its content; and that the answer which appealed to belief in the "American way" was preferred above all others.

Using Catholic and Jewish college women as subjects, Festinger (16) investigated group voting behavior before and after religious affiliations of the individuals were known. The girls were divided into small and large experimental and control groups, and in order to disguise the purpose of the experiment, the experimenter merely simulated a voting situation, telling his subjects that he intended to study voting behavior in general. After a vote had been conducted in the absence of information as to the candidate's religious affiliation, the experimenter made use of a device by which religious preference was casually made known. The vote was again taken, and comparisons made between voting behavior in the two situations, in an effort to estimate the degree of group belongingness manifested. Many of the subjects were interviewed, following the experiment, for purposes of checking results and adding to an understanding of the problem. Festinger found that, in general, Jewish girls were more conscious of the religious question, reacting in favor of their own group only when no open identification of the candidate was made, or when they themselves were not identified. Catholic girls, on the other hand, reacted strongly in favor of their own group, no matter what the experimental conditions of identification. From these results, the author hypothesizes that while Jews and Catholics are similar with respect to identification with their own groups, Jews are less secure than Catholics where acceptance or rejection in mixed groups is concerned.

HISTORICAL ANALYSIS

"Looking backward" has frequently proved fruitful as a method for studying social behavior and attitude. The analysis of records, personal and public, is after all the method of history, and is often useful in providing insight into social behavior of the past—insight which may be applied to problems of the present and future. Such analysis, unfortunately, maximizes the possibility of contamination of results due to the analysts' bias, but it is by no means deserving of rejection on those grounds alone. Two or three studies should serve to illustrate this technique sufficiently to the reader.

Using the method of "hindsight," Saenger (47) analyzed voting behavior in the presidential election of 1944. From his analysis, he arrived at the following general conclusions: (1) Social status, as determined by income and religion, largely determines political behavior. (2) Group membership of this kind supersedes party platform and propaganda in importance to the voter. (3) When the voter's opinion conflicts with the party line, the party program is rationalized to fit personal beliefs and desires. (4) Those voters least aware of differences among political parties and least convinced that election results will affect them personally are most likely to change parties.

Mead (40) surveyed the decade of the 1930's from the point of view of the light shed on changing customs and mores. She suggests that the period studied was characterized by a lowered level of expectation; an increasing shift toward federal initiative, accompanied by a decreased feeling, on the part of the people, of participation and individual importance; an increase in group antagonisms—heightened prejudice against Jews, Negroes, etc.; and finally, a decline in the "quest for learning," with increased atomization of knowledge symbolized by quiz programs and magazine and newspaper "know your facts" games.

Lundberg (38) compared the historical development of two "radical" communities with that of two conservative communities, in an effort to discover the effect of environment on political attitudes. Selection of communities on grounds of radicalism and conservatism was based on voting behavior with respect to the Non-Partisan League in the elections of 1916, 1918, and 1920. The radical communities (counties, in this case) were found to be newer, less developed, and less densely populated than the conservative communities. They had a more rapid rate of population increase, a larger foreign-born element, fewer and larger farms with smaller per capita values and more mortgages. They were, in short, in a position of greater economic insecurity than the communities with conservative voting records.

A method of "foresight" was evolved by Klingberg (*30*) in a study of relations among sovereign nations. Questionnaires measuring opinion toward probability of war, friendliness among the Great Powers, and attitudes of other nations toward the Great Powers were administered to specialists in international affairs over a 5-year period (1937-1941). Results indicated that attitudes of nations, in the eyes of the experts, may shift very rapidly and may not be as dependent on so-called basic factors (geography, form of government, economic organizations, etc.) as is generally supposed. The author concludes that this expert-opinion technique is a hopeful one, in that it may prove valuable in predicting future behavior of nations.

PERSONALITY AND DEVELOPMENT OF SOCIAL ATTITUDES

Considerable research has been conducted, much of it contradictory and inconclusive, in an effort to determine ways and means by which social attitudes are engendered. It is generally agreed that they are primarily cultural in origin, but as to when and how rapidly they develop and what constitute the basic sources from which they develop, agreement is by no means unanimous. We cite here a few studies representative of the kind of research being done in this area, again placing emphasis on techniques employed.

Allport and Kramer (*1*) attempted to get at some roots of antiminority prejudice. To 437 college undergraduates from Dartmouth, Harvard, and Radcliffe, they administered attitude scales concerning Negroes, Jews, and Catholics. In addition, certain personal data were gathered from the subjects, against which attitude scores were correlated. The authors found that

(1) racial or religious prejudice existed in four-fifths of their population; (2) anti-Semites were more accurate than the unprejudiced in identifying Jews by facial features; (3) prejudiced subjects had unpleasant memories from childhood of groups against which they held prejudice; (4) prejudiced students showed a greater tendency than the unprejudiced to cling to parental patterns; (5) bigots reported few school experiences favorable to minorities, and only 8 percent of the entire sample reported having been taught scientific facts about race; (6) most prejudice developed during school years, particularly in the age range from twelve to sixteen; (7) prejudice was lowest among Jews and those professing no religious affiliation, highest among Catholics; (8) women were less prejudiced than men, and children of college-educated parents were less prejudiced than children of noncollege parents; (9) students of the natural sciences were least prejudiced; (10) fear of fraud and trickery was positively correlated with prejudice, and prejudiced persons indicated little sympathy for the underdog; (11) prejudiced persons were not ashamed of their prejudice and tended to underestimate its intensity; (12) prejudiced persons were generally unfavorable to legislation designed to improve minority status.

In an effort to discover what makes attitudes liberal or conservative, Vetter (56) measured attitudes of 706 college students toward eight "basic" attitude objects: (1) capitalist wealth distribution; (2) communistic wealth distribution; (3) moralistic orientation; (4) "pagan" orientation; (5) favoring the new; (6) opposing the new; (7) individualism; (8) paternalism. His findings indicate the existence of definite attitude "sets," distinguishing the liberal and radical subjects from the conservatives and reactionaries. Liberals, for example, showed a greater degree of adherence to so-called individualism than did conservatives, individualism correlating -0.78 and -0.77 with moralism and paternalism respectively. The correlation between the attitude of favoring the new and that of opposition to trying the new was -0.85, with liberals holding the former point of view. Relating attitude toward capitalistic wealth distribution with attitude toward communistic wealth distribution gave a coefficient of correlation of -0.61, while moralistic versus pagan orientation yielded a coefficient of -0.95.

Krout (33) investigated personality factors in relation to the development of political attitudes in young radicals. His subjects were fifty members of the Young People's Socialist League and the Young Communist League, with 100 nonradical young people serving as controls. An autobiographical schedule containing 219 items was administered, and the following findings reported: (1) Both male and female radicals experienced greater rejection by parents than did nonradicals. (2) Early punishment of young radicals by parents tended to take the form of ridicule and like "mental cruelty," with less corporal punishment than that experienced by nonradicals. (3) Radicals tended less than nonradicals to emulate parents' behavior and beliefs. (4) Among the radicals, inferiority feelings in girls were intellectual, in boys, athletic. (5) Radicals manifested less general optimism than nonradicals.

In a similar study, Stagner (53) investigated the role of personal and family factors in the development of social attitudes. He found that the active radicals among his subjects had less satisfactory relations with parents and lower personal morale than the nonradicals; that there was a consistent tendency among college males with good family morale to be more conservative, aggressive, and nationalistic in orientation; and that, in general, men with a greater degree of antagonism toward parents were the more liberal and international in outlook. Stagner concludes that these data may be harmonized with the displacement theory of social aggression.

Using the interview method, Breslaw (6) studied the influence of various social factors on the development of socioeconomic attitudes. Subjects several years beyond the minimum voting age who had held conservative or radical opinions for some time gave information with regard to elementary school experiences, high school and college experiences, and experiences subsequent to formal schooling. The author emerged with the hypothesis that social, or cultural, factors are more important to the understanding of attitude development than so-called "personality" factors.

Kerr (28) summarized the literature bearing on correlates of politico-economic liberalism-conservatism. Citing research of such men as Allport, Brameld, Edwards, Gundlach, Remmers, Stagner, Kornhauser, Lentz, and Murphy, he recounts the following findings: (1) Politico-economic liberalism tends to increase with increased formal schooling. (2) Liberal college students tend to be better students than conservatives, and possess more special aptitudes. (3) Liberal college students and teachers are better informed than are conservatives. (4) Liberalism among college students appears to correlate positively with intelligence. (5) Socialists and older people are more consistent in their liberal attitudes than are young people and members of the major parties. (6) Children tend to emulate their parents' social views. (7) Adults over forty are more conservative than those under forty. (8) Among religious leaders, Jews, Unitarians, Universalists, Congregationalists, Episcopalians, and Reformists are most liberal. (9) Liberals are less favorable than conservatives toward religion and are less prejudiced against minority groups. (10) Students of the social sciences tend toward greater liberalism than those in other curricula. (11) Fraternity members tend to be more conservative than independents. (12) Liberal and conservative attitudes vary with shifting conditions of the country.

Horowitz (23) developed three interesting methods for investigating origins of attitude toward the Negro. His subjects in the study were several hundred boys in a New York City all-white school, boys in one grade of a nonsegregated school, a small group of children of Communist parents, children from urban Tennessee, and from rural and urban Georgia. Noting that popular theories emphasized sex factors, the historical derivation of the Negroes' present status, and economic factors in accounting for the existence of prejudice, Horowitz attempted to eliminate the influence of these factors by testing only boys, testing only very young children, and testing groups from different socioeconomic levels. His methods were as follows: (1) Subjects ranked pictures of children's faces in order of preference. (2) Children were asked to point to the faces of those children with whom they would like to engage in certain activities—e.g., go home to lunch, go to a party, play ball. (3) Certain social situations were depicted, and children were asked to indicate the ones in which they would like to join (for example, Negro and white children were shown sitting together at a meal). The author found that Southern children were no more prejudiced than the New York City boys; that white boys in the nonsegregated school were just as prejudiced as boys in the all-white school; that children of Communist parents indicated no apparent prejudices; and that beginnings of prejudice existed in children of preschool age. He concluded from these findings that anti-Negro prejudice develops not from contact with Negroes, but from early contact with the prevailing attitude toward them.

Blake and Dennis (3) studied the development of stereotypes concerning the Negro, using as subjects pupils from grades four through eleven in a Virginia all-white school. The children compared Negroes and whites in regard to sixty personality characteristics popularly supposed to constitute Negro or white "traits." His findings indicate that high school children are more homogeneous in their attitudes toward Negroes than are younger children, and that they reverse certain concepts held by the younger children. Younger children attributed to Negroes some traditional "white traits," expressing the view that Negroes are less religious, less cheerful than whites. The high school students contradicted this, propounding the stereotyped view of the Negro as very religious and happy-go-lucky. The author hypothesizes that young children acquire an attitude toward Negroes that is generally unfavorable, and do not attribute any "good" traits to the race. With increasing age, children tend to adopt adult stereotypes, which allow for the existence of some favorable characteristics.

SUMMARY

Attitude research in the area of community interrelations has been of a broad and varied nature. Employing such techniques as interviews, paper-and-pencil scales, sociometry, direct social action, and the method of historical analysis, workers have investigated attitudes of children and adults toward government, political and economic issues, racial and ethnic groups, crime and delinquency, marriage, morals, the church, occupations, and various ideologies, to mention only a few of an almost infinite number of social attitudes. This chapter briefly reviews some of the relevant studies, and closes with a cursory review of the literature pertaining to the development of social attitudes.

Questions

1. Can the ethnocentric tendencies of certain minority groups be modified? Could this lessen the prejudice of other groups toward them? Can you suggest a scientific testing of these hypotheses?
2. Is social distance between groups in this country increasing or decreasing? What evidence is there on this point?
3. What answers to the antifeminist attitude in business executive circles are justified by the available evidence?
4. Is intelligent treatment of children more likely to make them radical or conservative? What are some other factors that enter in?
5. What evidence is there for a "class structure" in this country?
6. Should churches conduct attitude surveys? Explain.
7. The American Federation of Labor (AFL) has often been characterized as being more conservative than the Congress of Industrial Organizations (CIO). How would you account for this?
8. What are the implications of the finding that the beginnings of racial prejudice exist in children of preschool age?

9. A number of studies found Jews to be more liberal and less prejudiced than other groups. How would you explain this?
10. What is a community? Is it possible to use attitude studies as an aid in identifying a community?
11. What questions would you ask to discover social class identification of individuals?
12. What questions would you ask of a rural family to classify it as to its specific community membership?
13. How might a group of psychologists tackle such a problem as world peace?
14. It is generally agreed that social attitudes are cultural in origin. Which years of life are most formative of such attitudes?
15. Can sociodrama be used as a technique of community attitude measurement?
16. Would it be better to attempt to raise the educational level or to increase church adherence in an effort to minimize racial intolerance?
17. Would examinations by boards of qualified psychologists and/or psychiatrists be desirable for governmental officials in order to determine their attitudes? Could this prevent power being placed in the hands of psychopathic personalities? (Consider some of the Nazi leaders who were found by competent psychologists to be psychopathic.)

Bibliography

1. Allport, G. W., and Kramer, B. M., "Some Roots of Prejudice," *J. Psychol.*, 1946, *22*:9-39.
2. Bernard, W. S., "Student Attitudes on Marriage and the Family," *Amer. sociol. Rev.*, 1938, *3*:354-361.
3. Blake, R., and Dennis, W., "The Development of Stereotypes Concerning the Negro," *J. abnorm. soc. Psychol.*, 1943, *38*:525-531.
4. Bogardus, E., "A Social Distance Scale," *Sociol. Soc. Res.*, 1933, *17*:265-271.
5. Bogardus, E., "Social Distance and Its Practical Applications," *Sociol. Soc. Res.*, 1938, *22*:462-476.

6. Breslaw, B. J., "The Development of a Socio-Economic Attitude," *Arch. Psychol.*, 1938, no. 226:96.

7. Britt, S. H., and Menefee, S. C., "Did the Publicity of the Dies Committee in 1938 Influence Public Opinion?" *Publ. Opin. Quart.*, 1939, *3*:449-457.

8. Cantril, H., "The Intensity of an Attitude," *J. abnorm. soc. Psychol.*, 1946, *41*:129-135.

9. Clark, K. B., "Group Violence: 'A Preliminary Study of the Attitudinal Pattern of Its Acceptance and Rejection: A Study of the 1943 Harlem Race Riot.'" *J. soc. Psychol.*, 1944, *19*: 319-337.

10. Crespi, L. P., "Public Opinion Toward Conscientious Objectors," *J. Psychol.*, 1945, *20*:321-346.

11. Davis, J., "Testing the Social Attitudes of Children in the Government Schools in Russia," *Amer. J. Sociol.*, 1927, *32*: 947-952.

12. Edwards, A. L., "Reactions of College Students to an Unlabeled Fascist Attitude Scale," *Psychol. Bull.*, 1941, *38*: 710(abstr.).

13. Fay, P. J., and Middleton, W. C., "Certain Factors Related to Liberal and Conservative Attitudes of College Students: Parental Membership in Certain Organizations," *J. soc. Psychol.*, 1940, *12*:55-69.

14. Fay, P. J., and Middleton, W. C., "Certain Factors Related to Liberal and Conservative Attitudes of College Students: I. Father's Occupation; Size of Home Town," *J. soc. Psychol.*, 1940, *11*:91-105.

15. Fay, P. J., and Middleton, W. C., "Certain Factors Related to Liberal and Conservative Attitudes of College Students: II. Father's Political Preference; Presidential Candidates Favored in the 1932 and 1936 Elections," *J. soc. Psychol.*, 1940, *11*:107-119.

16. Festinger, L., "The Role of Group Belongingness in a Voting Situation," *Hum. Relations*, 1947, *1*:154-180.

17. Forsyth, F. H., "Social Crisis and Social Attitude Toward Relief," *J. soc. Psychol.*, 1943, *18*:55-69.

18. Hamren, V., "Social Nearness Between the AFL and the CIO," *Sociol. Soc. Res.*, 1942, *26*:232-240.

19. Harding, J., Citron, A. F., and Selltiz, C., "Personal Incidents: 'A study of the Effectiveness of Various Types of Answers to Anti-Minority Remarks,' " *Amer. Psychol.*, 1947, *2*:336(abstr.).

20. Hayes, S. P., Jr., "The Interrelations of Political Attitudes: II. Consistency in Voters' Attitudes," *J. soc. Psychol.*, 1939, *10*: 359-378.

21. Hayes, S. P., Jr., "The Interrelations of Political Attitudes: III. General Factors in Political Issues," *J. soc. Psychol.*, 1939, *10*:379-398.

22. Hayes, S. P., Jr., "The Interrelations of Political Attitudes: IV. Political Attitudes and Party Regularity," *J. soc. Psychol.*, 1939, *10*:503-551.

23. Horowitz, E. L., "The Development of Attitude Toward the Negro," *Arch. Psychol.*, New York, 1936 (no. 194).

24. Horton, P. B., "The Church as a Socializing Agency," *J. educ. Sociol.*, 1941, *15*:46-54.

25. Humphrey, N. D., "The Stereotype and the Social Types of Mexican-American Youths," *J. soc. Psychol.*, 1945, *22*:69-78.

26. Katz, D., and Cantril, H., "An Analysis of Attitudes Toward Fascism and Communism," *J. abnorm. soc. Psychol.*, 1940, *35*: 356-366.

27. Katzoff, E. T., and Gilliland, A. R., "Student Attitudes on the World Conflict," *J. Psychol.*, 1941, *12*:227-233.

28. Kerr, W. A., "Correlates of Politico-Economic Liberalism-Conservatism," *J. soc. Psychol.*, 1944, *20*:61-77.

29. Kingsley, H. L., and Carbone, M., "Attitudes of Italian-Americans Toward Race Prejudice," *J. abnorm. soc. Psychol.*, 1938, *33*:532-537.

30. Klingberg, F. L., "Studies in Measurement of the Relations Among Sovereign States," *Psychometrika*, 1941, *6*:335-352.

31. Kornhauser, A. W., "Attitudes of Different Economic Groups," *Psychol. Bull.*, 1938, *35*:663(abstr.).

32. Kornhauser, A. W., "Chicago Surveys Concerning the Public's Beliefs and Desires About the War," *J. soc. Psychol.*, 1943, *18*:371-382.

33. Krout, M. H., "A Controlled Study of the Development and Attitudes of Radicals," *Psychol. Bull.*, 1937, *34*:706-707(abstr.).

34. Lapiere, R. T., "Race Prejudice: France and England," *Social Forces*, 1928, *7*:102-111.

35. Lentz, T. F., "Personage Admiration and Other Correlates of Conservatism-Radicalism," *J. soc. Psychol.*, 1939, *10*:81-93.

36. Levinson, D. J., "An Approach to the Theory and Measurement of Ethnocentrism," *Amer. Psychol.*, 1947, *2*:412(abstr.).

37. Link, H. C., "The Ninth Nation-Wide Social Experimental Survey," *J. appl. Psychol.*, 1944, *28*:1-15.

38. Lundberg, G. A., "The Demographic and Economic Basis of Political Radicalism and Conservatism," *Amer. J. Sociol.*, 1927, *32*:719-732.

39. McPherson, E. G., and McPherson, M. W., "An Exploratory Investigation of Tenant Reactions to a Federal Housing Project," *J. Psychol.*, 1945, *20*:199-215.

40. Mead, M., "Customs and Mores," *Amer. J. Sociol.*, 1942, *47*: 971-980.

41. Morgan, J. J. B., "Attitudes of Students Toward the Japanese," *J. soc. Psychol.*, 1945, *21*:219-227.

42. Mowrer, O. H., "Authoritarianism Versus Self-Government in the Management of Children's Aggressive (Anti-Social) Reactions as Preparation for Citizenship in a Democracy," *Psychol. Bull.*, 1938, *35*:660(abstr.).

43. Newcomb, T. M., "The Influence of Attitude Climate upon Some Determinants of Information," *J. abnorm. soc. Psychol.*, 1946, *41*:291-302.

44. Patrick, C., "Attitudes About Women Executives in Government Positions," *J. soc. Psychol.*, 1944, *19*:3-34.

45. Robinson, D., and Rohde, S., "Two Experiments with an Anti-Semitism Poll, *J. abnorm. soc. Psychol.*, 1947, *41*:136-144.

46. Rokeach, J. M., "Ethnocentrism and a General Mental Rigidity Factor," *Amer. Psychol.*, 1946, *1*:451(abstr.).

47. Saenger, G. H., "Social Status and Political Behavior," *Amer. J. Sociol.*, 1945, *51*:103-113.

48. Sargent, S. S., "Attitudes Toward the War and Peace in a Midwestern Agricultural Community," *J. soc. Psychol.*, 1943, *17*:337-345.

49. Smith, F. T., "An Experiment in Modifying Attitudes Toward the Negro," Ph.D. Thesis, Teachers College, Columbia University, 1933.

50. Smith, G. H., "Attitudes Toward Soviet Russia: I. The Stand-

ardization of a Scale and Some Distributions of Scores," *J. soc. Psychol.*, 1946, *23*:3-16.

51. Smith, G. H., "Attitudes Toward Soviet Russia: II. Beliefs, Values and Other Characteristics of Pro-Russian and Anti-Russian Groups," *J. soc. Psychol.*, 1946, *23*:17-33.

52. Stagner, R., "Some Factors Related to Attitude Toward War, 1938," *J. soc. Psychol.*, 1942, *16*:131-142.

53. Stagner, R., "Studies of Aggressive Social Attitudes: III. The Role of Personal and Family Scores," *J. soc. Psychol.*, 1944, *20*:129-140.

54. Stagner, R., Brown, J. F., Gundlach, R., and White, R., "An Analysis of Social Scientists' Opinions on the Prevention of War," *J. soc. Psychol.*, 1942, *15*:381-394.

55. Stagner, R., and Osgood, C. E., "Impact of War on a Nationalistic Frame of Reference: I. Changes in General Approval and Qualitative Patterning of Certain Stereotypes," *J. soc. Psychol.*, 1946, *24*:187-215.

56. Vetter, B. B., "What Makes Attitudes Liberal or Conservative?" *J. abnorm. soc. Psychol.*, 1947, *42*:125-130.

57. Walsh, W. B., "What the American People Think of Russia," *Publ. Opin. Quart.*, 1944, *8*:513-522.

58. *What the Soldier Thinks: A Digest of War Department Studies on the Attitudes of American Troops,* Washington, D.C.: Research Branch, Information and Education Division, Army Service Forces, *Periodical Publications,* December, 1942, to September, 1945.

59. Whisler, L. D., and Remmers, H. H., "Liberalism, Optimism and Group Morale: A Study of Student Attitudes," *J. soc. Psychol.*, 1938, *9*:451-467.

60. Zawadzki, B., and Lazarsfeld, P. F., "The Psychological Consequences of Unemployment," *J. soc. Psychol.*, 1935, *6*:224-251.

CHAPTER XII

· · · ● ● ● · ·

Applications in Education

INTRODUCTION

The measurement of attitudes and opinions has become a vital part of the educational system. Educators, especially those interested in the guidance area, are making more and more use of these devices. If progressive education had made no other contribution, its insistence on learning the needs and feelings of students would be a notable addition to educational methods. The need, also, for keeping in touch with parents' opinions and for informing them about school problems and plans has taught educators to make more use of the opinion measuring instruments. Democratic orientation of teachers and administrators has led them to encourage expression of ideas which can be evaluated and used in improving relationships within the school system. The result has been a steady growth, within the educational field, of attitude and opinion measurement.

Administrators are finding such measurement useful in their task of improving public relations. To keep a harmonious organization of teaching personnel, they are relying more and more upon the results of such attitude measurement. Guidance leaders, whether they are interested in vocational or in a more general educational type of guidance, are helped by interest questionnaires to learn the present and possibly the predictable interest of pupils and older students. In the classroom, teachers are learning to use opinion measurement. It is useful for making seating arrangements, for arranging project groups, for finding possible sources of tensions within the groups. The content of the curriculum has also been subjected to the measurement of opinions of students: This may be a source of information useful in providing more meaningful content.

The "public," always an important factor to be considered by the leaders of the public school system, can now be consulted by means of opinion measuring devices. Their reactions to many important aspects of education can now be heard and, what is more important, evaluated. The results have been to increase the avenues of communication between the "public" and the public school to a degree which would have been thought highly improbable by Horace Mann, although he would likely have been heartily in its favor.

Researchers in education have devised measuring instruments, applied them, refined them, and validated them. They have analyzed the data obtained by these instruments, and they have made the findings available for teachers and other interested members of the educational group to make use of them. The literature on research in education is vast. Evaluation instruments are being multiplied. Teachers are becoming increasingly aware of the techniques of surveying, polling and the whole area of attitude measurement.

Some of the areas touched on in this chapter will be: attitude measurement in the fields of vocational guidance; interpersonal relations within pupil-groups, pupil-teacher relations, administrator-teacher relationships; and understanding between the public and the school. Also important are the aspects of pupil-awareness of the problem areas of their community, their country, and the world.

The instruments used in educational attitude measurement include all of those discussed in Part One of this book.

This cannot be an exhaustive report of the applications of attitude measurement in education. Only illustrative and representative examples of such applications can be given. The best single listing of the instruments used is to be found in Buros's *The Fourth Mental Measurements Yearbook* (7).

Pupil-Pupil Relations

The chief environment for the school child is his classroom. It is here that he spends most of his school day. There has been a growing feeling that he ought to have some part in adjusting the classroom arrangement nearer to his own desires. An excellent device, developed by Moreno and his associates, and already described (Chapter VII) is the *sociogram*.

The chart derived from recording choices (for a teammate, for "the person whom you'd like to sit near," for the captain or leader of a project) gives the teacher a readily interpreted picture of his groups. It is an aid for arranging seating, for planning projects, and for any arrangements involving within-group relations. A very important aspect of such a method is also the revealing of "isolates" and others who are nearly or completely rejected by the group. It might be argued that any teacher is aware of these individuals. However, the objective measurement of the interpersonal pattern will give a more valid and precise basis for judgment. It will allow the teacher to provide means for improving the pattern.

Haas (*18*) in making such a study found that the learning situation requires a "dynamic" communication. He discovered that "telefactors" (as he describes them) exist in any group, and that the measurable degrees of communication, which these telefactors represent, are the revealing indices of the amount of dynamic communication between pupil and pupil and also between pupil and teacher. For the better understanding of interpersonal relationship, McLelland and Ratliff (*29*) used sociometric tests. Their aim was to improve social adjustment within a class. First, they made a sociogram of the class. Then, by personality tests they measured the "strength" and "weakness" of the personalities of individual students. Having learned them, they readjusted the structure of the class. Permitting time to elapse and the new structure to have its effect, they then made another sociogram. The implication is that this method could be used in many other school situations for improving the structure until the optimum arrangement is found.

Pupil-pupil relations are affected by homogeneous grouping. The purpose of this type of grouping is that it should allow students to be within a class somewhat similar to their own achievement level. Luchins and Luchins (27) used attitude measurement to investigate the effect of this kind of grouping on the individual students. The bright students, they found, wished to remain within their own class. Average and dull students, they report, felt that "their parents wanted them to be in the bright class." These results, the authors warn, may have been influenced by "a basic competitive philosophy in the school."

Pupil-Teacher Relations: The Teachers' Opinions

Teachers' opinions of pupils, I fear, still remain mostly at the report card level. This is not as objective as might be desired; yet it is an attempt at evaluating the pupil from the point of view of the teacher, on such aspects as academic achievement, coöperative attitude, sense of responsibility, and other important factors of the whole personality of the child. For this reason more instruments are probably necessary which will enable the teacher to express himself in terms which can be clearly interpreted. One aspect of behavior, at least, that which can be termed "objectionable," has been investigated by Clark (8). He discovered that elementary teachers rate behavior which interfered with the group as much more highly objectionable than any display of hostility toward the teacher. When we look at the question of teachers' understanding of pupils, we note two studies which deal with this subject.

Leeds and Cook (26) found a multiple correlation of .595 between a scale which they had constructed and three predictors: pupils' ratings, principals' ratings, and ratings by research workers. They found that teachers below age 40 were rated significantly higher than those over age 40. They also found that girls rated the teachers more highly than did boys. Gage and Suci (*16*), using the same Cook-Leeds Attitude Inventory,[1] related the ratings obtained by this measuring device to another variable—the teacher's ability to predict pupils' attitudes. They found that, among other results, "the scores on the Cook-Leeds inventory correlated .57 and .46 with our mean error and *r*-scores, respectively. This indicates that the attitudes and understandings concerning pupils tapped by that test are significantly related to ability to estimate students' opinions. . . . However in this school, at any rate, this test did not yield results in corroboration of the significant positive relationships with pupils' ratings (about .45) previously reported by Cook and Leeds" (*16:151*).

Bowers (*6*) in his book on teacher training research, reports fourteen experiments to determine the importance of each of fourteen variables in the selection and training of teachers. Some of these variables were "Growth of student-teachers in certain traits of personality during their training," "The feasibility of homogeneous grouping in a normal school," etc. His study is valuable especially for those who want to have interpreted for them findings of careful scientific investigation into teacher training. Bowers used ratings extensively and reports them clearly. Ringness (*49*) has related success in teaching to the attitudes held by the teachers. Sixty-three men and thirty-seven women in a University of Wisconsin School of Education course were used as subjects. A paired-comparison questionnaire and a comparison-of-professions questionnaire, all covering the same interest field, were administered to each person. A year later, when the subjects were actually beginning teachers, they were rated by university observers and the superintendents of their schools. The criteria were acceptability and efficiency. Factor-analysis techniques were used to discover group factors for the paired-comparison and ranking question-

[1] This Inventory is now published under the title *Minnesota Teachers Attitude Inventory*, Form A, New York: The Psychological Corporation.

naire. The general conclusions were: "Teachers are motivated to teach by certain wants, reasons and values, even though these may not all be the same for all teachers. Results of this study tend to substantiate the belief that teaching success is related to the nature of the reasons for the choice of teaching."

Wandt (58) revised sixteen attitude scales into one inventory. This inventory was administered to teachers. Their opinions on three phases of their interpersonal relations were examined and analyzed: attitudes toward administrators, toward pupils, and toward adults outside the professional group. He found that the experience of the teacher was not a significant factor in the forming or changing of his opinions. However, there was a correlation between the level of grade taught and the opinions held toward the three groups mentioned. In general the elementary teachers held a more favorable attitude to all three groups—administrators, pupils, and adults.

Pupil-Teacher Relations: The Pupils' Opinions

More work has been done in this field than in the previous one. At the elementary level, at the secondary, and at the college level, students are given an opportunity to express their attitudes in ways capable of being measured.

Tschechtelin (57) has devised, under Remmers' direction, a *Diagnostic Teacher Rating Scale* for elementary-school pupils. Questions are asked such as: "How well do you like your teacher?" "How fair is your teacher in grading?" "How well does your teacher keep order?" Anonymously responded to, this scale gives the teacher an opportunity of seeing how he compares with other teachers in these important aspects of his teaching behavior. Better than any teacher's subjective judgment, the scale shows how the pupil feels—that is, how the teacher appears to the child.

Baker and Remmers (2) have reviewed the progress of research in the specific field of personnel evaluation, with a stress on ratings of teachers by students. They describe the instruments, the *Purdue Rating Scale for Instruction,* the *Purdue Rating Scale for Administrators and Executives, How Teach and Learn in College,* and *How I Counsel*—all devices which were designed to aid teachers and counselors in self-government.

At the college level, the *Purdue Rating Scale for Instruction* (*3*) has been developed to meet a very real need. As the foreword states, "An instructor may or may not be aware of a possible 'poor reputation,' but the very nature of its derivation makes it impossible for him to do anything constructive about it. It is difficult to grapple with vague generalities. The *Purdue Rating Scale for Instruction* has been designed to help overcome this difficulty." In a word, it makes specific the opinions which a student may have of an instructor, his classroom characteristics, and his procedures. Thus it enables the instructor to go over his methods and approach them constructively, and makes it easier for him to improve. The scale has twenty-six items, ten of which first appeared as the *Purdue Rating Scale for Instructors.* It crystallizes the expressed needs of students in relation to instructors, and it was derived from an extended survey by Remmers and Elliott (*38*) of the literature on instruction and on the teaching-learning situation.

Some of the aspects of instruction rated are "Interest in Subject," "Liberal and Progressive Attitude," "Self-Reliance and Confidence," "Stimulating Intellectual Curiosity," "Suitability of Reference Materials," "How the Course Is Fulfilling Your Needs." Norms have been derived, and the Manual (*3*) provides the instructor a scale against which to rate himself.

By means of this scale Drucker and Remmers (*14*) tested the validity of the assertion frequently made that college students are too immature to be able to give valid opinions of the effectiveness of their teachers and that after they are more mature they often change their opinions. Using the ratings of instructors as given by 251 students and comparing these with ratings given by 128 alumni to the same instructors of the same courses (taken ten years previously) they found substantial agreement between the alumni and the students. They conclude that these two sets of ratings agree closely enough to establish the "permanence" or stability of student attitudes toward teachers and that, if the "mature" opinions of alumni are valid, then so are those of "immature" students.

Downie (*12*), using a faculty rating scale, investigated the attitudes of students toward members of the teaching staff of the State College of Washington. Those members who had doctor's and master's degrees, according to the students, had their courses better organized, were more effective in the presentation of material, and gave more appropriate assignments than did members with only the bachelor's degrees.

Opinion measurement which does not involve scales but which is still a revelation of pupil attitude is reported by Witty (*60*). He made a content analysis of 12,000 letters from children in grades two through twelve. These were submitted to officials of the Quiz Kid Contest on the subject, "The Most Helpful Teacher I Have Known." Important to the whole group was the coöperative, democratic attitude shown by many teachers. They also rated highly kindliness and consideration.

Teacher Rating: Bibliographies

For a critical evaluation of research in teacher characteristics and teaching efficiency (including the ratings of teachers by the administrator, the colleague, and the student) the review of the literature done by Baker and Remmers (*1*) can be consulted. Their conclusion is that much serious work has to be done, that too many trivial attempts at research are being made, and that the facts of the problems attacked are often too unimportant. However, they do cite the major work that is being done. Domas and Tiedeman (*11*) have issued an annotated bibliography of over 1000 titles, covering the research of the period 1929 to 1949. This is the most complete review of the literature to date. A more selective bibliography was published by Barr (*4*), who gives 141 titles of studies made in this area.

Teacher-Administrator Relations

A very important relationship in the educational system is that of administrator-teacher communication. It has been a commonly accepted idea that the administrator ought to evaluate the work of the teacher and to rate his personality, his ability to teach, his success in dealing with colleagues, and the other aspects of the teaching situation. However, it is only recently that the rating of the administrator by his subordinates has been provided for. Hobson and Remmers (21) developed a *Purdue Rating Scale for Administrators.* They had as subjects in the original study fifty-four college and university administrators in nine Indiana colleges and universities who were rated by their subordinates. The instrument yielded a reliability of .88, when a modified split-half technique was applied. Factor analysis revealed three factors which could be considered essential for good administrators. These were named: fairness to subordinates, administrative achievement, and democratic orientation. The same rating scale was given by Kirk and Remmers (23) to a national sample of eighty-eight administrators at the elementary and secondary school level, rated by 1153 teachers. For this group a reliability of .67 was obtained.

COUNSELING AND GUIDANCE

Since the days of the pioneering inventor, Benjamin Franklin, stress has been laid on the practical aspects of education. His efforts on behalf of the Philadelphia Public Academy, established in 1751, were just one example of the new emphasis which he and other American educators laid upon the training of the young for a useful participation in the life and work of the community. With the decline of the apprentice system, a method of education was dropped. A new method had to be introduced. Technical training was incorporated to some extent into the public school system. Along with the training, some means had to be devised for discovering who would be best able to perform certain tasks. Whether skilled labor, engineering, literary work, music, art, or some other field would be the happiest future for any one student became a pressing problem. To provide answers for the problem became the work of guidance, both educational and vocational.

Educational Guidance

Educational guidance, as contrasted with specifically vocational guidance, concerns itself with such problems as social-emotional adjustment, adjustment to the school system, basic choices of course of study, adaptation of training to the needs, and capabilities of all students in the public school system. Some of the instruments useful in such guidance are instrument inventories, personality questionnaires, and attitude scales. Such instruments as the SRA Youth Inventory (48), the SRA Junior Inventory (32), and the Mooney Check List (30) are designed to provide comprehensive measures of student adjustment.

Vocational Guidance

Of all aspects of the educational field, that which probably makes the most use of the attitude and opinion survey is the vocational guidance field. Surveys, projects, books, and pamphlets are constantly being written to describe some aspect of the application of measuring devices in this area. The two best known instruments are *The Kuder Preference Record* (25) and the Strong Vocational Interest Blank (56).

In his book, E. K. Strong, Jr. (53) has described the development of his Vocational Interest Blank. It was begun in 1923 at Stanford University. Since that time he has done research on thousands of subjects, using the data to validate and to improve his scale. Basically, the Interest Blank seeks to measure the interest of the newcomer or student in terms of the interests of people already successful in the occupational fields. The subjects are given 400 items against which to register their like, dislike, or indifference. The final tally gives them a rating of A, B+, B, etc., in each of such professions and occupations as physician, accountant, teacher, artist, etc., etc.

The Kuder Preference Record, by a somewhat different method, seeks to provide the same kind of information. Some 504 activities in brackets of three are presented, the subject being instructed to record his preference in each case. Again, as in the Vocational Interest Blank, tallies are made and the preference of the student found. Nine fields are covered in which he may have indicated a greater or lesser interest: *mechanical, computational, scientific, persuasive, artistic, literary, musical, social service, and clerical.* These are then rated against established norms suitable for rating the student's interest.

As has already been mentioned, much research has been done with these instruments. An example or two may be useful. Stability of interest ("Will my interest be the same later?") was a problem investigated by Fox *(15)*. He administered *The Kuder Preference Record* to 134 pupils in grade 9. Two months later, after an intensive guidance program, the test was readministered. Results showed that girls as a group had more stable interests than did boys (or possibly fewer alternatives in our society?). Also those who had an interest in the scientific and musical activities were least likely to change. Cross *(9)* investigated the possibility of faking an interest test. He administered the Kuder Preference Test to 600 high school students. He then administered the test to the high- and low-scoring students, suggesting that they deliberately try to make choices which would change their scores. He also gave the test to college students who had not previously taken it. He concluded that prospective employers using the test need to take into account the possibility of faking an interest.

DiMichael *(10)* found that only a moderate relationship existed between professed interest of vocational counselors and those interests as measured by *The Kuder Preference Record.* Stone *(52)* found that a vocational guidance program ought to include individual counseling in addition to the measurement of interests by questionnaires. Kirk and Remmers (24), using *The Kuder Preference Record,* investigated the interest patterns of students in seven schools at Purdue University. They discovered significant differences in the interest patterns of students in the different schools. For example, *engineers* showed a high interest in *mechanical* and *scientific* areas; home economics students, a high interest in persuasive and social service. *Low* interest was indicated by the engineers in *persuasive* and *social service*; for the home economics students, the *scientific* area had little appeal.

Attitudes: Specific Professions

As might be assumed, a great deal of research has been done in the area of attitudes toward teaching. The first profession to which students are exposed for long periods of time, it is natural that some attitudes must be created toward teaching as a profession. Yet it is not teachers who are the main influence of those who decide to enter the teaching profession. This is the finding of Richey and Fox (47), who investigated the opinions of 4000 Indiana high school students. They discovered that parents rather than teachers are the main influence in the lives of students who decide to go into teaching. Other findings were that (1) 48 percent of girls and 30 percent of the boys felt that teaching was less desirable than other professions and work requiring equivalent training; (2) as far as the teacher's personal life is concerned, the community ought not to interfere in it. The same authors (48) found that 969 university freshmen held similar views about the desirable and undesirable features of teaching. This was true even though the sample included three groups—those who were opposed to teaching, those who had decided to go into teaching, and those who were undecided about a future vocation. They also found that adverse attitudes toward teaching were formed early; favorable ones came later in the students' career.

Marzolf (28) found a relationship between areas of interest as defined by *The Kuder Preference Record* and choice of major teaching fields. When he tested 279 college freshmen, he found that future home economics teachers tended to prefer *social service*, business education majors tended to prefer *clerical* and *computational* areas, while for future elementary school teachers there was indicated a *low* interest in the *literary* field.

Another vocation which has been investigated from the point of view of interests is *pharmacy*. Remmers and Gage (39) in 1946 investigated the interests of 3200 entering pharmacy freshmen, distributed in forty schools throughout the United States. Their interest patterns agreed with those of drugstore managers, pharmacists, and advanced women pharmacy students. However, one significant difference was noted between the freshmen and the drugstore managers, with the freshmen rating much lower on the *persuasive* scale.

Many studies on the discovery of *medical* talent are reviewed by Stuit (56). He found that many interest tests were included in the batteries of tests of prediction. Strong and Tucker (55) followed up the interests of Stanford students over a period of 22 years. The investigators studied the physician interest ratings twenty years after graduation of 670 Stanford students, of whom 108 were physicians. Those who had had *A* ratings in the category "physician" had 53 chances in 100 of becoming a physician. Those who had reported *B*+ yielded 20 chances in 100; *B*, 12 percent, and *C* only 2. Once having learned the probabilities of a student's becoming a physician, the investigators looked at interests within four medical fields—internal medicine, surgery, pathology, and psychiatry. The subjects were asked to fill in two blanks: The Strong Vocational Interest Blank and the Medical Specialists Preference Blank. Criterion groups used were diplomates in the four specialized fields. As a control group, "Physicians-in-General" were chosen randomly from the American Medical Association list. They found that an *A* or *B*+ rating on the Internist, Surgeon,

Pathologist, or Psychiatrist Scale indicates that the subject probably has enough interest for this group, *provided he has at least an A or B+ on the original Physicians' Scale.*

Student's Personal Adjustment

Of prime importance to pupils, teachers, counselors, parents, administrators, and school psychologists is the problem of the student's personal adjustment. Lacking the facilities for a complete clinical analysis of these problems, many schools rely on inventories and attitude measurements to help them discover problem areas. Some of these inventories, already mentioned, have been described in Chapter VI. The whole structure of the SRA Youth Inventory (*46*), for example, has been described there. Other such measures are the *Minnesota Multiphasic Personality Inventory* (*20*), the Bernreuter Personality Inventory (*5*) and *The Mooney Problem Check List* (*30*), also described in Chapter VI. Projective techniques, such as the Rorschach Test (*50*), yield material which can help the counselor to find the early signs of maladjustive behavior patterns. Many other such tests, described more fully in Chapter VII, give similar aid.

The important point to note here is that schools are making use of these techniques. Not only adults, but also students and pupils at a younger stage, are being measured from the standpoint of adjustment. Anticipating "trouble spots" and even disastrous maladjustment, educators are able to prevent nonadaptive behavior by enabling the pupils to redirect their thinking and acting along constructive lines.

ATTITUDES TOWARD THE EDUCATIONAL PROCESS

The whole process of education is open to investigation and criticism. In a dynamic and continually changing society this is inevitable, as we may realize when we consider the breadth of its influence, the intimacy of its relationships, and the extent of its efforts. Whole generations pass through the process; its products are the whole adult population. The teacher and the school have touched the lives of all, and all feel qualified to pass judgment. Many aspects of the process are objects of attitudes, expressed in terms sometimes analyzable, sometimes vague. Here, also, attempts have been made to measure the opinions expressed. Specific instruments have been devised in order to improve the methods of educating. *How Teach and Learn in College,* developed by Remmers and Harvey *(40)*, is a scale for learning ways of improving teaching at the college level.

For teaching at the elementary and secondary levels, Kelley and Perkins *(22)* developed *How I Teach.* Problems of discipline, emotional adjustment, teaching methods, and general child psychology are dealt with in such a manner as to give the classroom teacher the benefit of expert advice.

The *High School Attitude Scale (17)* gives an opportunity for students to express their opinions concerning the high school.

The *Purdue Opinion Panel (34-45)*, based as it is on a carefully stratified national sample, has given an opportunity for students to express their opinions in such a way that it could be justly said that "this is how American high school students feel on this subject." The *Panel* has been used since 1941. It is given at least three times a year. The poll questions are usually administered by the classroom teachers to a unit (i.e., a class) at a time. Usually a whole school is reached at one time by this method. About a hundred schools or school systems well distributed geographically participate. In order to avoid possible bias, induced by the factor of self-selection, the sample once established is again sampled: A stratified sample based on available census data is drawn, finally yielding what is believed to be a group representative of the nation. From 8,000 to 15,000 provides the original sample: from 2500 to 3000 the final sample. A fuller description of the *Panel* is given in Chapter II.

Many topics relating to the educational process are dealt with by questions repeated at intervals. This shows trends where they can be traced, or reversals of earlier opinions by later "generations" of students. Some samples of this kind of question are "Should Federal aid be given to schools?" "Are public school teachers underpaid?" "Should tax money be spent to support students in college who could not otherwise afford to go?" The value of such a widespread expression of opinion is that it provides specific answers to the general question, "What do the present students think about school?" It also enables research workers to find what differences, if any, exist among different regions, different socioeconomic groups, different religious groups, etc. It provides much data for the drawing up of programs, for changing teaching methods, for measuring how well information is "getting through" to students. In one study conducted by the *Panel*, Remmers, Drucker, and Kirk (*36*), using as a basis the study conducted by *Life* magazine (*59*), compared the attitudes of high school students with those of adults on the subject of public education. The areas covered by the questionnaire may be judged from a sample of the questions used.

"Taking everything into consideration, would you say you are very satisfied, only fairly satisfied, or not very satisfied with the public school system in your community?"

"What things do you think you should learn more about or study more of?"

"Just considering your own community, in general, should people spend more of the money that goes for education on higher salaries for teachers, or on new school buildings?"

"In general, would you say you are in favor of the idea of Federal money being given to schools run by churches, or should the Federal money be given just to the public schools?"

The final results indicated that high school students over the country share basically the opinions held by the adults. There were very few significant differences between the adult and student groups. More clear-cut were the differences shown between students from different regions, socioeconomic backgrounds, religious preferences, etc. The divisions on important issues would appear to be less a factor of age and maturity (within limits) than of the region and cultural background which has been one's environment.

In a study of the opinions of faculty and students of Syracuse University, Downie, Pace, and Troyer (*13*) investigated the question of educational objectives. Their main concern was to get the objectives defined in the thinking of the students and faculty and then to ascertain how well these objectives were being met. Eighteen objectives of general education were rated by both groups. The conclusions concerning these objectives may be summarized as follows. Both faculty and students agree on the value of the eighteen objectives (good health habits, understanding scientific developments and processes and their application in society, understanding the meaning and values in life, preparing for a vocation, etc.). The majority of students feel that "some" but "not much" progress is being made toward the attainment of these objectives. Faculty members generally assumed no direct responsibility for the achievement of most of these objectives on the part of the students. The ratings of the importance of these objectives varied considerably from college to college in the university.

ATTITUDES TOWARD THE SOCIAL PROCESS

A final area of vital importance to the educator is that of citizenship attitudes. Are students more or less favorable to liberalism than they were 10 years ago? Are they inclining toward or away from socialism? Do they know the meaning of communism? Do they feel that progressive education has been useful or harmful? Do they have any understanding of what will be their responsibilities? Are they learning to make their own judgments? These and many other questions are asked, and answers are given.

A study of this nature is reported by Pace (*31*) in *Time* magazine. He first made a set of opinion scales labeled Politics, Government, Civic Relations, and The World. Each section contained six statements. These were rated by thirty to forty experts on history, government, sociology, etc., in terms of their agreement, disagreement, or "no opinion" on the best answer to the questions. The questions were then sent to approximately 10,000 college graduates, representative of the whole graduate population. Basic agreement existed between experts and graduates in the section on Politics, Civic Relations, and The World. However, on Government, opinions differed sharply. Understanding and interpretation of the terms "democracy," "fascism," and "communism" was very different as between the two groups. Pace's conclusion was that "if the experts are right, we need much better teaching in our colleges about the role of government in the modern world." He also found that liberal or general education was a better preparation for understanding of the civic and political affairs of the present day than was a technical-professional education.

Since a widely accepted theorem of social science is that the family is the most important social institution in transmitting culture to the oncoming generation, those concerned with the *Purdue Opinion Panel* decided to test the hypothesis that the *children* of fathers who had had a general or liberal arts college education would also be more in accord with the judgments of social scientists than the children of fathers technically-professionally trained.

Hence Remmers, Drucker, and Shimberg (37) asked some of the same questions of a national sample of 10,000 high school youth. They used twenty-six items, twelve of which were identical with those used in the *Time* magazine study conducted by Pace. The investigators found that the opinions of expert social scientists were not followed by a majority of the high school students. Two noticeable facts became evident. Those students whose fathers had attended college tended to agree more with the social scientists than did the other students. Also, the students whose fathers had taken liberal arts courses were significantly closer in opinions to the social scientists than their fellow students whose fathers were technically-professionally trained. The hypothesis was confirmed.

Besides the question of good citizenship, there exist many areas of attitude expression worthy of investigation. Courtship and marriage, the attitude of one race or group to another, the relations of parents and children, religious attitudes are some of the important meeting places of the student and adult thinking.

Remmers, Drucker, and Hackett (35) investigated the "parent problem" of young people. As a result of their findings, they reported that what the pupils *feel* is the situation in the home, rather than what might be objectively described as the real situation, provides the key to understanding the relationships between youth and their parents. This is further elaborated by Hackett (19). A follow-up study was made by Remmers, Horton, and Mainer (44), in which they investigated the problem of study at home and the factors interfering with it. Also, they learned the types of problems which students take to their parents and those which they take to their peers. Youth's knowledge and opinion of the Bill of Rights and other attitudes related to citizenship were presented in Panel Report No. 30 (42). National interest was aroused when *Look* magazine (February 12, 1952) published a report of high school youth's opinions on these matters.

The effects of our cultural background, socioeconomic status, and the individual's identifying with the mores of his group were investigated by Remmers, Horton, and Lysgaard (41). They stressed the importance of recognizing that the pattern which schools in general seek to impose on their students may be relatively foreign to a great number of the students. Different upbringing and emphasis on a set of values which may belong only to the teacher and not to a majority of pupils can lead to misunderstanding and a waste of effort. Panel Report No. 31 (45) had as its subject the contrast between "progressive" and traditional methods of education. Girls seem to favor the more old-fashioned methods more than boys; grade twelve students are more progressive than the earlier grades; rural students are less opposed than urban students to authoritarian methods.

The bringing up of children was the subject of a study by Remmers and Drucker (*33*). The opinions of students were gauged by the agreement or disagreement which they showed with the scale devised by Stedman, *How Bring Up a Child* (*51*). Girls showed more agreement with the experts on how to bring up a child. Senior students showed more agreement than did those in the junior grades. Children from higher-income homes also were in more agreement than were those from lower-income homes.

Remmers, Drucker, and Christensen (*34*) investigated the opinions concerning courtship conduct. Boys and girls disagreed on many aspects of courtship. Girls were more insistent on parental approval of their dates; boys stressed physical attractiveness more than did girls; boys more than girls felt that kissing on the first date is acceptable; girls claimed in far greater number than boys that their sex instruction comes from their parents or guardians. Differences also were found when comparisons were made between the groups divided on the basis of grade, religion, rural or urban residence, income level, and region.

A study has recently been made of the effect of the 1952 election on high school students. The importance of this topic was recognized by Remmers, Horton, and Mainer (*43*) when they polled the high school group on national issues as to the popularity of candidates. Findings were actually closer to the national vote for Eisenhower than were those of most national polls of adults. The high school poll gave Eisenhower 57.6 percent; the total adult popular vote for Eisenhower was 57.1 percent.

SUMMARY

The use of opinion and attitude measurement in education has become very widespread. It helps all concerned—pupils, parents, classroom teachers, guidance personnel, and administrators within the school system.

Interpersonal relations, vocational guidance, the area of personal problems, the evaluation of the opinions of students in general—all these afford much room for the application of the many techniques that have been devised.

Methods of developing in students responsible citizenship in a democratic society are receiving increasing emphasis and are greatly aided by the application and further development of opinion and attitude measurements.

Questions

1. The "public" should be kept informed of current educational methods, philosophy, and problems. Indicate three specific means for measuring the amount of information which a community has about its local system.
2. What were the main failings of the traditional one-sided rating of teachers by their administrators?
3. List the arguments for and against students' opinions being used as a factor in curriculum construction.
4. "The instruments used by education for measuring opinion are typically those devised for some other field, such as clinical psychology, industry, etc." Discuss this statement, and, if you disagree, point out specific examples of instruments suitable only for education.
5. Suggest five areas of attitudes toward education which have been partly investigated but which ought to be more thoroughly explored.
6. Design a questionnaire (suitable for a specific grade level) to investigate the attitudes of the pupils toward a specific projected change (method of instruction, classroom arrangement, etc.).
7. What evidence is there for assuming that parents and pupils are probably in greater agreement than the average member of either group may realize?
8. Suggest three suitable topics for long-term investigation of citizenship attitudes of students.

9. The concept of sociometry is probably a fruitful one for education. In what specific ways can it be applied?

10. What specific suggestions do you have for improving the present report card system of teachers' ratings of pupils?

11. Are teachers the main personal factor in prompting students to enter the teaching profession? Discuss.

12. List three opinion measuring instruments devised for helping teachers to improve their methods.

13. The *Purdue Opinion Panel* discusses problems of education, and the opinions of students toward the education system. What advantage can this have for future educators?

14. What advantages and disadvantages can you see in striving for unidimensional attitude measuring instruments?

15. In a high school with 4000 enrollment, what proportion of the total enrollment needs to be sampled to make the maximum sampling error not more than 2 percent?

16. In the 1952 presidential election the results of the *Purdue Opinion Panel* were less than 1 percent in error. Gallup, Roper, and other pollsters of adults predicted considerably less accurately. What explanatory hypotheses to account for this occur to you?

Bibliography

1. Baker, P. C., and Remmers, H. H., "The Measurement of Teacher Characteristics and the Prediction of Teaching Efficiency in College," *Rev. educ. Research,* 1952, *3*:224-227.

2. Baker, P. C., and Remmers, H. H., "Progress in Research on Personnel Evaluation," *J. Teacher Educ.,* 1951, *2*:143-146.

3. Baker, P. C., and Remmers, H. H., *The Purdue Rating Scale for Instruction and Manual,* Personnel Evaluation Research Service, Purdue University.

4. Barr, A. S., "The Measurement and Prediction of Teaching Efficiency: A Summary of Investigation," *J. exp. Educ.,* 1948, *16*:203-283.

5. Bernreuter, Robert G., *Personality Inventory,* Stanford: Stanford University Press, 1931.

6. Bowers, Henry H., *Research in the Training of Teachers,*

J. M. Dent & Sons (Canada) Ltd. and The Macmillan Company of Canada, Ltd., Toronto, Canada, 1952.

7. Buros, O. K. (ed.), *The Fourth Mental Measurements Yearbook*, New Brunswick, N.J.: Rutgers University Press, 1953.

8. Clark, Elmer J., "Teacher Reaction Toward Objectionable Pupil Behavior," *Elem. Sch. J.*, 1951, *51*:446-449.

9. Cross, Orrin H., "A Study of Faking in The Kuder Preference Record," *Educ. psychol. Measmt.*, 1950, *10*:271-277.

10. DiMichael, Salvatore G., "The Professed and Measured Interests of Vocational Rehabilitation Counselors," *Educ. psychol. Measmt.*, 1949, *9*:59-72.

11. Domas, Simeon J., and Tiedeman, David V., "Teacher Competence: An Annotated Bibliography," *J. exp. Educ.*, 1950, *19*:101-218.

12. Downie, N. M., "Student Evaluation of the Faculty," *J. Higher Educ.*, 1952, *23*(no. 9):496-497.

13. Downie, N. M., Pace, C. R., and Troyer, M. E., "The Opinions of Syracuse University Students on Some Widely Discussed Current Issues," *Educ. psychol. Measmt.*, 1950, *10*:628-636.

14. Drucker, A. J., and Remmers, H. H., "Do Alumni and Students Differ in Their Attitudes Toward Instructors?" *J. educ. Psychol.*, 1951, *42*:129-143.

15. Fox, William H., "The Stability of Measured Interest," *J. educ. Res.*, 1947, *41*:305-310.

16. Gage, N. L., and Suci, George, "Social Perception and Teacher-Pupil Relationships," *J. educ. Psychol.*, 1951, *42*:144-152.

17. Gillespie, F. H., *High School Attitude Scale*, Personnel Evaluation Research Service, Purdue University, 1936.

18. Haas, Robert Bartlett, "A Role Study from Pupil Motivations: Students Evaluate Their English Instructors," *Sociometry*, 1947, *10*:200-210.

19. Hackett, C. G., "Use of an Opinion Polling Technique in a Study of Parent-Child Relationships," *Purdue University Studies in Higher Education*, 1951, no. 75.

20. Hathaway, Starke R., and McKinley, J. Charnley, *Minnesota Multiphasic Personality Inventory*, New York: Psychological Corporation, 1943-1946.

21. Hobson, Robert L., "Some Psychological Dimensions of Academic Administrators," *Purdue University Studies in Higher Education,* 1950, no. 73:7-64.

22. Kelley, Ida B., and Perkins, Keith J., *How I Teach,* Minneapolis: Educational Test Bureau, 1942.

23. Kirk, R. B., "Guidance for the School Administrator," Sixteenth Annual Guidance Conference, *Purdue University Studies in Higher Education,* 1951, no. 79:65-69.

24. Kirk, R. B., and Remmers, H. H., *Interest Pattern of Purdue Students Measured by The Kuder Preference Record,* Division of Educational Reference Report 52-1, 1952 (mimeo).

25. Kuder, G. Frederic, *The Kuder Preference Record,* Chicago: Science Research Associates, 1942.

26. Leeds, Carroll H., and Cook, Walter W., "The Construction and Differential Value of a Scale for Determining Teacher-Pupil Attitudes," *J. exp. Educ.,* 1947, *16:*149-159.

27. Luchins, Abraham S., and Luchins, Edith H., "Children's Attitudes Toward Homogeneous Groupings," *J. genet. Psychol.,* 1948, *72:*3-9.

28. Marzolf, Stanley S., "Interests and Choice of Teaching Field," *Illinois Acad. Sci. Trans.,* 1946, *3:*107-113.

29. McLelland, F. M., and Ratliff, John A., "The Use of Sociometry as an Aid in Promoting Social Adjustment of a Ninth Grade Home-room. *Sociometry,* 1947, *10:*147-153.

30. Mooney, Ross L., *The Mooney Problem Check List,* Columbus: Ohio State University Press, 1941-1947.

31. Pace, C. R., "What Kind of Citizens Have Our College Graduates Become?" *J. gen. Educ.,* 1949, *3:*197-202.

32. Remmers, H. H., and Bauernfeind, R. H., *SRA Junior Inventory and Manual,* Chicago: Science Research Associates, 1951.

33. Remmers, H. H., and Drucker, A. J., "Teen-agers' Attitudes Toward Problems of Child Management," *J. educ. Psychol.,* 1951, *42:*105-113.

34. Remmers, H. H., Drucker, A. J., and Christensen, H. T., "Courtship Conduct as Viewed by High School Youth," *Purdue Opinion Panel Report No. 27,* Purdue University, 1950.

35. Remmers, H. H., Drucker, A. J., and Hackett, C. G., "Youth

Looks at the Parent Problem," *Purdue Opinion Panel Report No. 23,* Purdue University, 1949.

36. Remmers, H. H., Drucker, A. J., and Kirk, R. B., "Youth Looks Toward the Future of Education," *Purdue Opinion Panel Report No. 29,* Purdue University, 1951.

37. Remmers, H. H., Drucker, A. J., and Shimberg, Benjamin, "The Citizenship Attitudes of High School Youth," *Purdue Opinion Panel Report No. 22,* Purdue University, 1949.

38. Remmers, H. H., and Elliott, D. N., "The Indiana College and University Staff Evaluation Program," *School and Society,* 1949, *70:*168-171.

39. Remmers, H. H., and Gage, N. L., "The Abilities and Interests of Pharmacy Freshmen," *Amer. J. pharm. Educ.,* 1948, *12:*1-65.

40. Remmers, H. H., and Harvey, Jean, *How Teach and Learn in College,* Personnel Evaluation Research Service, Purdue University.

41. Remmers, H. H., Horton, R. E., and Lysgaard, Sverre, "Teenage Personality in Our Culture," *Purdue Opinion Panel Report No. 32,* Purdue University, 1952.

42. Remmers, H. H., Horton, R. E., and Mainer, R. E., "Does Youth Believe in the Bill of Rights?" *Purdue Opinion Panel Report No. 30,* Purdue University, 1951.

43. Remmers, H. H., Horton, R. E., and Mainer, R. E., "Youth and the 1952 Elections," *Purdue Opinion Panel Report No. 33,* Purdue University, 1952.

44. Remmers, H. H., Horton, R. E., and Mainer, R. E., "Youth Views Parents, Peers and Problems," *Purdue Opinion Panel Report No. 34,* Purdue University, 1953.

45. Remmers, H. H., Horton, R. E., and Scarborough, B. B., "Youth Views Purposes, Practices and Procedures in Education," *Purdue Opinion Panel Report No. 31,* Purdue University, 1952.

46. Remmers, H. H., and Shimberg, Benjamin, *SRA Youth Inventory and Manual,* Chicago: Science Research Associates, 1949.

47. Richey, Robert W., and Fox, William H., "An Analysis of Various Factors Associated with the Selection of Teaching as a Vocation," *Bull. sch. educ. Ind. Univ.,* 1948, *24:*59.

48. Richey, Robert W., and Fox, William H., "A Study of Some Opinions of High School Students with Regard to Teachers and Teaching," *Bull. sch. educ. Ind. Univ.*, 1951, 27:4.

49. Ringness, Thomas Alexander, "Relationships Between Certain Attitudes Toward Teaching and Teaching Success," *J. exp. Educ.*, 1952, 21:1-55.

50. Rorschach, H., *Psychodiagnostics* (Eng. trans. by P. Lemkan and B. Kronenburg), Bern, 1942.

51. Stedman, Louise A., "An Investigation of Knowledge of and Attitudes Toward Child Behavior," *Purdue University Studies in Higher Education*, 1948, no. 62.

52. Stone, C. Harold, "Are Vocational Orientation Courses Worth Their Salt?" *Educ. psychol. Measmt.*, 1948, 8:161-181.

53. Strong, E. K., Jr., *Vocational Interests of Men and Women*, Stanford: Stanford University Press, 1943.

54. Strong, E. K., Jr., *The Vocational Interest Blank for Men, Revised; The Vocational Interest Blank for Women, Revised*, New York: Psychological Corporation, 1938, 1946.

55. Strong, E. K., Jr., and Tucker, Anthony C., "The Use of a Vocational Interest Scale in Planning a Medical Career," *Psychol. Monogr.*, 1952, 66(no. 9).

56. Stuit, Dewey B., "The Discovery of Medical Talent," *J. Ass. Amer. med. Coll.*, 1948, 23:157-162.

57. Tschechtelin, Sister M. Amatora, "An Investigation of Some Elements of Teachers' and Pupils' Personalities," *Purdue University Studies in Higher Education*, 1943, no. 48.

58. Wandt, Erwin, "The Measurement and Analysis of Teachers' Attitudes," *Calif. J. educ. Res.*, 1952, 3:10-13.

59. "What the U.S. Thinks About Its Schools," *Life*, October 16, 1950.

60. Witty, Paul, "An Analysis of the Personality Traits of the Effective Teacher," *J. educ. Res.*, 1947, 40:662-671.

INDEXES

NAME INDEX

SUBJECT INDEX